Men, Women and Relationships

Making Peace with the Opposite Sex

John Gray, Ph.D.

Published by
Beyond Words Publishing, Inc.
Pumpkin Ridge Road
Route 3, Box 492-B
Hillsboro, Oregon 97123
Phone: 503-647-5109
Toll Free: 1-800-284-9673

Editing: Sara Steinberg
Art Direction: Principia Graphica
Page Layout: Deb Mecartea
Cover Design: Jerry Soga
Photography: Le Photographer

Printed in the United States of America by Arcata Graphics,
Kingsport, Tennessee.

ISBN: 0-941831-50-7
Library of Congress Catalog Card Number: 90-080256

The case studies in this book are real; however, the names and
circumstances have been substantially changed to protect the
anonymity and confidentiality of all cases.

Table of Contents

Preface

My father's death has become, in my mind, an allegory for the purpose of this book. My generous, compassionate father was robbed by a hitchhiker and then left to die in the trunk of his car of heat asphyxiation. He tried for several hours to get out. During that time his car was reported twice to the police by nearby residents who had noticed the abandoned car. The police responded to both calls, but didn't find the car because the directions to its location were not clear. After the third call they were able to find the car, but it was too late.

In some ways my father's death was symbolic, not only of his life, but of other's lives as well. He always gave help to other people but did not know how to really share himself or let anyone into his heart. Like him, so many people are dying of broken hearts, alone and abandoned. They are not being rescued because the directions are not clear. We do not know how to find them or help them. This book can help by dispelling the confusion in relationships and replacing it with clarity and hope.

There is still, however, another important part to this story. Returning home for the funeral, I went out to the car to see how my father died. I climbed in the trunk and pulled shut the hood to feel what he must have gone through. I ran my fingers over the dents where he had banged on the trunk top to get help. I felt his aloneness. Rarely in his life had my dad asked for help.

Still in the trunk, I saw where he had broken out the back light to get air. I instinctively stretched my hand out through the hole he had made. One of my brothers, who had been standing outside the car, said, "See if you can reach the button to pop the hood." I reached my hand out a little farther and opened the trunk.

If my dad had thought to open the trunk with his hand, he would have lived. I, too, being in the trunk and trying to get out, did not think to open the lid from the outside. It took my brother, who was already on the outside, to point the way.

In a profound way my father's death has inspired me in my life. It has prompted me to see my responsibility to help those who may be locked within their hearts, by pointing to the "button" by which they can free themselves.

Men, Women and Relationships is dedicated to all who are imprisoned within their own hearts. I hope that in reading this book, you will discover some of those buttons that go unnoticed when you are locked up within yourself. May you be successful in opening your heart to love and compassion. I hope that by your example you will inspire others to come out of their own trunks and share their love.

This book is also dedicated to those light bearers who are already on the outside trying to help others free themselves. May these pages support your efforts and enhance your work.

Writing this book and testing out its new insights, skills, and strategies has been for me a rich and fantastic journey. It has taken me to many heights, through many valleys and storms, into lands of sunshine, beauty, love, and trust.

I thank Bonnie, my wife, for sharing this journey with me and for her continued love and support. In developing the material of this book she has been my greatest teacher. Many of the concepts I have written about I learned directly from listening to her. Her love, vulnerability, and honesty has helped me to respect femininity and has inspired me to be a better and more loving man. Through her love I have learned to trust, accept, and appreciate my own masculinity. Most important, I have learned the transforming power of love.

My gratitude goes also to my daughter Lauren for teaching me to love in ways I could never have dreamed. I thank my stepdaughters Shannon and Julie for their acceptance of me and for their love.

I thank my younger brother Jimmy. His unconditional love has supported me throughout my journeys and his unfortunate suicide has taught me to value life. His suffering has taught me compassion, while his endless love fills my heart and motivates me to be of service to others less fortunate than I.

Heartfelt thanks go also to my mother, Virginia Gray, whose unconditional acceptance and continued support has helped me become the man I am. I thank her for her spirituality and for being an example of selfless giving. I could not imagine having a better mom. I also want to acknowledge Lucille for her continued devotion to my success and for always believing in me.

I thank my clients, whose stories I share in this book, and the many thousands of participants in my seminars, who have trusted the ideas in this book and have proven their effectiveness. To all of them goes my deep appreciation for sharing their stories and their wisdom. Most of the best examples and case histories in this book are taken from their heartfelt sharing. Their support has made this book possible and the many books to follow.

I thank Ann Weyman and Sara Steinberg for their expert assistance in editing this book. My thanks also to Richard Cohn and Cindy Black and the staff of Beyond Words Publishing for their gentle persistence in giving birth to this book.

In conclusion, I thank you for letting me make a difference in your life. Thank you for your courage and sincere commitment to find the light of love within your heart and to share that love, bringing light into the darkness of our world, bringing compassion to heal our collective hurt, and bringing joy to heal our sorrow. Always remember, you are special and your love does make a difference.

Introduction

Our world is changing.

The roles of men and women are changing. The rules for relationships are changing. Old ways are no longer working. Families are breaking up. Divorce is the norm rather than the exception.

We need a new way of relating, a new psychology for understanding the new man and woman. To make a relationship work today calls for a fresh vision that does not negate the ways of the past, but integrates their usefulness into an updated approach.

Men, Women and Relationships is the ultimate guide for enriching relationships. Although it focuses on our relationships with the opposite sex, its wisdom applies to all relationships, especially the relationship to self. It reveals creative and practical ways to love oneself and to successfully give and receive emotional support.

This new and innovative understanding profoundly assists us in releasing old resentments and mistrust. More importantly, it outlines strategies previously unknown for avoiding conflict and misunderstanding. The original approach of this book opens greater possibilities for growth and creates a powerful and inspiring impact.

Here at last is the definitive guide for understanding male and female psychological differences. In a respectful way, without taking sides, our respective strengths and vulnerabilities are revealed and explored. Through simple examples, we will discover how our masculine and feminine sides can enable us to complement and support each other rather than create unnecessary conflict.

This book puts an end to the frustration of trying to figure out the opposite sex. Revealing the secrets for understanding how to fulfill the unique

emotional needs of the opposite sex, it shows us how we can get the love we need without having to change our partners.

First we'll take an in-depth look at the importance of understanding our differences. We will proceed to explore these differences and how they create endless problems when they are not acknowledged and respected. Quite amazingly these conflicts begin to melt away once we stop fighting our differences and begin accepting and respecting them.

We will learn the art of having fulfilling relationships through practicing new ways to communicate and to give emotional support. We will observe the different ways men and women react to stress and how various kinds of support can either help or hinder.

Using examples of situations that many readers will find familiar, we will discover how we unknowingly sabotage our relationships. We will begin to master what may be the ultimate technique for achieving a truly successful, loving relationship. Just as important, we will learn how to receive support through the nine sources of love that are necessary for our full development.

This book is not only a practical guide, with tips on every page for improving relationships and neutralizing conflict, but an inspiration to be all that we can be. Relationships can either drain us or empower us. They can lead us to hell or be a ticket to heaven. It is up to us to create the positive and loving relationships that we all desire. To achieve this task the information in this book is invaluable.

Men, Women and Relationships repeatedly gives expression to our deepest feelings, insights, and convictions. It speaks from the heart and inspires us to try again when we are lost. It draws us back to that place of knowing within our hearts that can and will actualize our dreams.

The insights in this book are so powerful because they are self-evident and obvious. Yet they are new. As one of my teachers used to say, "Only a new seed can yield a new crop." The newness of this approach has a powerful influence on our relationships. But it can be temporary. Education theory states that to learn something new takes hearing it 200 times — 50 times if you are a genius. To sustain the positive and immediate results of reading this book, the information must be reviewed.

The changes inspired by this book can last only as long as we remember the insights and practice using the tools it supplies. Read *Men, Women and Relationships* once and notice how much better your relationships become. Notice how much better you feel about yourself. Then as you start to experience conflict again, read it once more. Let this book be your best friend on your new journey. Allow it to reinspire you again and again.

John Gray, Ph.D.
June 21, 1990
Mill Valley, California

CHAPTER ONE

The Art of Loving an Alien Being

PEOPLE ARE DIFFERENT

Recognizing this fundamental truth is essential for creating positive and loving relationships.

In practice, however, we do not fully acknowledge that people differ from us. Instead we are bent upon changing one another. We resent, resist, and reject each other's differences, as if the other is supposed to be like ourselves. We demand that the people in our lives feel, think, and behave as we would. And when they react differently we make them wrong or invalidate them; we try to fix them when they really need understanding and nurturing; we try to improve them when instead they need acceptance, appreciation, and trust.

We complain that if only they would change, we could love them; if only they would agree, we could love them; if only they would feel the way we do, we could love them; if only they would do what we ask, we could love them.

What, then, is love? Is love accepting and appreciating a person only when they fulfill our expectations? Is love the act of changing a person into what we want rather than what they choose to be? Is love caring for or trusting a person because they think and feel the way we do?

This certainly is not love. It may feel like love to the giver but not to the receiver. Real love is unconditional. It does not demand but affirms and values. Unconditional love is not possible without the recognition and acceptance of our differences. True love is obstructed as long as we mistakenly believe that our loved ones would be better off thinking, feeling, and behaving the way we do. Once we realize that not only are people different but they are supposed to be that way, the obstructions to real love begin to fall away.

HOW WE ARE DIFFERENT

Once we accept that people are different we can begin to seriously explore *how* we are different. A variety of personality theories quite accurately explore the ways in which we are different. Ultimately all human beings are unique and it is impossible to categorize them. But by creating a greater awareness of our possible differences, these systems are immensely helpful.

The study of morphology divides people into three body types that are associated with three major psychological differences: action oriented, feeling oriented, and mind oriented.

Hypocrites, Adickes, Kretschmer, Spranger, Adler, and Jung classified our differences by four temperaments, generalized by some as "physical, feeling, thinking, and intuitive." The widely used Myers-Briggs indicator expands these four into sixteen.

The ancient practice of astrology describes twelve psychological types. Sufi teachings recognize nine basic psychological types called the enneagram. Many contemporary personal growth and business seminars describe the following four types: supporter, promoter, controller, and analyzer. It is proposed that the individual potentially possesses all of these qualities, and with a greater awareness he or she can choose to develop and integrate them.

Some, however, oppose categorizing people since this may limit them or box them in. To say one person is analytical while another is emotional may give rise to judgment. This fear arises because experience tells us that when we are being judged as "less than another," it is because we are being categorized in some way; we are being seen as different. Hence, we fear being different.

In a symptomatic way, prejudice and judgment are always associated with categorizing another. It is, however, equally true that in praising and admiring a person we also tend to categorize them.

From one perspective, judgments and prejudice are associated with differences. But at a deeper level we can clearly see that the original cause of these judgments is nonacceptance and nonappreciation of our differences.

For example, a person might be judged as "too emotional" by an "analytical person" with the mistaken expectation that all people should be like him. This belief makes him incapable of truly appreciating or respecting an emotional person. In a similar way, an "emotional" person might judge an analytical person as "too analytical," because the emotional person is not appreciating their differences.

Though the acknowledgment of differences can be perceived as a threat, it is not. Through accepting that people are different we are freed from the compulsion to change them. When we are not preoccupied with changing others, we are free to appreciate their unique values. Ultimately, the recognition of differences among people allows us to release our judgments.

Another problem seen with acknowledging differences is the implication that one cannot perform a task as well as another. In the ancient caste system people were categorized and limited to the family caste. The four main categories into which families were divided were priests, soldiers, traders, or servants. In this way, people were prisoners of a system that defined within narrow limits what a person's role could be in society.

But we can acknowledge differences without being that rigid. It is incorrect to assume that if a person is an emotional type, they cannot also be analytical. They can develop that potential if they choose. These theories need not restrict the individual; instead, they can assist him or her in the integration of the whole person.

UNITY IN DIVERSITY

To accept our psychological differences frees us to experience an underlying oneness that permeates our relationships. In an abstract way, we are all the same. In every spiritual teaching is an acknowledgment of that oneness. Deep within we feel a spiritual oneness with our fellow man. When we read of children suffering from hunger, we feel in our hearts the pain we would feel if they were our own children.

We are all one, yet we are also different. Just as the five fingers are different, they are also the expressions of one hand. Through loving our differences we are capable of finding the mystical union that pervades mankind, uniting us as one family.

Ultimately we are all motivated to break free from the chains that separate us and to realize our oneness. This opening of the heart is really an awareness that what is outside us is also inside us. The quest to open the heart takes a variety of forms: the path to enlightenment, the quest for God, the dream of happy marriage, finding one's soul mate, or creating a loving family. In each example, one is inexplicably drawn to something and someone else.

The seeker of enlightenment is drawn to a teacher because the teacher embodies something within the student that the seeker is to realize. Through loving and understanding the teacher or the teaching, the seeker is indirectly loving and accepting those very qualities within himself. Gradually the seeker finds what he seeks within his own being. In this way we are inevitably drawn to that which we need to awaken within ourselves.

The devotee seeks God in the heavens, only to find the kingdom of heaven within. Through praying to God he finds the power of God emerging within himself. Longing to hear the voice of God, gradually he hears God through the silent whisper of feeling in the heart. It is always there but needs to be awakened.

A man separated from his female qualities becomes detached and cold. He seeks relief through union with a woman's softness and warmth. Their innate differences create an attraction or chemistry. As he blends his male energies with her female energies, he momentarily experiences the bliss of his own wholeness. Through touching the softness of her femininity with love, he becomes soft and gentle yet maintains his masculine strength and drive.

We may seek to find yet a deeper union with our soul mate, a special person with whom to share our lives, as if ordained by the heavens. We are drawn to this person not because they are similar to us but because they are different. Our soul mate embodies qualities and attributes that we unconsciously seek to find within ourselves. Through loving this person we begin to accept and awaken those same qualities hidden within our own beings. This discovery of self brings us greater fulfillment.

Through loving their children, parents have the opportunity to rekindle an awareness of their own childlike side. They are able to integrate being an adult while also enjoying the world through a child's eyes.

In each case, we search to find love and happiness outside ourselves, only to find that it comes from within. Through loving the differences in others we can incorporate their qualities without changing who we are. For example, if I tend to be analytical and I love a person who is more emotional, then automatically I will become more aware of my inner potential to be emotional. I will remain analytical yet become more emotional. Through loving someone who is different, I am able to remain myself but also express the qualities that attract me.

Although love allows us to integrate within ourselves the qualities of the loved, its prerequisite is an awareness of difference. We are drawn to that which is different. Our challenge is to understand, accept, and appreciate those differences, and then they will naturally emerge within ourselves.

This is a challenge because the process is not always easy. Intense attraction to someone is a sign that there are many differences to harmonize, many conflicts to resolve. Attraction is not under our control. We can be sure, however, that when there is attraction, there are lessons to learn and discoveries to be made. Because we are attracted to people who are unlike ourselves, the fundamental basis for enriching relationships is the acknowledgment that people are different.

This book will explore the common differences between men and women. Through respecting, accepting, and appreciating these differences, many of the problems that plague our relationships can be solved.

Certainly all women are not the same, nor are all men the same. But in very general ways, men and women differ from each other. Through increasing your awareness of these differences and how they apply to the people in your life, confusion between the sexes begins to clear up, important questions can be answered, judgments can be released, and conflict can be more successfully resolved and eventually avoided.

UNDERSTANDING OUR DIFFERENCES

Kathy, 32, is a successful musician and composer. Her career has taken off with opportunities opening in all directions. Like so many successful career women, she is not married and at times wishes she were. "I don't know what I do to turn men off," she says. "Somehow I am pushing them away. Maybe I make too many demands. What can you expect from a man? Men are very confusing. Relationships are confusing. I don't even know what a good relationship looks like."

Alise, a 36-year-old business consultant, and Henry, a 40-year-old land developer, have been married six years. "When we got married Henry was attentive, considerate, and so romantic," Alise explains. "Now everything is routine and boring. We don't even talk. Sometimes at night, after Henry has fallen asleep on the couch, I cry myself to sleep remembering how much I loved him and how special he made me feel. I don't understand why everything is so difficult now. We can't even have a conversation together. Occasionally he will open up and share, then something happens and he clams up. I wish I knew why."

Patrick, 42, a restaurant designer, is frustrated with his live-in girlfriend Jennifer, 36, who is an artist. He loves her and thinks about marrying her, but is unsure because they fight so much of the time. "Whenever I say something constructive about her or try to help her," Patrick says, "Jen reacts as though I am attacking her. Then when I explain myself, she gets more upset. I have no idea what to do. I feel frustrated because I really want to support her. I love her but when she overreacts to everything I do, I become mean and defensive. I don't know how long I can take it."

What is missing in each of these examples is a deep understanding of how men and women are different. Without this understanding it becomes nearly impossible to fully appreciate and respect the differences that make each sex special and unique. Keeping this in mind, let's review the three examples listed above:

Kathy Wants to Share, Tom Wants His "Space"

Kathy is frustrated because she is unable to fulfill her wants and needs with a man without offending him. For example, when she and her partner Tom get together after work, she wants to talk about their respective days, while he wants to forget his day and read a magazine or watch TV. The more she attempts to have a conversation and the more he resists, the more tension they both feel.

She says, "How was your day?" He says "Fine" while inside he thinks, "Ah . . . , now I can sit down, watch the news, and zone out."

She asks, "How did your meeting go?" He says "OK" while inside he thinks, "Oh no. Here we go again. She wants to interrogate me about my day. I don't want to talk about my day. If I did, I would talk about it. I just want to forget the day and watch the news."

She says, "Did you remember to renew your car registration?" He says "Yes" while inside he thinks, "I remembered it but I didn't renew it yet. I can't believe she keeps track of everything I do. I feel so smothered. Doesn't she trust that I can handle my own car registration?"

She tries again, "How was the traffic to town this morning?" He answers "The usual" while inside he thinks, "Who cares about the traffic. Why is she trying to bother me this way. Maybe she is trying to tell me I should leave more time to get to work. I hate it when she tries to improve and reform me. Give me a break, I just want to watch TV."

"Did you get to your meeting in time?" His response is "Yes." He thinks, "Get off my back, will you. You never trust me. Sure I missed part of the meeting, but the last thing I want to hear from her is a lecture on how I should give myself more time. I bet she is waiting for an opportunity to say 'I told you so.' "

Kathy senses Tom's irritation but has no idea why he is angry. She feels hurt and asks, "Are you angry with me?" He says "No!" while inside he thinks, "I just want to have some peace, and now she wants to talk about feelings. I hate it when she does this. Now I can't even enjoy watching the news, because she is upset with me. I was feeling fine about her until she did this to me. Why can't she just support me when we get together? Can't she tell that I've had a hard day? I don't bother her with a bunch of questions!"

Tom doesn't realize that Kathy *is* trying to support him, by treating him the way she wants to be treated. She is not trying to improve him with her questions; she is just trying to make conversation. Ultimately she wants him to support her by asking her caring questions. Unfortunately, he thinks he is supporting her by *not* asking questions and giving her "space," and doesn't understand why she is not respecting his "space."

On the other side, Kathy feels unloved, ignored, and taken for granted. She thinks, "I can't believe he doesn't want to share with me. He used to talk to me. He just doesn't love me the way he used to. Maybe I am boring to him. It hurts not to feel special anymore. I am so angry. He never listens to me. This is not the kind of relationship I want. Why can't I find a man who can love me. He knows I've had a hard day and I need to talk. I was so attentive to him, and he hasn't even asked me about my day. It's not fair."

Kathy doesn't realize how her attempts to support Tom actually make him feel unsupported. In various ways she mistakenly treats her male partners the way she wants to be treated, and then doesn't understand why it doesn't work. Kathy wrongly assumes that men will respond the way she or another woman would.

Alise Tries to Please, Henry Needs Appreciation

Alise is upset because she feels everything she does to help Henry is unappreciated and rejected. In truth, much of what she does is appreciated, but when it causes her to burn out and resent her relationship, then Henry would rather she do less.

For example, before Henry gets home Alise will do a variety of things to please him. She takes out the trash, she straightens up his desk, she cleans the house, she washes and folds his T-shirts and underwear, she thinks about his favorite foods and prepares a meal, she picks up after him and washes their dishes, she takes messages off the answering machine, and does anything else she can think of to please and make his life more fulfilling. In short, Alise anticipates Henry's every need and tries to attend to it. She then resents him for not doing the same in return.

Henry comes home from work already tried; when he feels his wife's resentment he becomes even more exhausted. He does not fully appreciate all that Alise does, because it makes her so resentful of him. He would rather she do less and be more appreciative for what he is doing to make her life easier. He needs her to be happier and have warmer responses to him. Henry is turned off by her martyr-like approach to their relationship.

Alise is confused because she is behaving in a way she knows would please her. In short, she is "doing unto him as she would have him do unto her." Unfortunately she doesn't ask Henry for more support. She assumes that because she is working so hard to please him, he should give back to her without her having to ask. She also assumes that if Henry loved her, then he would anticipate her needs. She does not understand that her doing more in the relationship, while resenting, makes him want to do less in the relationship. When she does ask for help — generally in a demanding tone — Henry just gets mad and smolders in silence.

Rarely do they talk except about practical matters. Whenever Henry does share about his day, Alise, in another attempt to please, tries to help him feel better. This turns Henry off; then he doesn't want to open up further to Alise about his day. For example:

Henry says, "We didn't get that new account at the office. I have to lay off about half of my crew. It's really a hard decision."

Alise, in an enthusiastic tone, says, "Well, now you have to decide who your best workers are and let the others go."

Henry's response is an immediate silence. He is turned off. Inside he thinks, "I wasn't asking her for advice. I am quite capable of handling this problem. Of course I will keep my best workers. Why can't she just listen and appreciate how hard I work. And why is she so enthusiastic?"

Alise is perplexed. She wants to help and doesn't grasp that Henry feels insulted by her trying to solve his problem. She is enthusiastic because she wants so much to please him, and this appeared to be an opportunity. At times like this she hasn't the faintest notion of what he really needs. She doesn't understand that he just wants her to listen and appreciate how hard he works. Just as she wants to feel special, he wants to feel as though he's her hero.

Patrick Invalidates Jennifer's Feelings

Patrick is frustrated because he doesn't understand Jennifer's angry reactions at times when he thinks he is supporting her. For example:

When Patrick comes home the first thing he does is to read through his mail. Then he listens to his messages and pets the dog. After looking at the newspaper for a while, he wanders into the kitchen where Jennifer is making dinner. The first thing Patrick says to Jennifer is, "Why are you mixing those spices together?"

Feeling angry and criticized, Jennifer retorts, "I feel like it, that's why." Inside she grumbles, "He hasn't even said hello and already he is criticizing me. He is ignoring me. He would rather read his mail than talk to me. He's not even excited to see me. I've been waiting to see him all day. I feel so embarrassed. He doesn't even want to give me a hug or kiss. He could care less. What a creep. He would rather pet his dog. And then he has the gall to come in my kitchen and complain about my cooking."

Patrick detects her upset and tries to make Jen feel better. He says, "Well, it's no big deal, but I just think those spices don't go well with red snapper. I think you should leave out the pepper." Inside he thinks, "Why is she defensive about a little suggestion? What's the big deal? She is so temperamental! Can't she take a little feedback?"

Jennifer says, "If it's no big deal, then why do you always insist on criticizing me when I've asked you not to! You are so mean. You don't even care how I feel. You don't love me anymore. Why should I even bother? All you care about is yourself."

Patrick then says, "That's ridiculous. I wasn't criticizing you. I can't believe you. Why do you make such a big deal out of everything? Of course I love you." Inside he adds, "I hate having to put up with your irrational outbursts. I wish you would grow up."

Patrick doesn't understand the valid reasons for Jennifer's feelings. He doesn't realize that comments like "that's ridiculous" or "I can't believe you" or "you're making such a big deal out of this" invalidate her feelings and make her feel worse. Even the phrase "Of course I love you" implies that Jennifer is insecure for doubting his love.

Jennifer overreacts to his suggestions because she feels neglected in the relationship. She is no longer being treated as she was in the beginning. He takes her for granted, then makes her feel foolish for becoming upset. He doesn't attempt to understand the real reasons for her sensitivity. His lack of respect for her feelings makes her feel invalidated, and her defensiveness increases.

Patrick is not an unloving man. He is quite capable and willing to respond to Jennifer's needs. The problem is that he doesn't know what her needs are, because they are different from his. Likewise, he doesn't respond well to her reactions because they make no sense to him. Since he would not be upset were he in Jennifer's place, he reasons, then she shouldn't be upset either. Not realizing how condescending he sounds, he invalidates her feelings. As a result, they start to fight.

Patrick mistakenly assumes that Jennifer would be happier if she were like him, so he tries to change her rather than to explore her needs and fulfill her. Like most men, Patrick does not understand that women are different and that they are supposed to be the way they are.

REEVALUATING OUR ASSUMPTIONS

Relationships are so puzzling because we mistakenly assume that our partners are like us. To some extent they are, but in many important aspects they are different. Let's look at four common ways that assuming men and women are alike negatively affects our relationships:

It Is Difficult to Nurture

When we expect another person to react as we would, we inevitably feel frustrated if they react differently. Out of frustration, we may automatically begin to invalidate our partner's feeling reactions even though our original intent was to nurture and support them.

When Jennifer and Patrick experience a crisis, it is difficult for Patrick to understand why Jennifer is getting so emotional. Under stress, he naturally becomes more detached. Jennifer, however, usually becomes emotional.

This particular difference between men and women is quite common. But their failure to understand this creates new problems. Patrick takes her emotional reaction personally, assuming that Jennifer doesn't trust his ability to handle things. He thinks that by saying "don't get upset" he is helping her, because his way of dealing with crises is to detach and not get upset. Instead, Jennifer gets *more* upset because Patrick doesn't share his feelings or validate hers. She cannot believe that he really cares because he seems so withdrawn.

It Is Difficult to Assist

We also may offend our partner by treating him or her the way we want to be treated. We mistakenly assume that "what is good for me is good for you."

For example, Alise commonly irritates her husband Henry by becoming overly caring. She is not trying to irritate him; as a matter of fact, she has no idea why he is annoyed. She is confused because she would welcome more caring from him.

By assuming that he would gladly welcome her caring influence, Alise unknowingly offends her husband. She thinks she is helping when, in truth, she is only making matters worse. It is nothing personal. Simply because he is a man, Henry feels smothered by her love. It is quite normal for men to feel smothered by too much caring. She cannot succeed in assisting him unless she first understands how his needs differ from hers.

Ultimately, every person has unique and particular needs. Understanding some of the basic differences between men and women has the advantage of helping you learn about your partner's needs and better identify some of your own.

It Is Difficult for Women to Appreciate, Accept, and Trust

Problems arise when we expect another to think, feel, and behave the way we do. Women frequently misinterpret a man's love by evaluating his behavior according to their feminine standards. For example, Patrick customarily prioritizes his problems and ignores those objectives (or commitments) that are not at the top of his list. When Jennifer's needs are then overlooked, it is hard for her to appreciate, accept, and trust that he loves her.

From his point of view, if her need were urgent, he would put it at the top of his list because she *is* so important to him. But since Jennifer doesn't understand Patrick's thinking and behavior, it is hard for her to believe him when he explains how important she really is to him. He doesn't understand that his way of handling problems frustrates Jennifer and doesn't support her needs.

This mutual misunderstanding arises because of one very fundamental difference between men and women. When under stress, men tend to prioritize and focus on what is most urgent. The drawback to this kind of stress reaction is that they forget other responsibilities or attach little importance to them. When Jennifer's needs are thus minimized, it does not feel very good to her. She cannot understand this reaction because she reacts differently under stress.

Under stress, women tend to become more acutely aware of the variety of problems and demands being placed upon them. To become oblivious to the needs of someone she cares about in order to fully focus on solving a problem at work is not one of her common experiences. Thus it is hard for her to trust that he really does care about her.

It Is Difficult for Men to Care, Understand, and Respect

It is equally hard to respond in a caring, understanding, and respectful way when you assume that your partner *should* think and feel the way you do.

Patrick has a difficult time respecting Jennifer when she feels unloved or unsupported. He knows how much he loves her, so when she doesn't feel his support, he takes it personally. He loses respect and judges her as ungrateful or irrational.

When she has had a long day and then reacts emotionally by feeling overwhelmed and hopeless, he feels as though she is complaining that he isn't helping enough.

From her point of view, Jennifer just needs to unwind and be heard. She merely needs to share; he assumes she needs him to solve her problems.

Because Patrick doesn't have the same pressing need to share his feelings, it is hard for him to respect her need to share. When he is upset he deals with it through problem solving. When she is upset, he assumes his strategy will help her too. Instead of listening, which is what she needs, he continually interrupts her with "solutions" to her problems. Jennifer doesn't get what she needs — simply to be heard — and Patrick doesn't get appreciated for trying to help. Because of faulty assumptions, they both end up frustrated.

No matter how committed we are to improving our relationships, it is impossible to make significant advances without reevaluating our hidden assumptions. The vast majority of conflicts between men and women stem from one basic misunderstanding: We assume we are the same when, in many ways, men and women are as different as aliens from separate planets would be. Without an understanding of how we are different, all our efforts to unravel the mysteries of keeping love's magic alive cannot even begin to bear fruit.

WHAT IF . . .
MEN CAME FROM MARS AND
WOMEN CAME FROM VENUS?

The communication gap between men and women can be so vast that at times our partners seem as different from us as beings from outer space. Let's pretend for a while that this is actually true. Let's pretend that men come from Mars and women from Venus.

Imagine that one day long ago Martians, looking through their telescopes, discovered the planet Venus. They had been getting pretty bored hanging around on Mars, but as soon as they spotted the strange Venusians, they started feeling quite excited. Quickly they built spaceships and flew to Venus.

When they arrived they were amazed at how they felt in the presence of these beautiful beings. The Martians began to feel powerful and more alive. A new sense of responsibility and purpose pulsed through their Martian muscles.

The Venusians reacted just as strongly to the arrival of the Martians. They had intuitively known that this day would come; when they saw the Martians, they felt a trusting love in their hearts that they had never felt before. Some said they felt like flowers opening to the warm rays of the sun; others felt more centered and clear, aware of their inner wisdom.

Together they decided to fly off in their spaceships and live happily ever after on the most beautiful planet in the solar system, Earth. For some time they lived in harmony, free from conflict.

The secret to their success was the tremendous appreciation and respect that they had for each other's differences. Neither Martian nor Venusian tried to change the other. They did not view their differences as superior or inferior, but greatly appreciated how their differences complemented each other. Through their loving interactions they all felt more powerful and fulfilled.

One morning, when the effects of Earth's atmosphere had finally taken hold, they all woke up with a peculiar kind of amnesia. They had forgotten that they were from different planets.

In an instant, they forgot that they were supposed to be different. They forgot that they spoke languages that sounded similar but were actually quite distinct. When they tried to communicate they were inevitably misunderstood.

The Martians and Venusians forgot that their needs and wants were different. They forgot that they had different motives, purposes, aims, values, drives, impulses, urges, and reactions. They forgot that they had divergent ways of thinking, feeling, recognizing, conceptualizing, perceiving, understanding, deciding, and concluding. They forgot that they had contrasting manners of acting and responding.

In one night, they had lost the awareness necessary to respect each other's unique qualities; differences were now interpreted as flaws and afflictions —

temporary manifestations of stupidity, sickness, craziness, meanness, immaturity, stubbornness, selfishness, weakness, or badness. Immediately a host of problems arose. Differences between the Martians and Venusians had become a source of conflict instead of joy, appreciation, and wonder.

In a similar way, men and women feel compelled to fix or change the other instead of supporting, nurturing, and validating. Needless to say, it becomes increasingly difficult to give and receive support. Relationships lose their magic and are filled with confusion and struggle. The bond of love diminishes as they are unable to understand, respect, appreciate, and accept their differences.

CONFLICTS IN HANDLING UPSETS

When men and women fail to understand how different the sexes are, a host of problems will predictably arise. Take Jennifer and Patrick, who experience a conflict that is quite common between men and women. This conflict arises because in some ways men and women are as different as beings from other planets, but have forgotten that they are supposed to be different.

When Jennifer is upset what she needs most of all is to talk about and explore her feelings, to have her feelings validated. Next, she needs to be touched, held, and comforted by someone she trusts and loves.

Patrick, however, handles upsets quite differently. When he is upset, he must have some space. He needs to pull away so he can think about what happened. In his mind he has a private cave where he withdraws to mull over what's bothering him. During this pulling-away stage he doesn't like to be touched.

When Patrick and Jennifer try to support one another without an awareness or respect for how they are different, unnecessary problems are sure to result. Let's explore a typical scenario between the two.

One day Jennifer becomes very upset. She needs to talk about what is bothering her. But when Patrick realizes she is upset, he gives her some space by leaving the room. Remember, for him, that is the loving thing to do.

Because Jennifer would never even think to walk away when someone she loved was upset, she misinterprets his behavior and thinks that perhaps Patrick doesn't care about her.

But since the relationship is new, Jennifer excuses his behavior by imagining that he didn't notice she was upset. She begins to cry, making sure to sob loudly enough for Patrick to hear. When he hears her crying, Patrick, again out of respect for her privacy, leaves the house.

Jennifer is now thoroughly confused. She wonders how this man, who appears to love her so much, could act in such an uncaring and inconsiderate way.

After some time Patrick returns. Jennifer decides to give him another chance and approaches him in an attempt to talk about her original upset feelings. But now she is even more upset, because she is afraid that Patrick's leaving the room and then leaving the house meant he doesn't care about her anymore.

Patrick listens attentively for a few moments, and then decides that by his standards, she is too emotionally involved with the problem.

"You're getting upset over nothing," he says. "How could you think I don't love you?" With a laugh he adds, "This is ridiculous, you must be kidding."

Patrick truly thinks he is giving some helpful advice. Jennifer, of course, finds his attitude anything but loving. Instead, she feels abandoned, insulted, and hurt. "I can't believe you love me," she responds. "Why do you treat me this way?"

Patrick, who has reached out to help, is naturally confused and frustrated. He feels unappreciated and gets upset. In typical male fashion, he silently retreats to his secret cave of the mind to figure out what just happened.

Now both Patrick and Jennifer are upset, confused, and frustrated. Each has tried the best way they know how to solve a problem, but the situation has only gotten worse. Neither of them has any idea of what really happened; both think the other is a bit crazy.

Neither Patrick nor Jennifer is crazy. They are just different.

MEN SHUT DOWN EASILY

As Patrick walks away, Jennifer begins to feel guilty for offending him, even though she has no idea of how she did it. She knocks on his door and in true female style says, "I understand you're feeling upset, Patrick. Let's talk. Tell me how you're feeling?"

He responds in typical male fashion. "I'm not feeling anything. I just want to be alone!"

Jennifer persists in her attempt to assist him in exploring his feelings, which women commonly do to help each other.

"I can tell you're angry with me," she says. "It's OK. Let's talk about it. I want to know what you are feeling." Jennifer is treating Patrick exactly as she would want to be treated.

Patrick, however, is offended and irritated by her concern. He needs space and she is crowding him. He barks, "Just leave me alone!"

Jennifer finally leaves him alone, terrified that she has lost his love.

In reality, Patrick is not nearly as upset as Jennifer imagines he is. He just needs a little time to cool off. Jennifer assumes something terrible has happened, because she would have to be extremely resentful to shut down as he has just done. She does not understand that shutting down happens to Patrick when he is just a little upset.

In fact, men tend to "shut down" completely in an instant and then open up just as quickly. Women do not understand this; once they open up to a person it takes them a long time to close down completely.

Because Patrick and Jennifer are unaware of their natural differences they end up misinterpreting, fighting, and resenting each other. Even though they love each other very much, they do not understand how to support each other. The real problem they have is not understanding their divergent needs.

HOW WOMEN LOSE SELF-WORTH

Henry and Alise love each other very much. However, after being married for six years, Alise is doubting her self-worth and resenting her husband, while Henry is no longer motivated to share in the relationship. He generally comes home, eats dinner while watching TV, and then goes to sleep. Occasionally they go out but they don't talk much.

Alise, like many women, has a particular vulnerability when she falls in love. When Alise is being loved, cherished, and treated with respect, she feels really good; from these good feelings come feelings of self-worth. But if her partner begins to treat her in a less respectful way and she doesn't feel loved, her attitude changes — she begins to feel as if she doesn't deserve to be loved after all.

The logic of this vulnerability sounds like this: "If I am being loved and respected, then I feel worthy of love and respect. Conversely, if I am not being loved and respected, then I have done something wrong and I am unworthy of love and respect." In order to compensate, the logic goes on, "If I am not receiving what I need, then I must give more before I deserve to ask for what I need."

This is exactly how Alise started feeling in her relationship with Henry. After the first year of their marriage, Henry became overly focused on his problems at work and gradually began to ignore her. When Henry came home from work, he didn't mention any problems. That was his male way of communicating that everything was fine. Each day, however, he became increasingly more distant. Alise assumed that something she had done offended him deeply and was causing him to retreat and to withhold his love. She imagined that he was secretly resenting her, because for her to clear up an upset, talking is generally essential; if you don't talk a problem out, you can't give up the resentment.

Out of fear of making things worse, Alise tried to be extra loving and giving to Henry. Ironically, the less Henry fulfilled Alise's needs, the more compulsively she tried to please Henry and the more she would give.

Occasionally, Alise would explode and demand that he be more loving. Henry's reaction was generally to become quiet and withdraw. This would scare Alise even more. From her point of view, she had tried everything to win back his love and was failing.

Since Alise could recognize that Henry was uncomfortable with her feelings and demands, she began to suppress them and tried to behave in a detached, reasonable, and nonemotional way. From time to time, however, she would lose control and again overreact emotionally.

When Henry pulled away, Alise would feel guilty for her emotional reactions and try harder to suppress her feminine nature in compliance to what she believed were his wishes. As her guilt and shame intensified, her compulsion to give more grew even stronger.

As this pattern repeated over the years, Alise gradually lost her sense of self as a woman. As a result, the couple got along, but she was unhappy. Henry occasionally wondered what had happened to the glow in her face and the sparkle in her eyes. Alise had lost her self-worth while Henry had lost touch with his loving feelings. Bored and unmotivated in his relationship, Henry had no idea what had happened.

HOW MEN LOSE MOTIVATION TO GIVE

Like most men, Henry overprioritizes his attention to such extremes that he appears to have tunnel vision. When there is a big problem at work he is apt to forget Alise's needs altogether and can only be motivated by the biggest or most urgent problems that are presented to him. After six months of marriage he started to feel that he had successfully solved the problems of the relationship — men tend to assume that once they please a woman, she will stay that way — and now he was drawn and consumed by the problems of work. He gradually became unconscious of his partner's ongoing needs.

Unfortunately the problem does not stop here. Just as being feminine has its weaknesses, so does being male. Feminine vulnerability causes Alise to give more when she receives less. Masculine weakness causes Patrick to give less when he receives more.

The logic of this common male weakness sounds like this: "If she makes certain sacrifices for me, I must have already done something to deserve it, so I can relax and receive for a while. If I am receiving more, then I don't need to give more, I can give less."

This is one of the reasons why, after winning or earning the love of a woman, men may become lazy in the relationship. As long as she continues to give with a smile on her face, he assumes that he is giving enough. He doesn't feel motivated to give more.

After a while, Henry's and Alise's relationship begins to look very lopsided. When Henry gives less Alise gives more, because she wants more. Alise assumes that her sacrifices to please Henry will naturally motivate him to give more back to her. Unfortunately her sacrifices have the opposite effect.

Henry is not encouraged or motivated to give more when he experiences receiving more by giving less. The price Henry pays in this cycle is that he loses Alise's genuine appreciation and acceptance. The price Alise pays is that she sets herself up to receive less and resent more.

Each time Alise gives in order to win Henry's love and Henry does not return her gift, she accumulates a degree of resentment. No matter how hard she tries to be loving, she cannot escape feeling resentful when she is giving from emptiness instead of giving from fullness. With each passing day her ability to appreciate, accept, and trust her partner diminishes; she is unable to give him the love he needs.

To a great extent, even Alise is unaware of this buildup of resentment. From time to time it slips out. Ironically, it comes out when one would least expect it. Whenever Henry goes out of his way to do something special or nice, her accumulated resentment prevents Alise from feeling her natural appreciation for his loving gesture. Or when she is asking for his help, her resentment intrudes, turning her request into a demand.

WOMEN, THE GREAT SCOREKEEPERS

What Henry doesn't know is that women have an incredible capacity to give without getting back. They can give and give and appear happy—because inside, they are keeping score. Women are great scorekeepers. They can keep giving because they assume that one day the score will be evened out. They assume that at some point their partner will be so grateful that he will return all that support. She will then be able to relax and be taken care of for a while.

A man generally has little conception that the score in the relationship is uneven. This is because when he does something for his partner, he expects something in return before he gives more. A man won't let the score get uneven. When the score is 3 to 1 he will begin to grumble about giving more or simply refuse.

A woman has the capacity to let the score reach 20 to 1 before she will begin to grumble. When Alise finally begins to complain about how unfair things are, Henry resents her because he has been thinking that the score is even. He resents her for withdrawing her appreciation, because he mistakenly assumed that she must have really appreciated him; otherwise, why would she have continued to give? He feels offended by her accusations. Henry feels she owes him an apology, when in truth he has been giving less in the relationship.

In resolving this kind of dilemma, the man must take responsibility to give more through understanding his partner's needs. He must also forgive her for not appreciating him and for storing up her resentment. The woman should take responsibility for being a martyr and allowing the score to get so uneven. Together, they must start a new score card.

Starting over again is achieved through the power of forgiveness. With this understanding of how they both contributed to their problem, Henry and Alise were able to turn their problem around. They are now planning to have a child, rather than get a divorce.

IF ONLY WE KNEW

These examples reveal very clearly how not understanding our differences creates problems in our relationships. With an understanding of their differences men and women can begin to construct new solutions to age-old conflicts.

Regarding the previous examples, Patrick could begin learning how to support Jennifer by listening to and exploring her feelings when she is upset. He would realize that treating her as a man invalidates her and makes her even more upset.

If Jennifer understood their differences, she would be less threatened by his male reactions, knowing that he isn't trying to be mean or intending to withhold his love. Jennifer could come to understand and support Patrick's need to pull away when he is under stress, while Patrick could learn ways to reassure Jennifer when he is withdrawing. Jennifer could find ways to share her upsets with Patrick without sounding to him as though she is blaming him.

Henry and Alise could discover new ways to handle their problems. If Alise understood men, she would know that men are like firemen: if there is a fire they give their all to put it out; otherwise, they get extra sleep to prepare for the next fire. Being aware of this, she would know that if she doesn't continue to communicate her needs, he will assume that everything is fine and give less to the relationship. She could then share her needs without resentment, in a way that Henry can understand.

If Henry understood how women are different, he would recognize that when women are not feeling centered, they give of themselves to the point of exhaustion and overwhelm. The next time Alise was overwhelmed he might not automatically blame her for taking on too much. Instead he could be compassionate and fulfill her need to be centered by listening to her.

Alise could understand that men react to resentment by becoming passive and lazy. The next time Henry was overly passive, rather than trying to rehabilitate him, she could take responsibility for her own resentment, come back to a loving place, and share her feelings of appreciation for the things he does do for her.

Having released her resentment, she would then ask for support. Asking for support with a tone of resentment in one's voice rarely works. A man is much more responsive to a request that is not backed by resentment, sacrifice, or suffering.

Henry would also understand that women tend to give more when they feel unloved. The next time Alise appeared especially interested in his day, he might get the message that Alise is unconsciously wishing he was more interested in her day. He could then respond by expressing his interest.

The next time Henry felt resentful because he wasn't being appreciated, he could remember that Alise really would be appreciating him if she weren't experiencing an accumulation of her own resentment. He would understand that she just needs to share her emotions in order to feel once again her love and appreciation.

The next time she resented him, she could remember Henry would give more if he really understood her needs. She would take responsibility for communicating her needs in a way he can hear. She would realize that men don't change their ways of doing things as quickly as women, but when they do change, it is solid. On the other hand, women don't change their feelings as quickly as men. Henry must learn to be patient in listening to Alise as she shares her upset feelings.

By understanding how women and men are different, Henry and Alise are gradually learning how to give each other the support they need. On this basis of approaching their differences as if they originated from different planets, they can more effectively nurture each other.

Of course men and women are not really from separate planets, but when we analyze the many ways we are different, we might as well be. Although both sexes are housed in human bodies, our differences far outweigh the obvious physical ones. Throughout this book we will explore these differences in great detail.

A way, then, to rekindle your desire to understand instead of to judge is to imagine that your partner or loved one is an alien from a far distant planet. Certainly if you met an adorable extraterrestrial, you wouldn't try to change him. You would probably feel an intense curiosity to understand his differences. In seeking to understand, you would be patient and tolerant. This desire to understand another with an attitude of acceptance is the basis of a positive and loving relationship. Giving your loved ones permission to be different opens a new dimension in which love can blossom.

In the next chapter we will explore four keys for creating cooperative and harmonious relationships.

CHAPTER TWO

Building a Relationship

There are four keys for creating mutually supportive and rewarding relationships:

1. *Purposeful communication* — Communicating with the intent to understand and be understood.
2. *Right understanding* — Understanding, appreciating, and respecting our differences.
3. *Giving up judgments* — Releasing negative judgments of ourselves and others.
4. *Accepting responsibility* — Taking equal responsibility for what you get from the relationship and practicing forgiveness.

These four keys can unlock the treasure of potential within you to create loving relationships and fulfill your hopes and dreams. They will help you realize why your relationships have had problems in the past, and provide a foundation to build stable and life-enriching relationships in the future.

PURPOSEFUL COMMUNICATION

Communication is essential if we are to learn about and respect each other's differences. In my first book, *What You Feel You Can Heal*, I explored in great depth the importance of telling the truth in our relationships, especially the truth about our feelings. Intimacy thrives on the communication of truth. But without understanding the underlying purpose of communication, even the best communication skills will inevitably fail.

What is this purpose and how can knowing it affect our communication? To answer this question, I will share with you how I experienced it one day. My wife and I were waiting in a restaurant during a lunch break at one of my relationship seminars. I had told the waiter we were in a hurry. He quickly seated us, brought us the menu, and we ordered. So far my communication seemed to be working well.

While we were ordering, another group was seated at the table next to us. As my wife and I waited for our food, we watched the new group leisurely order their meal and, within ten minutes, receive it. Even though we had ordered first, our food was nowhere in sight.

My temperature started to rise. After another five minutes passed and we still hadn't gotten our food, I began to boil.

I hunted down our waiter and with calculated restraint said, "I want to remind you that we are in a hurry. The people next to us ordered after we did and they've received their food." And then I blurted, "Where's our food?"

The waiter said, "Your food is coming, sir."

His answer didn't help, so I repeated myself, "The people next to us have already gotten their meal — where's my food?"

The waiter replied again, "Your food is coming."

Needless to say, I was furious. All of my compassion and good nature was gone, along with all my communication skills. I went back to the table wanting to start a war. As we continued to wait for our lunch, we watched the people at the next table finish their food and pay their check.

At this point, it was too much to bear. On the way to find the manager, I saw our waiter and approached him again. After explaining I was on a tight schedule, I asked again, "Where's my food?"

In a panic he repeated, "Your food is coming, sir."

Then fortunately, I asked, "*Why* is my food taking so long? *Why* were those people served before me?" I was finally addressing the real cause of my upset.

This time, the waiter explained, "Sir, those people ordered from our sandwich menu, which goes to a different kitchen. You ordered from our entree menu, which goes to the main kitchen. Although you can't see it from here, we're swamped by a graduation party in the next room. The cook has promised me your order is coming. I'm truly sorry it's taking so long."

In a flash my tension and distress were gone. They were gone because I could *understand* the situation. With this understanding I could feel compassion for the waiter. I could relax and choose to wait for my meal without feeling tense, resentful, and uncomfortable. I actually began to take pleasure in the view from our table and, most of all, I began to enjoy spending the time with my wife. You see, my communication with the waiter had been useless until I used it to seek more *understanding*.

Had I not taken the direction of *communicating to understand*, I could have made matters worse by communicating to manipulate or control. I could have said "I can't believe this has happened; it is disgraceful. I want to talk to your manager" or "If my food is not here in three minutes, I am leaving this restaurant and I will never come back."

When we feel upset or threatened, communication often becomes twisted and manipulative. Communication is doomed to fail when we employ it to manipulate or control. When we communicate to intimidate, threaten, disapprove, hurt, fault-find, or make someone feel guilty, we are misusing communication. We may succeed in controlling, but inevitably we will create resentment. True and effective communication has the intent to share our understanding and more thoroughly share another's understanding.

RIGHT UNDERSTANDING

Ultimately, it's not just communication that makes relationships work, but understanding. Communication is but a vehicle through which we can understand each other. Right understanding enriches our relationships, while misunderstandings ruin them. Purposeful communication allows us to increase right understanding.

How many times have you argued with someone you loved, and then found out later it was just a misunderstanding? One of the common problems in relationships is that after we get to know someone, we have a strong tendency to believe that the meaning we give to their words and gestures is accurate. We think we know what they mean, yet we frequently misunderstand their intended meaning. We jump to the wrong conclusions.

Many times, in counseling couples, I take on the role of interpreter. He says something and she hears it in a different way. She says something and he says she's wrong. In an instant they are beginning an argument. It is as though they are speaking two different languages that only sound the same. By rephrasing his meaning into words and expressions that she can understand, and vice versa, the conflict is resolved.

I remember once asking a client what she needed from her husband. Martha took a deep breath and began to cry, saying, "I just need him to listen to me . . . to hear me. I feel he doesn't love me."

As her husband Joe listened to what she said, I watched him appear to go cold. Then he silently shrugged his shoulders. I saw Martha's frustration and disapproval increase as he silently exhaled.

Next, I asked her what her husband's response had meant to her. She said, "It means he doesn't care. He's telling me that I'm wrong, that I'm too needy, and that if I had something interesting to say he might listen."

Joe started to defend himself, saying she was wrong about his response. I stopped him and asked him what was actually going on inside when his wife was feeling and expressing her need to be heard.

He said, "I was feeling frustrated. I was thinking about the things I did this week to let her know how much I love her. I was beginning to feel inadequate and disappointed because I don't know what to do. Then when she told you how she felt about my reaction, I got angry and started to make her wrong."

Martha had misunderstood Joe's detached reaction. She assumed that he didn't care and was judging her. Ironically, her misunderstanding of his reaction provoked him into actually feeling uncaring and judgmental — even though in the previous moment he had begun to soften in response to hearing her original hurt feelings. Without the assistance of a therapist, they would have continued to argue.

The original positive, caring, and vulnerable feelings we all have when we fall in love can be quickly forgotten due to simple misunderstandings and faulty assumptions. Wrong assumptions may actually provoke the behavior that, in the beginning, is imagined.

Most of the emotional tension in relationships arises from misunderstandings. Good communication lessens the chances of misunderstanding and ensures more positive relationships. Learning some basic communication skills will help, but what really makes communication work is the willing *intent* to understand.

There are many levels of understanding necessary for communication to succeed in a relationship. They are:

- A deeper understanding of ourselves and others.
- An understanding of how men and women react differently to stress.
- A deeper understanding of the true feelings that underlie what we say and do.
- An understanding of the true feelings behind the actions and reactions of others.
- A greater understanding that appearances do not always reflect reality. (For example, when our partner shrugs their shoulders, it may mean something different from when we shrug ours.)
- An understanding that what may be easy for us to ask, may be difficult for others to ask.
- An understanding that what may be easy for us to hear, may be painful for others to hear.
- An understanding that what we think should be helpful to others may not be — even if it is helpful to us.
- An understanding that people speak different languages, which may only sound the same as ours.

Right understanding starts with realizing that we are all individual and unique and that it is very easy to misunderstand each other. By understanding and respecting our differences we can truly build bridges that will unite us.

Fear of Being Different

One of the reasons we fail to acknowledge our differences is that while we were growing up, being different meant being laughed at or rejected. To become popular or powerful we needed to become like those who were already popular or powerful. As kids, we spent a lot of time trying to be like other kids.

Even though we're adults now, and even if we were very fortunate in having parents that could truly support us in our uniqueness, we're still apt to think being different means risking rejection and failure. To various degrees most people are insecure about appearing different. We are afraid that someone will come along and correct us or judge us as wrong, bad, or inadequate. Unfortunately, this is a valid fear. Most people use differences as a way to put themselves and others down. Insecure people are everywhere and quite automatically pounce on anyone who starts to step out and be themselves. For this reason, differences can be seen as a threat.

Differences Are Magic

But it's the differences between us that make for the attraction and interest in a relationship. Just like magnets, differences attract. As we grow in understanding, we can begin to appreciate these differences.

The true differences between men and women are actually complementary, giving each the opportunity to find balance. If I am overly aggressive, I may be attracted to someone who is more relaxed and receptive. Through relating with this more relaxed person, I am able to connect with the more relaxed qualities in my unconscious. These more relaxed and receptive qualities balance out, support, or complement my more developed aggressive qualities. These complementary differences are what draws us to each other and creates the mysterious feeling we call love.

The magic of difference creates yet another dimension to loving relationships. As we accept and appreciate the differences between people, we begin to also see the similarities. For although each one of us is unique, we are also, in many ways, the same. This seeming paradox points to a wonderful truth about relationships: The right person to share your life with is generally a blend of complementary differences and similarities.

There are many ways to express this mysterious blend. Here are a few I have heard from people who are both in love and in relationship.

- "We are both so different, but what keeps us together is that we are both so intense."
- "We are so different in many ways: he is a night person, I am a morning person; he is a dreamer, I am practical; he doesn't worry about things and I worry about everything. Yet, on some other level, we are one. It is as though we are on the same wavelength."
- "Sometimes I love her and sometimes I hate her. When I am not loving her, it is because I am not capable of loving at that time; I am not feeling good about me. In my heart I know it is right for us to be together."
- "Many of our problems are completely different, but what we have in common is, we have a lot of problems! We've learned to help each other cope with our problems without making the other person feel bad or unworthy. I think if he were perfect and had no problems, I would feel as though I was bringing him down all the time."
- "For two years our marriage was perfect. Then we fell out of love; the romance was gone. I woke up one morning realizing that we were two very different people with little in common. It was depressing and disappointing. That is when I began to learn about genuine love. Through

25

sharing our feelings and releasing our hidden resentments, we came to truly know and love each other. I began to love the real person rather than the person I wanted him to be."

In each of these examples, love was nurtured over time through acceptance and understanding. In this way, love fulfills its purpose to harmonize differences and creates positive and lasting relationships.

GIVING UP JUDGMENTS

Releasing negative judgments, the third key to creating a supportive relationship, is the inevitable outcome of right understanding. As we become able to understand our differences and successfully communicate our feelings, thoughts, and desires, we can then begin letting go of our negative judgments.

Negative judgments block our love and creativity. Our negative appraisals of ourselves and the results of our actions inhibit us from fully expressing our talents. Ultimately, deprecatory judgments keep us from fully enjoying all we have and our lives in general. Judgment and criticism are symptoms of low self-esteem and low self-worth.

When we feel that we are not enough, we begin to feel that what we have or what belongs to us is not enough; i.e., we do not have enough time, money, love, etc. We begin to feel that friends or family are not enough. Negative judgments ruin our relationships.

Judgment will continue until we understand, appreciate, and honor the differences between people. As we are able to love, accept, appreciate, and respect others, quite automatically we begin to accept and appreciate ourselves. This is the true secret of releasing judgment. Through loving others we are able to love ourselves, and through loving ourselves we can love others. Our self-esteem and self-worth grow daily when we are creating loving relationships.

. When we stand in negative judgment of others, it is a symptom of our own self-hatred. Most negative judgments are the projections onto others of the opinions we secretly have about ourselves.

Because the differences between men and women are not widely understood, many relationships only weaken our self-image and increase negative judgments. Men tend to make women wrong and women tend to make men wrong. Each sex feels that if only the other would change or conform, relationships would be wonderful. They could not be further from the truth.

Finding Our Oneness

True relationship is born from an awareness and appreciation of how we are different. From the vantage point of understanding and respecting our differences, we can more clearly appreciate our similarities. Recognizing our similarities gives rise to positive attitudes like compassion, empathy, understanding, acceptance, tolerance, and oneness. Acknowledging our differences creates attraction, appreciation, interest, respect, purposefulness, and excitement.

As we succeed in understanding each other, through honest sharing and heartfelt listening, we automatically begin to realize and release the negative judgments that separate us from each other. You see, it is not the differences that separate us, but our judgments around those differences — judgments born out of misunderstanding. Differences actually draw us together.

ACCEPTING RESPONSIBILITY

The fourth key for making relationships work is taking equal responsibility for what happens in the relationship and practicing forgiveness. Being responsible is the opposite of feeling as though we are a victim. Practicing forgiveness is next to impossible when we cannot see how we are equally responsible.

Have you ever felt "I gave and I gave and I got nothing back" or "I was having a great day until you ruined it." This is our victim side, a signal that we are not taking equal responsibility.

Victims think they are not responsible for what happens to them or for how they feel. Victims feel powerless to create change. Victims ignore their responsibility for provoking abuse in their relationships. The victim attitude not only ruins our relationships but also our lives.

A victim does not admit that had *they* handled things differently, they would have gotten better results. A victim is not willing to acknowledge how they contributed to their problem. A victim is not willing to see how they are misinterpreting a situation and making it worse. Moreover, they refuse to benefit in some positive way from a negative experience. They hold their past as an excuse for not being true to themselves.

A sign of a victim attitude is the feeling of resentment and blame; there is a denial of responsibility.

When we are resenting, in some way we are not willing to trust or accept the person we are resenting. We cannot trust, because we do not understand how we have provoked their behavior. We do not accept, because we mistakenly expect them to know what we need. Mind reading is sometimes easy from one woman to another, but it is almost impossible for a man to mind read a woman, or vice versa.

When we are resenting another, we do not take into consideration why they did what they did. We do not seek to validate why they may feel the way they feel. Simply put, we feel as though we are the victim and they, perforce, are the villain.

How We Unknowingly Provoke

Without thoroughly understanding how we are different, it is easy to conclude that we will unknowingly step on each other's toes from time to time.

Understanding that we are as different as Martians and Venusians opens us to seeing how we have offended others.

A close examination of what we do or do not do, in this context of respecting our differences, helps us to understand how our behavior affects others and why we get certain reactions. But responsibility for our behavior is not enough.

We are also responsible in less obvious ways. Just as our behavior provokes reaction, so do our thoughts and feelings. It is much more difficult to perceive how we affect others when our thoughts and feelings are doing the provoking, but they do have an effect.

When we openly or secretly judge another, they will tend to momentarily react in the way that we are judging them to be. If we judge them to be unloving, they may become momentarily unloving; if we judge them to be uncaring, they may react in an uncaring way, etc.

The more significant a person is to us, the more we are affected and provoked by their judgments. When we are dependent upon a person, the effect on us of their thoughts and feelings increases. Having had sex with a person also heightens their impact on us.

For example, when a woman judges a man as unloving and uncaring, he is apt to temporarily react that way. Even if she is pretending to appreciate what a caring person he is, if she secretly feels he is uncaring, the man will react to her in a more uncaring fashion. In that moment, his caring response is overshadowed by an uncaring reaction that is provoked by her negative judgments. The more bonded they are, the more he will be affected by her judgments and temporarily lose touch with his warm feelings.

Let's look at another example. When a man judges a woman as irrational and too emotional, she will tend to become irrational and overly emotional. Even if the man pretends to be understanding while a woman is sharing her feelings, if he secretly thinks she is not making sense, then she will lose her balance, disconnect from her intuitive center, and become confused.

Being provoked, however, does not mean the provoker is responsible for our reactions. We are always accountable for our own actions and reactions. Blaming the provoker is just another way of being a victim, not a justifiable excuse.

Nor does this understanding of how our thoughts and feelings can provoke a reaction mean we should condone or excuse the provoked behavior. It simply gives us a way to understand our partner's behavior; it creates an opening through which we can more fully relate to their reaction. It frees us from feeling like the victim of a chaotic and abusive world. It makes it easier to forgive.

There is still a more powerful way that we provoke abuse. Just as *judgments* provoke *temporary* dysfunction, *resentments* provoke *continuous* dysfunction. A man who resents his wife's emotions may provoke her into being continuously hypersensitive. A woman who resents her husband's uncaring attitude may provoke him into being continuously indifferent.

It is not uncommon for a man to come home feeling affectionate toward his wife, and then, when he enters her presence, suddenly become uncaring. She may be acting in a perfectly acceptable manner, but her hidden and unresolved resentments provoke in him an uncaring response.

In a similar way, it is not uncommon for a woman to come home feeling affectionate toward her husband, and then in his presence become overwhelmed with negative feelings. Again, in this particular example, his behavior may be perfectly agreeable, but his unconscious resentments provoke in her a negative emotional response.

When we resent we are holding on to our negative judgments. They stay firmly rooted until we experience some forgiveness. When we are unable to release our judgments, their power to provoke increases. No matter how good you think you are at disguising resentment, it is revealed in your actions, reactions, choice of words, body language, eyes, and tone of voice. It will seep out whether you are aware of it or not.

If you are free of resentment and you begin to negatively judge a person, it can easily be replaced minutes later with a positive judgment. But when you feel resentful, you are actually holding on to that judgment, either consciously or unconsciously.

Not only does resentment provoke negative reactions, but it also negates the effectiveness of communication. When you share your feelings and thoughts with an attitude of resentment, it is almost impossible for the person you are resenting to stay open to you. One of the reasons communication can be so easy at the beginning of a relationship is that there is no buildup of resentment.

Accumulated resentment undermines the growth of love in a relationship. The first step toward releasing resentment is to claim your responsibility; understand how you provoke the responses you get. Then, with a greater understanding of your partner and with better communication, forgiveness will become easier.

Responsibility and Repressed Resentment

It becomes easier to take responsibility when we realize that by misjudging others as wrong, unloving, incorrect, or not good enough, we unknowingly provoke their dysfunction.

There is yet another serious obstacle to accepting responsibility in our relationships. That obstacle is called repression. Both men and women easily repress their resentments. When a resentment is repressed, we become unconscious that it exists. Then it is very hard to accept responsibility for provoking dysfunction and abuse in our partners. The repression of resentments can make relationships very confusing.

When a person tries hard to be loving, understanding, and accepting without practicing good communication skills, they also become very good at repressing resentments. The harder some try to be loving, the more they repress their resentments. Then when their partner reacts as if they are being provoked by judgments and resentments, it is very difficult to take responsibility. In this case, the good intention of trying to be accepting (and thus repressing negative resentments) makes things worse.

If a man hits his wife over the head with a club and she bleeds, it is easy for him to take responsibility for how he has affected her. She can blame him and he will easily take it, because he can see how he provoked her response.

But if his repressed resentments have hit her over the head and she is bleeding and blaming him, it is very hard for him to take responsibility. Her reaction to his unseen, unconscious abuse will seem unjustified and irrational.

Good Intentions Are Not Enough

You may wish to be loving — you may even try with all your might — but your love will never be pure unless you are free from resentment. When we are free of resentment, loving is effortless. When we have to try hard to love, this is generally a sign that we are repressing our resentments.

Think of a time when you felt deeply in love. Was it difficult to love? When I first met my wife, I certainly did not have to *try* to love or appreciate her. When my daughter was a baby and she fell off the bed, I didn't have to try to care about her; every cell in my body came alive to rescue and protect her.

Think of people you deeply respect, who have achieved many great things. Do you have to try to respect them? Certainly not.

If a positive attitude is not automatic and effortless, then it is fabricated. When we feel resentful, there is no way we can hide it from the listener. It will always put the listener on guard to protect themselves from our blame.

With this knowledge about resentment, it is easier to be more responsible in our relationships. We become capable of taking responsibility when we recognize how our negative judgments, hidden or expressed, actually provoke much of the abuse or lack of support we get.

Linda, 38, had been married twelve years. After a few years of therapy, she realized how she was equally responsible for the problems in her marriage. For twelve years she had been feeling like a victim of her husband Bob's tendency to withdraw. She had resented that he was so cold, uncaring, and unloving. She now realized that her resentments had prevented him from hearing her feelings and needs. How could she expect him to be responsive when he was feeling her unspoken resentment?

Linda had believed that Bob would not feel her bitterness if she did not express it in her words or behavior. So from her point of view, Bob had no right to feel blamed by her, because she knew that she was not *openly expressing* her resentment. She did everything she could to cover it up, even to the point of making loving overtures toward Bob. When he didn't respond, her resentment grew.

Linda may have thought that her anger was hidden, but he could see it in the tightness of her jaw and hear it in the tone of her voice. As a result, his reaction, whenever she would ask for support, was to turn off and become uncaring.

Through therapy, Linda was able to see clearly how she was equally responsible for creating this problem. She realized that she had the power to change things and did. Once she stopped being the victim, her marriage dramatically improved

This is not to say that her husband Bob was not also responsible. It takes two sticks to make a fire; it takes two people to create a conflict. However, Linda realized that her job was to be responsible by communicating her feelings and needs from a truly nonresentful attitude. She had a lot of work to do on discovering and releasing old resentments and learning to genuinely love him.

Through practicing a technique you will learn later, the love letter technique, Linda was able to explore her deepest feelings and release her resentments. As she learned to communicate in a responsible way, she was amazed to see how quickly her husband responded to her nonresentful feelings by giving her the support he had always wanted to give. They felt as if they were on a second honeymoon.

This is only one of the thousands of transformations that I have witnessed as men and women learn to relate responsibly without resentment. In this case, the change was initiated by the woman and the man responded. In other cases, men have initiated this kind of change by learning to communicate thoughts, feelings, wants, and needs without resentment.

It is much easier to release our resentments when we thoroughly understand how we are responsible for what we get in our relationships. As long as we feel we are doing everything right but are still not getting what we need, we will stay victims.

Knowledge is power. The knowledge of how we are different gives us the power to be more accepting, understanding, respectful, and appreciative. The knowledge of how our secret resentments provoke others frees us to be more responsible for what we get and to practice forgiveness. With greater understanding of our differences, we can release the judgments that compel us to change our partners rather than to appreciate and support them.

In the next four chapters we will explore more deeply the psychological differences between men and women.

CHAPTER THREE

The Primary Differences Between Men and Women

The easiest place to start understanding the differences between men and women is with the physical. Most obvious, of course, is the difference in their reproductive systems. But ample research reveals other, equally significant physical differences. Look at these examples:

Men generally have thicker skin than women; thus women tend to get wrinkles at an earlier age than men.

Women have shorter vocal cords than men, so men tend to have deeper voices than women.

Men have heavier blood and about 20 percent more red corpuscles than women. This means men get more oxygen and have more energy. Men also breathe more deeply than women, while women breathe more often.

By and large, men have larger bones than women. Women's bones are not only smaller, they're arranged differently. The feminine walk we men find so enticing is really a matter of bone structure. A woman's wider pelvis, designed for childbearing, forces her to put more movement into each step she takes — causing a bit of jiggle and sway as she walks.

Men have a higher ratio of muscle to fat, which makes it easier for them to lose weight than women. Thanks to this extra muscle, men have quick start-up energy.

On the other hand, women have an extra layer of fat just underneath their skin, which keeps them warmer in winter and cooler in summer. This extra fat also gives women more energy reserves, so they have more endurance than men.

These are just a few of the physical differences between men and women. Although the physical differences are important, it's the psychological differences that give us new insight into the art of enriching relationships. These physiological differences set the stage for the deeper psychological differences.

GENERAL PSYCHOLOGICAL DIFFERENCES

Men and women are not only biologically and anatomically different, they are psychologically different as well. For example, it is universally observed that, compared to men, women are more intuitive, are more interested in love and relationships, and experience different reactions to stress. They also have different kinds of complaints and problems in relationships. To suggest, as many have, that these differences are entirely cultural and conditioned into us from childhood is absurd.

A multitude of studies clearly indicate consistently different behavior patterns between boys and girls. Statistically, for instance, boys demonstrate a greater aptitude for math skills while girls have a greater aptitude for language skills. This does not mean that every boy is better than every girl in math, or that every girl has better language skills, but it is common.

Certainly our cultural and parental conditioning affects how the sexes differ, but it is not responsible for our primary differences. From a pragmatic point of view these are determined physically by differences in our DNA programming. Then as children grow, they are further influenced by family and cultural conditioning.

In exploring our differences it would be absurd to assume that every male fits the description of a man and every female fits the description of a woman. Men are not all the same and women are not all the same in real life. Certainly, creating any stereotypical image of a man or woman ultimately would be misleading. A "real" man has a variety of qualities and characteristics that are both male and female. A "real" woman has a multitude of traits and attributes that are both female and male. There are, however, certain general differences that fit most men and most women. Men will generally relate to the male qualities, as most women will relate to the female qualities. These will be the focus of our exploration.

The problem with generalizing about the sexes is that people may begin to think something is wrong with them if they don't fit the description. But it is too cumbersome to continually qualify each generalization by stating that members of the opposite sex may equally relate if that particular side is more developed. To avoid this conflict, regard the generalizations about men to be descriptions of your male side and the generalizations about women to be your female side.

Initially, this categorizing necessary to our discussion may be confusing. This is understandable. Role reversal and gender confusion pervade our society. Women have denied aspects of who they are in order to develop aspects of their potential seen most commonly in men. In other words, they have rejected to various degrees their female side in favor of their potential to be more masculine. Likewise, men have rejected many of their male characteristics in favor of developing their potential to be more feminine.

Certainly, the development of our inner potential is a sign of growth. But to avoid creating new problems, we must learn to develop our potential without having to deny the primary qualities and characteristics of who we are as men and women (these primary male and female characteristics will be described in many contexts throughout this book).

Many women today are driven to be like men. They seek increased love, freedom, and respect at the expense of denying their own feminine values and qualities. Feminism has not only encouraged women to discover their potential to be like men, but has mistakenly implied that women *ought* to be like men. As a result, women have rejected to a great extent their essential feminine nature.

On the other hand, many men have responded by trying to be soft and sensitive in order to fulfill these women. This new, sensitive man has been rejected by women as "wimpy" or "nice but not desirable." In becoming more feminine, these men have denied much of their masculinity. They are frustrated because they have recognized that the values of the old fashioned fifties have not worked, but have not found clear examples of what does work.

It is impossible to give a particular stereotyped image that works for every man or for every woman. In general, however, we can safely say that to nurture and value one's self while pursuing the development of one's potential is the answer to this continuing quest. Giving up one's primary qualities and characteristics in favor of another's is not.

The confusion we are experiencing today is definitely due to the lack of acceptance of our differences. By accepting who we are and by embracing how others are different, we will learn to develop those different values and characteristics without compromising our true self.

For example, if a particular man tends to be rational in his assessments of the universe, he first needs to accept and appreciate that he is so rational. He will then be drawn to a more intuitive-type person, since intuition and rationality tend to be complementary. The masculine man tends to be more rational than intuitive. Through learning to love, understand, and respect the more feminine, intuitive person, he will naturally begin to develop his intuitive qualities without giving up his rational faculties.

On the other hand, another man may be predominantly intuitive. He needs to first accept and appreciate that in this respect he has more highly developed his feminine potential. Most likely, however, he has succeeded in developing his intuition through denying his rational, masculine side. To restore balance, he will be drawn to someone who tends to be more rational. Through learning to love, accept, and respect this person and her rational characteristics, he will naturally become more rational without giving up his developed intuitiveness.

As we explore common male and female differences through generalization, we should remember that these characteristics are based on what is "common" but not always the rule.

In some respects the description of men and women need be a caricature of typical differences between the sexes. These differences tend to show up the most when we are under stress (varying reactions of men and women to stress will be covered in Chapters 6 and 7). When we are more at peace we tend to be more balanced in our expression of male and female values, qualities, and characteristics.

Even when a man appears to have chiefly developed his female side, when he is under stress he will tend to react in a masculine way. He can safely assume that with some work, he can discover and develop the complementary masculine qualities within himself.

Likewise, a woman who primarily relates to the masculine qualities and characteristics described in this book can use the descriptions of feminine traits to validate and discover her rejected femininity. To whatever extent she has denied herself to develop her potential to be masculine, she can now work toward loving, accepting, and nurturing her female side.

COMPLEMENTARY DIFFERENCES

Take the example of a mirror to conceptualize how men and women can appear so similar yet be so different. The psychological differences between men and women can be likened to the reflection in a mirror. When you look into the mirror, you see yourself. At least, you think it is you.

When you look a little closer you find that although the image looks like you, it is very different. Your mirror reflection is backward! Everything is turned around.

The feminine psychology is a mirror reflection of the masculine psychology. They are exactly the same, but different. In many ways, men and women are like reflections of each other — different but complementary.

A fundamental way to understand this difference is in terms of two complementary forces that were defined by Newton. They are centripetal and centrifugal forces. Centripetal force moves toward a center. Centrifugal moves away from the center. These two apparently opposing forces are exemplified in male and female interactions.

In grade school you probably did a science experiment that involved filling a bucket with water and then, by a rope connected to the handle, swinging it around you in a circle. As you swung the bucket around you, quite mysteriously the water was held to the bottom of the bucket, even though the bucket was tilted on its side. This mystery is explained by understanding these two complementary forces.

Centrifugal force tends to pull a thing outward when it is rotating swiftly around a center. It is an *expansive* force. If it were not for centrifugal force, the water would pour out of the rotating bucket. If you were to cut the rope, or let go, centrifugal force would cause the bucket to fly out, away from you.

On the other hand, centripetal force tends to pull a thing inward when it is rotating around its center. A restraining force, or a pulling back, it is the force that keeps the rope tight. In a sense, it holds things together through being *contractive*.

These forces are paralleled by male and female psychologies. Like the expansive (centrifugal) force, a woman's awareness moves out from her center. Her fundamental nature is to move out from her self and connect with others. When she falls in love, it is easy for her to forget herself completely. In relationships, it is easy for her to become overwhelmed by the needs of others.

Men, on the other hand, tend to contract in relationships. Once a woman accepts him, he begins to pull back into himself. He tends to focus on his own needs and not hers. Like the centripetal force, he tends to hold himself together and is less likely to lose himself. In relationships, it is easy for him to be self-centered and inconsiderate of others without even knowing it.

WOMEN EXPAND, MEN CONTRACT

One of the most common problems women have in relationships is that they forget their own needs and become absorbed in the needs of their partner. A woman's greatest challenge in a relationship is to maintain her sense of self while she is expanding out to serve the needs of others. In a complementary way, a man's biggest difficulty is to overcome his tendency to be self-absorbed and self-centered.

While women tend to expand out, men tend to pull back, or contract. Like the centripetal (contractive) force, men usually move toward a center or point, not away from the point. This explains why men are often frustrated in communicating with women. Women are apt to expand with a topic, while men want them to get to the point.

For example, a man has little conception of how offensive it is to a woman when he looks at his watch while she is talking. She assumes that he doesn't care about her, when in truth he is just frustrated that she is not getting to the point. He expands by moving from point A to point B. She, on the other hand, needs to expand first upon a variety of topics, and then she may choose to focus on a point.

Generally, when a man speaks he has already silently mulled over his thoughts until he knows the main idea he wants to communicate. Then he speaks. A woman, however, does not necessarily speak to make a point; speaking assists her in discovering her point. By exploring her thoughts and feelings out loud, she discovers where she wants to go.

Just as men need to contract or pull away to mull over an idea, women find greater clarity by expanding out and sharing. When a woman begins sharing, she is not always aware of where it will take her, but she trusts that it will take her where she needs to go. For women, sharing is a potent process of self-discovery.

Many times men get frustrated with women simply because they don't understand this difference. They unknowingly interfere with this natural feminine process or they judge it as a waste of time. A man who understands this difference is able to nurture and support a woman through nonjudgmental listening.

CONTRASTING STYLES OF COMMUNICATION

For example, Harris came home and his wife Laura said, "Susie missed her soccer practice for the second time. She was very disappointed. Your brother Tom called and said they were planning to come visit in June. I didn't know what to say. I don't know where we are going to be. We may want to visit my mother in June; right at the beginning of summer break. When is the summer break? I still can't find those pictures my mom asked for. Remember, the ones we took at Yellowstone Park? Did you read the article I left for you about not feeding the bears at Yellowstone? The parks just aren't what they used to be. I remember feeding the bears with my hands. I hope we can find those pictures. Sometimes I feel everything is completely disorganized in our life. I think we need to take some time to work out our summer schedule together."

By first sharing a variety of associated ideas, Laura was then able to feel more collected and discover the point she wanted to express, that they needed to work out their summer schedule.

Harris's approach is much different. Rather than share aloud his thoughts and feelings, he will mull them over inside and then express the bottom line.

For example, Harris receives an offer to do some work in June. He wonders if it merits rearranging his summer plans. He reflects on how much greater his income would be if he takes the job. He thinks about all the extra things he can do for his family with that money. He then reflects on various summer plans with the family if he didn't take the job. He considers doing the job and joining his family for the last part of the vacation. He realizes that's not a good idea. He wonders when the kids are getting out of school. He wonders if there is some way he can do this extra work without disappointing his family. He wishes he didn't have to give up part of his vacation time to earn the extra money, but he concludes that the extra gain is worth the effort and that somehow he will try to do both. He thinks, "I'll talk to Laura and see how she feels about it."

In this way, Harris ponders his problem inside his mind, then later expresses his conclusion or bottom line out loud. He comes home and says, "I'm thinking of doing some extra work in June. We should plan our summer schedule."

Because neither partner understands the other's approach, these contrasting styles of communication result in unnecessary tension. Let's explore Harris's reaction to Laura's expansive approach. Then we'll review Laura's inner responses to Harris's focused approach.

When Laura begins talking, Harris can sense from her tone of voice that something is bothering her. She needs something from him. When she begins by saying, "Susie missed her game and is disappointed," he thinks, "So this is what is bothering her. Why is she complaining to me about it? I wasn't supposed to take Susie to the game. She thinks it's my fault and I should be more attentive to the children. I feel so frustrated, I am already doing everything I can."

38

Then Laura talks about Tom's call. Harris's inner response is, "What does Tom's call have to do with whether I am a good father?"

Next Laura mentions not knowing whether they are going to be in town. Harris thinks to himself, "How do you expect me to know our summer schedule, when we haven't even talked about it. Are you saying I should call Tom and give him an answer right away? Look, we don't have to answer him yet."

When Laura asks about the date of the summer break, Harris broods, "How am I supposed to know when school ends. Do you think if I was a more concerned father that I would know? Why don't you call the school? I can't believe you are upset about this and you waited for me to come home instead of calling the school."

Then when Laura mentions the missing pictures, Harris responds inside thinking, "Why is she bringing up these pictures again. I told her before that I don't know where they are. How does this relate to Susie missing her soccer game? What is she trying to tell me? Sure I am forgetful, but I didn't tell Susie I would take her to the game. I wonder if she is comparing me to my brother Tom, thinking that he takes his family on vacations while I don't even take Susie to her soccer game. What a ridiculous comparison."

After Laura mentions the article about how the parks are not what they used to be, Harris wonders "What does this article about bears have to do with my being there for the kids. Is she implying that the kids are growing up fast and I am somehow missing out by not being a responsible parent? Why is she upset that she can't feed the bears with her hands anymore — what does she expect me to do about that? I am so confused. Why does she do this to me?"

Finally, when Laura mentions that her life is disorganized and requests a planning meeting, Harris reacts by thinking, "That's it! I can't believe she is blaming everything on me. She accuses me of being an incompetent father and husband. Now I don't even feel like going on a summer vacation with her. Why would she even want to go with me if this is the way she feels?"

In a burst of frustration, Harris exclaims, "I'm sick of your nagging. Why does everything have to be so complicated with you? Let's try being spontaneous for a change."

Harris's increasing defensiveness stemmed from his original misunderstanding of Laura's expansive approach. Unfortunately, Harris had no idea how Laura actually felt. Laura had been sharing a series of ideas that inevitably led her to what she wanted to say, i.e., the bottom line. Harris, however, wrongly assumed that Laura's bottom line was in her first statement. Having associated her upset tone with her remark about Susie missing practice, he thought everything that followed was an elaboration on that original point. Harris has completely misread Laura's feminine communication style.

Let's now explore Laura's inner responses to Harris's male approach of expressing the bottom line first, i.e., getting right to the point. When Harris comes home after being offered an extra job he says, "I'm thinking of doing some extra work in June. We should plan our summer schedule."

Instantly Laura's feelings are hurt and her pride is offended. She exclaims, "You are so inconsiderate. How can you make such decisions without first talking to me. Don't you care about your family? All you care about is your work. You would probably be happier if you didn't have a family. Don't you know the kids get out of school in June? Even if you are going to be so rigid about it, the least you could do is ask me how I feel. At least take me into consideration." Needless to say, they are now in the middle of a big argument.

Laura wrongly infers that Harris has made a final decision and is not open to hearing her thoughts and feelings. She feels excluded, unimportant, and taken for granted. She doesn't realize that he has thought a lot about his family and her. In truth Harris is open to discussion, but unfortunately he assumes Laura would know that.

Why Men Appear Self-Centered

Another example of psychological contraction in men is a source of great confusion for women. It is hard for a woman to understand how a man can love her so attentively, and then suddenly shift and appear self-centered. Because this kind of shift is foreign to her, she takes it personally.

She does not realize how automatic it is for a man to become completely oblivious of everyone except his focus. When he is focused on pleasing her, he is very attentive to her. But when he thinks she is pleased, he finds a new focus, like a problem at work, and then directs all his attentiveness to that.

When under stress, men commonly increase their focus and become even more unmindful of others. This creates the appearance that they are self-absorbed or uncaring. At such times, they are not necessarily narcissistic or selfish, but may appear that way. They become absorbed in achieving their goal and forget everything else. To recognize that they really are caring, one can note that many times the goals they are absorbed in achieving are ultimately very altruistic or supportive of others.

It is hard for a woman to relate to this, because under stress a woman tends to expand out and become even more aware of others, especially the ones she loves. When a man is distressed at work he *appears* to forget that his family exists and focuses on solving the problem at work. Ultimately, though, he does care about supporting his family, and that is why he is so concerned about solving the problem at work.

A woman, distressed at work, compounds her upset, because she knows she is neglecting her family and may feel their needs even more strongly. Under stress her partner becomes more focused while she becomes more expanded. No wonder there is so much confusion in our relationships.

As we have seen, automatic focusing is an example of the masculine, centripetal force. It restricts or contracts awareness in order to increase focus. A woman falsely assumes that if a man loves her, he will expand, which is her normal reaction. She needs to understand that the way a man reacts has to do with his inherent balance of male and female forces, and is not a measure of his love. A woman who understands this will not feel so resentful when a man ignores her, but will apply skills to get his attention when she needs it.

THE NEED FOR BALANCE

Every man and every woman has both male and female energies. We could not exist without a combination of the masculine and feminine energies. The internal imbalance of these complementary forces determines many of the problems we experience in a relationship.

When a man has developed more of his masculine (contractive) tendencies than his feminine (expansive) tendencies, at times he will appear self-centered and selfish when, in truth, he is just blind to the needs of others. He will appear to be uncaring, but his real problem is his inability to access his feminine potential, through which he can easily be aware of the needs of others.

In a similar (but complementary) way, a woman who has an excess of feminine energy will be overly concerned with others and have little awareness of her self. When experiencing the stress of not getting what she needs, she expands even more. She becomes more responsive to the needs of others but forgets herself. She sacrifices herself, without even knowing that she's doing it. At a time when she needs more, she is unable to assert herself or share her wishes, because she is unaware of them.

Just as a man under stress appears ungiving or uncaring because he contracts, a woman appears unreceptive or unsupportable because she expands. To avoid these extreme states, men need to explore, develop, and balance both their male and female sides, and women must do likewise. Through blending these complementary energies, not only do our relationships improve but we individually become more creative.

To find greater balance within ourselves, we are naturally attracted to those qualities and characteristics that complement or balance what we have already developed. Male qualities are naturally attractive to the female, and vice versa. This is one of the secrets to understanding the "chemistry" of attraction between men and women.

Through learning to successfully love, appreciate, accept, and understand these differences, quite automatically we become whole within ourselves. Through loving the feminine, a man becomes more feminine while maintaining his masculine qualities. Through loving the masculine, a woman becomes more masculine without sacrificing her feminine qualities. By loving and respecting our differences we ourselves gain balance.

THE MYSTERY OF ATTRACTION

If we look to how we are conceived, we can understand the creative process. The male is attracted to the female; the female ovum sitting stationary attracts the moving male sperm. When the two connect, the creation of new life begins.

Every creative action is the product of complementary forces. Because living is a constant process of creation, we are constantly attracting and being attracted to the complementary forces necessary for the creative process.

In witnessing the birth of a child one can't help but be in awe of how nature alternates one- to two-minute contractions (masculine tightening) with minutes of relaxation (feminine expansion) in order to move the baby out. Even the process of breathing that gives us life is governed by the drawing in of breath (contraction) and the relaxing expulsion of air (expansion).

Another mysterious force that reveals this dual nature is magnetism. Although we have learned to utilize and describe this force, it is still a mystery. What we do know, put simply, is that opposite polarities attract and like polarities repel each other.

When we compare this to what occurs between men and women, we can begin to understand what we call "chemistry" or mutual attraction. Chemistry happens when a person feels a complementary force or quality in another. The two people are naturally drawn to each other, just like the opposite poles of two magnets. In this magnetic field of love, all it takes to generate the electricity of desire, excitement, and attraction is interaction.

KEEPING THE PASSION ALIVE

When partners are able to keep alive their differences through loving and respecting each other, they can sustain the passion in their relationship. When men and women become too similar they lose the attraction or chemistry. It is boring to be with someone just like yourself. To maintain passion in a relationship we must work to preserve our differences while gradually incorporating the qualities of our partner.

Passion in the beginning of a relationship generally tells us that what we are attracted to in our partner is also within ourselves. If we are attracted to their warmth, then that very warmth is seeking to emerge from our potential or unconscious self, to be integrated into our conscious being.

Tom, who is very cool and detached, is attracted to Jane, who is warm and feeling. Unconsciously he is attracted to her because she reflects qualities of his undeveloped female side. Through loving her he discovers his own inner warmth and feelings, to balance his coolness and detachment.

By connecting with her he feels whole and experiences an immediate surge of fulfillment. In loving a partner who is different but who mirrors a part of his emerging self, Tom experiences the elixir of fulfillment that only a passionate relationship can stimulate.

For example, a certain kind of man is attracted to women who are warm, receptive, vulnerable, feeling, loving, and yielding. The type of man attracted to this more feminine woman tends to be in some ways cool, aggressive, assertive, reasonable, successful, and decisive. These are aspects of his male side seeking balance through union with her female qualities of warmth, receptivity, etc.

Through loving and accepting a woman's feminine qualities, a man automatically becomes more loving and accepting of his own female side. Through touching her softness he awakens to his own softness, and yet remains hard. His cool is balanced with her warmth, his aggression is balanced by her receptivity, his assertiveness is balanced by her vulnerability, his power is balanced by her love, etc. By this process he is becoming whole and balanced. Through loving her he discovers within himself his own feminine qualities. And as she loves him, her own masculine qualities begin to be felt.

This paradox is integral to any loving and passionate relationship. By virtue of being different from our partners we are attracted to them. But through our inner potential to be like them, we are able to relate and have the possibility of intimacy, communication, and closeness. Without some differences there can be no relating; without some similarities there can be no joining.

HOW WE LOSE THE ATTRACTION

When partners do not respect and appreciate their complementary differences they lose their electricity, i.e., they are no longer turned on by each other. Without the polarity, they lose the attraction.

This loss of attraction can happen in two different ways. We either suppress our true inner self in an attempt to please our partner, or we try to mold them into our own image. Either strategy — to repress ourselves or to change our partners — will sabotage the relationship.

When we succeed in changing our partner we may get some short-term need fulfilled, but ultimately there will be no passion. For example, Tom says to Jane, "Don't be so emotional, you're getting upset over nothing." If she represses her feeling side to please and accommodate Tom, he feels less friction with her and she wins his love. The short-term result appears to be a good and harmonious relationship, but now Jane and Tom will be a few degrees less interested, excited, or attracted to each other.

As this process of gradually suppressing their true selves continues, more and more degrees of passion and interest will be lost until they feel almost nothing for each other. They will be friends but experience no passion. The good news is that this process can be reversed; we can learn to find ourselves again without always having to change partners.

To whatever extent a partner must suppress their ways of being, feeling, thinking, and doing to receive love or be safe in a relationship, the passion will fade. As we conform or reform, not only do we lessen the passion, but we also diminish the love.

Every time you suppress, repress, or deny yourself in order to be loved, you are not loving yourself. You are giving yourself the message that you are not good enough just the way you are. And every time you try to alter, fix, or improve your partner, you are sending them the message that they do not deserve to be loved for who they are. Under these conditions love dies. By trying to preserve the magic of love through conforming or reforming, we only make matters worse.

When in the name of love you seek to repress yourself or to change your partner, that is actually a kind of dysfunctional love. In later chapters we will explore real love as opposed to dysfunctional and manipulative love.

WHY WE CONFORM AND REFORM

When men and women are attracted to each other a tension is produced. The two, both separate, seek to fuse together. By getting closer through relating, being together, doing things together, communicating, sharing, touching, and sex, this tension is released and bliss, happiness, peace, inspiration, freedom, confidence, or fulfillment is immediately experienced.

The bliss is the result of awakening to our inner qualities, which in turn makes us feel whole. Unfortunately, however, this bliss is not lasting. It is but a glimpse of how we will feel when we are truly whole and balanced. But to actually become whole, these potential qualities must begin to emerge into our conscious being. To whatever extent we resist these emerging qualities, we will lose the bliss and may even experience its opposite.

For example, when Tom loves Jane he becomes more considerate, compassionate, caring, and feeling. At first, this makes him feel happy and confident. But to whatever degree his past conditioning tells him, "It is not OK for men to be feeling or considerate," his unconscious mind will automatically resist the emerging qualities of his feminine side.

Inner alarm bells go off, announcing, "Danger, danger, you are becoming a wimp. Watch out, do not proceed in this way. Pull back. . . ." This inner resistance gives rise to a host of negative symptoms. He may suddenly feel resistant to his partner, dissatisfied, unhappy, distressed, oppressed, smothered, anxious, depressed, or empty.

What was so wonderful now becomes painful. To escape from these natural growth pains, Tom will seek to "avoid relationship." This is most easily accomplished by reforming or conforming — he may try to change his partner or give up being himself. In both cases he will find temporary relief, but in the long run the relationship will become less loving and passionate.

Thus when a man is attracted to a woman, at some point he will resist his partner and may then seek to change her or deny himself in order to find relief. There are, of course, other means to obtain relief, like moving from one partner to another, having secret affairs, or developing any addiction that can numb the growing pains of resistance. In any case, to whatever degree he is resisting the emergence of the very qualities he was attracted to, he will seek to avoid true relating.

Reforming, one measure commonly taken to escape the distress of inner resistance, is an increasing demand for her to be like himself. He will expect her to want what he wants, feel the way he feels, and react the way he reacts.

Out of his need to control or change her, he is unknowingly hurting her as well as reducing the original polarity and attraction.

She, on the other hand, may also contribute equally to this process. It is not all his fault; as the saying goes, it always takes two to tango. As her own resistance to relating emerges, she may seek to ease her discomfort by denying herself.

Women who are attracted to controlling and reforming men tend to be equally good at conforming, complying, and denying themselves. They become overly dependent on their partners for a sense of identity. Of their own accord they offer up their sense of self and will to their partners, to earn love and create harmony.

For example, if Tom feels Jane is selfish or inadequate, she releases her own self-image and agrees with him. If he wants her to like the movies he likes, then she rejects her own preferences. If he thinks she is being unrealistic or demanding, she agrees and loses touch with her own values and needs. As he tries to change her, she yields to his control in order to be loved and feel lovable.

Surrender is one of women's greatest virtues. But as this typical example illustrates, she often surrenders far too much — so much that she begins to deny her sense of self in order to earn her man's love. Over and over again she gives in to his wishes and needs while postponing her own. She believes this will make things better. But by reducing the original polarity between them, this way of relating decreases the attraction. If she succeeds in becoming more like him, she may create temporary harmony, but the attraction will diminish.

The opposite case also occurs. A man whose female side is well developed may surrender overmuch to his partner's wishes. This type of man is generally considered the "sensitive type." The problem they often complain about is that women "like" them but are not attracted to them. They make great friends but women don't want them for an intimate relationship.

The woman who is initially attracted to this type has developed more of her male side. She is predominantly independent and aggressive. Unconsciously she begins to control and dominate him and gradually, as he complies, she may lose interest.

When the independent type of woman begins a relationship with a "sensitive" man, after some time her suppressed female side begins to emerge. To whatever extent she has rejected her female side she will tend to reject her partner. She may begin to feel, "I need a real man," when in fact she needs to accept and develop her own female side. She is not really rejecting him, but her own female side, which he has already developed.

In a similar way, when the sensitive man rejects an aggressive woman, he needs to accept and develop his own male side. In rejecting her he may say that he wants a soft and vulnerable woman. In truth he doesn't need a woman to make him feel like a man; he needs to work on developing his emerging masculinity, which she is already helping him to find.

WHY WE RESIST OUR DIFFERENCES

This understanding of resistance helps us to understand why men and women typically seem so eager, loving, and giving in the beginning of a relationship, and then later pull back. Commonly partners put forth their best selves in the early stages of a relationship. As their resistance to each other increases, they tend to conform and reform. Knowledge about the underlying causes of this resistance unveils many of the mysteries of relationships.

The four basic categories and causes of resistance are:

1. *Macho man* (masculine resisting feminine)
2. *Martyr woman* (feminine resisting masculine)
3. *Sensitive man* (developed feminine, repressed masculine)
4. *Independent woman* (developed masculine, repressed feminine)

In the following sections we will look at examples of each of these types and some of their possible causes. Some people fit only one of these categories, while others may shift from one to another. Men commonly swing back and forth between being macho and sensitive, while women swing between martyrdom and independence.

Macho Man

Generally, a macho man is drawn to a woman because she reflects parts of his undeveloped feminine side. Through relating to her, he feels more whole and complete and thus turned on, excited, curious, or interested. This is the good part of getting closer to a person. But then the problems of getting close also emerge.

Through uniting with her, it is inevitable that he will begin to resist her differences. His loving union with her facilitates the emergence of his own feminine side. To whatever extent his past conditioning has rejected his own feminine qualities, as they begin to emerge he will begin to reject her.

For example, as a man loves his female partner, he may become more vulnerable, feeling, and in need of love and reassurance. These are qualities of his female side. If he has been conditioned to believe that feelings are a sign of weakness, he will resist this natural growth process.

This conditioning may have begun when he observed the way his father reacted to his mother's feminine side. If his father was judgmental or disrespectful of her feelings and vulnerability, then unconsciously the little boy may have resisted being vulnerable or expressive of feelings as he grew up. It could also be that his father didn't show his feelings, and so the little boy got a clear message again and again that men don't cry or show feelings.

These kinds of messages are unconsciously received thousands and thousands of times. Then as an adult, when macho man falls in love and his soft feelings begin to emerge, that early conditioning restricts the natural growth process. At such a time, he doesn't know what is happening. This inner resistance to his emerging feminine side is happening unconsciously. He experiences becoming uneasy, overly defensive, controlling, judgmental of his partner, overly frustrated, righteous, demeaning, condescending, impatient, or he simply shuts down — and doesn't know why.

Resisting his emerging female qualities, he rejects his female partner or tries to change her by "fixing" her or by invalidating her feelings and needs. Quite unconscious of the real cause of his discomfort, he imagines it to be his partner. To whatever extent he judges his own femininity, he will project those judgments onto his partner.

Without some kind of training manual like this book, it could take macho man a very long time to understand his feminine side. To overcome his inner resistance, the macho man needs to practice respecting the feminine qualities, values, and needs. Learning to listen to women with respect, caring, and understanding, and then patiently learning to accept his own feelings will help him overcome the occasional resistance produced by early childhood conditioning. Compassion and empathy for women and children will emerge as he takes the time to understand what women really feel. He may even need to do some healing with his mother. Remember, before judging a woman he should try walking a mile in her high-heel shoes.

Martyr Woman

Much the same resistance process occurs to women. For example, when a martyr-type woman loves her male partner, she may naturally become more assertive, strong, detached, and autonomous. These are qualities of her male side. Through loving, trusting, and accepting his aggression and assertiveness, she naturally begins to connect with those qualities within herself.

If she has been conditioned to believe that women who show strength will be rejected, she will unconsciously resist this natural integration process. She may have been programmed from early childhood on that women should not be assertive, women should stay at home, women are subordinate to men, women must never show a man that she is intelligent, women should be submissive, etc.

This kind of conditioning is most dramatic when a little girl watches her mother repressing her masculine qualities. When she sees her mother being a martyr, that is the feminine role she learns. When Dad treats Mom and her sisters one way but he treats her brothers another way, she learns by example that her place is in the home, that she is subordinate and should wait on Daddy, that she is to always comply with his wishes, that Mom's will is always subordinate to Dad's, that women should not be successful, etc. In thousands of ways she may get the message that it is not safe for a female to act masculine.

In adulthood when she loves a man, her masculine side will begin to emerge. Because of her negative conditioning, she will not feel safe opening up to her male qualities and may become increasingly protective, critical, opinionated, mistrusting, manipulative, or resentful of the man she loves the most. All of the negative judgments toward her own masculinity get projected onto her partner. Although she is unconsciously resisting herself, consciously she compulsively begins to resist, resent, and reject her partner.

To overcome her inner resistance, the martyr woman needs to practice being autonomous and assertive. She needs, above all, to practice asking for support, and to give up expecting men to anticipate her needs just as she does for them. As her tendency in relationships is to keep score, she needs to take responsibility for her role in letting the score get too uneven. When it does get uneven she needs to practice forgiveness to release her resentments. She needs to honor and heal the repressed feelings of anger and resentment stored up from her past. She generally needs to do some healing with her father.

Sensitive Man

As this sensitive-type man gets closer to a woman, his repressed masculine qualities begin to emerge into consciousness. At some point — if his conditioning says that aggression is destructive and not creative, or assertiveness is selfish and not positive, or that being reasonable is not loving — he will instinctively try to repress his emerging male qualities.

This kind of negative conditioning may occur in childhood. For example, by experiencing his father being abusive with his aggressive energy rather than being creative or productive, a young child may reject masculinity as evil and bond more closely with his mother. He may experience his father's assertive energy expressed in a selfish, controlling way and thus seek to repress his own assertiveness. He may observe his father justifying abuse and thus experience the power of the intellect as negative.

As a child, this sensitive man has been powerfully affected by the examples set by his parents. He may also reject his masculinity when he perceives his mother being hurt by men. The mistrust she feels toward his father the boy begins to feel toward his own masculine side.

When a man has repressed his masculinity, he is generally attracted to women who have already developed to some extent those qualities. Again the union of opposites creates passion, but as his male energies begin to emerge a shift takes place. Due to negative conditioning surrounding masculinity, aggression, assertiveness, power, etc., he will begin to experience an inner resistance. This resistance gets projected onto his partner. He unconsciously becomes defensive, critical, mistrusting, manipulative, resentful, and disapproving.

To overcome his inner resistance, the sensitive man needs to practice giving up blame in his relationships and being completely responsible and accountable for what happens to him. He needs to practice being decisive, rational, and logical. He should rely less on his feelings and more on his mind to make decisions. He should practice doing little things to support his partner that require some extra effort. Most of all, he needs to practice following through and keeping his word.

To strengthen his masculinity, the sensitive man can do more things with men, hang out with men, see action male movies, or participate in some competitive sport. Healing his relationship with his father is very important, as well as having male teachers, guides, or mentors.

Independent Woman

When a woman who has repressed her feminine qualities becomes involved with a man who has developed more of his female qualities, inevitably her feminine traits will begin to emerge. Her conditioning brings up misleading ideas: that being soft and vulnerable is weak, or "feeling" people go crazy, or it is not safe to need others, or that people who need others are victims. As her feminine feelings, needs, and vulnerabilities emerge she panics inside and begins to resist her partner.

The overly independent woman doesn't feel it is safe to reveal her female side. She is afraid of being judged or hurt in some ways. She may long for a more masculine man to "make her feel like a woman," when she really needs to heal the emerging woman in her. Out of resistance she may become judgmental, critical, controlling, demanding, and disappointed with her partner.

This conditioning to suppress her feminine side may have come from observing her mother being victimlike or unfulfilled. The very same feminine vulnerability and softness that can make a woman so nonthreatening, attractive, and receptive may have been distorted by her dysfunctional mother and expressed in a powerless, helpless, and unfulfilled way. To protect herself from turning out like her mother, she represses her feminine side. If, moreover, her father was rejecting, condescending, or invalidating of her mother's feelings, she probably concluded that feelings are irrational and unworthy of respect.

To overcome her resistance, the independent woman needs to practice being vulnerable and work on expressing her feelings and emotions in situations where she feels supported. She also needs to heal her relationship with her mother — in a sense she needs to accept the part of her that is like her mother, and acknowledge that it is lovable and worthy of support.

Trust is a major issue to overcome in her life. Trust means letting oneself be vulnerable, which involves being hurt from time to time. This woman must learn to feel her negative emotions and heal them as they gradually come up to be healed. Through persistent sharing of her feminine feelings she will gradually overcome her shame and embarrassment around being feminine, and learn to respect her feminine qualities as she already values her male side.

She needs to recognize that even when she feels independent and strong, deep inside she fears that others will not love her. Secretly she may feel unworthy or not good enough. By opening up gradually, she will gracefully learn to balance her developed masculine side with her newly developed feminine side.

In a variety of ways, children are programmed to favor and reject different aspects of their male and female sides. Deepening our understanding of our male and female sides frees us from the prison of negative childhood conditioning. Through learning to understand, accept, respect, and appreciate our gender differences, not only do we become more successful in loving and supporting our partners of the opposite sex, but also we learn to love ourselves. This kind of self-love liberates us to be all that we are.

MAINTAINING THE ATTRACTION

A relationship that sustains the magic of love is one in which we do not try to change the other nor deny ourselves. Through understanding our complementary differences we release the tendency to mold our partners into our own image. We are also able to accept and appreciate our own uniqueness without judgment, shame, or guilt.

A relationship blossoms, and attraction is sustained, when we can both support our partners in being themselves and receive support for being ourselves. Just as we must learn how to give support according to our partners' unique needs, we must also learn how to receive support without giving up who we are. Learning to appreciate and respect our differences is essential if we are to have mutually supportive relationships. It is this growing love and respect of our differences that supports us through the inevitable periods of resistance, resentment, and rejection.

In the next three chapters we will explore these differences in greater detail. In Chapter 4 we will explore how men and women see the world differently. Chapter 5 will look at how men and women develop self-esteem in different ways. Then in Chapter 6 we will compare male and female reactions to stress.

CHAPTER FOUR

How Men and Women See the World Differently

Men and women see the world as if each sex was wearing different glasses. In a generalized way, men see the world from a "focused perspective" while women see the world from a more "expanded perspective." Both perceptions are, however, equally accurate.

Masculine awareness tends to relate one thing to another in a sequential way, gradually building a complete picture. It is a perspective that relates one part with another part, in terms of producing a whole.

Feminine awareness is expanded; it intuitively takes in the whole picture and gradually discovers the parts within, and it explores how the parts are all related to the whole. It places more emphasis on context rather than content.

This difference in orientation greatly affects values, priorities, instincts, and interests. Because the "feminine open awareness" perceives how we are interrelated, women naturally take a greater interest in love, relationships, communication, sharing, cooperation, intuition, and harmony. Likewise, because the "masculine focused awareness" perceives how parts make up a whole, men have a greater interest in producing results, achieving goals, power, competition, work, logic, and efficiency.

FOCUSED AND OPEN AWARENESS

Focused awareness can be conceived of in terms of a spiral moving toward a center or point. You could imagine an archer with his arrow pointed at the center of a target. Open or expanded awareness can be visualized as a spiral moving out from a point. To grasp open awareness, picture a radar dish receiving from all directions and reflecting in all directions. Open awareness is like a floodlight, while focused awareness is like a laser. Both have their own unique value. Let's look at some everyday examples of how men are focused and women are open.

Boy Scouts and Girl Scouts

As her awareness expands out into the future, a woman is naturally concerned for what potentially could happen. She is motivated to prepare for the future. On the other hand, focused awareness makes men more concerned with efficiently achieving their goals. While the men are worried about getting to their destinations, the women are more concerned about what will happen when they get there.

This can be noticed quite clearly through observing Boy Scouts and Girl Scouts. While the young Boy Scouts are busy figuring out how to get from point A to point B, the little Girl Scouts are already preparing what they are going to eat when they get to point B.

When the Boy Scouts get to point B, one turns to the other and enquires, "Who brought the food?"

In response he hears, "I don't know . . . I forgot . . . I thought you were going to."

They were unprepared — oblivious of what they were going to do once they got there — because they were so focused on getting to the goal. Because they are born without an abundance of expanded awareness, Boy Scouts repeat daily as their motto, "Be Prepared!" It is even sewn into their uniforms. To mature properly little boys are trained to be prepared.

Little girls, on the other hand, need not be trained in this attitude; their open and expanded awareness makes them already preoccupied with being prepared. Like radar, their expanded awareness alerts them to all the possible things that could go wrong.

In preparing to such an extent, however, the Girl Scouts tend to be late in arriving, or they may feel the journey is too risky and let their fears hold them back. It is much easier to be courageous when you are unaware of the possible consequences of an action.

Wallets and Purses

Contrasts in how males and females confront the world are most visually apparent when we compare a woman's purse with a man's wallet. Women carry large, heavy bags with beautiful decorations and shiny colors, while men carry lightweight, plain black or brown wallets that are designed to carry only the bare essentials: a driver's license, major credit cards, and paper money. One can never be too sure what one will find when looking into a woman's purse. Even she may not know. But one thing is for sure, she will be carrying everything she could possibly need, along with whatever others may need too.

When looking in a woman's purse the first thing you find is a collection of other, littler purses and containers. It's as though she carries her own private drugstore and office combined. You may find a wallet, a coin purse, a makeup kit, a mirror, an organizer and calender, a checkbook, a small calculator, another smaller makeup kit with a little mirror, a hair brush and comb, an address book, an older address book for really old friends, an eyeglass container, sunglasses in another container, a package of tissue, several partially used tissues, tampons, a condom package or diaphragm, a set of keys, an extra set of keys, her husband's keys, a toothbrush, toothpaste, breath spray, plain floss, flavored floss (her children like mint), a little container of aspirin, another container of vitamins and pills, two or three nail files, four or five pens and pencils, several little pads of paper, a roll of film in its container and an empty film container, a package of business cards from friends and experts in all fields, a miniature picture album of her loved ones, lip balm, tea bags, another package of pain-relief pills, an envelope filled with receipts, various letters and cards from loved ones, stamps, a small package of bills to be paid, and a host of other miscellaneous items like paper clips, rubber bands, safety pins, barrettes, bobby pins, fingernail clippers, stationery and matching envelopes, gum, trail mix, assorted discount coupons, breath mints, and bits of garbage to be thrown away (next spring). In short, she has everything she could need and carries it with her wherever she goes.

To a woman, her purse is her security blanket, a trusted friend, an important part of her self. You can tell how expanded a woman's awareness is by the size of her purse. She is prepared for every emergency, wherever she may find herself.

Ironically, when she is being escorted to a grand ball she will leave this purse at home and bring a little shiny purse with the bare essentials. In this case, she feels, this night is for her. She is being taken care of by her man and she doesn't have to feel responsible for anybody. She feels so special and so supported that she doesn't need the security of her purse.

Entering a Room

Men and women will tend to enter a room differently. A man will walk into the room, pick a spot, move to it, then look out to one thing, then another, and yet another, until he gradually builds up a picture of his environment (this may happen in just a few moments). His innate tendency will be to first focus, and then expand and open.

A woman, in contrast, will walk into the same room and in a quick glance, notice lots of things almost simultaneously. In a sense, she will take in the entire room before she is concerned about where her spot will be. She will notice the color of the walls, interesting people or pictures, friends or family members, how the room is set up, etc. Then, when she has a picture of the whole environment, she will find a spot in which to settle.

A more dramatic example is the behavior of men and women at an exposition or convention. You can observe the masculine focus as he very pointedly and purposefully moves from one display booth to another. A woman, on the other hand, seems to spontaneously flow from one thing to another as if taking everything in. For her, it is a process of exploration and discovery, while for the man it is a process of achievement and accomplishment.

He is focused on experiencing what he considers the most important or relevant booths; she is having a good time, eager to take everything in and, for that matter, eager to take things home with her. It is the feminine nature to shop and collect.

Shopping without a particular focus or deadline is very relaxing for women but tends to be very draining for men. Conversely, men are energized if they maintain a sense of focus and purpose as they shop. With this perspective, let's observe how men and women behave differently in shopping malls and grocery stores.

Shopping

When a man is focused he is energized. A woman, on the other hand, can burn out very quickly if she is too focused, especially when she is in a very busy, expanded environment. Likewise, a man burns out or tires when he is too open and is not focused. For this reason, women generally enjoy shopping more than men.

A woman becomes more centered through shopping, because there are so many things to take into her awareness. This "taking in the environment" fulfills her need to expand and relate. As she experiences all the various items in the shopping arena, her awareness expands out and yet is constantly related back to her self and loved ones. She sees a dress and her awareness soars, reflecting on the romantic occasions when she could wear it. She imagines herself in it. She tries it on. She enjoys its beauty, puts it away, and has had a fulfilling experience.

Thirty minutes of unfocused shopping is the maximum a man can take before he begins to tire. For women, a few hours of unpressured shopping can be relaxing, centering, and rejuvenating. Acknowledgment of this difference is steadily growing; notice that in most women's stores there are now chairs strategically placed for the husband or boyfriend to sit in.

Another shopping difference can be observed in grocery stores. Women are busy saving money by using discount coupons and buying what is on sale. Men certainly enjoy the conquest of a good deal, but in general they are more concerned with making money rather than saving it. Men are more concerned with getting to a goal, while women are more concerned with responsibly possessing what has been obtained. That is why a man is not instinctively motivated to carry a packet of discount coupons. When he grocery shops his goal is to buy food; when he is at work his goal is to make money.

Phone Conversations and Car Trips

Men don't like to be talked to while they are busy talking to someone else on the phone. Women are generally bewildered when a man resists being interrupted while talking on the phone. It is difficult for a woman to understand why he becomes so frustrated or irritable. She fails to realize that he does not easily keep track of two things at once, i.e., what she is saying and what is being said on the phone.

Masculine energy wants to concentrate on one thing at a time; the interruption destroys his focus. Conversely, a woman is able to talk on the phone, keep dinner from boiling over, comfort a child, and understand what the man is saying to her — all at the same time. Her expanded awareness allows her to keep track of many things at once. Of course a man could allow his awareness to expand and do many things at once, but his general instinct is to focus on one thing at a time.

Driving the car is another situation that brings up these differences. Never try having an intimate conversation with a man while he is driving. He is so focused on getting to his goal in the most efficient way possible that it is difficult to keep his attention. Because his female partner doesn't readily relate to his focused awareness, she misinterprets his not listening to mean that he doesn't care. As a result, for many couples driving in the car can become a very tense experience. This little misunderstanding creates a resentment that causes conversations to turn into arguments and vacations into disasters.

These are simple, everyday illustrations of the masculine tendency toward focused awareness and the feminine inclination toward wide-open awareness. But as simple as these examples are, they can provide the basis for resolving many of the difficulties in communication that can occur between men and women.

GETTING HIS ATTENTION

If a woman knows a man usually operates better when he focuses on one thing at a time, she can avoid conflicts by not distracting him. Or, if she needs his attention, this information can allow her to interrupt in a way that works. For instance, she can acknowledge the interruption and ask for his attention, which allows him time to change his focus.

Instead of just beginning to talk, she might say something like this: "Honey, I know you're busy, but I need some help right now. Would you take a minute?" This gives him a choice and a chance to switch his attention fully to her.

With this understanding she knows that if a man is not giving her his full focused attention, it is not because he doesn't care, but because his attention is already focused somewhere else. For example, if a man is watching the news it is unrealistic to seek his full attention as long as the TV is on. Instead you could ask, "When would be a good time to talk?" If he says "We can talk now" and doesn't turn off the TV to listen, then he is also unaware of his limitation. He may honestly believe that he can watch TV and give you his full attention. Don't be fooled and then resent him later for not fully listening.

STRESS AND THE EMOTIONALLY ABSENT MAN

Under stress focused awareness becomes more focused while open awareness becomes even more open. This simple difference can give rise to a host of misunderstandings. For example, when a man is under stress at work, it becomes difficult for him to release his focus. His mind fixates on a particular problem and it is hard for him to think about anything else. He comes home but his mind is still at work. When approached, he seems distracted and is thus inattentive and emotionally absent.

The more stress a man has at work, the more detached he may be at home. When spoken to, he may pick up a magazine and begin to read it. This is not a conscious insult, nor does it mean that he is not interested in you. He is unconsciously picking up the magazine to distract him from listening to you, because most of his mind is still focused on the problems of work. It can help greatly if you politely ask for his full attention. If he gets distracted, pause until he notices that you are waiting for his complete attention.

For his part, a man can begin to realize that he is not giving a woman what she needs when he listens to her with a distracted mind. The deliberate decision to give her his full attention and remove all distractions will assist him greatly in shifting his focus from work to his partner. Without a conscious decision to remain focused and give her the attention she needs and deserves, he will easily be distracted.

I suggest that men get in the habit of putting down the newspaper or magazine — not just in their lap but completely out of their hands — when listening. If there is a TV on, it is best to turn it off until the exchange is complete. These little physical actions increase your ability to turn off work and shift your focus to the family or relationship. If you have children it is important to realize that they too need to be heard.

MISINTERPRETING A WOMAN'S OVERWHELM

Because women have open awareness, they are more easily overwhelmed by the needs of others. Just as a man becomes absorbed in one problem, a woman becomes overwrought by a multitude of problems. One of the ironies in being overwhelmed is that she temporarily loses her ability to prioritize, which leads to more overwhelm. She feels overly responsible, even compelled, to do "everything" and then feels powerless to do it all. This gives rise to the ancient adage, a woman's work is never done.

Without an understanding of this feminine vulnerability, men react to overwhelmed women by becoming frustrated. A man feels that he is being blamed for her unhappiness or that he is somehow responsible for the upset feelings she is experiencing. He defends himself by making her wrong for being so overwhelmed, judging her as "making a big deal out of nothing."

Men need to understand that when women are overwhelmed they are not necessarily trying to accuse or blame, but are just trying to talk about their problems in order to feel better. At times like these a woman really needs to be heard. Unfortunately, most men don't know this secret. Instead, they try to make their partner feel better by explaining to her that she shouldn't be upset, or they suggest solutions to her problems. This attempt to fix her only makes matters worse.

For example, one afternoon on his way out the door, Tom hurriedly asks Jane, "Would you pick up my dry cleaning? I'm running a little late."

Jane responds in an upset and overwhelmed tone by saying, "I can't pick up your dry cleaning; I'm already in a hurry. I have to pick up Mary at school, make two bank deposits, return Timmy's library books, buy groceries for tonight's dinner, and try to get home in time to do my exercise program. I just don't know how I can do it all. Our bank account is almost overdrawn and the bills are piling up. There are so many things I have to do. I still need to give you your phone messages."

Hearing Jane's upset, Tom gets frustrated. In a rather judgmental and angry voice he says, "Look, it's no big deal, I'll pick them up myself." This is Tom's instinctive response to solve the problem of her being upset. He thinks that by saying this he has made everything all right. But it is not. Not only does he feel blamed, but she feels judged.

As he walks out the door with a frown on his face, Tom thinks to himself, "Why does she have to make such a big deal out of saying no. Couldn't she just have said it in a pleasant tone, instead of giving me a lecture on all that she is doing? Is she trying to make me feel guilty or something? I'm not making her do all those things today. All I did was make a simple request. It's not my fault that she is so overwhelmed. She acts like I am 'so-o' lazy and she is 'so-o' responsible. Just because I don't complain about all my problems, it doesn't mean that I am doing nothing."

In this example, Tom's response ("It's no big deal . . .") made Jane feel worse. He thought he was being nondemanding and thus supportive. Jane, however, assumed that he thought she was wrong fore being upset about her day. This made her feel as though Tom didn't care about her distress. She ended up feeling unloved and unsupported.

In truth, Tom is upset about Jane being upset, but for different reasons than she imagines. Tom is resentful because he thinks she is making him wrong for asking her to pick up his cleaning. He thinks she is saying his request is unfair and demanding and has caused her to feel overwhelmed. Tom is not upset that she is upset; he is angry because he thinks she is blaming him for her upset.

Tom has misunderstood Jane. She is not trying to make Tom responsible, she is just trying to be heard. She is not trying to tell Tom that he is lazy and demanding. His asking her to pick up his cleaning has merely given her an opportunity to express how overwhelmed she is. She unconsciously seeks relief by sharing everything that is overwhelming her.

As a result of this misunderstanding, Jane is not only upset about her day, but is even more upset because she thinks Tom doesn't care about her feelings. She also feels bad because Tom, who was feeling fine before, is now leaving for work in a frustrated and angry mood. Neither Tom nor Jane feels loved or supported. They do love and desire to support each other, but because they misunderstand each other they are at odds.

FEELING BETTER DIFFERENTLY

When they are under too much pressure, men and women help themselves feel better in different ways. Women undergoing stress feel better by talking about their problems and being heard, while men feel better by prioritizing their problems, focusing on one, and then developing a plan of action or a solution.

Let's look at an example of how, when a woman attempts to share and feel better but her partner keeps interrupting with solutions, they both end up frustrated.

How He Invalidates Her

One day Mary is looking for the form to register her children at the local pool. As she searches she is also beginning to doubt whether they can afford to pay for pool memberships at this time. Because there is a limit to the number of pool members, if she pays in advance her children will be assured acceptance, but if she waits, they might miss out. As she looks through the mail she finds a $1,400 VISA bill. She becomes even more concerned and wonders whether this is the right time to pay for pool membership.

By the time Bill arrives home, Mary is rather upset. She says, "We got our VISA bill today. It's $1,400. I just don't know how we are going to pay it."

He says, "We'll manage. We've got plenty of time to pay it." He assumes she will feel better now that he has offered a solution to the problem, and he mistakenly thinks the only thing bothering her is this $1,400 bill.

Then Mary says, "We already owe on our American Express bill and the mortgage is coming up soon." She is continuing her attempt to share her various worries.

Bill responds in an annoyed tone, "Don't worry, we still have ten days." Irritated because she hasn't accepted his solution, he now begins to feel a little attacked. He wonders inside, "Is she upset with me for spending too much money or for not making enough money? She spends just as much as I do."

What Bill doesn't know is that Mary is just airing her feelings about money so she can feel good about buying the kids swimming passes.

At this point in their conversation she is feeling hurt and invalidated by his comment not to worry. Saying "don't worry" is Bill's attempt to help her feel better or to "fix" her. It is his way to solve the problem and feel better. What he doesn't understand is that this approach only makes matters worse for her.

The last thing Mary needs is to be told not to worry. What she hears is that she doesn't have good reasons to be worried and is thus foolish, unworthy of respect, irrational, or inadequate in some way. She feels that he is condescending to her and that he doesn't care about her feelings. She needs him to understand her worries, but instead of feeling heard she feels put off and put down.

In spite of her hurt she continues sharing her financial concerns and says, "You know we promised the kids that we were going to Disney World this summer."

With increasing frustration Bill says, "I know, I know. It will be fine." Misunderstanding her hurt tone of voice, he thinks, "How dare she accuse me of being a lousy dad. I keep my promises to the kids. Is she saying I am not a loving father? Is she criticizing me? Why is she bringing all this up?"

Bill feels attacked and rejected. What he doesn't know is that Mary feels he is a great father. She is just concerned about their finances and needs to be heard.

Mary, feeling brushed off, continues to share her concerns. "We even owe for Laurie's hospital bill."

He says with increasing annoyance, "Look, I told you before that I am getting a bonus this month. Don't make such a big deal out of this." He is annoyed and irritated because he thinks she is accusing him of being irresponsible and undependable. He is taking her upset personally.

Mary responds in a mistrusting tone, "What if you don't get a bonus?"

He says, "You worry too much."

She says, "You promised your parents you would visit home. When are you planning to go?"

He barks, "Get off my back, will you." By this time Bill feels persecuted and interrogated as if he is the bad guy. He does not feel loved or appreciated. Indignantly he thinks, "Why is she telling me that I don't keep my promises?"

She persists, "Taxes are coming up in two months. Have you thought about how we're going to pay them? How much are we going to owe this year?"

He says defensively, "Of course I've thought about it. It will work out fine. It always does." He grumbles to himself, "Does she think I am an idiot? Of course I've considered my taxes."

She says, "I hope we can afford a membership at the pool this summer. But I think I lost the registration form. Have you seen it?"

By this time Bill is so angry that he doesn't want to talk to her. In a moment of frustration he says, "No, I haven't seen it . . . but if we are so broke why are you thinking of new ways to spend money!"

As a result of this conversation, Mary's feelings are hurt and Bill is unwilling to talk to her. What could have been a very simple conversation turned into tension and conflict.

If Bill had understood that Mary needed to talk for a while to feel better, he wouldn't have been in such a hurry to identify and solve her problem. Let's see how they could have had this conversation turn out in a positive way.

Mary says, "We got our VISA bill today. It's $1,400. I just don't know how we are going to pay it."

Bill nods and says, "Um hum. Gee, that's a lot." Inside he thinks, "I wonder if this is the problem that is upsetting her. Generally the first thing she says is a warmup to what is really bothering her. She probably needs to talk for a while. I'll just practice listening without interrupting.

Mary then says, "We already owe on our American Express bill and the mortgage is coming up soon."

Bill nods again and says, "Um hum. You're right." Inside he thinks, "I guess she needs to talk about our finances. Remember, don't interrupt. I'm sure I can support her if I minimize my comments and try to understand how she is feeling."

"You know we promised the kids that we were going to Disney World this summer. We even owe for Laurie's hospital bill."

Bill nods again and says, "We owe a lot."

She says, "What if you don't get a bonus."

Bill says, "If I don't get my bonus . . . we are in big trouble." With each response Bill remembers to not minimize her worries. If he wasn't being diligent in his support he could have easily slipped back into a put-down statement like "Oh, you worry too much" or a Mr. Fix-it statement like "If I don't get the bonus, then we'll get it next month or the month after . . . the bills will just have to wait." Fortunately, after much practice in listening, Bill has learned to not interrupt her flow with solutions or invalidating comments.

Mary then says, "Taxes are coming up in two months. Have you thought about how we're going to pay them? How much are we going to owe this year?"

He says, "I know it's a lot." In each case he is prudent in his comments. Bill recognizes that she just needs some time to be upset. He knows that his every comment is helping her to gradually feel better as long as he doesn't try to fix her.

She then remarks, "I hope we can afford a membership at the pool this summer. But I think I lost the registration form. Have you seen it?"

"Humm, no, I haven't seen it around," he says thoughtfully.

She then asks, "Do you think we should buy the membership now or wait?"

"I'm not sure," he says. "Maybe we should wait till I get my bonus. That will still give us time to register in advance." Bill is careful not to sound too confident in his response. One part of him actually feels that the swimming passes are a minor expense and can easily be purchased now. But another part, having listened to her concerns, realizes it would be a much better idea to wait.

Mary then says, "That makes sense." She gives him a hug. "Thanks for listening to me. I feel like you really understand. I just love you." To himself Bill thinks, "Wow, it really worked. I did it again. Once you get the hang of it, listening sure makes things easier."

In this example Bill has learned the secret of improving communication — listening. It is a skill that takes time to learn, just as learning to speak did. Mary, too, needs to learn the art of listening; otherwise she can make the same mistake of offending him when he speaks.

How She Offends Him

Just as well-intentioned men mistakenly try to "fix" women, women tend to misguidedly "improve" men at those times when a man talks about what is bothering him. All it takes is one or two objectionable comments and he will become silent. At such times she generally has little idea of how she antagonized him. She doesn't realize that any attempt to "help" or "improve" him will be offensive. Let's look at four examples.

Bill and Mary: Bill is worried because he went into debt while doing a remodel of his home. Now he is trying to figure out how he is going to pay his tax bill. When he comes home, he says in a rather defeated tone, "I don't know how we are going to pay our taxes this year."

Mary responds by saying, "I knew we should have spent less on our remodel." Bill now becomes silent and won't talk anymore. Mary feels bad and has no idea of how she hurt Bill.

If Bill was centered and not upset, he probably would not have been bothered by Mary's comment. He would have said, "You're right, we blew it." But because Bill is already upset and feeling defeated, her mentioning the remodel makes him feel as though she is trying to teach him a lesson on being responsible. He is also hurt and offended because he reads additional meanings into her remark.

"I can't believe she would say that," he thinks. "Does she think I am an idiot? Does she think I don't already know we overspent on the remodel? How dare she imply that I am irresponsible with money. Everybody overspends on a remodel. What's the big deal? I hate it when she treats me like a child and tries to change me. This is the last time I'll talk to her about my worries. Why can't she just listen and support me. Every chance she gets to criticize me she takes it."

Since men can shut down after just one wrongfully taken comment, let's look at more examples of the innocent ways a woman can hurt a man.

Joe and Martha: Joe, frustrated with low sales at the office, comes home silent and withdrawn. Martha asks, "What's the matter, Joe?"

Joe says in a depressed tone, "We didn't make our sales quota this month."

Martha responds, "Well, every business has its ups and downs. I don't think it would be so bad if we would plan for such times."

At this point, Joe stops talking. He feels unsupported and angry. Inside he thinks, "I didn't ask for her advice. I hate it when she gives me a lecture on how I could be a better businessman. Does she think I'm stupid? I already know every business has its ups and downs." At such times Joe needs Martha to just listen and let him talk. Any unsolicited advice will be offensive.

Even advice that attempts to broaden a man's understanding can backfire, as the following scenario demonstrates.

Steve and Janet: Steve comes home and is very quiet. He seems tense and irritated. Janet, hoping to soothe him, says, "What's the matter?"

61

He says, "Oh, nothing. I'm just having a hard time with my secretary. Her resistance to my requests is driving me nuts."

Janet understands his frustration, but she also understands his secretary's frustration in dealing with Steve. She feels he will be able to handle the situation better if he understands his secretary's point of view. She is right, but this isn't the time to tell him. He needs her to be sympathetic to his side of the problem.

Hoping to help, Janet says, "You know, I bet your secretary would respond better to you if you would take some time to listen to her. You rarely talk to her. Tell her what you are really feeling."

Immediately Steve goes quiet. He is first stunned and then angry. He feels betrayed by his wife. "How dare she take sides with my secretary," he thinks. "My own wife thinks I am the problem. She never thinks I talk enough. I talk with my secretary — that's the problem. She doesn't listen. I was already furious with my secretary; now I am furious with my wife too."

In her attempt to help Steve by expanding his understanding, Janet unknowingly turned him off. Let's look at one more example of the type of comment that men find unsupportive.

Rick and Sharron: Rick took his wife Sharron out to a nice restaurant. During a 45-minute wait for their table, Rick got increasingly annoyed. Several times he spoke to the maitre d' in an attempt to speed up the process. A number of people who came in later were seated before him. Each time Rick would become more upset, even though he knew the recent arrivals had reservations and he didn't.

Sharron eventually mentioned the unmentionable. Rick was grumbling about how terrible the service was at this restaurant. He said, "I can't believe they are so slow here!" Sharron countered, "Do you think we would be waiting this long if we had made reservations?"

Rick's response was anger in his eyes and immediate coldness. He mumbled, "No!" and then fumed inside.

All of his anger at himself for not making reservations, which he had displaced onto the restaurant, was now displaced onto Sharron. Furious at her comment, he thought, "What a stupid thing to say. I can't believe her. If she's so smart, then next time she can take me out to a restaurant. If she wants reservations, let her make them. I'm not going to bother. I hate it when she picks at me. Does she think I don't realize that I forgot to make reservations? She acts as though I am supposed to remember everything. I don't even want to talk with her."

Rick had wanted Sharron to be on his side, not to take this opportunity to improve him. Her comment was intended to reveal to him how he could avoid waiting in the future and to help him be more responsible. Instead, it offended him because it started the obvious, implying that he was foolish. What he needed her to say was, "Yes, they are slow."

In each of these examples, the man was looking to feel emotionally supported by his partner, and was turned off by any attempt to help, offer advice, or improve him. It is important to note that in each example the man wasn't asking for advice or help. He was just talking, and wanted his partner's passive support. Instead, she tried actively to help him be a better person in some way.

This is a mistake that women commonly make, having no idea of how they offend the men in their lives. Men have a feminine side and from time to time need to share their thoughts and emotions to feel better. At such times women mistakenly shut their men down. All it takes is a few such experiences and he will stop sharing what he needs to share.

When He Does Want Advice

There are, however, times when a man *is* looking for advice and a woman's attempt to help may still unknowingly turn him off. When he has thought a problem through but has not found a solution, he may talk about it. After he has presented the problem he will say something like "What do you think?" This is a signal that he is asking for a solution. A male listener would suggest something the man could do to solve his problem. This is what he is looking for, and he will feel supported.

A woman, on the other hand, may make a number of mistakes when trying to help a man who is looking for a solution. She may try to nurture him, which turns him off, or she may try to help him see the bigger picture, which can offend him.

Women listeners often offend men inadvertently because females, as a rule, instinctively approach their problems differently from men. Women may talk about how a problem was created or how the problem could be avoided or even make the problem bigger by describing how it affects them. In each of these ways a woman may turn a man off so that he doesn't want to discuss his problems with her.

In addition, a woman may frustrate a man by wanting to explore how the problem makes him feel, and by listening in an overly concerned and sympathetic way. If a man is asking for a solution by saying "What do you think," he doesn't want to be nurtured with caring understanding of what he is going through. What he wants is a concrete suggestion.

Let's replay the above four examples differently, imagining that the men are coming to their partners not for emotional support, but for a solution.

Bill and Mary: Bill comes home and says to his wife Mary, "I don't know how we are going to pay our taxes. I didn't get my bonus and the house remodel has put us too far in debt. We could spend less on our vacation or take another loan against the house. What do you think?"

Mary responds, "If only we hadn't spent so much on the remodel. Henry warned us that it would cost more. We should have planned to pay a lot more." Bill is now intensely frustrated. Mary is sharing her feelings about what caused the problem, while Bill wants to focus on a solution.

To himself he thinks, "I know, I know we spent too much. I got that a long time ago. Why does she do this to me? We can't talk about anything!"

63

Bill has signaled his desire for a conversation to solve the problem. He wants Mary to say something like "I think we should try to spend less on our vacation and try to avoid going further in debt" or "I don't know what to do. Are there any other options?" Mary could also offer a new option by saying, "Maybe we should try selling our boat. We've talked about that before."

In short, when Bill asks what Mary thinks, he wants her to focus on ways to solve the problem as he presented it.

Let's look at another example.

Joe and Martha: Joe comes home frustrated, wondering why he didn't make his sales quota. "I don't know what's happening," he tells Martha. "I didn't make my quota this month. I even expected to do better this month. Why do you think this is happening?"

Martha replies, "Well, I think we should have planned on this happening. Every business has its ups and downs. We should have a backup fund to carry us through times like this."

Joe's response to Martha's good advice is frustration. She has not responded to the problem as stated by him with a suggestion regarding why sales were low this month. Instead, she has brought up another issue that she is worried about, namely, how can the couple better prepare for lean times. Rather than answering Joe's question, Martha has replied to an unasked question, "How do you think we could avoid being affected by job setbacks?"

Joe needs Martha to give a specific answer to his question, such as "Well, that new product line you introduced may have overwhelmed some of the buyers" or "I just don't know why (little pause), you have worked so hard and your products are so good. Maybe it is the economy" or "I read an article yesterday that said we have recently entered a recession. Maybe that's why."

These comments are all directed at the problem that Joe was focused on. To be supportive of him, Martha needs to stay focused on the problem as he has described it.

Let's look at how another wife's advice did address her husband's question, but still went off the mark.

Steve and Janet: Steve comes home and says to his wife Janet, "I've been having a hard time with Phyllis (his secretary). She is resisting my requests, and it is driving me nuts. What do you think I should do?"

Janet responds by saying: "I think she is resisting you because you are so closed. You need to be more open. You never sit down and really talk with her. If you understood her point of view, I don't think she would be resisting you."

Steve is frustrated and offended by Janet's response. He feels blamed and judged as incompetent. He thinks, "Well, that's the last time I'll ask you for advice. Why do you have to blame me for not being open. I talk with my secretary...."

Janet has given Steve good advice, but has worded it in a way that makes him defensive. She has told him how he could have avoided the problem, instead of telling him what he can now do about it. Steve could have heard and appreciated the same suggestion had Janet worded it in terms of what action he can now take, instead of focusing on what he did wrong.

Steve would be more open to Janet's advice if she focused not on the cause of the situation, but on its resolution. She might say, "I think you should sit down and have a talk with Phyllis. Schedule some time and really listen to what she is feeling inside. Take the time to listen to her and I think she will want to listen to you."

Finally, when a man asks for another's opinion or advice, the last thing he wants is consolation or sympathy. Here's an example of how kind words can backfire.

Rick and Sharron: While Rick and Sharron are waiting for their table at a restaurant, Rick says, "I can't believe this place is so slow. What do you think we should do? Should we try another restaurant?"

"I know you've had a hard day," Sharron responds. "We've been waiting at least 45 minutes. It must be pretty difficult to wait this long. You're probably really hungry. Did you eat lunch today?" Sharron has responded to Rick's feelings instead of the problem, because that is the way she would want him to console her if she was upset about waiting.

Rick is now even more furious. He feels as though Sharron is treating him like a child. Inwardly he gripes, "Don't mother me this way. I can't believe that you are not furious with this restaurant too. Who cares if I ate lunch. . . ." He does not want her to console him. He wants her to respond directly to his question with an answer.

Sharron might reply, "Well, we've waited this long. We might as well wait a little longer" or "I think we should stay but get the menu, so at least when we get seated we can order right away" or "I think that's a good idea. What about going to that new restaurant along the freeway?"

Each of these responses will feel supportive to Rick, because his problem is being addressed instead of his feelings.

With the help of the above examples it is easy to see some of the common ways men and women unknowingly create tension and conflict when they are simply trying to help each other to feel better.

Men Need Solutions, Women Need to Share

Men instinctively look for solutions. When a man has a problem, the first thing he does is to go to his "cave" and try to find a solution on his own. If he can find a solution or plan of action, he will feel better. If he doesn't find a solution, then he will come out of his cave, find another man that he greatly respects, and talk about it.

When he shares a problem with another man, he is generally looking for another opinion to solve his problem. If he receives a good solution, he will immediately feel better. Thus when a woman is upset and starts talking, he assumes that she is looking for a solution to her problems. He has no reference point to let him know what she really just needs to be heard for a while. So he tries to help by solving her problems, which usually ends up invalidating and frustrating her.

When a woman is upset, her first need is for it to be OK to be upset for a while. She needs him to listen to her feelings without trying to fix her. Through sharing her problems in a nonfocused way, she will naturally feel better. Her feeling of overwhelm will diminish even if all the problems remain unsolved.

A man mistakenly assumes that all a woman's problems need to be solved before she will feel better. This is why he gets so frustrated and exhausted when listening to her talk about all the things that are bothering her. He feels he is being expected to solve all of these problems, but he feels powerless to help her.

He especially becomes frustrated when she is bothered by problems that nothing can be done about, or that have not happened. Some common masculine attitudes toward getting upset are:

1. "Why get upset if there is nothing you can do . . . what good will it do to feel upset?"
2. "Don't get upset until you know for sure it has happened."
3. "Since it's already happened, there is no sense in getting upset . . . there is nothing you can do about it now."

These three mottos keep men mainly in their heads and out of their feelings. Being in your head is useful for solving problems, but it is not always good for your health and emotional well-being. Women instinctively understand that feelings need to be shared if we are to successfully release the tension produced when our desires and expectations are frustrated. Even if there is nothing you can do about a situation, it is important to talk about the feelings involved. Sharing feelings is essential if we are to create and sustain intimacy.

Through understanding this difference, a man can learn to relax when a woman is sharing. Instead of feeling responsible for solving all her problems, he can simply focus on solving one problem: he can fulfill her need for a fully focused listener, which will help her to feel better even if none of her problems are solved.

MALE FORGETFULNESS

Without the ability to focus or concentrate, a person can be immobilized. Focus is necessary to get a job done, but it's possible to have too much concentration. When masculine energy isn't balanced with feminine energy, it tends to focus on one thing to the exclusion of everything else. In the pursuit of one objective, nothing else gets done. This pattern is especially troublesome in relationships.

For instance, even though a man may love his wife very much, if his masculine and feminine awareness is out of balance, he may forget important dates like their anniversary or her birthday, or simple things like picking something up at the store or taking phone messages. It is not that he doesn't care, but his awareness is focused in another direction.

This forgetfulness is understandably hard for women to accept. A woman assumes that forgetfulness connotes lack of caring or interest. It's hard for her to believe that a man who forgets birthdays and anniversaries could really love her. After all, this kind of behavior is so foreign to her experience of loving someone. Women remember things not according to their priorities, but according to the importance of the person and the relationship. Unfortunately, when men get overly focused, they tend to remember their most urgent priority and forget everything else. Men prioritize in the context of achieving their goals, while women prioritize according to the importance of their relationships. With this perspective it is easy to see how men can unintentionally hurt the feelings of women.

SPINNING OUT AND SPACING OUT

One of the biggest areas of conflict and frustration between men and women is communication. This is because men listen and talk for different reasons than women. Men listen to gather information in order to solve problems, while women listen in order to relate or share. Men talk when they have a specific point to make, or when they are helping another to solve a problem. Women talk in order to explore a topic as well as to discover themselves.

From this simple perspective, it is easy to see why men get frustrated when listening to women. A woman expands in search of the point she wants to make, whereas a man expects her to get right to the point, the way a man would. He assumes something is the matter with her for rambling on, or he feels that she is wasting his time. Neither is true.

Women explore their thoughts and feelings *as* they share them, gradually discovering the point they want to make. Men tend to be intolerant of this because men generally don't speak unless they have a specific point to make. When they do speak they try to come to the point as efficiently as possible.

When a conversation is underway and the man falls silent, the woman often mistakenly assumes that he is slow, stupid, withholding, or just unconcerned. None are true. He is doing what is natural for him. He is mulling over his thoughts, to formulate a point to make. This is hard for her to recognize because she processes her thoughts and feelings through sharing them outside himself.

Men need to occasionally mull things over, just as women need to talk out their thoughts and feelings. As a result the man comes back clearer and more directed, and the woman comes back more centered.

The drawback of both these approaches is that men can sometimes "space out" and forget that they are mulling over a problem, while women can "spin out" and lose themselves in exploring tangents, getting far off the subject.

When a man spaces out he can easily forget what he considered to be very important. For instance, he may forget birthdays, appointments, promises, his schedule, his priorities, etc.

67

When a woman spins out she loses the ability to discern what is really important to her, tending to make everything equally important. At such times she may become overwhelmed and overreact to situations. She feels the needs of others are as important or even more important than her own. She may make her children's every need more important than her spouse's romantic needs. She may overreact to his shortcomings by displacing all her frustrations of the day onto him. While sharing her thoughts and feelings, she may spin out and never make an actual point.

Because we are not perfectly in balance at all times, it is realistic to expect men to occasionally space out while mulling things over, just as it is perfectly normal for women to occasionally spin out while sharing their feelings. This understanding is important because it helps women to be more tolerant of men when they space out and forget things. It equally helps men to realize that women are not crazy when they spin out and become overwhelmed.

Without this understanding, when a man detects that a woman is "spinning out" he panics and worries that she could go on forever. In most cases, she just needs to spin out for a while, and then she will find her center again.

Sometimes a woman will spin out and become confused when she doesn't feel safe enough to explore and share what she is really feeling, or if she has shared it but it has not been heard. Ironically, the very process of sharing that can lead her to greater self-awareness can also create confusion.

On the other hand, when a woman realizes that a man has spaced out, she panics and worries that he doesn't care. Generally what has happened is that he didn't have enough information to arrive at a solution to the problem at hand; he has spaced out and forgotten everything, unconsciously waiting for more information.

To remember what he was mulling over, he just needs some more information. If he feels judged or made wrong for spacing out, he loses touch with his positive intent to serve or support. He may become defensive. To find his focus again, a man needs to feel trusted, needed, and appreciated.

If a man spaces out a lot in a relationship, a woman can help by trying to be tolerant of his problem. At such times when he spaces out and may even forget what she wants or forget what she is talking about, she has to work hard to continue trusting his caring intent to serve her. If she gets frustrated she can say to herself, "I *can* trust that he cares; his forgetting does not mean he doesn't care. I *can* trust him to remember more and more as he feels more loved, accepted, trusted, and appreciated."

Likewise, a man must work hard to not judge a woman when she is spinning out. He needs to listen with patience and remember that she needs more caring, understanding, and respect at such times.

If he starts to become too frustrated, the male partner could say, "Would you please pause for a moment. I need some time to think about what you are saying." Or he could say, "I want to hear what you are saying but I need some time to think about what you have already said." In most cases he won't even need to ask her to pause; as she expresses herself she will pause. At those times he should practice saying nothing and continue trying to understand her point of view. He can say to himself, "She has a right to her emotions. As I understand her feelings, she will feel better and her emotions will become more positive. I *can* find the good reasons for her feelings. I *can* listen without making her wrong. She needs my silent support."

As he is able to more fully understand her feelings, he can more effectively focus on her. His attentiveness and focus will help her to become more centered.

A PROCESS OF UNFOLDING

Regarding communication the male motto is "Don't speak unless you have something to say." This intimidates women, because for them communication is not just a means of conveying a point, but also a means of discovering a point.

When women need to share, they don't know exactly what they want to say. Sometimes they have so much to share, they don't know where to start. Or they may need time to share a progression of feelings and thoughts before they discover the point they want to make. A man also goes through this preparation process, but in a different way. He ponders things within, comes to a conclusion, then shares it outwardly.

Does this sound familiar?

Woman: "We never talk."

Man: "OK, let's talk. What do you want to talk about?"

Woman: "I don't know, you go first."

He goes nuts. He does not understand that for her, talking is an unfolding process. He assumes that if she wants to talk, then she must have something in particular to say. He expects her to have a point or a series of points to make.

She, on the other hand, just wants to share and connect. She wants to enjoy being together. For her, communication is not just a sharing of information, it is a sharing of her self. It is a basis for intimacy. It is fulfilling and centering.

For a woman, sharing is a gradual unfoldment and she may need to be drawn out. She may not know exactly what she wants to say, but (1) she wants to connect and feel in a relationship, and (2) communication is her major means of connecting and relating.

To use an analogy, when an upset woman shares her feelings, it is as though she is sharing the contents of her purse. She needs time to clean out that purse without being judged for having so much in her purse, or for not knowing exactly what and how much she has inside, so if she begins to spin out, a man can imagine that she is just taking everything out of her purse. When it is all out, she will feel much lighter and he will have served a very important role.

When a woman is sharing what's inside of her, if she has a respectful, attentive, and caring listener she will feel safe to empty out her purse (her inner feelings). Once everything is out, she will feel much more centered and loving. She will greatly appreciate the support.

MIND READING

Throughout this book, we'll see that faulty communication between the sexes is largely due to mistaken assumptions. One of the most common of those assumptions manifests as what we can call "mind reading": Because men and women do not realize how different they are, they assume that they already know what the other is thinking or feeling before it has been clearly stated.

True, women are quite accurate when mind reading other women, because they are already so similar. Likewise, men can accurately mind read other men. But when men and women start mind reading each other, trouble is inevitable.

A man prematurely decides that he knows what a woman is saying. His error lies in assuming that she started out making the point she wanted to make, as a man would. So he may be listening and then, before the speaker is finished, says, "I got it, I got it." This works fine with another man, but to a woman, his statement is preposterous. She knows that he can't know what she intends to say, because many times *she* doesn't even know. While sharing, she is *in the process* of finding out or discovering what she feels, thinks, or wants.

There are additional reasons this kind of mind reading doesn't work. Men need to understand that if a woman needs to talk, and if his desire is to support, then his purpose in listening is not just to get the gist of what she is saying, but to support her in getting it out. As she gets it out, without being interrupted, her view might change midstream or she might completely change the subject. She may ask questions and then start answering them.

By expecting this to happen, he can avoid feeling frustrated. He needs to remember that just as he has to mull over his problems before talking about them, a woman needs to talk about her problems before she will have a definite opinion. If she feels overwhelmed by difficulties, just by talking about them she may feel better.

Sometimes she will even find out that there is no problem. But the last thing she needs when she is upset is for a man to tell her that there is no problem. The next-to-last thing she needs is for him to offer a string of solutions to whatever she is saying. Finally, the next-to-the-next-to-the-last-thing she needs from him is "OK, I got it!" To be interrupted by "I got it" sounds like "OK, OK, will you shut up, I don't want to hear it anymore."

Women also mind read, but in a different way. They tend to attribute negative interpretations to a man's behavior patterns. When he is quiet, she assumes he doesn't care. When he is distracted, she assumes he doesn't love her. When he is late, she assumes that she is no longer important to him. When he forgets to do things, she assumes he is getting even. When he shuts down, she assumes he is leaving her.

Because she is not a man she has no reference point to help her understand why he does what he does. It is understandably hard for her to trust his love. But she could look for the real and positive reasons for his behavior; she could share her fears in a way that avoids blame but asks for reassurance. In later chapters we will explore how she can more successfully ask for this kind of support.

It is important to work at new ways to communicate that take into account these differences. Just as women are especially vulnerable to being interrupted, men are particularly sensitive to being doubted or mistrusted. When a woman is interrupted again and again, or subjected to an impatient listener, she will close down and become unwilling to share vulnerable feelings. Her love is replaced with doubt and mistrust.

When a man is mistrusted by his female mate, he tends to react in a most confusing way. If he is being blamed and punished for a crime he didn't do, his reaction is to commit the crime to get back at the punisher. If she assumes that he is uncaring when he is trying to be caring, at least in his male way, then eventually he becomes cold, impatient, and uncaring.

As you can see, this negative pattern fuels itself. The more uncaring he becomes, the more untrusting she becomes. The more untrusting she becomes, the more uncaring he becomes. This is a major communication trap, but we can end the cycle through increasing our understanding of each other with respect, trust and compassion.

Another female form of mind reading is the expectation that others already know and anticipate their needs. It is very unrealistic to expect a man to anticipate a woman's needs. With this expectation she will surely end up disappointed. On the other hand, men expect women to know their loving feelings by looking at what they do. Women need to be reassured again and again through communication that they are loved and special. In a similar way, men need to be reminded again and again of the woman's needs, wishes, and wants.

MALE TUNNEL VISION

Their focused awareness can make men incredibly determined and efficient, but it can also make them oblivious to other's needs and to priorities not directly related to their primary goal. Having "tunnel vision" is becoming so focused on a task that one cannot see or give attention to anything that does not directly contribute to their most effectively achieving a goal.

Consequently, when a man is focused on a particular task or problem, he may not notice the signs of growing distress in his environment, family, relationship, or even within his own body. He does not feel pain or hurt, nor does he acknowledge this in others. He unconsciously negates the importance of needs that are not directly related to his focus. If his wife and children are hurting and upset, his reaction is that they shouldn't hurt and they shouldn't be upset. This kind of invalidation and denial is very hurtful to others and destructive to relationships.

Thus it is quite common for a man to get sick on the first day of vacation or when a major project is completed. He may have ignored his body's needs until the job was done, and now the body cries for help through falling ill. Or he may become emotionally depressed because he has not been creating the emotional support he needs.

A man can also begin to feel his inner emotional poverty if he fails at his task, or if he retires from it. Statistically, most men die three years after they retire. They have been running on empty without knowing it. When the job is complete, their debt to their bodies and to others must be paid.

The solution is not finding another job in which to bury oneself, nor masking the problem through drinking or drugs. The cure for this man's physical or emotional pain is to create the emotional support he needs and to reassess his priorities and values. He needs something to work for, a new goal and a purpose to live. He needs to balance his work needs with his emotional and health needs.

Another consequence of tunnel vision is that men tend to neglect the needs of others — not because they don't care, but because they are unconscious of the part of them that does care. He, his wife, and their children all suffer from his neglect. Many a man, after his kids have grown up, says, "I didn't realize how quickly time passes. I feel that I missed out on something very precious." Guilt, regret, sorrow, and shame often accompany this realization.

How Women Can Deal with Tunnel Vision

Women are naturally gifted with an intuitive awareness of the needs of others. But her open awareness can be a mixed blessing when her partner is experiencing tunnel vision. While the man thinks everything is fine in the relationship, the woman is burdened by her awareness of all the problems.

When he is not sharing this burden, she mistakenly assumes that he is happy with the relationship. When he acts as though everything is fine, while she sees problems, she gets the message that she is much too demanding or that he doesn't care and thus will never do anything to change.

This feminine awareness of a relationship's problems becomes a burden to her when he is not willing to hear and validate her awareness. When he denies the validity of her needs and perceptions, she then feels the burden of the relationship and the family rests on her shoulders. She feels alone and unsupported. No wonder women become frustrated when men act as though everything is fine.

With this new understanding of tunnel vision, a woman can correctly conclude that her partner appears satisfied only because he is unconscious of the problems. She can realize that in most cases if he was aware of the problems, he too would be upset or would be motivated to improve things.

Both partners are equally responsible for creating a good relationship. However, their roles are different. The woman will naturally be more aware of the relationship's needs and problems.

She should remember that he is more easily distracted from relationship needs by the demands of his work. She cannot realistically expect him to know when her needs are going unfulfilled unless she communicates them to him. Sometimes he will not even know if his *own* needs are not being met.

For relationships to work, women need to be aware of this male vulnerability, recognize the importance of good communication skills, and persist in communicating their needs and wishes. They must be willing to ask for support — and continue to ask.

This is probably the most difficult task for women in having positive relationships with men. Women don't want to ask. They expect men to anticipate female needs and to feel obliged to fulfill them. Women commonly fall prey to the negative myth, "If he loves me, then he will know what I want." This kind of expectation is destructive to relationships.

Even with good communication techniques, a man may at first tend to minimize the importance of her needs and wishes. This resistance is not from lack of caring; it occurs because he does not readily relate to and therefore cannot understand her needs. Tunnel vision has turned off his awareness of emotional needs. If she wrongly thinks that he does not care, she will too easily give up trying to communicate her needs and the needs of the family. She may stop asking just when it is beginning to work. Understanding his tunnel vision can help her to accept his valid need for her to be gently persistent in asking for his support.

This kind of responsibility, however, must not be misinterpreted. Women in general already take on too much responsibility for the feelings and needs of others. Just as a man becomes resistant to fulfilling the needs of others, she feels compelled to fulfill the needs of others at the expense of not fulfilling her own needs.

Furthermore, I am not implying in this discussion that the needs of the relationship are her responsibility to fulfill. I am saying, however, that she carries a responsibility to herself to persist in communicating those needs, striving to do it in new ways that don't make him wrong.

For example, he needs to be reminded of how important time shared with him is to her. This is hard to do, as we have said, because she believes that if he really loved her as much as she loves him, then she wouldn't have to ask. The truth is, if he were a *woman*, then she wouldn't have to ask him for more participation in the relationship. As she learns to ask for his participation without secretly resenting him, he can more readily remember his and her needs for relationship. He can recall how much better he feels when he is receiving her love and giving his.

A woman's biggest mistake in a relationship is to give up communicating her needs and to start doing everything by herself. In the short term this is easier, but in the long run she is not developing the necessary communication and understanding in her relationship. Ultimately she will feel a consuming compulsion to do everything, while wrongly assuming that her partner doesn't care to help or participate.

If, instead, she persists in communicating, she can help a man become aware of the relationship problems that his tunnel vision prevents him from seeing. Tunnel vision is like a spell that can take over a man. He is released from that spell when he is able to *hear* the needs of others. When he is not mistrusted and rejected for his tunnel vision, but loved, trusted, and talked

73

to in a positive way, he can come back to his caring self. This kind of loving communication frees him from the spell.

A metaphor of this is contained in the fairy tale, "Beauty and the Beast." To save her father's life, Beauty promised to live with the Beast. One day she asked permission to visit her family. The Beast warned her that if she didn't come back he would die of heartbreak. She decided not to return and the Beast started to die. Realizing her mistake, Beauty went back to him. She begged him not to die, she expressed her deep love and her desire to marry him. In an instant the Beast was transformed into a handsome and articulate prince. Her love for him and her acceptance of his limitations allowed his true self to emerge.

Transformation is possible. Through accepting and understanding each other's differences with love, our relationships can be transformed. We become more of who we truly are: loving and caring beings.

A similar metaphor comes from the story of Sleeping Beauty. The kiss of the young prince, it is foretold, will awaken her from a deep sleep. But before he can awaken her with his love, he must overcome many obstacles. Through performing a series of valiant deeds, his love becomes stronger and eventually capable of awakening Sleeping Beauty. But he must cut through miles of thorns to reach his bride. In real life, a man must be willing to work through his resistance to communicating and listening before he can enjoy the love of his beloved. A good relationship requires hard work at times, balanced by periods of enjoying the fruit of that hard work.

A MAN'S RESPONSIBILITY

For a man to enjoy a good relationship with a woman, he must adjust his expectations. Instead of thinking his work is over when he comes home, he must realize that having a relationship is also a part of his work. There will always be obstacles to overcome in sustaining a loving relationship. Too often men assume that once they are married, the work of having a relationship is over. Realistically, that is when it begins.

A man's major responsibility is to counteract his tendency to be overly focused (tunnel vision) and strive to be caring, respectful, and committed to understanding his partner's feelings and needs, while maintaining his masculine sense of self. Through gradually learning to hear her feelings, he will become more motivated to support her and will become aware of his own needs in the relationship.

A WOMAN'S RESPONSIBILITY

Even though a woman is more aware of the needs in a relationship, that does not make her solely responsible to solve its problems. But she is responsible for getting her own needs fulfilled — in two main ways. First, she must communicate her needs and wishes without resenting her partner.

Second, she must get her needs fulfilled from a variety of sources, and not make him the source of her dissatisfaction, or the sole source of her fulfillment.

Consider the woman who tries to improve a suffering relationship by giving to the man, while expecting him to give back to her in the same way. She takes on the responsibility of pleasing him, but ignores herself until it is too late. By denying her own needs, she prevents him from being able to support her. Men are drawn to where they are needed, trusted, and appreciated. A man runs from the needs of a woman when it appears that he cannot satisfy her needs. The signal that he has failed is her resentment.

Women typically do not communicate their needs until they have sacrificed for so long that resentment has set in. Then, no matter how they communicate their needs, it will sound like nagging, complaining, bitching, blaming, or demanding. This just increases a man's resistance to hearing that he must continue to work on his relationship.

It is very difficult for a man to react in a positive way to resentment or a "guilt trip." He cannot contribute to the relationship when he is considered the "bad guy." To enrich the relationship, a woman's major responsibility is to share her feelings, thoughts, and needs without secretly harboring resentments, but with a loving, accepting, trusting, and appreciative attitude. She also must not expect him to meet all her needs, creating instead many avenues of fulfillment in her life. With this extra love and support from family and friends, she is not as needy for his love and reassurance, and can be more accepting of his particular limitations.

Men commonly expect there to be no more problems once they are in a relationship, and women expect the men to fulfill their needs without having to be reminded again and again. When these mistaken assumptions are corrected, communication improves. He can more easily hear about problems, and she can share her needs in a more supportive way. With better communication, they are then able to share more equally the burdens — and the joys — of the relationship.

MAKING DECISIONS

Just as a man can be too focused, women can be too open. Being too open or too focused greatly influences how men and women make decisions. Overly open women tend to be aware of so many possibilities that they can't focus on one and make a decision. For example, they may spend days looking for *exactly* the right birthday present for their spouse, seeing so many possibilities that they are unable to make a decision.

A man might find such behavior incomprehensible. Instead, he would concentrate on buying a gift and get it done quickly, perhaps missing a better present because he didn't take the time to explore at least some of the options.

Because women are more relationship-oriented, they tend to include others in the decision-making process. Before a decision is made, they talk with others, including everyone affected by the decision, and then finally they reach a conclusion together. In contrast, men first make a decision on their own, and then are open to changing it according to feedback from others. First a man makes his decision privately in his "cave," and then he checks it out with others. If his first conclusion is not accepted, then it is back to the drawing board.

Without a true understanding of these different decision-making styles, conflict, confusion, and resentment are sure to follow. When he makes decisions before exploring how she feels, she ends up feeling excluded, disrespected, and unimportant. In reality, he is not aware that she is waiting to be included. He mistakenly assumes that if she has something to say, she will just say it. He does not realize her need to be included and drawn out.

She does not offer any feedback because she assumes that he has rigidly made his decision and excluded her. She does not realize that he has come up with his best decision on his own, and now he is open to feedback. This is confusing to a woman because she first collects all the information and then makes a decision — one that is much more final than the kind of decision a man makes.

For example, a man might say to his wife, "I think we should take a vacation in June for 10 days. We can go camping and have a great time." Hearing this, she is stunned. She can't believe that he hasn't even asked her if, when, and where she would like to have a vacation.

He assumes that she will speak up if she doesn't like his idea. So when she doesn't respond, he thinks his idea has been accepted. She, however, is still recovering from the shock of someone else being so selfish as to make a major decision without including her before the final say. It sounds to her as though he is saying, "I've decided that we are going camping for 10 days in June and I don't care what you want to do. My mind is made up." It is important to note that this is not what he is saying, but in feminine language that is what it sounds like. Emotionally she will react to his decision as if he is not willing to include her, when he is in truth open to feedback.

Some women understand this; when a man makes a decision, they know that he is now open to feedback and open to change. Most women, however, do not understand this difference. They either resent him for it, or they are intimidated by it. If he is resented or mistrusted, then he becomes fixed and rigid, but if he is appreciated for making a decision, then he is open to changing it. Women don't get a lot of chances to see this flexible male side, because as soon as he makes a decision alone, women feel they have to fight to be heard. When they start fighting, men lose their openness to change and protect themselves through righteousness and rigidity.

On the other hand, men get frustrated with a woman's more democratic decision-making process. It seems long and tedious. A woman generally wants to explore by asking lots of questions before she makes a decision. Often the man assumes she is pretending not to know what she wants, when in truth she needs time to explore all possibilities and various points of view before making a decision. He may become furious because he feels controlled through her lack of knowing.

For example, Joe has decided that he would like to go camping with the family during the summer. He says, "I think it would be a good idea for us to go camping this summer." Martha responds, "I don't know. I haven't thought about our vacation yet."

"I don't know" is a very creative state of mind. From this state of mind Martha is able to access her intuition as well as be open to many sources outside herself. Free from being locked into the limits of her mind and logic, she can respond to her inner feelings.

Joe, however, thinks that "I don't know" means she is rejecting his suggestion. In frustration he thinks, "I hate it when she stalls me. She takes such a long time. If she doesn't want to go, why doesn't she just say so? She is so controlling."

To ease his discomfort at her needing more time to make a decision, Martha could say, "I think it's a good idea, but I need some time to think about it. I appreciate your patience" or "That sounds like a good idea. Let's talk to the kids and see if they also want to go" or "We haven't been camping in several years. What a good idea. Before we decide, would you give me a few days to think about it?"

These kinds of responses can help him to be more patient. But he too can make her life easier if he respects her valid need for more time to make decisions.

Sex and Decision-Making

Sex is one area in relationships where this is particularly important. Generally a man definitely knows when he is open to having sex. A woman however, may be open to having sex but may need more time to discover whether she really wants to. Men don't readily understand this because when they are open to having sex, they also simultaneously want it.

When a husband asks his wife whether she would like to have sex that night, if she says "I don't know," it is very easy for him to misinterpret and think she is saying "no." While he thinks he is being rejected, she is just warming up to the idea. She may be quite open to having sex, but needs some time for her inner feelings to emerge before she can make the decision.

For example, Bill says to Mary, "I'm in the mood to make love tonight. Would you like to?"

Mary, starting to experience rush of feelings, says, "I don't know." Inside her are various layers of feelings yet to be discovered: "How nice, making love sounds good, but I am tired tonight, I still have to make those calls, I'm not sure I want to get sexual tonight, I don't know if I have the energy, I may just want to be cuddled, another part of me would love to have sex, you are such a wonderful lover, I would love to have sex tonight. . . ."

But when Bill hears "I don't know" he hears rejection. Feeling hurt and defensive, he says, "Oh well, forget it. Tonight is probably not a good night."

Inside Bill thinks, "I hate it when she rejects me. If she doesn't want to have sex, why doesn't she just say it! Well, that is the last time I am going to ask. If she doesn't want to make love to me, I'll just take care of myself."

If he understood this difference between men and women, he could remedy the situation. To her statement, "I don't know," he could respond, "Is there part of you that wants to make love?" Then she might say, "Part of me would love to. I just need a chance to feel whether this is the right time."

If Mary understood how men hear "I don't know," she could respond to his suggestion by saying "I love making love with you. I need some time to discover whether tonight is the right night for me" or "Making love sounds like a wonderful idea. I don't know if tonight is the right time for me. Give me a little time to see."

After she responds in one of the above courteous but still indefinite ways, she will want him to be reassuring and patient and to gently persist in his interest. He could say "OK, we'll just take it as it comes" or "You take all the time you need, Honey" or "I understand. We could just cuddle for a while and see if anything happens" or "Do you want to talk about anything?"

With sex as with many other areas of life, it is essential for men to understand that when a woman says "I don't know," she is not saying no.

FORMING OPINIONS

Similar to the decision-making process, men and women form and express opinions in different ways. Understanding these differences can avoid much conflict.

Just as when making decisions, women take longer in forming opinions. They take additional time and care to consider various points of view and to gather all available information. Even when they express their opinions they tend to be open to other points of view, and are careful to let others know that they do not claim to be absolutely right.

When she is centered a woman has a gracefulness and flexibility that leave a door open for others to have differing beliefs. She uses phrases such as, "It sounds to me like, I feel as though, it could be that, it looks to me like, what I see is, what I hear is, it seems to me that, etc." Her style of expression reveals that she is open to seeing the value or truth in other points of view.

Men form and express opinions in an opposite way. A man quickly forms an opinion or conclusion based on what he already knows. Then he tests it out by proclaiming it *as if* he were absolutely certain. Through experiencing how others react to his opinion, he then reassesses its accuracy. If others agree with his opinion, he feels more definite. If others have differing opinions, he may weigh their merits against his own and then change his view. Through gathering more information, a man may change and improve his opinions.

When a woman hears a man's opinion she may react negatively, because she does not realize that he is open to hearing others. It sounds as though he thinks he is absolutely right, and that any other view is foolish, irrational, or unintelligent. Because her conclusions are the result of careful consideration, she tends to be intimidated or offended by a man's quick conclusions and opinions. To her, he appears narrow-minded, arrogant, and unwilling to hear others.

This man, however, may be quite open to changing. He merely appears rigid because his process of forming conclusions is different. He is quick to form conclusions, but he is also quick to change if presented with more information. Although he is not absolutely certain, he appears that way to women.

For example, Bill says in a definite tone, "Our children are completely spoiled." Dismayed, Mary says, "They are not. I can't believe you would say that." They are now headed in the direction of an argument.

Mary assumes that Bill is not open to changing his point of view. She prejudges him as a righteous, opinionated, and self-centered person. To her, having a discussion after Bill has voiced such a definite-sounding opinion is out of the question. If she wants to be heard she thinks she faces the formidable task of *convincing* rather than *sharing*.

Without a prior understanding of how men reason things, Mary interprets Bill's statement as arrogant and rigid. Because she fears she must fight him to be heard, she becomes opinionated and aggressive. This aggressive attitude, in turn, makes him defensive and resistant to her point of view. Her fear becomes a self-fulfilling prophecy.

If, however, Bill said to his friend Tom, "My children are completely spoiled," Tom might respond, "I know what you mean. Kids today are very different from our generation. I don't think they are spoiled, I think they are just more assertive. In the long run I think they will do fine."

In this case, Tom heard Bill's point of view, but Tom knew instinctively that Bill was also open to other opinions. Thus Tom was able to express his differing point of view without defending his own or attacking Tom's. He trusted there was room for him to differ in his opinion. Tom knew that Bill would compare the merits of the differing ideas and possibly form a new opinion.

With this understanding Mary would have responded to Bill in a nondefensive manner. When Tom said, "Our children are completely spoiled," she could respond in a supportive and open manner, saying, "They sure do make a lot of demands. I don't think they are spoiled. They are very responsible in getting their homework done. They're just different from our generation." In this example, Mary felt safe to express her point of view; the couple could have a conversation and not an argument.

Through understanding our differing styles we can respect and integrate them both. Thus in forming opinions and then making decisions, truly balanced men and women understand the creative value of openly sharing thoughts and feelings, yet they also respect the value of self-reflection and of thinking a problem over before seeking input from others. The intention to be open and respectful of our partner's differing style of reasoning is very helpful in avoiding conflict.

These differences of awareness not only style our thinking processes but even affect our sexual experience. Let's look at some examples of how our focused and open awareness manifests in the sexual needs and experiences of men and women.

FOCUSED/OPEN AWARENESS AND SEXUAL EXPRESSION

In sex, men tend to skip foreplay in favor of reaching the goal of orgasm, whereas women favor the pleasurable process of foreplay. Even their physiologies express this difference. Men need two to three minutes of genital stimulation to reach climax, statistics show, whereas women need an average of eighteen minutes. These figures are staggering: she needs six times as much duration and attention to reach climax.

If a man doesn't understand this difference, he can easily and mistakenly assume that his partner does not enjoy sex as much as he does. Most important, if he does not know that she needs six times as much foreplay, then he will not be motivated to give it to her. Without this foreplay, she certainly will not enjoy lovemaking as much. When she is not fulfilled in sex, it stops being fun and energizing, and becomes difficult and tiring for both.

Because a woman has open awareness, it takes more time for her to relax and open up to enjoy sex. If a woman doesn't understand and accept this difference, she can easily believe that something is wrong with her. She may even imagine that she is frigid or unable to be aroused, when in reality she is not getting the relaxed foreplay that she needs.

In many cases, because a woman takes longer to experience intense arousal, she will fake arousal to give her man a sense of accomplishment and also to avoid appearing inadequate. This sets up a negative loop. When a woman appears satisfied without enough foreplay, a man gets the wrong message. He thinks what he is doing works and will continue doing the same thing. Rather than give more foreplay, he may give even less foreplay. This is certainly a delicate subject to talk about, but if a woman is pretending or exaggerating her pleasure, she is setting herself up to not get what she needs.

Getting to the Goal vs. Enjoying the Ride

When a woman is overwhelmed from her day, it is more difficult for her to relax enough to have a sexual climax. At these times, what she needs is to be cuddled. She needs lots of hugs, affection, and intimate embracing. Through being held and loved in a nonsexual way, she can just relax without any demands being made of her. This is a heavenly experience for her and is closely related to how men feel after they have a climax.

This is important to understand; otherwise, men don't take the time to give this kind of loving support to their partners. This nonsexual, non-goal-oriented physical touching is highly valued by women in ways that men do not understand. Touching is as important to women as sex is to men.

This does not mean that women don't like sex. They love it just as much as men. The difference is that when women are tense they relax through non-goal-oriented hugging and cuddling, yet when men are tense they feel a compulsion to intensify that tension through goal-oriented sex. Then it gets released and they can relax. Open awareness wants to expand the process of pleasuring each other, while focused awareness wants to get to the goal as efficiently as possible.

Men are goal-oriented in sex and sometimes get impatient with foreplay. Women sometimes need a lot more than eighteen minutes of foreplay to have an orgasm. In fact, sometimes sex can be quite satisfying to a woman even if she doesn't have an orgasm. This nonorgasmic experience is much different from what a man would suspect.

It is hard for a man to conceive how a woman could sometimes feel sexually satisfied without having an orgasm. A way men can relate to this is by comparing her nonorgasmic sex to his "quickie." Just as a man can be satisfied by getting right to the goal (a five- to ten-minute quickie), a woman enjoys the ride or the process of moving toward the goal. Arriving at the goal (orgasm) is not primary to her fulfillment just as the process of getting there (foreplay) is not primary to a man.

This does not mean that women don't enjoy orgasm. In general, though, she does not fully enjoy orgasm unless she first enjoys foreplay. Sometimes she is not even interested in orgasm, but rather wants to savor the sensual play of enjoying and pleasing each other. At times she may be very goal-oriented and at other times she may just enjoy the process of getting closer.

A man also experiences different desires in his sexual experience. Sometimes he wants to take time and enjoy tantalizing his partner. Gradually his whole body is filled with pleasure, and then when he climaxes, he experiences the joy, sensuality, and ecstasy of a full-body orgasm.

This full and ripe experience is contrasted by having a quickie. In a quickie — five to ten minutes of foreplay — he focuses on getting to climax as fast as he can. Although in either extreme he is satisfied, the quickie is not as deeply fulfilling as indulging in the sensual pleasure of foreplay. It is like comparing fast food to gourmet food. Sometimes we want fast food and other times we want the finest.

At times a woman just wants to cuddle. She wants to be held and touched and doesn't care about having an orgasm. Understanding this makes it easier for a man to feel successful in lovemaking if his partner does not have an orgasm. He will also be more motivated to create times when they can just cuddle without having to be sexual at all. This is very important to women.

In a similar way, sometimes a man just wants a release and he is satisfied. It is important to men to forget all the foreplay and experience quickies from time to time.

This balanced understanding relieves a woman from feeling pressured to perform as a sex goddess whenever they make love. He does not demand that she have an orgasm each time. She does not expect him to relish long, drawn-out lovemaking every time. During quickies, a woman doesn't have to resent not getting foreplay if she knows that at other times they will cuddle and sometimes, when they are both feeling more balanced, they will enjoy gourmet sex.

Our sexual needs change in cycles like the weather or the phases of the moon. These cycles are then interrupted by the varieties of stress in our daily lives. A healthy sexual relationship demands flexibility and tremendous acceptance of our differences.

The Logistics of Foreplay

Because their awareness is so expanded and open, women are easily distracted or affected by their environment, especially when it comes to their own needs. When it is her time to relax and enjoy, a woman may find herself worrying about unpaid bills or wondering if the house is safe.

Men need to recognize that for women, environment is essential in the lovemaking process. Beautiful surroundings go a long way. Lighting a candle, sweet smells, low light, soft music, all can make a tremendous difference.

For an overly open woman to relax (and remember, most women become overly open after a stressful day), she may need her whole body touched before she is focused enough to enjoy direct stimulation to her erogenous zones.

When a man is tired he can be sexually satisfied by a quickie; a woman may be equally satisfied by a loving massage all over her body. By feeling throughout her whole body, she is brought back to her center.

Understanding the different kinds of awareness helps us to identify some of our common differences, but it doesn't determine how sex or making love should look. Styles of making love are very personal and it is not possible to say what is right for everyone. At most, this discussion can help you explore your partner's needs and be more open to looking for and accepting his or her differences.

LIVING IN THE PROMISE

Open awareness is capable of recognizing the potential of someone or of a situation. The ability to see what one could be is a great virtue, but can create a variety of problems when it is out of balance. When a woman is too open she can fall in love with a man's potential. If she lacks focus, she will react today to things she expects to happen in the future — she imagines she is happy today because she expects her needs to be fulfilled in the future.

Certainly it is normal to be happy when you expect something good to happen. This becomes a problem, however, when anticipatory happiness masks the unhappiness in the moment. It is hard for an overly open woman to have enough focus to experience what she is feeling in present time, when she is borrowing her happiness from an unrealized future.

She may even be in a relationship with a man whom she does not love, imagining that one day her love will change her man. She imagines he is her ideal partner. Through perceiving his potential to be loving, supportive, understanding, etc., she begins to feel as if he has already changed. She lives in a fantasy world. She sees what she wants to see rather than what is.

For example, imagine that someone offered you a check for a million dollars. That would be quite exciting. The only hitch is that you have to wait a month before the check will clear. Even though you have to wait, you will probably be very happy and excited. In much the same way, being in a relationship with someone who holds a lot of promise can excite you and make you very happy, regardless of what you are getting in present time.

As you go home with this check for a million dollars, even though it will take a month to clear, you will feel like a millionaire. If you have any credit cards you will probably start spending your money before it comes in. This living in the future is like counting your chickens before they hatch. It leads to certain disappointment, especially if the check never clears.

Let's look at an example of one couple "living in the promise." Daniel, 32, a writer, married Susan, 33, an executive secretary. Daniel was never sure that he wanted to be married to Susan. He also loved another woman. But Susan was sure that he was perfect for her. She even left her previous husband, who was quite famous, to be with Daniel. She said, "I have never met a man as wonderful as you. I know it is meant to be. I can't live without you. Everything is so perfect now in my life."

The message Daniel received was that he could do no wrong. Daniel couldn't believe how easy this relationship was. Susan accepted him unconditionally. She would listen to him, praise him, agree with him, satisfy him, and basically wait on him hand and foot.

Susan was seeing in Daniel her idealized perfect mate. She was immeasurably happy. In Daniel she saw a man who would love her the ways she had always dreamed of. He was kind, considerate, responsible, creative, spiritual, and would be very successful one day. He had tremendous potential. He was loved by everyone. But most of all, he needed her love.

The problem was that Susan did not love Daniel. She was in love with the perfect partner she thought Daniel would become if she was successful in loving him. The other half of the problem was that Daniel did not love her. He loved what he was getting; he needed love and he loved being loved.

Susan's vision of Daniel's potential was very accurate. He was potentially kind, considerate, responsible, etc., and given the right kind of loving support, those qualities would develop. What she didn't see was that he was not "right" for her. She only imagined that if she could be "the one" to love him and support him, he would reward her with his love and they would live happily ever after.

During their relationship, Susan was preoccupied with being a "perfect loving partner," while Daniel was absorbed in being loved. She had a picture of what a loving partner does and she did just that, determined to earn his love. Susan was so consumed in being loving that she never really saw who Daniel was.

On the other hand, Daniel did not really love Susan. Instead, he loved the way he was being treated. As long as she poured on all her love and devotion, he would love her. But when he felt mistreated, he would get upset and withhold his love until Susan apologized and promised to change.

Most of the time, Susan actually felt as though she was getting the love she needed. In truth she was not. For instance, Daniel would ignore her while she was talking. Deep inside she would be hurt. But on the surface she didn't mind, because she believed that if she loved him enough, he would change. Her strong expectation of one day receiving his love acted to suppress her pain.

Just like the person waiting to cash their million-dollar check, Susan faithfully waited with a devoted smile on her face. Her denied feelings of unhappiness and dissatisfaction were eventually expressed in momentary glares of disapproval and resentment. Over time, she unconsciously began trying to mold him into her ideal image.

This underlying tension gave rise to increasing conflict. Susan thought she was loving Daniel, but deep down he felt rejected. He received a very confusing double message. On the surface she was happy with him and said that they were perfect "soul mates." But at a more unconscious level, she was dissatisfied with him and sought to control, change, and rehabilitate him. In subtle ways she would tell him what to do, correcting, nagging, demanding, and complaining.

After two years of marriage, Daniel was no longer attracted to Susan, while Susan realized that she was in love with another man, her doctor. He was now the "perfect partner," the willing recipient of her devotion. Daniel was extremely intolerant of her feelings for another man and they got a divorce.

In counseling, Daniel learned the difference between real love and conditional love. He realized that he had not loved Susan, but instead had loved how he felt when she was adoring him. He later married a woman he truly loved and gradually learned to give love unconditionally.

Susan too went into counseling, where she recognized her pattern of falling in love with a man's potential and then trying to earn his love. She learned that in trying desperately to earn love she was not truly giving to a man, but was actually rejecting him. What she thought would ensure a successful relationship was actually counterproductive.

When a woman is living in the promise, she may appear to be happy and loving toward her man, but she is only loving his potential self, not the real man. What she doesn't realize is that he won't change as long as he is getting the message that she is happy with his behavior.

There is a paradox here. As I have mentioned before, men need to feel loved and accepted the way they are before they can change. Being accepted "as one is" does not mean being accepted "as one will be." Certainly men need appreciation and acceptance. But on the other hand, they need honest feedback to determine how they can become more supportive of their woman's changing needs. This is accomplished through loving but honest communication and persistence in asking for support. Then the love, acceptance, and appreciation he receives is real.

Love doesn't require being happy about everything your partner says and does. A woman can be loving and accepting and also express feelings of frustration, disappointment, concern, anger, hurt, sadness, and fear. She can be very happy some days and less happy on others. A part of her can be angry and yet another part is happy to be with him. When she is in touch with her true feelings and needs, then when she is happy and appreciative, those feelings will be real and will affect him in a positive way. Only then will he be able to truly respond to her needs.

No man can grow and realize his potential with a woman unless she is real. When a woman "lives in the promise," she behaves to her partner as if she is getting her dreams fulfilled. She acts like a millionaire but each day her account gets emptier. On an unconscious level, she is becoming increasingly dissatisfied, frustrated, and disappointed. Outwardly she is loving and happy, but her love becomes clingy and has a false ring to it.

He gets mixed messages. On the one hand she seems so happy with him; and on the other he feels that nothing he does can truly satisfy her. She is always trying to improve him and mold him into her ideal image. He becomes increasingly turned off. He cannot truly respond to her because she is not communicating the truth. She is not communicating her needs, nor does she share how it feels to not get her needs fulfilled.

At some point, she wakes up and feels the void in her life. The pain becomes so great that she cannot deny it anymore. She goes from elation to depression.

It is not uncommon for a woman to feel she has a happy marriage, then after ten years wake up one day and realize how unhappy she has really been. She then rejects her partner for not fulfilling her. This blame is certainly her experience, but it is unfair. He is shocked when he finds that she is so unhappy. He says he is willing to change and she says she is tired of trying to make the relationship work.

Her fatigue arises from years of trying to make it work by pretending that it was working. She was trying to be loving and nice when deep inside she was furious and resentful.

Some women spend years living in the future, denying the pain in the present, while others go through much shorter cycles. She may flip from elation to depression in one week, twice a month, or once in ten or twenty years. The longer she denies her pain, the greater is her depression when it comes up.

If a woman is to find more stability, she needs the opportunity to share her insecure feelings and be reassured by her husband or intimate friends. When an overly open person is happy, it may seem to them that they are always happy. When they feel bad, it seems as though *everything* is bad and it always will be that way.

To find greater stability she needs to remember how changeable her reality is. Keeping a journal of feelings, experiences, and impressions is very helpful, as are support groups and therapy.

In most cases, when a woman suddenly discovers that she is not getting what she needs, she feels like a victim. She blames her husband rather than taking responsibility for the mixed messages she was sending the whole time. It is important to note that when she does wake up, to find balance, she has a valid need to feel like a victim for a while. Then she can work on taking responsibility.

This is not to say that "living in the promise" is all her fault. Just as women can live in the future, men can live in the past. A man may make his partner happy once and then expect her to stay fulfilled. Men do something nice and they imagine women will be happy forever. Men feel and say "I love you" and think that the loving part of the relationship is handled. They expect women to always know that those loving feelings are there.

Men also can live in denial. Tunnel vision causes them to deny themselves. They also may be unhappy in their relationship and not even know it. They will minimize the importance of problems in the relationship. Like an ostrich that buries its head in the sand, men bury themselves in work and don't even know there are problems in their love life. Some are so lost in work, they don't even know they need love and are not getting it. They don't realize that although their bank account may be getting bigger, they are emotionally empty.

Like women, men can also live in the future. When they are richer and more successful, they imagine, they and their mates will be happy and fulfilled. The hard truth is that in many cases success actually puts a greater strain on relationships. After "making it" these couples are confronted with the problems they ignored to become successful.

Just as women may wake up and realize that they are unhappy, so, too, men can experience a shift when their inner pain becomes too great. A man wakes and realizes that he wants more from a relationship. The problem is, he thinks he has to find it elsewhere. He doesn't realize that by learning to communicate better, he can heal the pain and fulfill his needs in the present relationship.

Too often the impulse to get a divorce is just burying one's head in the sand — denying that the problem is within and blaming it on the relationship. I have witnessed literally hundreds of couples on the verge of divorce who, through learning to communicate more successfully, were able to create a more loving marriage. When someone wants to get a divorce, I recommend they get help instead. If a couple feels they are tired of trying, they may simply have been trying ways that don't work.

SELF-BLAME VS. BLAMING OTHERS

Yet another common difference between men and women is that women tend to blame themselves first, while men blame others first.

Whenever there is a problem, conflict, or negative experience, women tend to feel too much responsibility. They first see themselves as responsible, and then they recognize how others share in the responsibility. They are especially hard on and judgmental of themselves, before they look to see how others contributed to the problem. This "blaming inward" is a symptom of open awareness.

Men are apt to accuse others before they look at their responsibility for problems. They tend to be immediately aware of the shortcomings of others, and then they become aware of their own. This "blaming outward" is a symptom of focused awareness.

Focused awareness sees problems as obstacles to achieving a particular outcome or goal. From this focused perspective, any obstruction is perceived first with blame.

On the other hand, open awareness sees problems in a larger context — as outcomes that need to be corrected. From this perspective, a woman is quick to see all the possible ways she could have done something differently in order to have produced a different outcome. Thus she easily feels responsible and accepts blame.

These basic differences give rise to much confusion in relationships. When a man reacts to a problem with blame, the woman mistakenly assumes that he has already considered his responsibility first, as a woman would do, and that his final conclusion is that she is at fault. This gives the impact of his blame much more weight than it really carries. If she can learn not to react defensively to his blame, it gives him a chance to cool down and explore his own responsibility.

When a man poor self-esteem, his insecurity prevents him from becoming aware of his responsibility; he stays stuck in blame and self-righteousness. Women fail to recognize that a male's sanctimonious attitude is sometimes just a defense mechanism to hide his insecurity. The more insecure a man is, the more confident he may appear. Women don't see through this because when they are insecure, they tend to criticize themselves even more (blaming inward) rather than faulting others (blaming outward).

When a woman does blame her partner, he may ignore her complaints because he assumes that she will later see her side of the problem, as a man would do. Many times, a man doesn't take seriously a woman's valid grievances because he assumes that she is totally blaming him without accepting any responsibility herself. He does not realize that she has already looked at her side of the problem and has tried her best to correct it.

In concluding this chapter's exploration of how men and women see the world in different ways, it is important to note again that no person is exclusively masculine or exclusively feminine. Within each person all sorts of combinations of focus and openness are possible. A man or woman may be overly focused in one area of their life, have a balance of openness and focus in another, and be overly open in still another.

Recognizing these differences in awareness helps us to understand how and why relationships with the opposite sex can be so difficult. This increased understanding gives us greater compassion for each other's vulnerabilities, as well as greater clarity to work toward finding solutions to our problems as they arise.

In Chapter 5 we will continue to explore our differences and vulnerabilities by taking a look at the divergent ways that men and women develop self-esteem.

CHAPTER FIVE

How Men and Women Develop Self-Esteem Differently

Men and women perceive themselves in different ways. A man knows himself through his work. The realm of work, doing, effort, action, achievement, accomplishment, decisions, efficiency, and results is a major source of his self-esteem. When a man's work, etc., is valued, it is like the door through which love can enter in to touch his soul.

On the other hand, a woman knows herself through her relationships. The quality of communication, intimacy, honesty, sharing, cooperation, feelings, mutual respect, understanding, and compassion deeply influences her self-esteem. When a woman is valued through her relationships, her self-esteem is most deeply influenced. Just as a man identifies more with his "doing," a woman identifies most with her "being." This difference in self-awareness makes men more result oriented while it makes women relationship oriented.

WOMEN VALUE SELF THROUGH RELATIONSHIPS

As a woman's awareness expands outward, to maintain a sense of self she *relates* to others. By seeing degrees of her self in others she is able to know herself. For example, through relating to the beauty of nature she is able to connect with her own inner beauty. By relating to the loving qualities of others she is able to feel her own loving qualities. Through watching and relating to her mother and father, she is able to discover the qualities within herself that she observes in her parents. This way of knowing oneself is also true in men, but it is not their primary way.

Because a woman's primary nature is to expand, as her awareness expands outward she may easily forget herself. Relationships become an essential mirror by means of which she is able to draw her awareness back in order to see herself.

To the extent that she is unable to truly know herself and her own feelings and needs, a woman is generally more conscious of the needs and problems of others. Her low self-esteem or insecurity may manifest as increased concern for her loved ones. This increased concern can cause her a lot of confusion when dealing with a man.

Because of her increased concern for him, she expects him to be equally concerned about her needs. If he really loves her, she tells herself, he should be just as concerned about her. What she doesn't realize is that most men, when their self-esteem is low or they feel insecure, become more concerned regarding their work rather than their relationships. Thus she takes his apparent detachment to the relationship to be a symptom of not loving her instead of a reflection of his own low self-esteem. This misinterpretation causes a lot of tension in relationships.

June and Al had been married five years. June had been a real estate agent before becoming a mother of two children. Al is a doctor. When Al would become absorbed in his work, June would begin to feel unloved and insecure. She began to feel unworthy of Al's love, as if his work were more important than her and her wants and needs. The more she doubted his love for her, the harder it was for June to feel good about herself.

As she looked onto the mirror of their relationship, she saw herself becoming more insecure and inadequate. From this attitude of unworthiness she did not feel capable of asking for more time and attention. She began to doubt the validity of her feelings and kept them to herself. She did not want to appear negative or demanding. To avoid the pain of her feelings, she buried herself in activities designed to win Al's love. He seemed happy but didn't treat her any differently.

What June didn't know until much later was that Al thought she was happy; he thought the relationship was great. From his point of view, his only problems were related to work.

In therapy, June felt safe and supported enough to share her true feelings of hurt, insecurity, and resentment. At first this was very hard for Al to hear. He initially thought she was being irrational and demanding. Gradually he began to listen and understand.

When Al was able to recognize that June needed validation, recognition, and strokes in their relationship just as he needed strokes, recognition, and appreciation at work, he became much more attentive to and tolerant of her needs in their relationship. He could now listen with open ears. June felt empowered to share more of her feelings and needs.

June's reaction to Al's absorption in work was only one of many potential problems that could arise. Some women consider their increased "loving concern" for others to be a healthy standard for relationships, rather than a symptom of low self-esteem. There is, of course, a fine line here. A woman's expectations of loving concern for and from her partner may be very appropriate, or under other circumstances may be very unrealistic. Without a basic understanding of our differences, this is obviously very difficult to determine and can be very confusing.

To our feminine side and especially for women, "relating" is a primary source of self-awareness, self-esteem, and self-worth. Relationships are a woman's major source of love and support. Relating is also a means for her to "collect" herself. Through actually collecting things or people within her awareness, she has a stronger sense of self. As a result of culturing and nurturing positive and loving relationships, she expresses a gracefulness in her life that inspires and empowers others, especially men.

When a female is not attentive to her need for loving and supportive relationships, it is very easy for her to lose touch with her femininity and grace in favor of developing her masculinity. To sustain her feminine gracefulness is an ever-increasing challenge in our current society — a task not unlike swimming upstream. Everything in our society says to become masculine. Feminine values are not respected by men or women.

Why do women find it much harder than men to sustain high self-esteem in our so-called modern society? Here are two reasons:

1. Women are pressured to succeed at work and spend less time developing and nurturing relationships, yet they are expected to raise a family at the same time. By working harder and putting less attention and energy into her relationships, a woman's self-esteem is sure to suffer. This contrasts with a man's self-esteem, which is bolstered by an increased focus on work.

2. Women who are successful at work are respected more than women who focus primarily on their family and relationships. This puts even more pressure on women to neglect their feminine needs. Because femininity is not respected in our society, women are drawn to becoming more masculine to earn respect for their success at work. Then at home they are rejected by their male partners because they are not feminine enough. After a grinding day in the competitive work world, it is difficult to instantly become soft, warm, graceful, fulfilled, relaxed, orgasmic, and feminine. This imbalance caused by the pressures of our society is a major source of frustration in sexual relationships.

Changing economic situations have of necessity given rise to the two-paycheck family. This situation, coupled with the increase in single mothers who must support their families, makes succeeding at work just as important for women as it is for men. But a woman's success, unlike a man's, does not fulfill her self-esteem needs. A successful day at work empowers her masculine side by does nothing for the feminine side. A man can feel very good about himself after a fruitful day at work, while a woman still needs to have nurturing relationships.

Although society expects women to change, they cannot alter their fundamental feminine nature. *Women primarily need to have nurturing relationships if they are to feel good about themselves.* Women today must be especially attentive to balance the energy put into work with the energy put into supportive relationships.

When a woman's worth is derived from her work, her ability to form loving and lasting relationships is diminished. The workplace as it is today cannot fulfill her feminine relationship needs for caring, understanding, validation, and respect for feelings. As the work world evolves from an arena motivated solely by greed into a place of mutual respect and caring, it will become much easier for a woman to form loving and supportive relationships in her work environment.

Without the support of loving and caring relationships, a woman loses her ability to be graceful, attractive, warm, receptive, loving, vulnerable, soft, and feeling. These are the qualities that create nurturing relationships, which in turn help to develop her self-worth.

A woman's self-worth primarily arises through her relationships, especially in the ways she is treated and viewed. If she is treated with respect and love, then she feels worthy of love and respect. If a girl's mother or father sees her as a joy, she is then able to see herself as a joy. But if her parents see her as a burden, she will see herself as a burden. The more relationship-oriented she is, the more dependent she is on how others perceive and experience her.

When a woman is not receiving the support she needs in her relationships, she easily loses touch with her femininity and tries to earn love in a masculine way. Unfortunately the love she receives for her accomplishments cannot truly fulfill her feminine side; it cannot heal her deep insecurities and fulfill her soul. Without an understanding of what can truly fulfill her, she may seek recognition solely through her achievements. In this way she cuts herself off from her true and primary source of self-esteem — quality relationships.

Julie, 38, is a television producer. Although she has achieved great success, she doesn't feel fulfilled. As she gets older, her work seems less satisfying. She says, "When my marriage failed in my twenties, I was determined to be independent. I would never need a man again. I buried myself in work. Now I feel as though I have sold my soul. I feel tired and burned. In my marriage, I gave and gave and got nothing but hurt. Now I have given myself to my work and I feel even more empty."

Julie learned the hard way that she had a problem with receiving. When she did not receive back the love and support she needed, she would desperately seek to be more worthy of it. She was unable to relax and enjoy. When people attempted to enter the protected fortress around her heart, she would reject them. She didn't want to be hurt again. To avoid feeling the pain of her aloneness and emptiness, she would drown herself in work.

This does not mean that a woman cannot be fulfilled through her work. Julie was unfulfilled because she used work as a way to avoid or deny her natural and real needs for love through relationships. Once she gained a deeper understanding of her feminine needs for relationship, Julie admitted to herself that she was missing love. Readjusting her priorities, she was able to begin the gradual process of learning to love herself and letting others love and support her. When a woman is able to know herself through the quality of her relationships, she is not compelled by insecurity to prove herself through outward achievements. Instead, she is free to achieve at a pace that brings her inner fulfillment.

MEN VALUE SELF THROUGH ACCOMPLISHMENTS

Whereas women let in love through relating, men let in love that comes to them in response to their actions. This is because men identify with their actions. This identification is a symptom of the masculine focused awareness.

As a man's awareness focuses on a point, to have a sense of self he regards the point of his focus in a context of cause and effect. He knows himself in terms of how he can affect a person, object, or situation. Quite automatically and unconsciously, he views himself in terms of how he can be used by the object of his focus, or how it can be used by him.

A man sees everything in terms of how he can affect change. He affirms his value through the results he creates and values others through their effectiveness. He knows himself in reference to what he causes, affects, changes, creates, or controls.

The power to create results is the key for a man to have a positive sense of self; the ability to sustain relationships is what determines much of a woman's self-worth. In this sense, failure in the workplace is a man's biggest fear, while failure in relationship is a woman's.

The male side of us knows itself in terms of its achievements and accomplishments. A man's worth primarily comes, as it were, from the notches on his belt. Our female side knows itself through relating in a positive way to its environment.

MEN AND SPILT MILK

Because men are result-oriented they tend to focus on solving problems and are apt to ignore feeling reactions. For example, if there is nothing they can do about a particular problem, they will have little or no need to talk about or even feel the effects of the problem. Their motto is "why cry over spilt milk; what's done is done." They are only concerned with what can be done about the situation. Their attitude sounds like this: "If there is nothing you can do about it, then why complain or be upset about it?"

The man who expresses a balance of male and female energies might answer, "By being upset you are only acknowledging the truth, and by exploring the truth of feelings, you may find that there is something you can do, or at least you will end up being more careful in the future." By denying upset feelings a man loses touch with the creative power of balancing his male side with his feminine side. Moreover, when a man turns off his feeling self, he inevitably turns off his ability to feel good as well.

WHY MEN WANT TO BE RIGHT

Because a man's self-image is so tied to creating results, he identifies with his decisions and actions. When someone tries to correct or control his actions, it is like saying that he is wrong or inadequate. To avoid the pain of being inadequate he may aggressively defend his behavior or rebel against any control. He is especially defensive regarding his "doing" because to him, actions are a primary reflection of his self.

On the other hand, a woman will tend to have this same sensitivity regarding her feelings. Just as correcting a man's behavior is painful to him, correcting a woman's feelings is equally distressing to her. Feelings are an essential part of relating, so when a man invalidates a woman's feelings he is hurting her in a most vulnerable place. Without this understanding men and women unknowingly mistreat each other; they do not give due consideration to their valid vulnerabilities.

Men always have to be right, women complain. This is generally true. Because a man identifies with his actions and decisions, to make his actions and decisions wrong is to make him wrong. He tends to take this kind of feedback more personally than a woman would.

Just as men want to be "right," women want to be "good." Being good makes them feel worthy of love. Many times a woman will make great sacrifices to reveal to a man how good she is, hoping that this tactic will make him more supportive. Unfortunately it backfires. By trying to be "good" she tells him by implication that he is "bad" if he is unwilling to make the same kinds of sacrifices. The message he receives is that this relationship is too demanding.

Mark is a 36-year-old engineer and Jill, 38, is a publicist. They have been married six years. While they were engaged Mark had a final fling with an old girlfriend. After they were married Jill found out about it. She was deeply hurt. Unfortunately, after six years she continues to bring up the issue.

Jill wanted Mark to take her to lunch, but Mark said he was too busy that week. Then on Thursday, Jill called his office only to find that he was gone, helping a woman in the office pick up her car. This upset her very much.

When Mark arrived home that night, Jill asked in an incriminating tone, "Where were you today? I called your office and you weren't there."

"I gave somebody a ride to pick up their car," Mark said.

With mistrust in her voice, Jill continued, "Was 'somebody' a man or a woman?"

Irritated, Mark said, "It was Mary. She works in the accounting department. It was no big deal! Look, I don't like being treated this way. I didn't do anything wrong. I feel mistrusted."

"You were too busy to take me to lunch, but you could take time out of your schedule to help her," Jill accused.

"When you asked me about lunch, things were very busy," Mark explained. "But today a major account cancelled and then Mary asked me for a ride."

"Everybody is more important than me," Jill said reproachfully. "You don't love me. You are always flirting with women. How can I trust you? I've never had an affair. I've always been faithful to you."

In a tone both cold and furious, Mark answered, "I've had it with you. I can't believe you are bringing this up again. . . ." They were now well into a major argument.

In this argument, Jill has brought up how faithful and committed she is and how Mark is not. This kind of tactic will never work. By harping on how "good" she is, it makes him feel bad. Expressing how much better she is than him does not motivate him to give more. At such times he does not feel loved or supported by her. Rather than inspire him to be loving, her allegations only make him feel unappreciated and mistrusted. Eventually he will become the "bad" person she thinks he is. He will react to her by becoming mean and uncaring.

If Jill wants Mark's support, she needs to approach him in a way that encourages his love and attention. She needs to be approachable. To become more receptive to his support she must forgive him for his past mistakes.

Here is a much more direct way Jill could have approached the problem:

When Mark comes home Jill says, "I called your office today and you were gone. I was upset when I found out that you were helping a woman pick up her car. I feel jealous. I want you to take me to lunch if you have extra time. I want to feel that I am the special woman in your life."

This nonaccusatory approach allows Mark to hear Jill without feeling blamed or inadequate. He can then understand her feelings and feel supportive and compassionate. He will probably remember next time to invite his wife out to lunch when he has the opportunity.

Just as trying to be the "good" partner is a mistake many women make, being right also backfires for men. Men do not realize that when they are trying to be right they indirectly make women wrong. When a man takes the time to explain his actions, often the woman just concludes he is making her feelings wrong. If a man wants to appear right in a woman's eyes, his best strategy is to take the time to listen to her side and make *her feelings* right. In return she will naturally be more accepting and appreciative.

Let's look again at the example above.

When Mark comes home, Jill says, "I was upset when I found out that you took the time to help another woman. I feel jealous. I want you to take me to lunch if you have extra time."

Mark says, "You shouldn't feel jealous. It was no big deal. I didn't know that I would have the extra time. If I had known in advance, I would have taken you to lunch."

Mark thinks he is supporting Jill by explaining why he did what he did. It is a logical explanation but it doesn't support her. Jill feels discounted and unheard. She feels as though he is saying she does not have the right to feel jealous or upset. What she needs is for Mark to first be understanding of her feelings, and then he can explain what he did.

To be more supportive, he could have said, "I understand you feel upset and jealous. I'm sorry it looks as though I made her more important than you. A casual relationship with Mary does not compare with our intimate relationship. You are the most special woman in my life. Having lunch with you is also a priority for me. Let's schedule a lunch next week. (Now he can give his explanations.) If I had known in advance that I would have the time off, then I would have scheduled lunch with you."

Mark's habit of "being right" and explaining why Jill should not be upset is deeply ingrained. It is a habit that will take time to change, but through practice a more supportive mode of expression can be learned. Similarly, it will take time and practice for Jill to express herself in ways that do not make her look "good" and Mark look "bad."

By making Jill's feelings right before explaining himself, Mark will be more successful in supporting her. Likewise, as Jill learns to express her upset feelings in a nonaccusatory way, she becomes more approachable and supportable.

As we continue to explore male and female differences, it becomes more evident that men and women have different vulnerabilities related to self-esteem. Men are more sensitive to any criticism of their behavior, while women are more sensitive to any criticism of their feelings.

Let's look at various examples of problem areas related to criticism.

Shutting Down During Sex

The more result-oriented a man is, the more sensitive he may be to correction and control. This is especially true during lovemaking. Most men are very sensitive to corrections in this area because during sex, men are most definitely result-oriented. He wants his partner to be happy and fulfilled, but on the other hand, he wants to feel that *he* is doing it *to* her. This works fine for the woman as long as he knows what she wants and needs. But many a man is very closed to feedback. He expects himself to know what she needs. This is unrealistic. Not only is he not a woman, but even if he were he could not know her needs — they are always changing.

If a woman makes a specific request that corrects what he is doing, a man may suddenly shut down in defense. She might innocently say, "Could you touch me a little softer, that hurts." In an instant he turns over and is silent.

She says, "Is something the matter?" and gets no response except cold silence. He shuts down and forgets all his communication skills. Although his feelings are hurt, he doesn't want to admit that he is hurt over something so minor. If he could express his feelings, he might say, "I don't like it when you tell me what to do. It is painful to be corrected."

Because he doesn't say anything, she pursues the problem and says, "What are you feeling?"

"Nothing."

After a long silence she says," Weren't we just making love?"

He says, "Yes" and nothing else.

By this time she is panicking and wants to talk. She says, "Do you want to talk about it?"

He mutters, "No."

She has no idea of what she did to upset him. She then feels inadequate and becomes even more afraid to communicate her needs and feelings in the relationship.

Through understanding the male sensitivity to correction, a man can become more receptive to input while a woman can become more tactful in the way she gives feedback.

A large part of this problem stems from the unrealistic notion that a man should always know what a woman needs. This certainly is a symptom of the overly macho mentality — which holds that a man is an expert at pleasing a woman just because he has a penis — but it is also a reaction to the unrealistic and immature notion, held by many woman, that if a man loves her, then he will know just what to do.

Just as it is unrealistic to think a man can always know what a woman needs, it is equally idealistic to believe that a sign of true love is when a man knows a woman's needs. A real sign of his love is that he is willing to understand her needs and then respond to them. A sign of her love is when she does not demand that he always remember her needs. She understands that because his needs are different, it is easy for him to forget her needs. When a partner disappoints you, real love trusts that he really didn't understand.

When His Is the Only Way

When a man is overly masculine or result-oriented, he may believe that there is only one way to do something. From this perspective there is only "one right way," which is the most time-efficient or energy-efficient way to get from point A to point B. He does not see that there are thousands of equally valid ways to move from A to B that would serve a variety of other purposes besides his own.

People with too much result orientation must be in control at all times. They also tend to think in terms of black or white. Hence it is easy for them to control others, because they have an arrogance about them that says, "I can do anything and my way is the best. If you are not doing it my way, then you are wrong. There is only one way and this is it."

In contrast, a more balanced point of view would sound like this: "I can relate to what you are saying. I can see that your way is best for you while my way is best for me."

A person lacking in result orientation who is overly relationship-oriented might say it like this: "I can relate very well to what you are saying and to everyone else's ways. I can't make up my mind about who to follow. I guess I will follow you, since you are so sure of yourself." People who are deficient in the masculine quality of being result-oriented are very easily intimidated and controlled by the dogmatic and self-righteous absolute attitudes of the overly result-oriented person.

Correction Under Stress, His Achilles Heel

A person who is overly result-oriented will hate it when someone corrects them or tries to control them. In fact, their own insecurities will motivate them to try to control others. Because men are primarily result-oriented, they generally hate to be corrected under stress. It is their secret Achilles heel. Women unknowingly create resistance in men by correcting their behavior or trying to assist them before they have been asked. Unsolicited advice is usually very hurtful to the masculine ego.

Men typically resent being told what to do unless they have specifically requested assistance. However, a man does not resent another man giving him orders if he respects the accomplishments of that man. In respecting that man he is also respecting his own masculine abilities. For this same man, it can be threatening to receive orders from a woman, unless he relates to her as if she is a man.

The more a man respects his own female side, the more he is able to accept and respect the equal power that women wield. Until men feel this secure, however, a woman can wisely respect this male vulnerability and support him — to support her — by being "suggestive" rather than "controlling."

When Helping Isn't Helpful

From the previous discussion it follows that a common problem crops up in relationships when women try to help men solve their problems without first being invited to do so. A man can automatically shut down when a woman tries to come up with a solution to a problem that he is upset about. If her suggestions are really good, this may make him feel unmanly and inferior.

A woman can relate to this masculine vulnerability by comparing it to how easily she is wounded when a man invalidates her feelings. When he tells her that she should not react the way she naturally does, it is often the most painful experience a woman can have. This does not mean that she cannot offer advice. It means that her timing is critical — she should wait till he is capable of receiving it.

Women must be equally tactful when it comes to offering sympathy. When a person is upset, a woman will instinctively offer sympathy, empathy, and understanding, which will make another relationship-oriented person feel better. To a result-oriented person, however, such sympathy may be offensive. He may feel as though he is being smothered or locked into a feeling of weakness. This is an ongoing source of discontent in male/female relationships.

From this perspective it is clear to see how people with the best intentions may fail the most in relationships. Men commonly do not know that when a woman is hurting she needs validation for her feelings: She needs compassion, empathy, and understanding; she needs to be sure her feelings are heard and respected. A man's instinctive reaction is to try to solve her problem or talk her out of being upset.

Just as men do not understand a woman's needs, so also women do not understand the needs of men. When men are hurting they need to withdraw and think about what happened. Men do not necessarily need to talk about their feelings right away. He needs a compassion that comprehends the source of his pain, which is generally a failure to achieve his goal. He does not need his partner to make excuses for him. He needs to feel appreciated for what he has done, even though he might have failed. He generally does not need the sympathy that she would want if she was upset.

SOME CONSEQUENCES OF IMBALANCE

The overly masculine person worries about avoiding the pain of failure; the overly feminine person is more afraid of abandonment and the pain of rejection. The result-oriented part of us tends to be offended, while the relationship part feels hurt.

A man who feels overly hurt by others will be weak in his masculine power to create real results. He may be very loving and empathetic to others but lacks the strength to really contribute to their needs. Although he is able to relate well, women will sense this lack of masculine energy and be unwilling to commit to him.

He's Nice But Not Exciting

This relationship-oriented man is many times perplexed. He has listened to and related to women's complaints about overly result-oriented men. He hears how women feel abused by the "Macho Man" and does everything to not be like him. Yet when it comes to sex and commitment, these women go for the result-oriented macho kind of man. Moreover, they continue to complain to the sensitive man about the abuse they receive from the macho man. It just doesn't make sense to him.

A balanced man is both result-oriented and relationship-oriented. In his life, he is always juggling these two priorities.

Striking a Win/Win Balance

A man who is overly result-oriented may wield great power, but lacks the empathy to contribute to others in a significant way. He will tend to be preoccupied with work, achievement, competition, wealth, status symbols, and success. He can be ruthless and cold to others simply because he truly is unaware of the sensitivities of those who are more feminine.

He will tend to adhere to a win/lose philosophy: I win and I don't care if you lose. He is insensitive because he does not consciously relate to the pain of losing. From a deeper perspective, his compulsion to win is in itself a desperate attempt to avoid his own feelings of being a loser.

The opposite of being overly result-oriented is being overly relationship-oriented. In this case, one may feel so much empathy that they give up winning to avoid hurting another. This is a lose/win philosophy. It is most commonly demonstrated by the housewife who mistakenly believes she is being loving by continuing to sacrifice and to lose herself. The "sacrificer" is the female counterpart to the ruthless and selfish businessman. He denies or hurts others; she denies and hurts herself.

When the male and female sides are in balance, a person is still success-oriented, but from a win/win perspective. He feels that he wins when everyone wins. He is committed to creating solutions to problems in which everyone benefits. He also so relates to others that if they lose, he feels the loss. In this way he is both patient and compassionate.

MEN NEED TO BE APPRECIATED

Result-oriented people need lots of acknowledgment, appreciation, and gratitude for their actions and achievements. In return they can become more open. Men often feel greatly offended when women do not appreciate their way of doing things or trust in their abilities. When a man is upset by a woman's reactions, it is most often because he assumes she does not appreciate his actions or trust his willingness to fulfill her. In many cases, however, he is not entirely mistaken: her appreciation is overshadowed by her accumulated resentment.

Ted is 35 years old and a commercial artist, and Cathy, 34, is an accountant. They are quite happily married with three children. They have been married before and have healed much of their past hurt. They go regularly to counseling to improve their communication and to ensure that things stay good.

One morning Ted rose early to finish a project. While reflecting on his strategy he took a long shower. When he was done he noticed that the water had overflowed onto the floor. He quickly wiped most of it up and rushed off to his office. When he got home Cathy was furious.

She said, "I can't believe that you left the bathroom in such a mess. There was water all over the floor. There were hairs everywhere. I feel angry. I think you should clean up after yourself. I hate it when you expect me to be your maid. It was your mess. Susie could have slipped on the floor and hurt herself."

When Ted hears her upset, at first he takes it too personally. He thinks, "How dare she say I am an incompetent father? Does she think I am out to hurt my children? Is she saying I am a bad father just because I didn't finish cleaning the bathroom floor? I don't expect her to clean up after me. I didn't ask her to clean it up. Does she think I do nothing for her? I can't believe this mistreatment."

Ted's reaction is quite common for men. He takes her upset as a sign that he is not appreciated for all the good things he does. But he has misunderstood her. Cathy is not saying he is an incompetent father or that he is not supportive of her. She is saying that she is hurt and upset about this particular incident, and is expressing the various factors that are upsetting to her. She needs his understanding to feel better about it.

If he can just give her permission to be upset, she will be able to release the upset and remember all the wonderful things about him. If he makes her wrong, then they will argue.

Part of learning to hear better is understanding how to respond effectively to upset feelings. Ted is learning to listen without expressing his gut reactions. This is called containment. He contains his reactions until she is finished speaking. Then, before explaining himself, he reflects back his understanding of her feelings and expresses some concern and reassurance. Then he can explain the situation from his point of view.

To successfully support Cathy, Ted says, "I understand you feel angry about my leaving the floor wet. I'm sorry that it looks like I take you for granted and expect you to be my maid. I understand that this is very upsetting. I was careless and inconsiderate. You are not my maid and I don't want to take you for granted. You are right to be upset. Six years ago, I would never have left the floor wet (now he can explain). I did not realize it would upset you so much. I was just in a hurry to start my project. I hope you don't really think I am an incompetent father. Do you?"

Cathy, having been supported, can now express her support. "No, I think you are a wonderful father. I was just expressing some of my fears."

Having this way of responding gives Ted more patience. But he must also understand that when Cathy is upset, she needs to share how she feels without him interpreting everything to be a statement about him.

WHY HEARING HER UPSET IS PAINFUL

It is hard for men to listen to upset feelings because they immediately infer that they are not being appreciated. He assumes that she is asking him to resolve her problems. He gets the message that what he is doing is not enough; therefore he feels he is not being appreciated. In his mind there is no room for her to be upset and also appreciate him. It is so painful for a man to feel unappreciated that when a woman is upset, he feels a compulsion to make her feel better.

Men are also over-sensitive to female upset for another reason. Being result-oriented, a man feels successful when his wife is happy; he feels like a failure when she is not. If she is upset, he automatically assumes responsibility for this result. He takes it personally, not realizing that other factors besides himself may be affecting her.

Sometimes all a man needs is a reminder that he is appreciated be*fore* a woman shares her upset feelings. In many instances it would help if she could remind him that (1) she *does* appreciate what he does, (2) she is not asking him to do more, and (3) she is just sharing her feelings so that he can be aware of her situation and she can become more centered and clear.

On the other hand, it is essential for men to understand that from time to time a woman needs to emotionally purge herself. In that moment she may not be appreciating him. But if he can back up and give her the space to move through her emotional purging, she inevitably will become more centered. She will be able to see clearly again and focus on all the good that he brings to her life

WHY WOMEN OVERREACT

When someone is upset, a man will tend to tell them why they shouldn't be upset. If, however, the upset person is a woman these "helpful" explanations will only make her feel worse. Men commonly try to talk women out of being upset. They think they are helping when in truth they are making matters worse.

When his logical solutions fail to make her feel better, he typically becomes frustrated, judgmental, or offended. Then he sulks. This pattern is apparent to most women, so they are afraid of getting upset. They try to control and suppress their upsets until inevitably they lose control and erupt like a volcano.

As we have seen, women generally have a much greater need than men to spend time exploring and sharing their feelings. To feel centered they need to explore their various emotional reactions to the people, places, and things around them. For this reason, communicating is not only a process of conveying ideas, but a process of discovering how they are feeling.

Men tend to think first about what they are feeling. Then when they want to convey an idea, they will communicate it as a point or as a logical progression of ideas to make a point. Women often share not to make a point, but to discover what they are feeling inside.

As a woman is sharing, her feelings and ideas gradually come into focus and start to make sense. A man, however, will "make sense" of his feelings and ideas *before* he speaks, through silently mulling them over inside. When a man hears a woman speaking out her ideas or feelings before they "make sense," he mistakenly judges her as being irrational and illogical. When he hears a woman share her upset feelings he may think, "Why is she making such a big deal out of things. She is overreacting."

In the above example, Cathy became upset when she saw the mess Ted had left. When she expressed her feelings, Ted couldn't believe she was infuriated over one simple little mistake. If there was just one reason for her upset she probably would not have reacted so strongly. But on that day there were many reasons for her upset; the mess in the bathroom merely triggered an eruption of her feelings.

The reasons Cathy was upset were very complex.

- She was upset that he left the mess and didn't clean up after himself.
- She was upset because a part of her believed that she was responsible for cleaning up after Ted and that she should not complain. After all, he was in a hurry to go to work to help support her.
- She thought about all the other chores she had to do that day and become more stressed.
- She thought about how her children took her for granted and expected her to clean up after them, and became more upset.
- She thought about how this same kind of thing happened in her previous marriage.
- She felt guilty for being so upset and thought she was being too demanding.

- She got angry because she had to demand support, which felt so humiliating.
- She felt afraid that Ted didn't love her as much as before. She was afraid it would make matters worse to bring up her feelings. She was afraid that if she didn't, she would lose herself.

When she expressed that she was angry, she did not know all this was inside. Through sharing her upset she came to discover the variety of complex and sometimes conflicting reasons for her reaction.

From the point of view that she was upset because he left a mess, Cathy was overreacting. But from the point of view that Ted's mess triggered her upset about various other issues, she was not overreacting. The better men can understand this, the less judgmental and impatient they will be when a woman is upset and needs to talk.

There is yet another reason that women tend to overreact: Unresolved feelings from the past surface and compound her present feelings. When something stressful occurs, women not only experience a variety of feeling reactions, but these reactions may be intensified by related feelings from past experiences.

This means that when something hurts 20 "degrees" in present time, she may automatically remember a similar experience in the past when she hurt 30 degrees. She may then confuse the past with the present and feel as though she has just been hurt 50 degrees.

WHY MEN UNDERREACT

In an opposite way, men who are overly result-oriented will "underreact" to stress in their lives. As a general rule men tend to automatically prioritize their problems and then direct all their upset feelings to whatever problem is most immediate and demanding. If a stress factor is not directly related to the problem he is seeking to solve, either he will not notice it or he will automatically dismiss and minimize the stressor as irrelevant and unimportant.

Even so, a man is still affected by these other sources of stress. He is just not aware of how they are affecting him. When a woman gets upset, she becomes aware of all the things that are upsetting her; a man is outwardly upset about the one problem he has prioritized, but his other problems build up stress on a subconscious level.

For example, Ted is trying to save money to take his family on a vacation. To reach this goal he must make more money at work, but he is behind schedule. There are other problems in his life, but this is his major stress. When he goes home his wife Cathy reminds him that the home is a mess, the plumbing needs repair, the kids' grades are not so good, one of the children is sick, his car needs to go in the shop, and they haven't gone out in a long time.

As his wife reminds Ted of all these problems or stressors, he appears to be unaffected. He says in an irritated tone, "Don't bother me with all these little details. Stop nagging me. You worry too much." He has no idea that when he minimizes these problems he minimizes her. When he makes these smaller stressors unimportant, she feels as though *she* is unimportant and that he does not care about her.

Let's say that his goal to take his family on a trip creates 30 degrees of stress. Now let's say that all the other problems they share (messy house, plumbing, etc.) add up to 60 degrees. Then Ted comes home and experiences the home-related stress, this 60 degrees of stress is pushed into his subconscious. When he is confronted by these problems consciously, he experiences indifference. He treats Cathy as if she is nuts for being so upset.

Ted's conscious experience of these problems is that they do not bother him, but *subconsciously they do.* The effect of this suppressed stress is that he becomes more worried about the one problem he has prioritized, earning more money at work. Now, instead of being 30 degrees stressed, he is 90 degrees upset about his work-related problem.

He becomes consumed by his frustration to make more money and take his family on a nice vacation. His normal reaction to home stress is minimized but his reaction to work stress intensifies. The only way he can find peace from work stress is to avoid thinking about work (he has already avoided thinking about home stress). Consequently, Ted "turns off" by focusing on TV or burying himself in the newspaper.

A man can, however, use this understanding to his advantage. He can work at learning to listen with caring and understanding to his partner's upsets. By supporting her in resolving her upset feelings about their problems, his subconscious stress will be automatically released. He will be able to handle the pressures and anxieties of work and home, and participate more with his family. He will also be more effective and creative at work. He will begin to feel more fully, enjoy life more, and feel better about himself, even if he has not solved his prioritized problem at work.

WHEN A WOMAN IS OBSESSED WITH SACRIFICE

While a man under stress suppresses much of his feelings, some women under stress suppress their needs. When a woman has an excess of feminine, relationship-oriented energy, under stress she tends to make too many sacrifices to improve her relationships. For example, her partner's needs become more important than her personal needs. This approach can only work for a while, until she begins to feel her inner deprivation. At this point she unfairly blames her partner for her unhappiness and he reacts defensively with little compassion.

Instead of a win/win relationship, hers is a lose/win approach. She loses so he can win. In the early stages of a relationship this appears to work — she makes him happy. But later on she begins to feel that he should do the same. She expects him to give more. When he doesn't, she is easily hurt. Moreover, by this time he has gotten used to getting all her support and resists any changes. She approaches him from the point of view that he has not given enough; he then feels unappreciated and becomes defensive.

This kind of woman may become obsessed with changing herself in an attempt to please her partner. If her needs and wishes upset him, she minimizes their importance. Her self-esteem becomes increasingly dependent on the approval of others. This tendency makes her overly vulnerable to their comments, attitudes, and behavior. The more she denies herself, the more easily she can be hurt. What would not be painful to most is painful to her.

Because she is so dependent on others to know her self, each time a woman sacrifices or minimizes her own needs she is disconnecting from some part of her self. This sacrifice makes her more sensitive to being hurt.

The problem with this sensitivity is that she overreacts. As she shares her pain she blames others for not supporting her more. Feeling that she is too demanding, too sensitive, they become defensive and frustrated. In general men are drawn to vulnerability, but in this case they are repelled. It is extremely difficult for a man to listen when a woman is too vulnerable and overreacts with blame. The irony is that to heal this problem, she needs to be heard. When a man understands this explanation for why women overreact, he can become more tolerant.

Myra was always a sensitive child. When she would hurt, no one understood her. Her family thought she was getting upset over nothing. They would make fun of her or become annoyed and frustrated. Because she never got the love and understanding she needed, she grew up overly vulnerable.

The price Myra paid to stay open in an unloving environment was low self-esteem. Each time she was hurt and didn't get the understanding she needed, she would feel somehow defective and unworthy of love. Being so sensitive, Myra was overly protective of others. She would give and give, then not understand why she was mistreated in return.

When Myra would share her hurt, she *expected* others to hear her, understand her, and change for her in the same ways she would change for them. When they didn't she would feel disappointed and more hurt. Not only would others not sacrifice for her, but they would get turned off to her and give her less.

In short, Myra was a martyr. When others didn't sacrifice for her she felt they didn't love her. The more hurt she felt, the more she disapproved of others in return.

This kind of disapproval is most painful to men. When she would feel hurt in her marriage with Don, she would share her hurt with so much condemnation in the tone of her voice that he could not hear her: he felt blamed, attacked, manipulated, resisted, rejected, and criticized. The message he got was that he was responsible for her pain and that he was bad and unworthy of her love. Myra was not deliberate in sending this message; she merely shared her hurt. Her tone of voice and facial expressions did the rest.

Eventually, being overly vulnerable became a way to control Don and other people. Instead of asking for Don's support she would give her all, then become painfully exhausted and expect him to support her. Also quite unconsciously, she attempted to use her hurt to motivate others to support her. To Don this was manipulation and control. When he would rebel and turn from her, she would feel hopelessly misunderstood.

Myra changed this pattern by learning to give less and ask for more support. It took years for her to learn how not to sacrifice herself. She began by taking responsibility for her role in creating this problem.

She had always thought that this was being done to her. As she became aware of her unvoiced expectations and demands, she could understand why Don felt so controlled and unappreciated. She saw that much of the time she did not ask for support, and then resented him for not helping her. She saw how unforgiving, cold, and bitter she had become.

Myra worked on becoming less *giving*; at the same time she worked on becoming more *forgiving*. As she sacrificed less, she found that she felt less resentment. As she practiced forgiveness, she found that Don was more willing to listen and caringly understand her hurt. As Don sensed her willingness to forgive and accept his limitations, he even began to apologize more.

WALKING ON EGGSHELLS

The self-sacrifice we have just discussed is closely related to self-denial. To avoid the pain of rejection and invalidation the overly relationship-oriented person denies her own needs and wants. For this reason, it is very common for women in a relationship to walk on eggshells at all times. Certainly men behave in certain ways to avoid a woman's upset reactions, but in general women are much more concerned with not upsetting their men. Being more relationship-oriented, they are much more aware of how people can be hurt.

What this kind of woman doesn't realize is that by denying herself (walking on eggshells), she becomes less attractive to her partner. The natural attraction that he felt for her gradually diminishes as she develops a false persona. As she pretends to be someone else, she loses touch with who she really is. Gradually her self-worth diminishes. Even when she is being loved she cannot let it in, knowing it is not the true self that is being loved. Yet she is afraid to share her true self because she so fears losing the love that, ironically, she can't let in.

VICTIMS OF THE PAST

Women become overly vulnerable and dependent on others when as children they were abused in some way. (When a boy is closer to his mother and he is abused, he will react in a similar way.) Depending on the amount of love and understanding she received at the time of her abuse, she will need to experience those victimized feelings again and again to eventually heal them. Unfortunately, until her early pain is healed all subsequent pain is processed in a victim-like way. She feels the powerlessness of a young child even when she is a powerful grown-up.

It is hard for this woman to develop a normal sense of responsibility, because all subsequent hurts trigger her victimized feelings. Let's look at Myra's life as an example.

At four years old Myra is rejected, resented, and ignored. Naturally she feels hurt. Three things occur:

1. She feels worthy of being rejected and thus unworthy of love.
2. She feels powerless and helpless to change the situation.
3. She suppresses the pain to survive, but feels unworthy and helpless.

At age seven, Myra may complain that no one loves her. She may feel inadequate and unworthy of love. Each time she feels the pain of rejection, she will regress back to her earlier pain and feel powerless to change the situation.

Because as Myra grows she is now more responsible for creating what she needs, when she shares the pain of how hopeless and helpless she is, her chances of being understood dwindle. Her parents teach her how to make friends, when what she needs is to be held while she cries like a baby. Because this support is not available and never was, she will again suppress the pain to survive.

At sixteen when she is rejected by her boyfriend, she again feels deeply hurt. She feels unworthy and inadequate — powerless again to change the situation to get the love she needs. Another 16-year-old, suffering the same rejection but without the childhood trauma, would not be hurt as deeply and would not feel so unworthy and dependent. They would bounce back more quickly and shift their love needs to another partner. The abused child in Myra will keep seeking love from the person who rejected her.

Any kind of abuse is very confusing to a child. Even an adult struggles to determine what is fair to expect; imagine how difficult this is for a child. Unfortunately, a little girl commonly reacts to abuse by feeling worthy of such abusive treatment. It is as though she takes on the unacknowledged guilt and shameful feelings of the abuser. In order to make sense of her world, she justifies the abuser by assuming that in some way she is worthy of abuse. When her mother yells at her and sends her to her room, she thinks to herself, "If Mommy doesn't love me then I must be bad."

Later on as an adult woman, still feeling worthy of abuse, she may *unconsciously* seek it out and even provoke it. Studies have shown that abused women tend to repeat circumstances similar to their abusive pasts (unless they were able to heal their hurt). This is not to say that if a girl is molested, she will be molested again. But a high percentage of raped women were molested as girls. Those who were abused as children but have sufficiently healed the trauma are not prone to repeat the unfortunate circumstance.

It is important to understand that an abused woman is not consciously or practically accountable for the abuse. Instead, she *unconsciously* attracts or is attracted to the abuse in order to bring up the repressed wounds of the past for healing. Ultimately, her wounds are healed when she is able to recount the experience and not feel worthy of such treatment. At such a point, she is able to truly feel the abuse was wrong and unjustified.

Although we have seen that a woman may unconsciously attract abuse, the abuser is still considered accountable for their abusive behavior. It is irrational to consider the victim accountable, just because her past trauma is being unconsciously repeated.

VILLAINS OF THE PAST

In a complementary way, the abused result-oriented person will tend to become like the "villains" of his past. While the female side of us justifies an abuser by feeling worthy of such treatment, the male side justifies an abuser's actions by validating and unconsciously incorporating the behavior. If a boy was abused and holds onto his resentment, he will tend to automatically abuse others in the way he believes he was mistreated.

This principle became clear to me one day while taking a cab in New York. The cab driver was from Yugoslavia. As we talked, he complained about the irresponsible behavior of American youths. I asked what he thought the reason or cause was. Very adamantly, he replied that Americans were not punished enough. He went on to explain that the reason he did not end up in jail was that his father had beaten him everyday. If he was a minute late for dinner he was beaten. If he looked the wrong way he was beaten. If he was lazy or fooling around he was beaten.

I was surprised that he described all this abuse with pride in his voice. I asked if he liked the beatings and he emphatically said no. In fact, he said, he had hated his father, but because of the beatings he had learned to respect authority. I then asked if he had beaten his children. Very proudly he replied, "I beat my son everyday and he has never once been in jail! He now has his own family." I asked if his son beat his children. "Of course," he said.

In that moment it became clear to me that as long as violence is seen as a solution and not the problem, violence and war will be perpetuated. The problem with trying to change abusive behavior patterns is that our male side tends to react to maltreatment by justifying the abuser's actions, while the female side justifies abuse by seeing the victim as worthy of it. No human being is worthy of abuse. When they are "bad" they need healing, education, transformation, and rehabilitation. One wrong does not justify another.

The result-oriented person who has been ill-used tends to get revenge through punishing others. He believes "an eye for an eye" is the only justice and does not comprehend the true meaning of forgiveness. Needless to say, this type of person is attracted to the "victim of the past."

When a person repeats the injustice of their past they are apt to justify their behavior based on the way they were treated. Certainly, their past is influencing them; ultimately, they are unconsciously repeating the abuse they received. But as adults they are accountable for their actions. The abusive male side of humanity needs to be transformed; the abused female side needs to be healed. Transformation occurs through understanding the pain of the abused while recognizing and feeling one's accountability for abusing. Healing occurs when the abused person is fully heard and understood.

OUR DIFFERENT NEEDS FOR SUPPORT

When a man truly understands that a woman's primary support comes through relationships, he will spontaneously begin to respond to her needs for attention and sharing — not because he loves her more, but because he now realizes that this is a genuine need on her part. He does not label it a sign of weakness, but a valid and important aspect of femininity. Through understanding her needs he naturally becomes more caring and considerate.

When a woman thoroughly understands that a man's primary support comes through his work and achievements, she naturally becomes more appreciative of his efforts and accomplishments. It is not that she loves him more, but that she now realizes how important it is to him to be appreciated, accepted, and trusted. She realizes that the greatest gift she can give him is to support him in being her hero.

SOURCES OF FULFILLMENT

Men love to feel that they are responsible for a woman's happiness. In this light, the greatest gift a woman can give a man is to let him to be her primary outer source of fulfillment. When she does this, however, she must be careful not to go out of balance and forget that she is the *inner* source of her fulfillment.

As a woman becomes more dependent on her mate, she may not only forget her inner source of love and fulfillment, but also the many other sources outside herself. She may even continue her other relationships, but makes her happiness and fulfillment primarily contingent on her male partner's love.

What commonly happens in relationships is that after some time all the unhealed needy feelings from childhood begin to get projected onto our primary mate. We make them responsible for our happiness. For example, women may demand from their spouses the attention and affection they needed as children. It is appropriate for a child to be this needy, but it is an impractical expectation to put on a mate. When a man begins to feel these kinds of demands being made of him, he will tend to reject, withdraw, withhold, or even punish. He may get the message that he is not enough, and give up.

The solution to this problem lies not in a woman's becoming more independent by denying her valid needs for quality relationship. The answer lies in satisfying this feminine need. She needs to practice allowing others to fulfill these deep needs, realizing that it is an impossible task to give to one man. Women must solicit the support of other women for the nurturing they need to heal their pasts. This support can also be found in therapy, support groups, and supportive seminars.

In seeking out this support, it is important to keep in mind the male/female differences discussed throughout this book. Because men and women are primarily dissimilar in how they are able to know themselves, the methods and strategies they use for healing and growth need to reflect these differences. With all good intentions, a therapist, teacher, or guide may point you in the wrong direction simply because they do not recognize and understand these fundamental differences.

For example, it is essential that a woman learn to love and accept the needy part of her. If she does not learn to fulfill this part through a variety of relationships, she will be compelled to consciously or unconsciously demand fulfillment from her partner.

In rejecting her neediness she becomes strong and independent. But when she embarks on a relationship and starts to open up sexually, she begins to feel the relationship needs she has been denying to be independent. She becomes like an emotionally starving person, hungry and needy.

She unfortunately has little support for this part of her, except for the man who has assisted her in opening up. Unless she has other sources of support she will demand more from him than he can fulfill. Inevitably she will feel the same disappointment she felt as a child. He no longer feels like her hero, but is the enemy. In response, he feels pressured and constricted and begins to withdraw or withhold. He becomes, ironically, the enemy that he doesn't want to be.

Men are equally prone to bringing their childhood neediness into their adult relationships. The greatest gift a man can give a woman is to make her feel special. In making her special he feels he has no need for anyone else. In this way, he cuts himself off from other sources of support.

To feel good about himself, he becomes dependent on making her happy. He feels too responsible for her. When she is happy he feels good, but when she is unhappy he feels bad. He becomes too reliant on her fulfillment to feel good about himself. When she is upset he becomes defensive, seeing her mood as a reflection of his competence. He stops appreciating, accepting, and trusting himself.

If his mother was consistently unhappy during his childhood, he would have felt the pain of not being able to make her happy. Later, as an adult, he will be overly sensitive to his partner's upsets, experiencing the intense pain he felt as a child when he was powerless to help his mother.

To have successful relationships, then, both men and women need to continue building various kinds of support so they do not become too dependent on their partners.

Just as important as understanding our differing primary needs to know and value ourselves is understanding how we uniquely react to stress. Men and women need to recognize and validate each other's natural coping mechanisms. In the next chapter we will explore how males and females react differently to stress, and how we can best support each other at such times.

CHAPTER SIX

How Men and Women React Differently to Stress

As we have seen, males and females see the world and develop self-esteem in disparate ways. The third major category of complementary differences between men and women is the way they uniquely react to stress. In a nutshell, masculine awareness reacts to stress in a more objective or analytical way while feminine awareness is more subjective or feeling in its reactions.

Masculine awareness is primarily concerned with what happens in the outer world: *by changing the outside objective world, the masculine nature attempts to reduce stress.* A man reacts to stress by withdrawing into his thoughts to determine what needs to be done to reduce the stress.

The feminine psyche is more concerned with the inner subjective world: *by changing herself the feminine psyche attempts to reduce stress.* A woman primarily reacts to stress with an upsurge of feelings. These feelings allow her to center herself, explore her attitudes, and make changes within herself so that she can reduce her stress. For example, if something is upsetting her she can reduce her stress by becoming more flexible, tolerant, forgiving, patient, understanding, etc. By changing her attitude she reduces stress and feels better.

BASIC DIFFERENCES IN HANDLING STRESS

Under stress a man will be motivated to affect or control his environment to fulfill his purposes. When undesirable things happen to him, to maintain his control he needs to objectively analyze how his actions are responsible for what happened and realize what he can do to change things.

To understand how he is responsible, he first needs to objectively review the situation. He becomes very alert and attentive to what happened in his external environment. Then he is able to determine what *he* did that led to the problem. His objectivity can then be put to determining what he can do to solve the problem. In this way, he can begin to understand and accept responsibility for his part in creating what happened.

Unlike a man, when under stress a woman first needs to center herself through exploring her feelings. She can then figure out what happened, why it happened, and what should be done about it. If a woman feels and understands her emotions, then her thinking will be open, flexible, and clear.

DESTRUCTIVE EMOTIONS

To react objectively is to detach, observe, and analyze what happened and why it happened. To react subjectively is to feel and explore one's emotional reactions to a problem or stress; it is to explore how one is affected by what happened and why.

When a man reacts to stress immediately from his feminine, emotional side he tends to lose his positive attitudes. His negative emotions may make him destructive, moody, and self-centered. Negative emotions are not bad. They are a part of healing or de-stressing. But when a man experiences his negative emotions *and* has lost his objectivity, his emotions become mean, threatening, and unloving. For example, when a man is angry it is easy for him to lose control and become violent, break things, or say cruel things. This is his dark side.

This is not to say that men should not be emotional. It is saying that when a man under stress gets into his feelings before he has established an objective perspective, then his emotions will tend to be unloving or destructive. When a man prematurely goes into his feelings there can be other symptoms besides meanness, coldness, cruelty, and violence — he may become moody, needy, wishy-washy, indecisive, apathetic, and apt to procrastinate. The main symptom is that he loses control of himself. He loses control because by indulging in his emotions he has disconnected from his primary source of power, i.e., his ability to be objective.

A woman, on the other hand, doesn't necessarily lose her positive feelings when she becomes angry. She has a greater ability to feel angry but maintain a caring and respect for the other person. She can be angry and still be quite capable of hearing and understanding another's point of view. While anger may make men overly self-righteous and defiant, it can assist a woman in discovering what she deserves.

When a woman is under stress the most important thing she can do is to look inside herself to her feelings. Being more subjective, women first need to react emotionally and then they are able to view a situation more objectively. Ideally she will process her subjective feelings before drawing a conclusion about what is happening objectively. In processing her feelings she explores and identifies her reactions, then questions their validity and corrects whatever feelings are not consistent with her true self. If she becomes too analytical or objective without considering her subjective feelings, she may experience rigid thinking and become controlling, opinionated, confused, demanding, petty, negative, and frustrated. This is the dark side of a woman.

A man who does not honor and support his objective reactions automatically experiences negative and destructive emotions. A woman who doesn't honor and support her subjective reactions becomes rigid and opinionated in her thinking.

As long as a woman is in touch with her positive feelings and attitudes, her thinking will be clear and flexible. As long as a man's thinking and attitudes are positive, then his feelings will be loving and supportive.

BOTH ARE VULNERABLE TO ARGUMENTS

When a woman is emotionally upset but she denies or suppresses her feelings in an attempt to be logical and rational, she is bound to experience many arguments with men. At such times, her statements will be rigid and opinionated. This is not only offensive to a man, but threatening. It tells him there is no room for his ideas to be true and that his differing point of view is not being appreciated. While she thinks she is making sense to him, he becomes angry and "dumps out" his negative emotions.

On the other hand, if a man just dumps out his negative feelings without considering objectively his partner's point of view, he can create in a woman serious defensiveness. Here again, she will tend to be opinionated and rigid. From this perspective, arguments are a "no win" situation and should be avoided.

In an argument, a man can sometimes just dump out all his negative emotions and feel much better, but leave the woman feeling like a wreck. He can easily apologize for all the mean things he has said, and expects her to forget it, just as he has. That is easier said than done. She will probably remember what was said and the pain it caused her for a long time.

In a similar way, if a woman becomes very opinionated, critical, and controlling, it can shut a man down for days. He generally does not know what happened, but he does know that he doesn't want to become open to her again. He decides to keep his thoughts to himself.

Both men and women are very vulnerable to arguments, but they are unaware of the injurious effect they have on each other when they argue. The impact of arguments should not be taken lightly. Although the parties are not physically damaging each other, on a psychological level they are bruising each other and it takes time to heal. The closer we are to someone, the easier it is to be bruised or to bruise.

Because men derive their power from their objective analysis of a situation, they are naturally unaware of how delicate and vulnerable a woman's feelings are. He does not sustain his sense of self through his feelings. Hence he will disregard her feelings as if they are not important, and stress what he experiences as important, namely, his ideas and beliefs. When a man is emotionally upset he is generally incapable of arguing in a way that would not hurt a woman's feelings. Men commonly have no idea of how they hurt a woman's feelings. It is as though they are the proverbial bull in a china shop.

It is equally true, but less known, how women with their rigid opinions can hurt men. One disapproving comment like "you should have" from an upset or defensive woman can stop a man dead in his tracks. Men just instinctively shut down. One minute he is open and caring, and in the next he is cold and offensive. The big difference between men being hurt and women being hurt is that men are much more *unaware* that they are being hurt.

It is only by reading a book like this that a woman could even begin to understand how she is hurting him. He certainly can't tell her. He doesn't even know. This understanding is vital for men: at least when they are shutting down, they can become more objective by understanding what is happening to them. It is when men lose their objectivity that they move into their dark side; women move to their dark side when they lose their subjectivity.

STRESS MANAGEMENT FOR MEN AND WOMEN

These two complementary viewpoints, objectivity and subjectivity, are the two ways to decrease stress. The masculine way to reduce stress is to change or eliminate whatever object or situation is causing the stress. The second, feminine way is to adjust one's self or attitude so that one is not affected in a stressful way, i.e., change the belief or attitude that is causing the stress.

For example, changing one's behavior is the masculine way to reduce stress, that is, improving the situation by doing something differently. An example of the way our female side reduces stress is to change our attitude — to improve the situation through forgiveness, love, gratitude, or tolerance.

HOW WOMEN GO OUT OF BALANCE

What typically happens in a relationship is that a woman will tend to repeatedly compromise and adjust herself to preserve harmony and avoid confrontation. On a conscious level she will try to change herself. After she has sacrificed or surrendered her position repeatedly, she will begin to feel resentful that he is not doing the same. Now, on a more unconscious level, she will begin to try to change her partner. All communication at this point becomes somewhat manipulative and very distasteful to him. He will inevitably reject her or rebel.

A woman shifts into manipulating when her first means of getting what she needs fails. Her problem is that no one ever taught her what to change about herself to get what she needs. To change herself does not mean to give up herself; it does not mean to act a certain way. The emphasis is not on changing her behavior and speech, but on changing her negative attitudes, such as resentment and mistrust. It means to purify or release her negative feelings so she can be more of who she truly is. This self-discovery can be difficult if she has not been taught how to transform negative feelings. In childhood most girls only learn how to suppress, deny, and repress their feelings. They learn to be good, nice, and happy all the time, even when that is not how they are truly feeling. Suppression may appear to make her more loving and positive, but in truth disconnects her from her true self, being, or "center." To effectively cope with stress a woman needs to center herself. If she remains resentful or uncentered for long, she will inevitably become more manipulative or controlling.

HOW A WOMAN CHANGES

In coping with stress a woman can change herself in a very natural way. In a sense, she is really not changing, but becoming more of who she already is. Being subjective in nature, she changes herself through sharing and expressing her feelings, thoughts, and wishes without being invalidated. To do this she needs to be heard with caring, understanding, and respect. These very important aspects of love nurture her and help to center her.

But if she keeps her feelings to herself, she will gradually lose touch with who she is. Her thinking will become shallow, superficial, and rigid. She will not be able to lovingly and gracefully adapt to the stresses of life, work, and relationships. She will become consumed in trying to adjust her behavior and speech to win the love of others. From this place of seeking to earn love, she will try to change others to get the love she needs. At this point she loses her ability to adapt and change in response to stress. She is unable to sustain a truly loving and positive attitude.

At times of stress, it is easy for a woman with low self-esteem to adjust her behavior and speech in relating to others. What is most difficult is to change or transform her feelings. She may put up the appearance of a loving and giving person, but deep inside she is hiding a storehouse of resentment, mistrust, and dissatisfaction. These negative feelings are weakening to herself and her relationships.

HOW MEN GO OUT OF BALANCE

In a different but complementary way, men in relationships will at first be objective and then become subjective. This means that in the beginning of a relationship a man tries to improve things by making his partner happy when she appears unhappy. His instinctive strategy is to change the object: if she is unhappy, then he tries to make her happy by fulfilling her needs.

This is a positive reaction for him; it motivates him to give more of himself to make a positive difference. In this way she gives purpose to his life.

If, however, he begins to feel that he can't make a difference, he goes out of balance, becomes more subjective, and his attitude changes. He may feel self-righteous, defiant, resentful, spiteful, punitive, unforgiving, and judgmental. As a result he becomes weak, moody, insecure, and more passive. He loses his confidence and is no longer willing to take risks. He may even develop negative patterns for "getting his way" through emotional outbursts and tantrums. It is hard for him to shake off his negative mood when he has lost his objectivity.

HOW A MAN CHANGES

A man, being objective in nature, can best change himself through recognizing and solving problems outside himself. For example, rather than trying to *be* more loving and sensitive, a man *becomes* more loving and sensitive by recognizing how others are hurt or affected by certain things he does or does not do. Through a willingness to change his behavior he becomes a better person. By solving the problem, he automatically changes.

When he sees "himself" (as opposed to his behavior) as the problem, it is very difficult for him to change. This is hard for a woman to recognize because, being subjective in nature, if she identifies something about herself that needs to change, she can begin to change it by just choosing to *be* different. A man changes by deciding to *behave* differently. While self-awareness is the basic ingredient enabling women to change, objective awareness is necessary for men to change: he needs to understand the problem outside himself. Then he can change most effectively.

A man feels compelled to change when he feels appreciated and accepted but also recognizes that he is not creating the desired result and that he is responsible. A woman succeeds in changing the way she feels when she feels loved, understood, and safe but also recognizes that her feeling reactions are not true expressions of who she truly is, i.e., they do not reflect her loving and responsible self.

When a man repeatedly fails to satisfy his mate after trying everything he thinks should work, inevitably he gives up and becomes passively accepting. Instead of coping by changing his behavior, he defends his actions and blames her. This is weakening for a man. He needs to understand how he can make a difference; then he is inspired and remotivated.

HOW SHE UNKNOWINGLY TURNS HIM OFF

Let's review in greater detail what happens. As a man continues to fail in satisfying and fulfilling his female partner, he gradually changes his approach. He begins to deny his natural masculine impulses. He stops being responsible and decisive, feeling that whatever he decides is never good enough. He begins to turn off this part of him because it is too painful to make mistakes for which he might be corrected. He stops taking risks because it is most unpleasant for a man to think he is not being appreciated, accepted, or trusted by the people he loves and who know him best.

When his plans fail and a woman corrects his decisions without being asked to, she unknowingly hurts him and lays a foundation for him to become less motivated and uncaring. He begins to feel unwilling to give of himself, because it is too painful to experience her correcting him. When she corrects him or is disappointed by him, deep inside he feels inadequate and powerless.

Women correct men because they think it will motivate or assist them in changing. The truth is, it just makes them more stubborn and unwilling to change. Women have no idea of how they affect a man when they try to improve him.

When a man fails he needs time to mull things over and gradually assume responsibility for his mistake. Unfortunately, at such times a woman has a compulsion to make some offensive comment, like "I told you so," or some correction like "You should have . . . ," or one of those famous last words "You know that . . . ," or a rhetorical question like "Why didn't you . . . ," or a generalization like "You never . . . ," or a sympathetic gesture like "I know you must feel bad" (I feel so sorry for you).

She mistakenly assumes that these kinds of comments will get him to realize and remember his mistake. Their actual effect is to stimulate his self-righteousness and forgetfulness. Even if he acknowledges his mistake, he will forget the lesson he should have learned. A man remembers and learns from his mistakes when he is not corrected or rejected for them. He needs the support to correct himself.

What makes the above statements ineffective is that they are all attempts to help him feel or perform better *when he hasn't asked for help.* One of the most valuable things a person could say to a man under stress is "What happened?" This helps him to center himself by becoming more objective. Then, if and when he becomes talkative, ask him "why" he thinks it happened.

WHAT A MAN NEEDS

During a stressful situation a man needs time to mull over his thoughts and feelings until he is able to understand what he did and how he could have done it differently. Then he will feel comfortable in talking about what happened and why it happened. At this stage he becomes more accountable for his mistakes. Then he can change himself without repressing his masculine nature.

It is as though a man cannot admit he erred unless he can figure out a way he could have acted differently. He can recognize he has made a mistake when he realizes, "If I had known then what I now know, I could have and would have done things differently."

WHAT A WOMAN NEEDS

When a woman is upset she needs time to explore her feelings through sharing before she is able to be her loving, appreciative, accepting, and trusting self. When she is unable to explore her feelings she becomes overwhelmed, overreacts, and then feels exhausted. At that point she requires even more time to come back to her center. What she needs most from a man is his caring and attention, respect for her needs, and understanding.

Men typically go into judgment and blame when a woman is upset. She needs instead for him to listen and support her without trying to fix her or correct her feelings. He must consciously resist trying to give advice or telling her how she should feel. When men truly realize how they unknowingly hurt women, they automatically become more considerate and respectful.

HOW MEN HURT WOMEN

Just as it is hard for a woman not to correct a man when he is irresponsible and fails her in some way, it is equally difficult for a man not to judge a woman's upset feelings as weak, crazy, foolish, bad, stupid, bitchy, and selfish. Little does he realize that when he casually makes his judgments he is hurting her in a much deeper way than he imagines.

A man's judgments cause a woman to go off center and lose herself. She begins to take on the negative qualities he judges her to have. For example, when he judges her as selfish and unloving it can have the effect of making her more selfish and unloving. He judges her as crazy; she begins to actually feel crazy. In a similar but complementary way, when a woman criticizes a man by telling him what he should do, he will become even more rigid in his ways of doing things. Judgments that arise from resentment never serve to improve one's partner.

When a woman is upset or under stress, she needs the time and support to discover for herself how she can change to be more loving, accepting, appreciative, and trusting. This will naturally happen when she is able to share and explore her inner feelings.

Because men and women do not understand their respective stress reactions and the unique needs that they possess, many times they lose touch with their true or more mature selves and become possessed by the grip of their "dark sides": their inherent positive characteristics become overshadowed by negative feelings, beliefs, perspectives, and attitudes.

OUR DARK SIDES

When a man is unable to support himself or get the support he needs as he is going through his stress reaction, inevitably his dark side will be provoked when he feels hurt, offended, or wounded. Similarly, when a woman doesn't get the support she needs her dark side emerges. Generally a man's dark side surfaces when he loses his objectivity. A woman's dark side emerges when she loses her centeredness.

When a man is unable to be objective, he starts to withdraw — and eventually shut down — his feelings, to assist him in becoming more objective. By being objective a man is able to recognize his responsibility in creating what happened. *At this point it is now safe for him to be subjective*; he can safely explore how he has personally been affected (his emotions) and also explore how he could change.

As we have discussed before, if a man is unable to maintain his objectivity when his subjective feelings emerge, then his feelings will tend to reflect his dark side. He may become moody, irritable, cruel, unfair, and violent. "Shutting down" prevents these feelings from coming forth. It is like a breaker switch that prevents a circuit from overloading.

Many times a woman will try to get a man to share his feelings when he needs to be silent and mull things over in his mind. She has no idea that she is fanning the fire of negative and dark reactions in this man by trying to draw out his feelings. She does this instinctively because being essentially feminine or subjective, she knows that she needs someone to draw her out when she is upset and she especially needs to explore her feelings.

MASCULINE VIOLENCE

When a man is hurt, if he indulges in feeling hurt emotions before he objectively analyzes what has happened, why it happened, and what he can do about it, he will tend to overreact with inferior emotions. This overreaction is not so terrible, except that men tend to act it out. When women overreact they do not act out as much; rather, they are drawn to communicate or talk out their feelings.

Probably the most negative form of acting out hurt is revenge. When a man is hurt he generally feels a compulsion to release his hurt by inflicting it on someone else. This is a very important observation about the male psyche. Violence is generally the compulsion of the male psyche to release its pain and feel better. *Breaking something or someone is a backward or subconscious way of saying "this is what you have done to me."* As men learn to communicate more effectively this tendency gradually lessens.

In a primitive way, when a man is possessed by his pain, by inflicting it on others he can objectively experience his pain and release it. This means that he can see, hear, or feel the pain of another, and it reflects his own.

Dick and Lynn were married two years when he found out she was having a secret affair. Dick felt a compulsion to hurt Lynn back and make her suffer the pain he felt. To punish her, he became violent. He slapped her and called her abusive names. Eventually he felt better and all was forgiven. In this example, Dick began to feel better when Lynn appeared to suffer as much as he had suffered. In a primitive way he felt, "Now she understands my pain. She will not do that again."

In more extreme cases a man may even delight in another's pain and suffering. The most common example of this we can see in the movies. When the good guy, whose children were murdered, finally kills the really bad guy, everyone rejoices. They feel better. The pain of injustice is magically released when the "bad guy" suffers and is abused. This phenomenon is also true in women but it more strongly relates to men.

Ultimately, one can only rejoice in the suffering of another if one is deeply wounded and unable to heal their wounds in a more civilized manner. This observation helps to explain the mysterious satisfaction the male psyche gets out of hurting others or getting even.

WORLD PEACE

This tendency of releasing pain through hurting back is the basis of all violence and war. As men learn to communicate their pain they will become less violent. There is, however, a condition that must be met before men can communicate their pain. To communicate their pain they must first be able to feel it. To feel his pain a man needs to develop his feminine side.

Through listening to and feeling the pain of others, a man's feminine side (subjective awareness) is awakened, and he is able to feel and communicate his own pain. Then through sharing his pain he is able to heal his hurt and find relief without resorting to revenge.

In teaching my seminars on improving relationships, I witness men who have never cried open up and feel their pain and find relief. Without this heartfelt experience of listening to others share their pain in a safe, supportive, and respectable situation, men cannot access and heal their own inner turmoil and pain. Their fathers were alienated from their own feelings, and so the next generation, too, is unable to feel. As a result, men remain trapped in a cycle of hurting back whenever they are hurt.

Taking seminars or being in a group that is safe and supportive for sharing is the fastest and most effective way to develop this ability. Personal therapy and counseling can only be effective to the degree that the client is in touch with his feelings. It is a long process for a man to develop the ability to feel, especially if his therapy is limited to personal counseling. As he is able to feel more, the effectiveness of personal counseling increases dramatically.

Throughout our society support groups are becoming increasingly popular. Civilized man is becoming less dependent on getting even or hurting back to feel relief. This gradual transformation not only leads to more loving relationships but is a real basis for truly creating peace in our world. Our personal success in being free of violence will be mirrored in the world when we are able to maintain love and nonviolence in our relationships. From this perspective, peace in this world is a real possibility.

INFLICTING PAIN

When a man is hurt through some interaction, if he is unable to feel and communicate his pain (and thus heal it), then he is compulsively locked into hurting back. He can only react to meanness with meanness. He cannot express an appropriate firmness and justice from a compassionate place in his heart. The tendency to hurt back runs deep.

When Dick feels betrayed by Lynn's infidelity he is compelled to hurt her back. He wants her to suffer as he has suffered. This compulsion gives rise to violence, vindictiveness, revenge, and cruelty. Once she has suffered in reaction to his revenge, and he can see and feel her pain, he is able to feel relief. The cycle is complete.

This is, however, a negative cycle, because whenever Dick is hurt he feels the urge to hurt back in order to feel better. Also, in hurting back he is not really healing his wounds, just repressing them. The healing he needs will occur only when he is able to feel and share his feelings.

To break out of this uncivilized cycle of revenge and payback, a man must be able to feel and communicate his pain. If Dick can communicate his pain to Lynn, the compulsion for revenge will be fulfilled without hurting back. Instead of acting out his hurt through revenge, he has communicated back his hurt.

If Dick can communicate his sorrow, Lynn may naturally feel an empathetic and compassionate response. This compassionate response shows him that his pain has been acknowledged. When she feels his hurt — which she can do if she is not attacked with it — he will feel healed and be capable of forgiveness.

Most men, however, cannot communicate their upset feelings in a nonthreatening way, especially if they have been deeply wounded. To begin to develop an ability to communicate pain in a safe way, a man needs to listen to the pain of others who have suffered similar injustice. In hearing the pain of others, he is able to feel, share, and heal his own pain without taking revenge. As a result, he becomes more capable of hearing a woman's pain. He becomes more compassionate and understanding.

It is important to point out here that when a man is incapable of being compassionate, this does not mean that he does not care about his partner. When a man becomes detached, a woman often assumes that he doesn't care about her hurt. In truth, he does care, but becomes detached because he is getting in touch with his resistance to feeling his own pain. His apparent resistance to her is not a sign of his uncaring, but a symptom of his inability to feel his own feelings.

As men learn to listen and then feel and communicate their own hurt, they can be free of the unconscious compulsion to inflict pain. Men who cannot communicate and release their subjective pain will continue to inflict hurt on their partners to feel a relief within themselves.

PASSIVE AGGRESSION

Some men reading this description of masculine violence may feel they are exceptions to this. But if they look deeply into their behavior they may see the various ways they withhold giving themselves to secretly punish or get even with others. Revenge may even be disguised as helping a person by teaching them a lesson. Many times a person is completely unaware of their aggressive tendencies. This unconscious aggression becomes passive aggression. Rather than *acting* in a way that inflicts pain, their *inaction* causes pain.

Some common examples of passive aggression are being late, forgetfulness, loss of sexual appetite, fatigue, unwillingness to share thoughts and feelings, uncaring attitude, stubbornness, rebellion, secret judgments, having a holier-than-thou attitude, spiritual or self-righteous arrogance, and feeling satisfied when somebody "bad" suffers rather than feeling compassion for their pain.

RIGHTEOUS AGGRESSION

Another way men express their aggression is through being self-righteous. A man will justify his punishing behavior by blaming it on another. In a relationship he may withhold his love, sex, kindness, and attention, or he may directly punish through violence, meanness, and name calling. The deeper abuse, however, is that he makes her responsible for his negative and unloving behavior.

Certainly his negative behavior can be *understood* by hearing what was done to him, but this does not *justify* it. He feels he is right in hurting her because she has hurt him. He believes she is responsible for his destructive and negative behavior, and deserves to be punished. This is never true. Two wrongs do not make a right.

At a global level, to justify their inner urge for violence, men imagine an enemy worthy of such treatment. In truth, no human being deserves to suffer. Men justify violence by defining it as a solution rather than the problem. As long as violence is seen as a solution, it will persist.

Until men are able to heal their pain, they will feel a compulsion to inflict their pain on others as a means to create change; they will continue to rationally justify their violence as a necessary evil. In reality, violence will only be a solution until man is capable of feeling and communicating his pain without inflicting it. The old way (violence) will be with us until we become adept in the new ways (healing and effective communication and negotiation).

In this context, we can understand the function violence has served in the development of man. In a very primitive way it communicates one man's pain to another. As man develops we can look forward to a world in which man can effectively convey his pain and hurt through verbal communication. From this perspective, peace in our relationships and our world hinges on the development of our feminine side. In the future, compassion for the pain of others will motivate the decisions of the powerful, rather than this unconscious compulsion to punish.

FEMININE VIOLENCE

Woman can of course be violent, but this generally occurs when her feminine side has been hurt so much that she becomes more masculine to protect herself. Violence is not their first reaction. When females are being violent, to whatever degree, the cause is their masculine side controlling them.

Essentially nonviolent, women may instead subject themselves to violence. When they are abused, instead of hurting back their inclination is to make others feel guilty or responsible for their hurt. Through this process, the female side feels relief. Just as the male side of us obtains relief through hurting back, the female side finds relief through making the abuser feel bad or look bad.

To truly assuage her hurt, though, a woman primarily needs her pain to be heard, shared, or felt by others. She needs compassion and understanding to release her pain. When she is unable to elicit enough compassion, she unconsciously seeks that compassion through trying to get sympathy. The strategy employed by the female psyche is to induce guilt in others, hoping that they will change their ways. Also, by making another feel guilty, a woman is able to prove to herself that she was not worthy of such abuse. Instead of making matters better, this strategy hurts a man and he then seeks revenge.

As women are becoming more enlightened, they are beginning to become more aware of how they may be indirectly abusing men. The most powerful way to hurt a man is to take away your trust, acceptance, and appreciation of him through opinionated blame, doubt, criticism, resentment, and judgment. When women retaliate by abusing men through negative feelings and attitudes, they generally don't realize how much they hurt men. They may not even be aware that they are doing it. In an equally abusive relationship, women generally feel the man is much more hurtful, because male abusiveness is so much more obvious. A woman can project guilt on her partner by the tone of her voice, while a man tends to abuse more overtly.

As we explored earlier, when the female psyche is abused and she is unable to share her hurt and be heard, she falls into feeling guilty and unworthy. She is unconsciously driven to release her guilt by showing how others are guilty or responsible for her hurt. This relieves her of some of her pain, but only temporarily. Real healing has not occurred.

Women have felt compelled to be victims so as to warrant the sympathy of others. A woman may feel that she does not have the right to receive compassion unless she has been unjustly and unfairly treated or abused. *In a backward way, by being victimized she feels more worthy of love, compassion, and support.* This attitude needs to change. Through learning to communicate her pain without making her partner a bad person, she can release this attitude and experience receiving compassion without having to be an abused victim or martyr.

In some cases a woman will begin to punish herself when her hurt goes unhealed and unheard. There are a variety of ways and degrees to which a woman hurts herself. She may deprive herself of fulfilling experiences or engage in self-destructive behavior. She may get sick or berate herself through criticism, doubt, and judgment. She may continue to give more in a relationship although she is getting less.

One way of viewing illness is recognizing it as an expression of unhealed psychological pain. Disease is the "self" punishing the "self" through the body.

From this perspective, illness and disease are manifestations of the dark side of our female self. Just as the male side punishes externally, the female side punishes itself.

Every person has a male and female side. When our male side is wounded it tends to seek revenge and punish others. When our female side is wounded it may punish itself. Sickness is one of the ways we punish ourselves when our female side is wounded.

In a positive sense, the male side of us is responsible to be of service to others, while the female side of us is responsible for self-healing and personal growth. Through hearing the pain of our female self the tendency toward sickness and suffering is healed.

From this perspective, war and violence are the expressions of man's inability to heal his hurt; disease and weakness are the outcomes of woman's inability to heal her hurt. Of course these are very broad generalizations. Just as women can be violent, men do get sick. But ultimately it is our male side that abuses outward through actions and our female side that inflicts abuse on itself. Men primarily react from their dark side by inducing pain while women induce guilt through conscious or unconscious self-abuse.

NEGATIVE SELF-TALK

The main way a woman hurts herself, however, is subjectively. Through negative self-talk she abuses herself. As a result she may decide to outwardly and objectively punish or deprive herself. The major symptom of negative self-talk is a feeling of unworthiness, helplessness, and self-pity. Through self-pity she denies her power to create more in her life and indirectly blames others, thus affirming her powerlessness.

For example, feeling self-pity, she may say, "Poor me, no one appreciates me; no one knows how hard I work and how much I sacrifice." In affirming "poor me" she is denying her inner potential to be happy and improve her life. In this way, self-pity is a form of inner violence. Just as outward violence restricts another's potential to be happy, through self-pity we restrict our own ability to be happy.

There are many ways we hurt ourselves through self-pity. Let's look at a few:

"Poor me, if only my partner were not so mean and uncaring I could be happy."

"Poor me, because he didn't call my whole day was ruined."

"Poor me, there is nothing I can do about it, I am completely powerless."

"Poor me, I didn't make that investment."

"Poor me, I have so much to do and I can't do it."

"Poor me, there is no one to love me; I am all alone and no one cares."

"Poor me, I give so much to my children and I get nothing back."

"Poor me, for years I gave and gave and gave and I got nothing back."

"Poor me, I am such a loving person but I'm the one without a relationship."

"Poor me, I have so much talent but no opportunity."

"Poor me, I didn't buy real estate in the 1970s."

"Poor me, they have money and I don't."

"Poor me, I gave the best years of my life and now I am alone, while he remarried in six months."

"Poor me, I am so good and noble and I have been betrayed."

"Poor me, I work twice as hard and I get less."

In each of these examples, through self-pity we limit ourselves to the experience of unhappiness by denying our potential to feel good about ourselves and our lives. Our ability to love and feel grateful is restricted. In addition, through feeling sorry for ourselves we indirectly send out the message of blame and induce guilt in others. The victim or martyr does not realize that when they feel sorry for themselves, they may get more love, but they are reinforcing the pattern of being a victim to feel worthy of love, attention, and compassion.

As women learn to share their hurt without self-pity and resentment and consequently receive the compassion they need, they gradually can release the tendency to feel self-pity. As men learn to share their pain and listen to and understand the pain of others, they gradually release the tendency to be mean or violent. Given the needed understanding, love, and support, it seems almost miraculous how quickly a person can begin to release these deep and unconscious patterns. In teaching weekend seminars I have repeatedly witnessed such transformations.

The better we can learn to understand our different reactions and needs while under stress, the more there is great hope for our relationships as well as for the world. As men learn to listen to the feelings of women they become more aware of their own feelings; they become more compassionate, caring, understanding, and respectful of women. As women feel this compassion, they are able to share more of themselves and heal their hurts in a journey of increasing love, trust, acceptance, forgiveness, gratitude, appreciation, and empowerment.

Through learning to take care of ourselves at times of stress, rather than demanding that our partners fix us, we release the impulse to make others responsible for us. We then enjoy the beautiful experience of feeling responsible to be all we can be and skillfully supporting the ones we love, especially at those times of greatest stress.

In summary, under stress a man needs time and space to find objective solutions (positive behavior), and a woman needs time and attention to find her subjective solutions (positive attitudes). When they are unable to give themselves the support they need, they run the risk of being possessed by their dark sides. To avoid the negative tendencies of our dark sides, it is essential to recognize the distinct symptoms of increasing stress.

In the next chapter we will explore these different symptoms of stress in men and women. Understanding these differences can make it easier to support each other in times of stress. Through recognizing your own stress symptoms, you will be better equipped to come back to balance.

CHAPTER SEVEN

The Symptoms of Stress

There are three major symptoms of stress in men. It is important to recognize these symptoms because women tend to take them personally and then mistakenly assume matters are worse than they are. These three symptoms of stress are withdrawing, grumbling, and shutting down. At such times a woman generally feels unloved and afraid that things in the relationship are not as good as they really are. A correct interpretation of these symptoms can help a woman relax and more skillfully support her partner in coping with stress and coming back into balance.

Likewise, there are three major indications of stress in women, which men tend to take personally and misinterpret. Her symptoms of stress are overwhelm, overreaction, and exhaustion. When a woman gets upset, instead of knowing how to support her a man usually gets upset that she is upset, making matters worse. Through learning to recognize these stress reactions and interpreting them correctly, men can also relax more and learn to better support their partners.

First we will explore the three male stress reactions and then the three common female stress reactions.

MALE STRESS REACTION #1:
HE WITHDRAWS

A male's first stress reaction is that he withdraws and detaches from the situation. While under stress a man tends to deny his feelings and emotional pain, and automatically withdraws. The overall symptom of withdrawal is that communication stops. He is unwilling to talk. Inevitably his female partner takes this personally, not recognizing that he is withdrawing because it is his way of coping with stress.

She mistakenly assumes the problem to be much worse — she assumes he does not love her. This is understandable, because for her to withdraw would be a symptom of increased resentment in the relationship and a lack of caring and concern. She does not naturally relate to his feeling less concern for loved ones when under stress. Just the opposite, the more stressed she becomes, the more concern she feels for the welfare of those she cares about. His detachment at such times is, for her, very confusing and obviously very hard to relate to or understand.

Just as he is unaware of his pain, he becomes blind to the pain of others. He is unable to be compassionate. He minimizes the importance of problems that come up around him. When his empathy is needed, he automatically withdraws to avoid feeling his own pain.

He acts as though everything is fine; yet because he is suppressing his feelings, he becomes distant and withdrawn. He will reject all forms of intimate communication or any attempts to assist him. A woman needs to understand that when a man is distant or withdrawn, he is struggling inside to resist his painful feelings. Any attempt on her part to help him may be resisted or rejected.

For example, when Bill is unable to solve a problem at work, he seems preoccupied and distant because he is in this first stress reaction. When he starts to withdraw, his wife Mary generally takes it personally and assumes that he no longer cares about her. In truth, he does care deep in his heart, but his caring is being overshadowed by his need to withdraw.

MALE STRESS REACTION #2:
HE GRUMBLES

Any attempt to make Bill change his mood may cause him to become irritable. If he does not release his stress and find balance, things just get worse. He becomes grouchy and grumbly, especially if his wife Mary tries to cheer him up in an effort to make him feel better, or tries to create more intimacy. Any attempt to change him or any request for him to do something will be met with resistance and grumbles.

In resisting Mary's attempts to change him or help him, he may become more testy. In this stress reaction Bill also seems dissatisfied with everything. Nothing excites him or turns him on. Much of the time when he is in this space he has no idea of how intimidating, threatening, unloving, and resistant he appears.

If he is asked to do something, he may moan, groan, scowl, growl, or mumble various expressions of resistance. Women generally misinterpret these grumbles as an unwillingness to support. They are not.

When a man is under stress he becomes increasingly focused. If he is focused on achieving a goal and he is interrupted by a request to do something not pertaining to his present focus, he will feel a resistance to shifting gears. The symptom of this resistance is grumbling.

For example, Bill is sitting on the couch relaxing and reading a magazine. His focus is reading the article. Seeing that he is not busy, his wife asks him to empty the trash. He acts as though his wife's request is a major interruption and an intrusion.

Mary cannot understand this reaction because under stress, women are much more capable of shifting from one thing to another. Men, however, tend to adhere rigidly to one task or concern at a time. Then when that is finished, they go on to focus on something else. Thus when a man is asked to do something that interrupts his present focus, he will tend to complain. The more stress he feels in shifting goals midstream, the more he will protest.

These grumbles are actually a symptom of his unfolding willingness to support. If he does not grumble at all but sits in silence, that is a sign that he is thinking about whether he is willing to do it. If he grumbles, that means he *is* willing to do it but is resisting. This resistance is natural and common in men under stress.

This increased male resistance is related to one very important difference between men and women. Women have more corpus callosum in their brains. This is the connective tissue that joins the left and right hemispheres of the brain. Recent discoveries have revealed that because women have more corpus callosum, they are able to access more quickly and more readily different parts of the brain. This makes women more flexible in their ability to shift goals in midstream.

A woman only grumbles in response to a request if she feels that she is being unfairly used. Her grumbling has little to do with shifting goals. A man under stress grumbles because he is being asked for shift goals. He will grumble even if he feels the request is fair. He will even grumble if he is willing to do it. His grumbling is his way of *shifting gears*. One minute he is focused on one goal, and then the next, he is being asked to do something different. The more stress he is feeling, the greater will be his resistance to shifting gears.

Women are generally intimidated by men in this stage. They are afraid to ask for support to help because they can sense a man's put-upon attitude. She assumes he will think her request is unfair or invalid and feel resentful, because that is what would cause her to grumble. When a woman is asked for support and she grumbles, this indicates that she feels the request is unfair and she resents the requester. If she actually does what is asked of her, she will resent him even more. Women misinterpret a man's grumbles to have the same meaning they have for a female.

As I was just writing this section, my wife entered my office and said in an almost playful way, "Interruptions, interruptions. I need your attention for just a moment. We can schedule your (medical) appointment on Monday at 6 or Wednesday at 11. What do you want me to do?" I observed myself feel incredible resistance to her interruption. I put my hands up to my face with a sigh of frustration, and then shifted gears. I noticed she was very accepting of my frustration. She was able to correctly interpret my frustration without taking it personally. With this understanding she was able to be light and playful about her request; and even anticipate my cranky reaction. As quick as my grumbles came on, they went away.

There is another reason a woman misinterprets a male's grumbles. When he reacts peevishly to a request she assumes that he is saying the score in the relationship is uneven. Women assume this because they themselves are great scorekeepers. Just as they are good at giving and giving, they tend to be just as good at keeping track of how much they are getting back. They keep score.

A woman has the amazing talent to continue giving with a smile on her face even when the score is 20 to 0. When the score becomes 30 to 0 (in her opinion), then she will begin to grumble the way men do. What women don't realize is that when a man complains, it has little to do with them or the score in the relationship.

When a man grumbles at a woman's request she takes it personally. She assumes he thinks the score is 30 to 0 in his favor. Rather than risk his grumbles, she will avoid asking for help — and add another point to the score.

The Womanly Art of Asking

To get support from a man, a woman must learn to ask. If she doesn't ask, she will not get. Women presume that if they just keep giving more and more, he will surely feel more generous and give more in return. It certainly increases your chances of receiving if you give of yourself in a relationship. But more important is learning the art of asking without demanding, and asking directly rather than indirectly and subtly implying your needs.

Women are afraid to ask. Those grumbles are intimidating. She is not only afraid of not getting the support, but she is even more afraid of how much worse things will be if he does support her and then feels even more resentment. If she asks and he does help her with a grumble, what she doesn't know is that after a short time, he will recover and the grumble will not get worse.

As Bill begins to achieve his new goal (emptying the trash), he starts to feel better. If he comes in and she is appreciative, then his grumbles are long gone and he probably feels better than before.

This is an idea foreign to women, because if they were to be in a state where they felt like grumbling, and they responded to another request, they would generally feel even more fatigued and resentful after achieving the goal. Because this is a woman's reality she projects it onto a man. She is afraid to ask for support because she imagines he will feel even worse and grumble more.

To overcome this intimidation, a woman needs to practice asking for help, if she wishes it, and then to practice giving her partner the "space" to refuse. Giving someone the "space" to say no is an essential part of the art of asking. Without this kind of acceptance and openness a request becomes a demand; it becomes an obligation or a "you should." To ask without being open is apt to make things worse.

If he says no and she doesn't make him wrong, that does not go unnoticed. He will feel a greater willingness to support her next request. Asking for support, openly, will at least let him know that the score is slowly becoming uneven. It will let him know that he is needed but not criticized or judged. It will let him know that she is gracefully deferring her needs for his, but continuing to want his support. It will give him more opportunities to help her and make her life easier.

This is the opposite of what many women do. They don't ask for help but secretly resent a man for not being helpful. Then if the score is 20 to 0 they will ask, and if he resists, they react with disdain and resentment: "How dare he complain when I have done so much for him while he sits around." Even when they make a request, in anticipation of his grumble, they toughen up inside and demand, rather than ask. It is hard for a male to respond to a demand or a guilt trip. He wants to give freely, not because he is under an obligation.

This analysis helps women to understand why men generally appear lazy in relationships. Often a man assumes that the score is even because a woman continues to give when she is not getting. He can't imagine that the score is 20 to 0 when she continues to do things with a smile on her face. After all, if a man thinks he is giving more than he is getting and thus the score is uneven, he tends to immediately stop giving until it it even again.

The other instruction for a woman to remember when dealing with a man's grumbles is to ask for support and then be quiet. Maintain silence. Don't defend the request with all the reasons why he "should" do it, or it is his turn to do it, or you have done it twenty more times. Just ask and be silent. This is the famous pregnant pause. It contains all possibilities.

Let him grumble as he gets dressed and bangs out the door. Then after he has gone, feel your appreciation for his love and support. When he returns let him be your knight in shining armor who saved you from having to go out into the night. Next time he will grumble a little less, until eventually he will look forward to doing supportive things for you because you are so appreciative. This loving acceptance of his grumbly side is what helps to heal him of it.

MALE STRESS REACTION #3:
HE SHUTS DOWN

If Bill is feeling even more stress, eventually he will completely "shut down." It is as though in an instant his feelings are completely gone. He becomes unfeeling and cold.

When a man shuts down it is an automatic reaction. Women do not understand this reaction correctly, because if a woman shuts down she does so by conscious choice. She feels a man is unfairly punishing her when he shuts down. She imagines that he has some control over it. In truth, a man shuts down automatically when he feels painful emotions arising into his consciousness. It is a defense mechanism over which he has little control. When a man is shutting down he is just asking for some space, but a woman interprets it as a declaration of complete rejection.

In Native American tradition when a brave was upset, he would withdraw into his cave and no one was to follow. They understood that men under stress need to be alone. The brave needed to go inside and mull over the problem that was disturbing him. His squaw was warned that if she ran after him, she would be burned by the dragon that lived in the cave. The brave would come out when he was ready.

When a man shuts down, that is a warning sign not to try and help him in any way. Just give him space and understand that he is silently dealing with his pain and frustration. Appreciate that he cares so much that he wants to solve his problem. Trust that he has the resources to handle what he needs to handle. Don't touch him. The Indians warned of the dragon, because when a man is shut down and he is provoked and drawn out, he will move into his dark side.

Why Men Shut Down

Most men react to intense stress by shutting down their feelings and looking objectively at a situation. Even if a man's female side is overly developed in many areas of his life, when he is under stress he will most likely react by pulling back and trying to figure out what has happened. This is called mulling it over. His whole awareness contracts and becomes focused. He then tries to pull out of it by detaching himself from his emotional reactions. By becoming objective in this way he can begin to recover.

Because a man's essential nature is masculine, to combat stress he needs to pull back and take some alone time. This pulling back intensifies his masculine strength. This is not a time for him to explore his emotional reactions. His imbalance during stress makes him inept at processing his subjective feeling reactions. For most men, if they are confronted with stress, their automatic first reaction is to disconnect from their feelings in order to objectively review what has happened.

Women are greatly threatened by a man's withdrawal, because for a woman to shut down, she must be feeling so upset that she wants to reject a person. This is not the case for a man. Whereas men shut down automatically in reaction to stress, women shut down as the result of a conscious decision. She would only shut down after she had given up on a person. If she had been repeatedly hurt by someone and had lost all trust and acceptance, then she would make a conscious decision to shut down to her feelings. Women do not realize that a man becomes detached just to regain his balance and avoid the weakening onslaught of "negative emotions."

A man has the capacity to close down completely in an instant. A woman, on the other hand, gradually closes down over time. For her it is a gradual process of building a wall of accumulated resentment, brick by brick. Eventually, when a wall of resentment is built, she chooses to shut down to protect herself from further abuse. Men may also build up resentment over time. The main difference is that a man closes down to recover from stress; a woman only closes down if she has built a wall of resentment.

Just as a man can close down in an instant, he can open up again in an instant. Women generally mistrust a man when he opens up that readily. They assume that he is just pretending to feel better. From a female's perspective she could never close down and open up so quickly. When a woman closes down she needs to do a lot of talking and healing to open up again. When a man closes down he generally just needs a lot of space, and then he can quickly open up again.

If a woman tries to pull a man out of his shutdown, it automatically provokes his dark side. To ask him what he is feeling — at a time when his feelings are shut down — is asking for trouble. When a man is upset he will naturally tend to shut down and go to his "cave" to cool off and figure things out. To try to pull him out and get him to talk is to provoke his dark side. Every human being has a dark side. In normal situations it comes out only when provoked. When a woman tries to pull a man out of his "cave," she inevitably gets burned.

After a woman has been burned a few times she becomes even more scared of a man when he shuts down. She does not realize that the dragon only comes out when he is being pulled out of the cave before he is ready.

Men need to understand that because women don't readily shut down, she instinctively misinterprets when he does, and assumes she is in big trouble. She imagines the problem to be much bigger than it is. With this insight he can help matters by simply reassuring her that when he shuts down, he will be back and then he will talk about it.

I suggest that when men shut down, they say to their partner, "I need some time to think. I'll be back and then we can talk." In the early stages of practicing this, it may be that all he can say is, "I need some time to think and I'll be back." At such times, to say "and then we'll talk" is too big a commitment and too much against the male nature. As men become more balanced it becomes easier for them to talk about what was upsetting them.

When a man comes back from being shut down, he may have nothing to say because he has realized there was nothing to be upset about. He realizes that he was overreacting or viewing something the wrong way, and now everything is fine. In most cases, when a man says things are fine after he returns from shutting down, a woman needs to trust him and relax.

WOMEN AND STRESS

When a man experiences stress he will tend to draw back into his mind to reconnect with his true self and find balance. A woman, however, needs to feel her feelings to reconnect with her true self. If she is unable to process her feelings, she will tend to go further out of balance and will experience three common stress reactions: overwhelm, overreaction, and exhaustion. In a sense, they are the female equivalents of the male stress reactions, namely, withdraw, grumbles, and shutdown.

It is essential that a man learns to correctly interpret a woman's stress reaction. Otherwise he tends to make her wrong and defend himself when that is not necessary. Having one's stress reactions misinterpreted throws a person even more out of balance, especially when they are in a relationship. Let's explore these three female stress reactions in greater detail.

FEMALE STRESS REACTION #1:
SHE BECOMES OVERWHELMED

In coping with stress the female psyche becomes more emotional. If she is not used to being in touch with so much feeling, she is thrown out of balance and is unable to draw a clear line between her feelings and the feelings of others. She quite automatically feels an inner compulsion to respond not only to her feelings, but also to the feelings and needs of her partner and others.

She begins to feel overwhelmed. It is as though she has too much to do, and she can't rest until "everything" is all done. She feels pulled apart in many directions.

As she denies her needs in favor of respecting his wishes and the wishes of others, she becomes even more overwhelmed. She keeps giving and giving but doesn't take time to receive or to give to herself. She may even become compulsively submissive to the needs of others. She cannot say no until she is completely burned out.

In the state of overwhelm, a woman loses her ability to prioritize the various pressures and requests and responsibilities she feels. It is increasingly difficult to separate her needs from the needs of others. It is as though everything is equally important: from paying the late bills . . . to cleaning under the bed . . . to watering the plants . . . to folding his T-shirts . . . to returning a few calls for him . . . to getting ready to go out that night . . . to getting the directions for a picnic next week . . . to walking a friend's dog.

Let's look at an example. When Mary goes into overwhelm, Bill might innocently ask her to make a call for him, a call that is not very important to him. (Bill is used to asking Mary to do little things that "aren't that important" because she generally says yes with a smile.) If she were to say, "Sorry, I'm running behind," that would generally be a fine response. Bill would make his call and make nothing of it. He might even see if he could help her in some way. Unfortunately, when Mary is in overwhelm that is not the response that pops out of her mouth.

As soon as he asks her, she reacts with a frustrated and helpless tone of voice. She says, "I can't right now, I have to cook dinner. I already have too much to do. I have to call Julie's teacher, I have to change the baby's diaper, I have to clean up this mess, balance the checkbook, finish the wash, and tonight we are going out to a movie. I have so much to do. I just can't do it all."

In an instant Bill reacts to her stress reaction with his stress reaction. He withdraws and detaches. It is hard for him to go back to sitting on the couch and watching TV without detaching from his inner feelings and connectedness to her.

Rather than wanting to support Mary's needs he resents her neediness. He resents her for different reasons than she would imagine. Yet he resents that she has not asked for help sooner. He resents her for making him feel like a failure (or in Martian language, he resents her for "bumming him out" or "bringing him down").

In truth she has not brought him down. He has brought himself down by misinterpreting her overwhelm. But being "bummed out" is nevertheless his experience. He is bummed because he feels he has failed her in some way. When she is happy he feels as though he is responsible, but when she is unhappy he feels that he has failed. In this way he takes her overwhelm personally, as if he has caused it or should have been able to avert it. He does not realize that overwhelm has nothing to do with him.

To Bill, Mary's overwhelm sounds as though she is blaming him for not giving her more support. As she complains about all the demands being placed on her, he assumes that he is being reprimanded for not supporting her more and expecting too much from her. None of this is her intent. This is not what she is saying.

When a man "withdraws," what a woman hears is that he doesn't care about her. In truth he is not saying anything — just taking care of himself. Similarly, when a woman becomes overwhelmed, she is not saying anything but taking care of herself. She is trying to share her feelings in order to feel understood. Through being understood, she feels more centered and less overwhelmed.

What Happens to a Man When a Woman is Overwhelmed

When a woman is overwhelmed a man tends to withdraw and detach from her to be free of the feelings of guilt and inadequacy that he feels in response to her. He has taken her unhappiness, overwhelm, and helplessness personally. He feels that he has failed her in some way. But he does not know how to say this without losing face.

He does not tell her that he is frustrated because she is so unhappy, and that he wants her to be happy. He does not say he is disappointed that he has not done more to make her life easier. He does not say that he is worried for her and doesn't want her to feel so alone and unsupported. He doesn't say, "I understand how hard it can be around here." He doesn't give her a hug and say, "I love you, let's talk about it."

This is how he feels. But he doesn't say it because he doesn't know how and he doesn't know that it is needed. What a shame. Because he does not understand what she needs at these times and because he has not learned to communicate his feelings, he automatically withdraws. The irony is she imagines that he is feeling the very opposite. She imagines that he doesn't even care. Inside he is unhappy that she is unhappy, but on the outside he acts as

135

if everything is fine, OK, and all right. And all along his resistance to her increases. As a result, she now feels even more abandoned, upset and helpless.

The fact that a woman in overwhelm pours out her problems as if they were all major crises helps to explain why men tend to misinterpret this state and feel blamed. A man holds his overwhelm inside and focuses his upset on one "big" problem. He will only list out a lot of problems if he is blaming someone for them. For this reason, he assumes a woman who does this is blaming him. As he withdraws, she does begin to blame him for being so cold and insensitive. This is another example of how our incorrect assumptions become self-fulfilling prophecies.

In this way, two people who love each other very much but don't understand how they are different may in a short period of time begin to resent, mistrust and fight each other.

When a woman is feeling overwhelmed she needs her partner to be a sounding board. He can help her find balance just by listening and understanding her frustration. However, he thinks she is asking him to rectify the situation. He typically hears a few of her problems and then attempts to offer solutions, assuming that if his solutions are good, then she will feel better.

He expects this because when a man is upset and he realizes a good solution to his problem, he will generally feel better right away. When she continues being upset and listing out even more problems, he starts to feel rejected and helpless.

From his perspective it seems impossible to please her. She is rarely happy, and she appears to demand more than what he can give her. Even though he may want to help her, he will resist because he feels blamed and accused of having not helped her already.

Bill generally becomes impatient with Mary when she is overwhelmed. To him it just sounds like complaining and self-pity. He feels like saying, "Don't worry about everything. You are getting upset over nothing. Everything does not have to get done. It doesn't matter so much. Can't you be happy? Everything is not so difficult. You always have too much to do." Saying this, however, just makes matters worse. when Mary is in overwhelm she does not need a lecture. What she needs is an understanding and compassionate ear.

To get this kind of support she must realize that Bill easily misinterprets her overwhelm as blame and rejection. She can ask for his support, but should warn him that right now she is rather overwhelmed and *it is not his fault.*

These five little words can make a huge differences to a man: *IT IS NOT YOUR FAULT.* She can simply say, *"If this sounds as though I am blaming you, I am sorry. It is definitely not your fault."*

After a man has listened for a little while, he needs to desist trying to fix her and understand that she doesn't need to be fixed. She is already in the process of healing, even though it sounds to him like she is complaining. Through being heard, her attitude will shift automatically. One phrase from him can be particularly helpful: after listening for some time he can say, *"I just don't know how you do it."* This backfires, of course, if it is not done with sincerity.

Getting What She Needs

What an overwhelmed woman needs — to have someone understand and validate her pain and discomfort, to explore and share her fears without being made wrong for them — is almost impossible to receive from a man unless she reminds him that it is not his fault and that she appreciates his help. It is hard for a woman to get support in overwhelm because when she shares what she is feeling, it all comes out sounding like blame.

Generally speaking, however, another woman listening to such feelings can and will immediately understand. For this reason it is important that women look to each other for more support, and not expect it solely from their male partner. It is a worthy goal for men to learn to fully understand overwhelm. But until that skill is developed, she should mainly look to her female friends for support at such times.

FEMALE STRESS REACTION #2:
SHE OVERREACTS

As a result of being overwhelmed, a woman naturally moves into the second stress reaction. She begins accumulating emotional upset and thus overreacts to situations. Easily mistaken as to the reasons she is upset, she may confuse cause with effect. If she is upset from a long day filled with stressful calamities and her husband walks in, she can forget that the day is bothering her and react as if he is the cause of her upset. In a sense, the weight of the day gets focused on the man.

Eventually, by talking about all the other things that are upsetting her, she can and will start to lighten up. But until that happens it will sound as if whatever she is talking about is solely responsible for how she feels. She will appear to be blaming him and punishing him.

In this state an overreacting woman will tend to say things that are irrational, unfair, inconsistent and illogical — things that she will later on forget or say she did not mean. A few minutes later she may laugh about it. This is similar to how a man responds under stress. He will become irritable and grumble, but if you don't resist him or make him wrong, it will quickly pass. Just as a woman must learn to ask for support and ignore the grumbles, a man needs to ask how she is feeling and listen without taking it personally, without defending, without fixing her, and without interrupting her with corrections, explanations, and lectures.

Even though she appears to hold him responsible for her upset feelings, that is not her meaning. She is in the process of sorting out what is bothering her. She truly doesn't know what is bothering her and how much of it is her partner's fault, or how much of her upset stems from ten other sources.

Denise is 38 and the mother of three children. She is also a bookkeeper. Her husband Randy is an architect. One day he came home from work fifteen minutes late. When he walked in his wife was cold and silent. He said, "Is dinner ready? I'm starved."

She then dumped his food on the table saying, "Here, it's burned."

His inner response was to become furious and indignant. He felt, "How dare she be this upset with me, when I was only fifteen minutes late. I could understand her being a little upset but not this much." He scraped his chair back and stood up, said a few profanities, and stalked out to eat elsewhere.

Randy's response to Denise's overreaction was equally confusing to Denise. Unfortunately, when women overreact, men feel punished. In return, men feel, "If I am going to be punished for a crime, then 'let the crime fit the punishment.'" A man then commits a crime to fit the punishment she has dished out. He treats her in a way that deserves her intense reaction.

This inner compulsion to punish her back, by treating her in a way that would rationally warrant a negative reaction from her, is the source of major problems in relationships. As a man comes to understand that she is not deliberately dumping all her upset feelings on him and that *there is always a long list of other things bothering her when she overreacts,* then he doesn't take it personally. He can graciously realize that she is not as upset about his being late as it appears. In truth, she must have really had a long and upsetting day, and he has arrived home at the end of it. She finally has someone she can talk to and it all comes out on him.

Let's look at what really happened to Denise on that day. As Denise was balancing the checkbook, she realized that a couple of check entries were missing and thus she couldn't balance it. She assumed the culprit was her absent-minded husband, who would occasionally do this. At this point in the day, she was more upset that she didn't have the information than she was about Randy's absent-mindedness. This was her first upset. Let's call it a 20-degree upset.

A half hour later she made some tea in the kitchen and saw that her daughter Katherine had left her lunch. Now Denise faced a new stress. Should she bring the lunch to school, or should she let her 12-year-old starve. Let's call this a 10-degree upset. Because Denise is already 20 degrees upset, this new problem is experienced as a 30-degree upset.

This is called accumulating emotional charge. It does not just occur in women who are bookkeepers, but in all women when they are experiencing overreaction to stress. This is the rational explanation for a reaction that to men appears extremely irrational and unfair.

Let's continue reviewing what happened that day to Denise. After pondering over her decision, she decided to bring Katherine's lunch to school. She got into her car and it wouldn't start. The battery was dead. Someone had left the car door open all night. Now she had a new stress. Let's call this a 30-degree stress. But because of what preceded this upset, it becomes a 60-degree upset (30 plus 20 plus 10).

Imagine for a moment that Katherine called home just then and asked Denise to bring the lunch. What kind of reaction would she get? Instead of a 10-degree upset, which is what Denise originally felt about the forgotten lunch, she would now be the target of a 60-degree upset reaction. Fortunately for Katherine, she didn't call home.

Denise headed back toward the kitchen to call the motor club to come out and recharge the battery. On her way into the house she picked up her mail. As she was making the call she noticed a letter from the bank. She opened it and found an overdrawn statement. Normally an overdrawn statement would be a 30-degree upset. But on this day it automatically accumulated with what preceded it, becoming a 90-degree upset. As Denise called the motor club, which would normally cause her to feel 30 degrees of frustration and embarrassment, she now felt 90 degrees of upset

Now imagine what would happen if Randy called home just then to tell her he had forgotten to enter a particular check. Instead of being 20 degrees upset, which is how she originally felt, she would now feel 90 degrees upset. Instead of being mildly frustrated by his absent-mindedness, she would now resent him for being such an irresponsible, inconsiderate, and immature idiot. Fortunately, Randy didn't call home.

After Denise finished her humiliating call, she went to her cupboard to find relief. As she looked for her hidden stash of cookies, she found a trail of mouse droppings on her kitchen shelf. "Mouse turds" she screamed as she hit the ceiling with frustration and rage. Keep in mind that for the past three weeks, Randy had been trying to trap the little culprit. On another day, when Denise was not so upset, this discovery of a mouse in the kitchen would rate about a 15-degree upset. But today it registers 15 plus 90, or 105 degrees.

Certainly if one was to observe Denise's reaction to mouse droppings, one could think she was quite irrational. But what has preceded her experience of the mouse droppings, her overreaction is very understandable. This very understanding is what she needs when she is in overreaction.

At such a moment it is not within her power to rationally discriminate that she is only 15 degrees upset about the mouse, and 10 degrees upset about Katherine's lunch, and 20 degrees upset about the missing checkbook entries, and 30 degrees upset about the car battery, and 30 degrees upset about the overdrawn account. It all flows into one feeling reaction of 105 degrees.

When men are able to understand this process they are less inclined to take a woman's overreaction so personally. Let's continue to review what happened that ill-fated day in Denise's life when she dumped Randy's food on the table.

After the motor club man recharged her battery, she got in her car. As she drove off she realized that she had forgotten Katherine's lunch. She pulled up the driveway, parked her car, and ran into the house. When she returned to the car, she couldn't start it. Another dead battery. Well, earlier in the day a dead battery rated 30 degrees. This time it made her feel 105 plus 30 = 135 degrees. Denise felt completely humiliated in calling the motor club back. She painfully endured the man on the phone saying, "Didn't you just call 45 minutes ago?" On a different day she might have felt a little embarrassed and made a joke of it. But because she had already accumulated 105 degrees of upset, this was a major setback for her.

Becoming exhausted from so much inner turmoil, Denise headed for the bedroom to lie down and wait for the second tow truck to arrive. As she closed her eyes she felt a moment of peace. But when she got up for a drink of water, she saw on the floor another little trail of mouse droppings. Never before had she seen them outside the kitchen. "Mouse turds," which was previously a 15-degree upset, was now a 150-degree calamity.

In that moment Denise panicked. Her mind raced with fears and concerns: How many more mice could there now be? How were they getting in? What kinds of diseases were they carrying? Were they in her children's rooms? Did they crawl over her children in their sleep? Were there other creatures in the attic? Instead of being a little afraid of a mouse invasion, she was now 150 degrees upset about it. Needless to say, she was now unable to relax and enjoy her rest.

After the battery was recharged, Denise was more determined than ever to bring Katherine's lunch to school. She had only ten minutes to get there before her daughter's lunch period would start. On the way she got stuck in road repair traffic for an extra five minutes. Such a minor delay would generally rate a 10-degree upset or perhaps a 30-degree upset if one was in a hurry. On this day, however, it rated 30 degrees plus 150 degrees, which made it 180 degrees upsetting to Denise.

By the time she reached the school, Katherine had already left to eat lunch off campus with a friend. A wasted 10-minute trip to school would certainly warrant a 20-degree upset. That brought the total up to 200 degrees.

It was now time for Denise to pick up her three-year-old. Susie whined the whole way home that she wanted to go swimming, but Denise explained repeatedly that it was too cold. Susie picked this day of all days to throw a big tantrum. Children seem to do that. They can sense the buildup of feelings that want to explode and they act it out. All day Susie was especially whiny and needy. This kind of treatment from their child would make most mothers react with at least 20 degrees upset. For Denise it was now a 220-degree upset. She regretted the day she had wanted children.

She was determined to do something right. So now she decided to fix a very special meal for her husband Randy. Making the meal was particularly frustrating because little Susie kept pulling her and needing so much of her attention. When Randy didn't come home on time, she left the salmon in the oven to keep it warm. Then she was distracted again by Susie. When Randy walked in she remembered the salmon. She rushed to the oven and found that it was burned.

Randy noticed his wife was cold and silent. He said, "Is dinner ready? I'm starved."

On a normal day when Denise had not accumulated so much upset, Randy's being 15 minutes late would have been a small matter — generally about 10 degrees of upset. But today it was 15 plus 220, which equals 235 degrees. She was boiling upset with him. If Katherine had walked in the room, Denise would have been 235 degrees upset with her. If she had seen a picture of a mouse, she would be 235 degrees upset about the mouse invasion.

When Randy asked if dinner was ready, Denise's inner reaction was, "Is that all you have to say to me? After all I have done for you. You walk in here late.

You don't even call. You don't even greet me or ask me how my day went. You're so selfish, all you care about is yourself. I hate you. I could care less if you are starved. I hope you do starve." There was so much upset feeling inside that she didn't know what to say. She remained cold and silent and just dumped his food on the table saying, "Here, it's burned." The look she gave him communicated her 235 degrees of upset. That and the tone of her voice said it all.

Randy's response was to become 235 degrees mean and furious. Indignantly he thought, "How dare she be this upset with me, when I was only 15 minutes late. I could understand her being a little upset but not this much." He then got up, said a few profanities, and silently went out to eat. He fumed, "She will pay for that overreaction."

What a man in this situation doesn't realize is that a woman has already paid for it. She has lived it all day. What she needs is some compassion for what she has gone through. Instead of assuming that she is punishing him, and instead of becoming defensive, he needs to back up a little bit, take a few breaths and try to relax. Then he should proceed with caution, carefully attempting to empathize with her but not attempting in any way to fix her, correct her or defend himself.

The "What Else" Technique

What he can say, perhaps while holding her, is "How are you feeling?" or "I can see you are upset. What's the matter?" After he listens for a while and when she stops talking, instead of responding to what she has said with a list of explanations as to why she shouldn't be so upset, he must remember the magic phrase, "*What else* is bothering you?" Or he can simply keep asking "What else?" or "Go on" or "Tell me more." Then he should listen some more.

These questions tell her that he cares and that he is interested in understanding. "What else" also helps keep her from getting lost while focusing on only one source of her upset. Too, these questions help to validate her pain, which is what she needs the most. As she talks, it allows the listener to truly understand what she is going through with more empathy and compassion. The more she feels heard and understood, the intensity of her upset will decrease. She may even start laughing about what an awful day she had.

When a man uses this technique he must be responsible to ask only if he truly can hear. He should respect his tolerance for hearing complaints. If he can only listen for two minutes before he becomes defensive, frustrated, and angry, then he should *not* continue to ask, "What else is bothering you." He should back off and take some space. He should try to be civil and say something like, "I know you're upset, but I need some time to think about what you've said. Then we'll talk some more." In the quiet time that follows he can help himself by remembering that he is unnecessarily taking her upset personally. He can remind himself that this is not her intention.

If he has not reached a point of complete frustration, he could try two other approaches. He can ask, "Is my listening to you helpful?" If she can say, "Yes,

I do appreciate it," then he can continue to listen longer. Just a little appreciation can dramatically help a man to not take these overreactions personally.

He might also say, "I know you are upset and I want to support you. After a while, though it starts to sound as if you are saying it is all my fault. Is that what you are saying?"

Generally she will say, quite surprised, "No, I'm not saying that."
Then he can say, "Thanks. Tell me more."

When a man has this understanding, he can listen and truly understand and feel a growing compassion. When he does practice listening, the last thing he should try to do is to rationally explain why he is not responsible for her hurt. If he does, then her mind will begin looking for all the reasons he could be the cause of her upset. Then they will argue about that. When he listens he must consciously choose a non-explaining but investigative or explorative posture. His job is not to defend himself but to give her a chance to unwind. When she feels heard without blame or judgment, quite automatically her attitude shifts and becomes more loving, positive, centered, and accepting.

In a similar way, when a woman learns not to blame or judge a man's grumbles (the male equivalent of overreacting), quite automatically his grumbles go away as he succeeds in doing something to please her. If a woman makes a man wrong for grumbling he will justify why he should complain, then grumble some more. When a woman overreacts and a man defends himself — thus making her feelings wrong — she will overreact even more to his immediate lack of support. If his invalidating her is normally a 30-degree upset, on Denise's terrible day it would cause her to feel 265 degrees of upset.

Avoiding the Buts

Many times when a woman is experiencing the stress reactions of overwhelm or overreaction she will become confused. In this confusion she will tend to ask questions. If this doesn't sound like blame, then it generally sounds to a man as though she is asking for a solution. The man assumes she is expecting him to make her feel better by answering her questions. She could be upset and begin talking about what is bothering her; he will listen for about two minutes maximum and think he now understands her problem and has a solution to her problem.

In reality she is in the process of figuring things out. Regardless of how good his solution is, she will say "but" and continue talking about things that are bothering her. This is frustrating to a male because he assumes that once he gives her a good solution to her problem, she should feel better. This, of course, works for men but not for women.

He must remember that when she is upset she will not feel better until she has talked things out for a while. She does not want nor is she capable of appreciating solutions. This is hard for a man to remember, because when *he* talks about problems it is generally to ask for help in finding a solution.

If someone gives him a good solution he feels great. When *she* doesn't feel great he takes it personally. He gets upset because she doesn't appreciate his brilliance.

Another male/female difference helps to explain why many men have the mistaken idea that women are incompetent. Most of the time when a man talks about a problem, it will be something that he has thought about for a long time before he utters it out loud. To utter out loud what is bothering him is to acknowledge that he is somewhat stumped by this problem. He is loathe to admit this, because if someone were to come along with a simple solution, he could be quite embarrassed. He might feel very foolish and inadequate.

When a woman starts talking about what is bothering her, she may need to talk about 10 to 15 difficulties before she has a clear grasp of what really is upsetting her. Then she feels better. From a more centered place she looks at how she can solve it. For this reason a woman shamelessly shares her list of problems without feeling threatened that she has not figured out solutions to them. After listening to a women unwind this way a man commonly begins to form two very incorrect judgments or conclusions.

How He Misinterprets Her Unwinding

The first mistaken assumption a man makes when a woman shares a long list of things bothering her is that she must really be incompetent not to see the solution to these "petty problems." A man assumes that the degree of upset expressed indicates one's frustration in trying to solve a particular problem. But the extent of a woman's upset as she mentions a problem has little to do with her inability to solve it. Rather, it has to do with the accumulation of stress that has been building up. It points to her need to sort things out. Unfortunately, if in listening he assumes she is upset about this one thing, then he begins to doubt her overall competence in handling problems.

The second false assumption he makes is that she can't be happy unless all of her problems are solved. Because he cares about her he wants to make her happy, and believes that the way to make her happy is by solving her problems. He mistakenly believes that in talking about her problems she is asking him to solve them. To him her long list of woes and difficulties sounds like a series of demands, complaints, and criticisms. He feels attacked, as if she is saying he is responsible.

As he listens to her roster of problems, he becomes frustrated because he knows he cannot solve them all. He then concludes that she has too many problems. He makes her wrong for having too many problems, when all she really needs to be happier is to be heard and understood. He takes it all too personally.

As a woman's stress increases, her awareness opens and she sees more possible problems. This is why women tend to worry so much about many things.

Men worry just as much, as we have seen, but they tend to focus on one particular problem. Just as she associates her accumulated degree of upset with an increasing number of external problems, he will take the accumulated degree of upset in his life and place it on one problem, overly minimizing the importance of other things in his life. When focused on one problem he will seem indifferent to other problems. If, however, he is distracted from this overly focused state, he will seem very indignant; he will grumble, complain, resist, or throw a tantrum.

A woman makes two mistaken assumptions about his stress reaction. She concludes that he doesn't care about her or her needs, or that he doesn't love her. She also errs in assuming that he resists responding to her needs because he sees her needs as invalid. After grumbling for a while, he will remember that she does deserve more of his support and he wants to give it to her. Likewise, after overreacting a woman will realize that her partner is not to blame.

How Both Sexes Can Handle Overreaction

When a woman overreacts, if her partner would give her some understanding and a sign of empathy for her stress and struggle rather than make her wrong for it, she would quickly recover. The most powerful way to do this is with a hug. Women need to be touched and hugged. It is one of the most powerful ways to communicate his support. Many times a man doesn't know what to do or say. That is either his cue to take a deep breath, relax, and feel his love, or it is the time to quietly hold his partner and give them a hug. Correspondingly, if a woman can give a man "space" to grumble he will more quickly recover.

Just as his tantrum disappears and he feels better, her overreacting can disappear if she gets the understanding she needs. Understanding to a woman is the equivalent of acceptance for a man. Men under stress need lots of space and acceptance, while women in their stress reactions need lots of understanding and validation.

In addition, when a woman gives a man the space to grumble she should also give him the opportunity to be her hero. So many times women think of asking their partners for support, but because they are so afraid of his resistance, they don't. In this way they keep him in a box as the uncaring, selfish, bad guy.

Likewise, when a man gives a woman understanding, he must also give her the opportunity to feel special, worthy, and loved. He can from time to time do and say things to make her feel loved and special. When she is actually talking about her upset he can use reassuring phrases like "you deserve that" or "you have a right to feel that way" or "You deserve to feel . . ."or "you have a right to do that," etc. Besides understanding, what she needs is validation, empathy, attention, and compassion. One useful way to think of validation is "to understand with respect."

A woman needs to share outside herself to the same degree a man needs to go into his "cave" and mull things over alone. While "mulling" a man quickly identifies the problem and then looks to find a solution. Finding a solution makes him feel better. A woman, on the other hand, needs to discover what she is feeling and then what she is feeling upset about. Instead of looking for a solution, she explores the possible relationships between what she is feeling and what is happening to her.

Just as a man tries on for size many possible solutions to his problem, a woman will try on or explore many possible relationships between her feelings and what is happening around her until she finds one (or more) that fits. Her awareness expands and reviews all the possible external happenings in relation to her upset feelings. When she can clearly see her true relationship to her environment, then she is able to take responsibility for her feelings. At this point she is able to realize that no one is externally responsible for her feelings. She can now change her negative feelings to positive feelings.

While a woman is sharing in order to discover what she is feeling, if a man tries to solve her problems not only will he feel as though nothing can please her, but he will interrupt her from finding balance.

How Men Are Misled

What men find so misleading when trying to support an overreacting woman is that when a woman is upset she will ask many questions as she talks. She will say things like:

"Why do you think my boss does that?"

"How am I supposed to know . . .?"

"Why doesn't she realize that I am trying to help?"

"What am I going to do?"

"I just don't know why I am so upset?"

"What am I supposed to do when that happens?"

Hearing this, a man naturally thinks she is asking for an explanation or solution. On the contrary, she needs his silent understanding or empathy to support her in exploring and discovering what is going on inside of her. Men typically respond to this idea by saying in frustration, "Well, if I am not supposed to solve her problems, then what am I supposed to do?" The answer to this question is generally obvious to women, but not to men.

It can be a very difficult task for a man to listen without "doing" something — especially when he is being asked questions. The following are some ways a man can make listening into something he can "do":

1. He can make a decision to give his full attention.
2. He can practice not saying anything that might sound like a solution.
3. He can nod his head.
4. He can make reassuring responses like "hmm," "uh-huh," or "tell me more."

5. He can use the phrase "I understand." A word of warning: don't use this too often or she will get the idea that she is being patronized. She may feel, "How can *he* understand when I know that I haven't gotten to the heart of the matter."

6. He can avoid answering questions. He should assume that she is asking rhetorical questions, which make a point rather than require an answer. If she insists on an answer, be indefinite. Say things like "I'm not sure" or "I need some time to think about that" or "I don't have a ready answer." Certainly it is appropriate to ask and answer questions, but when a woman is upset it is best to stay in the posture of listening and understanding rather than explaining and fixing.

If he tries to solve her upset he is not helping; he is only resisting her natural process of exploration. When he does give solutions he will expect her to feel better. But when she doesn't he will start grumbling and blaming her for being upset. When she says "but" in response to his solutions, he feels rejected.

She is not really rejecting his ideas or solutions. She is merely saying, "I still need to be upset; I haven't gotten to the real issue. I need you to continue supporting me and not expect me to feel better right away."

He can't hear this message because he already thinks he knows the real issue. He becomes frustrated when she does not agree. What really disconcerts him is that even if he is right about what is bothering her, his telling her will not help. This is something she must discover for herself.

The reality is that when she is upset, confused, and out of balance, she needs to come back to balance. No one can do it for her. She can, however, be assisted by a loving and attentive listener who serves as a sounding board. In the literal sense, a sounding board is a thin plate of wood built into a musical instrument to increase its resonance. When a person serves as a sounding board they increase the speaker's self awareness, which allows them to find their most loving and accepting self when they have gone off-balance.

It greatly aids a woman to share in her journey back to center. This is very difficult to do unless a man understands that she is not asking for solutions and that at this time she is not even capable of appreciating them.

When a woman has become overwhelmed and her upset increases to the point that she overreacts, if she doesn't get the support she needs, then inevitably she will move into her third stress reaction, exhaustion.

FEMALE STRESS REACTION #3: SHE BECOMES EXHAUSTED

As a result of being upset and overwhelmed, Denise may instantly break down, feeling completely exhausted. She feels hopeless, like giving up. In this reaction, she is truly reaching out for support. Unfortunately the message others get — especially men — is that they have failed to support her and that nothing they could do would please her.

The major symptom of this third stress reaction is that she begins to feel exhausted and drained. Up to this point she may have appeared to have things "together," then almost instantly she appears completely drained, powerless, miserable, and bitchy.

A man feels very threatened by an exhausted woman, because it is extremely painful to think he has been negligent in fulfilling her. He doesn't realize that exhaustion is an inevitable consequence of her being out of balance. He needs to realize that it is not his fault. He must also realize that because she is human, she will go out of balance again and again, no matter how successful he is in providing for her.

Just as men "shut down" from time to time in response to stress, a woman becomes exhausted. Just as women misinterpret and are threatened by a man's shutting down, so also men misread and are threatened by a woman's exhaustion. Whereas a man can open up instantly after he has shut down, a woman can be energized and positive immediately after she has been exhausted.

One way a man can understand a woman in exhaustion is to realize that metaphorically speaking, his male physiology is equipped with a pressure gauge that warns him when he is giving out more than he is getting back. It tells him to rest and take care of himself to avoid burnout. But women do not have these pressure gauges. The more stressed they feel, the more they forget themselves. Her solution to burnout is to center herself through feeling heard and supported. In a practical sense, she needs a little help!

At such a time she needs to feel she is not alone. She needs the assistance of others. Most men are greatly threatened by this. A man sees the burden she is carrying and assumes that to make her feel better, he has to carry the whole load. He presumes that she has no more energy to fulfill her responsibilities. This is a huge mistake. In truth she has just reached her limit. Actually, he can make her feel much better by just taking on a few of her responsibilities and then later handing them back.

When a woman reaches her limit, she appears to be completely empty and powerless. The truth is, she still has energy — she is just disconnected from it because what she feels she "has" to do, she knows she cannot do alone. She needs help. Until she feels supported, she is disconnected from her energy resources.

The Straw that Broke the Camel's Back

Women break down when they go beyond their limit. The actual factor that causes the breakdown can be likened to the straw that broke the camel's back. It is not the whole weight of the load that causes her to break down, merely one or two straws. If a man can listen to her tell of all the pressures and responsibilities that are weighing her down, and then offer to lighten her load by carrying a few straws, he will help her tremendously. She may not feel better right away. But she will appreciate it greatly and recover much more quickly than he could imagine.

A man is generally reluctant to help a woman in this state, because he assumes the way to help is to identify and then do the most difficult tasks. This is not necessary. Moreover, he will resent doing her most difficult tasks. What he can do is pick those chores on her list that would be easiest for him to do. All she needs is two or three straws lifted from her back and her strength will return.

This works because when she is exhausted, every straw seems to weigh the same. What she needs is for someone to carry a part of her load. What she doesn't need at this time is his resentment toward her neediness. If he realizes that he doesn't have to fix *everything* to assist her, then it is much easier for him to offer his support without feeling resentful.

At such times men are notorious for giving lectures on how a woman shouldn't do so much. They say things like:

"You take on too much."

"Relax, you worry too much."

"All this is not that important."

"It's no big deal if we are late."

"That's not your responsibility."

"Well you don't have to do that."

"Life is not this difficult."

"Lighten up will you."

Not only is this kind of advice not helpful, it makes matters worse. She will be hurt in the same way that he may be offended when she tells him after he has made a mistake, "I told you so" or expresses some truism like, "Well, that's what happens when you don't plan."

Sometimes it is next to impossible for a man to listen and respond lovingly to an exhausted woman. After all, he assumes she is blaming him and/or is expecting him to solve all her problems. If he too is under a lot of stress, he is apt to immediately shut down.

This is why it is essential that women have many areas of support in their lives. It is unrealistic to expect a man to give her all the support she needs, especially when she is experiencing her stress reactions. He would have to be in balance all the time, which is quite unlikely.

People are generally drawn together because their degree of inner pain is similar. To the extent she goes into her reactions, he will generally follow suit. When he goes into shutdown she becomes exhausted; when she becomes overwhelmed he withdraws and detaches.

At such times, Denise should be responsible to come back to balance on her own or through the support of others. After she is in balance she can successfully support Randy if he is still in need. In a similar way, Randy may be the first to come back to balance, and then he can have the strength to support her if she is still in need.

A HEALTHY RELATIONSHIP

The reason for pointing out our different stress reactions in so much detail is not to excuse our partners, but to free ourselves of taking their reactions personally. As we have repeatedly observed, without this knowledge of how we are different, even with the best intentions we can easily make matters much worse.

We sometimes need to be reminded that when we relate with real love we see ourselves in our partners; we do not judge them as less than. With this feeling of connectedness and oneness, when we support their needs we automatically receive back. It is through giving with an open heart (or with real love) that we experience joy in our lives.

When loving is not joyful, then we are confused about love. When love is difficult or a strain, then we are demanding that our partner fix us. So many of us confuse love with needing. We get things backward. We assume that being loved means having one's needs fulfilled. In reality a healthy relationship supports both members healing themselves.

The real joy of a special, intimate, or committed relationship is the opportunity to share and celebrate the good times, and give to your partner when they are in need. When we are in need and our partner is not giving to us, we can safely assume that they are also in need and thus unable to actively support us.

CHAPTER EIGHT

Finding Balance

So far we have explored how our male and female sides determine how we experience others and ourselves, and even influence how we react under stress. Through identifying our different sides it also becomes easier to find balance. Simply recognizing that we are out of balance helps us to automatically move in the direction of greater equilibrium. Regardless of whether you are a man or women, to find greater love and effectiveness in all your life's pursuits you need to balance your male and female sides.

When both sexes are able to balance focused awareness and open awareness, their creativity is enriched. When they are able to balance their work activities with relationships, greater fulfillment and success is assured. When they can react from their mind as well as their heart, then they can respond to others with love and other positive attitudes.

How can this balance be achieved or discovered? To find balance, a person needs to understand, accept, appreciate, and respect both sides of themselves, masculine and feminine. Ideally, it would happen this way:

As a boy naturally developed his masculine energy, his feminine energy would be allowed to simultaneously and spontaneously unfold. He would swing back and forth naturally between his male and female sides. As he grew in his manhood, he would have the freedom to express both his feminine and masculine sides. His feminine energy would support in harmony what he does and who he is.

For example, as Billy grew up in an ideal environment, he would witness, thousands of times, his father successfully supporting his mother. Through his father's example he would learn to honor and respect femininity. When his mother was stressed, overreactive, overwhelmed, or exhausted, he would see his father respond with compassionate understanding and respect, rather than with indifference or judgment. His father would hug her, hold her, and listen to her. In this way Billy would learn how to listen to his own feminine feelings.

As he grew up he would feel secure in simultaneously developing and expressing his masculine and his feminine sides. For example, he would not be judged for crying or showing his feelings. Not only would his mother hold him and hug him, but also his father would hold and hug him and understand his feelings. His father would feel proud of him for both his masculine qualities of competence and efficiency and his feminine qualities of goodness and love. In addition his father would know that to support his son, they would need to do things together. Billy's dad would make the time to teach him sports and other hobbies, take him on outings, and enjoy his son's activities. He would not demand success, but would rejoice in his successes and empathize with his losses.

Regrettably, many fathers hesitate to show affection to their sons, fearing that they may become homosexual. This could not be further from the truth. As children, male homosexuals were generally deprived of any loving or affectionate contact with their fathers. As adults they still need and seek to find that male energy that only a father can give his son. Crying will definitely *not* make a boy a "sissy." But judging him for being a "sissy" will.

In an ideal environment, a boy is appreciated for his male qualities and respected for his feminine qualities. If he is respectful of his environment and nurturing to others, he is appreciated for that. If, however, he is more masculine and self-centered, he is not judged as defective by his mother. He is not seen as bad, and when he does bad things he is forgiven. Boys with a lot of masculinity will tend to be mischievous and need a lot of acceptance and forgiveness.

His ideal mother will learn how much trust and space to give Billy and where to take control. She respects that he has a need to feel independent and in control of his life. She trusts that he has to learn his own lessons, knowing that overprotection can weaken him and undermine his self-confidence. She accepts his differences and is appreciative of him. She does not take anything he does for granted. She allows him to be decisive and feel important. She respectfully asks him for support, rather than demanding it through guilt and disapproval. She believes in him and trusts his process of development.

Most important, Billy gets to experience his mother loving his father. As a result the masculine qualities within him have a chance to come forth and be developed. He does not need to apologize for being the way he is, or deny himself to win his mother's love. He feels safe in exploring his aggressive tendencies by asserting himself and taking risks. He is not made to feel bad for being selfish, withdrawn, grumbly, or irritable. Above all, he does not have to be different from dad in order to be loved by mom. He feels secure in his masculinity because he sees his mother repeatedly loving and appreciating his father, who represents his male side.

In a similar way, ideally a girl would naturally develop her female energy, and as she grew into womanhood, she would discover and allow for the full expression of her masculine energy as well. Her masculine energy could then support who she is and what she does.

For example, as Sharron grew up in an ideal environment, she would repeatedly observe her mother successfully supporting her father. Through her mother's example she would learn to trust and appreciate her own masculine side. She would feel safe being feminine in ways that she would see her mother being feminine. When her father was stressed, withdrawn, grumbly, or shut down, Sharron would experience her mother continuing to love herself, accepting Sharron's father with trust and appreciation.

Free of resentment, her mother would be assertive and yet forgiving. In this way Sharron would learn how to get her wants and needs fulfilled in a relationship without resorting to manipulation. She would see her mother acknowledging and appreciating her father for all the ways he contributed to the family. By this example she would feel secure in her own masculine power to contribute to others and make a difference.

As she grew up she would feel safe in concurrently exploring and developing her feminine and masculine sides. She would not be judged as unladylike if she wanted to achieve great things and make a difference. If she was good in math, she would be appreciated for that and not shamed. If she was assertive, precocious, or demanding she would be admired for her strength and will. And yet when Sharron felt emotional, tender, or vulnerable, she would be nurtured and reassured. Her mother would spend the needed time sharing with her, listening to her, and comforting her.

Sharron's mother would not expect her to be "grown up" while still a child, but would allow her to develop in her own time. She would also teach Sharron to respect her boundaries by respecting her own: her mother would not be a martyr and resent giving to others. She would teach Sharron how to ask for what she wanted and how to share feelings when she was upset. Sharron would grow up staying in touch with and trusting her feelings.

In an ideal environment a girl is both respected for her feminine goodness and admired for her masculine strength. When she is assertive, creative, and aggressive she is admired and acknowledged. When she is loving, good, sweet, cute, and pretty she is adored and praised. When she is not good, however, she is still loved. She does not feel pressured to be good or happy all the time. If she is tender and vulnerable, she is not made wrong and told to grow up. She feels safe to express anger as well as to be afraid or to cry. She can be selfless or selfish and still be acceptable to her parents.

Sharron's ideal father is careful to respect her feelings, vulnerabilities, and needs. He knows that she is supposed to be different from him and he respects those differences. And yet when her masculine qualities emerge, he is right there to play games with her, teach her, and do things with her. He thinks about her day and asks questions that let her know he is interested. Just as he has learned to support her mother with little presents, he also surprises Sharron with little gifts from time to time. This makes her feel special. As a result she will feel secure in her worthiness. She will grow up without feeling a need to control, but with a trusting willingness to empower others with her love.

He understands that little girls have a strong tendency to blame themselves, and so he is extra careful to show concern or apologize when he makes mistakes or upsets her in any way. In this way he helps her to respect herself. In the presence of her daddy she feels safe to express her feelings, opinions, and wishes. She can speak without his ignoring her. When she gets overwhelmed and overreacts he does not put her down; he knows how to listen and comfort her without trying to fix her. She feels safe being pretty and attractive. She feels comfortable asking for support. He is able to set limits and yet make her feel deserving.

Most important, Sharron gets to experience her father loving her mother. She learns that being feminine is lovable. This makes it safe for her feminine self to emerge and develop. She does not need to hide herself, deny herself, or pretend to be someone she is not. She also does not need to change herself to win her father's love; she sees her mother being herself and being loved by a man. This is a very important experience. She does not have to be different from her mother to be loved by dad. She feels secure in her femininity because she sees her father repeatedly loving and respecting her mother, who represents her female side.

Children brought up in such a loving and respectful environment have an opportunity to develop simultaneously their male and female sides. This balanced interaction of male and female energies is later reflected in every aspect of their lives. Thus they are able to actualize more of their human potential. In particular, this internal harmony is reflected in their ability to have harmonious and mutually supportive relationships.

THE INFLUENCE OF REPRESSION

Of course, few if any of us grew up in this ideal way. Every time little Billy experienced Mom rejecting Dad, he had a choice: "Do I reject Dad and thus reject the part of me that is like him, or do I reject Mom and reject the part of me that is like her?"

Every time Billy himself is rejected or opposed, he has another choice: "Do I choose to deny myself or do I choose to lose love?"

When Dad gets angry and yells at his daughter Sharron, does she realize Dad is dysfunctional, or does she assume that something is wrong with her and that she should be more like him to protect herself?

Does little Billy reject his masculine side because Dad hurt Mom?

Does Sharron reject her female side because she sees how weak and helpless her mother is?

These are just a few of the multitude of examples that reveal how our childhood shapes us. No one escapes childhood without repressing or denying some part of themselves in order to survive, be secure, be free, and be loved.

Consequently, we have repressed the natural development of different aspects of our male and female sides. If while he grows Billy's male side is not loved, appreciated, accepted, and trusted, he may begin to repress his masculinity to get his mother's love. In this case his female qualities have a greater chance to develop. But if schoolmates make fun of him or he starts feeling rejected by his father, he may then deny aspects of his female side. Boys generally grow up fluctuating from normal and balanced to overly sensitive (or nice), and then over to macho (or unfeeling.)

As little girls develop, some parts may mature in balance while others are judged and rejected. By repressing her female side she becomes more masculine or overly responsible. This can give her a lot of power, but at the price of feeling disconnected from her true self. She feels as though she does not know herself and experiences an emptiness or lack of fulfillment. If she then rejects her masculine side, she becomes not only disconnected but also weak, needy, and hopeless. She becomes overly vulnerable to others and overly dependent. She may feel unable to take care of herself. In many ways she feels like a little girl, unable to assert herself.

When a boy represses his masculinity, his masculine qualities remain undeveloped. When as an adult he chooses to awaken these qualities, he must also recognize that they will need time to develop into appropriate behavior. For instance, by being aggressive and breaking things, a little boy gradually learns to be more respectful. If this aggression is pent up for years and then comes out in adulthood, one must be careful to channel it appropriately.

Similarly, if a little girl grows up too quickly and takes on the role of Mommy because Mom is dysfunctional or not available, then that little girl and her neediness may suddenly engulf her as an adult. This is the price she pays to heal her past and become whole and complete. Fortunately, this is a temporary phenomenon that may recur but gradually goes away. If she can love and accept this "disowned" needy part of her, it can be integrated into her awareness and make her more whole and complete.

It is important to note that it is possible and very common to selectively repress different aspects of masculinity or femininity. Thus in reading the examples throughout this book of male and female tendencies, a man might relate to many of the male examples but sometimes relate to the feminine examples (and vice versa for women).

SEXIST ASSUMPTIONS

Unfortunately, because we haven't had clear role modeling for being fully male or female, we often get confused about who we are. Consequently, since we haven't been taught how to balance and express our male and female energies, we fall into sexist assumptions about ourselves and others. These assumptions limit the expression of our innate potential. They are limiting because we think they're true, and we try to conform. But to conform, we must suppress parts of ourselves.

Listed below are seven common (faulty) sexist assumptions:

1. Women are loving and men are heartless.
2. Women are irrational and men are intelligent.

3. Women are supportive and men are destructive.
4. Women are weak and men are powerful.
5. Women are submissive and men are dominant.
6. Women are dependent and men are independent.
7. A person's role is predetermined by their sex.

These general sexist beliefs give rise to thousands of other, more specific, unfair assumptions such as, "a man should work in the world while a woman stays home" or "women make better nurses and men make better doctors."

These seven categories of sexual discrimination are significant because they directly inhibit and restrict our potential, which ultimately transcends our manifest sexual differences. Certainly, our particular sex influences the expression of our potential, but it in no way determines who we are or what we can do. Our particular sex determines how we know ourselves and others, and also determines how others can most effectively support us, but it in no way limits how we can express ourselves to support others.

Our true, inner potential to give transcends our sexual differences. This shared potential can be expressed in the following seven categories. Each one of us is meant to:

1. Be purposeful
2. Be intelligent
3. Be creative
4. Be loving
5. Be powerful
6. Be decisive
7. Be self-reliant

Each and every one of us has our own, unique blend of these essential human qualities. Naturally, every person has their own limitations, but those limitations are not determined by sex. To assume our sex determines our ability to love, or to express power, or to understand is a great mistake. It does everyone an injustice. Such attitudes box people into imaginary categories and inhibit the full expression of who we are and what we can do.

THE TRUE MEANING OF EQUALITY

Men and women are created equal; ultimately, the essence or spirit of men and women is the same. All men and women have intelligence and loving hearts. The qualities of who we are and what we can do — of our potential — are the same. But how we develop and express our individual potential is different for each person.

Our greatest power is to love and support each other. Every person is unique and has a special gift to offer. It is unfortunate that in order to find equality, we assume we must be the same as others. Through respecting and appreciating our singular differences, we give ourselves a chance to fully blossom and discover our true gifts. In reality, we're all different and inter-dependent. It's through the recognition of this interdependency that we can come to express our full power. Our highest potential is to give of ourselves in love.

As human beings, we are all purposeful. We possess within us a distinctive purpose to fulfill and have been given a unique intelligence, no matter what our sex is. The more we understand and accept our male and female energies, the more able we are to discover the sacred treasure of knowing who we are and what we can do. We can unlock this treasure chest by exploring the male and female energies within us. This exploration leads to greater under-standing, which opens the door to greater self-esteem, self-worth, confidence, happiness, and peace.

Without this knowledge, trying to love ourselves and others can be very confusing. Sometimes, even when we are trying to support ourselves and others, we unknowingly sabotage our success. In the next chapter we will explore how men and women unwittingly restrict their ability to love in re-lationships.

CHAPTER NINE

Why Women Feel Unloved

Women often complain of feeling unloved, whereas their partners have no idea what they are talking about or how to change things. Typically, the man will ask, "How could she possibly feel unloved? Look at all I do for her!" He then proceeds to list everything he does to support his family, such as earning a regular paycheck, concentrating on making his business grow, taking her out to the movies, etc. He truly doesn't understand why she feels unloved.

Let's look at an example that reveals how men's and women's differences could create this confusion.

MASCULINE AND FEMININE AWARENESS

John, a football coach, tends to focus on a single point or goal at a time. He is aware of all the factors relevant to his goal, but in the process of focusing exclusively on one aim, in masculine fashion, he becomes unaware of the people and circumstances in his life that are not directly relevant to his goal. His awareness is restricted to the distance or path between himself and his point of focus. For the most part, nothing matters but the goal.

When his focus changes from one goal to another, his awareness shifts dramatically, bringing in the information he needs for the new goal. His awareness is redirected, but still focused on a single goal or point.

Since John has not balanced his male and female sides (focused and open awareness), each change in focus means he becomes unaware of anything other than his new goal. He can even forget what he was doing just a moment ago, if it doesn't have some relevance to his new point of focus.

John's view of his own worth is determined by how well he thinks he's moving toward whatever goal he has in mind. In fact, his very sense of himself comes from how he affects his environment. He identifies with his actions, his "doing." You could almost say that as long as he's doing something, he stays in touch with himself. All his information about his environment is filtered by his aim, to the exclusion of everything else.

John's wife Pam, on the other hand, with her feminine awareness, takes in the whole picture. If she's aware of John's goal, she'll not only see his goal, but see how it relates to her and to other people in their lives. She'll automatically be concerned with how his goal may affect their relationship with each other and their children. She will tend to be even more aware of how his focus on this goal affects his health. She'll also have some sense of what will happen if he is successful or if he isn't. John's focused awareness doesn't readily envision all these consequences. He is first concerned with the possibility of getting to the goal; she sees all the possible consequences of going after the goal.

Pam's open awareness allows her to see a multitude of possibilities in any situation. But because she doesn't understand John's focused awareness, she jumps to the conclusion that he doesn't care about her or the family when he makes a decision without first considering how it would affect them. She knows that she would consider her family because she loves them. And so she wrongly assumes that he doesn't love the family.

WHEN HIS WORK IS HER LIFE

Each year in mid-August, John begins drilling his football team for the fall season. During the first part of the school year, he spends extra hours at team practice, extra time at home watching videos of the team's performance, and even extra time tutoring the star place kicker who is close to failing algebra.

When football season is over, he spends after-school time watching other high school and junior high sports events in hopes of spotting a potential football star for the next year. At the beginning of summer vacation, John is finally able to relax. But within a couple of weeks, the new season will become his primary focus again.

Chances are, with all the attention John is paying to his job, he'll have a winning team. His high school will be happy with him and he'll eventually receive tenure, securing his income for many years ahead.

Meanwhile Pam is home, raising the kids and trying to support John and his goal of a winning football team. She fixes a hot breakfast every morning so he'll have plenty of energy; he bolts it down and rushes off to school. She spends time shopping carefully for his favorite foods and prepares dinner every night. (Often John is late for dinner when practice runs longer than expected.) She makes sure the kids behave when he gets home so he can enjoy some peace and quiet, and she's always careful to hold discussions about the family when John's work is going well.

Pam makes sure John has clean, pressed clothes, taking care to remove as many of the grass stains as possible. She listens as he describes the problems he has with various players, and often helps him understand how to approach a recalcitrant team member. She goes to all the games. As a matter of fact that is the only time they go out together.

HOW BOTH CONTRIBUTE TO THE PROBLEM

As you might expect, eventually trouble erupts between the two. At first glance, it looks as if John is the "wrong" party in this situation, but in truth, both are just doing what their respective energies direct them to do. John has no understanding of the problem, and Pam has no idea that her way of coping with the problem is only making matters worse.

Pam has gradually lost track of herself and her own needs, and resents that John does not respond to or consider them; John is so totally focused on his goal of winning football games that at first he doesn't know there's a problem, and when he finds out, he doesn't understand it. He has no idea that Pam's needs aren't being met — in part because she has not communicated what those needs are. She thinks she has expressed her needs. Unfortunately, she did so in a way that John could not hear. Let's look at what happened.

As John gets involved in the new season, Pam tries to be loving and accepting. After some time, when he doesn't seem to notice or appreciate the sacrifices she is making, she feels resentful. Pam begins to complain about all the things John isn't doing around the house. Sometimes he tells her she shouldn't worry about it; sometimes he promises to get something done and then forgets about it. Occasionally she suggests ways he might spend some more time with his kids. He nods distractedly or comments that everything will be OK.

Pam feels unloved when John doesn't respond to her needs. She reacts at first by working even harder to understand and fulfill his needs. But he hardly notices, because it's just not in his nature to notice anything that isn't part of his goal of winning football games.

Eventually, Pam can't take this anymore and she explodes, telling John she feels totally unloved. He becomes defensive and points out how hard he works to support the family. If she pushes, he negates her feelings entirely, saying that she is overreacting and being irrational.

SHARING NEGATIVE FEELINGS WITH LOVE

Pam doesn't understand that in an attempt to be loving, accepting, and supportive, she has merely withheld her negative feelings of anger, frustration, sadness, disappointment, fear, and worry. These feelings build up inside until she finally shares them with an attitude of rejection, which says "I have done all this and you do nothing. I love you but you don't love me back."

No one has ever taught Pam how to share her negative feelings *with* a loving attitude. She oscillates back and forth between two extremes: either she suppresses her negative feelings to be loving, or she becomes unloving (resentful) and expresses her negative feelings.

Neither of these formulas work. If John is to respond to her needs and problems, he needs to hear the truth of how she feels. If she has an unloving, resentful, unaccepting, unappreciative, or untrusting attitude, he will not be able to take in what she is saying. But if she pretends to be loving, happy, and accepting, that won't work either; he will assume that everything is fine and remain focused on his work.

Pam needs to practice sharing her negative feelings before they have built up, and John needs to practice listening to her feelings. When verbal communication is not working, the next step is to try writing. The best way to begin learning to communicate upset feelings *with* love is to write them out and later read them to your partner.

In Chapter 16 of this book I will describe a technique for writing feelings in a way that both centers a person in loving feelings and communicates their experiences and needs. If writing fails, then another workable option is getting the help of a counselor.

Unless John creates time to listen to and support Pam, and unless she learns to share her feelings and needs without resentment, it is inevitable that Pam will continue to meet John's resistance.

HOW PAM CAN CHANGE

Pam will feel unloved as long as she doesn't understand her responsibility to communicate her feelings, wishes, and needs. But it is almost impossible for her to accept this responsibility unless she first realizes that a man's focused awareness causes him to behave very differently from her.

Because her open awareness naturally motivates her to keep track of the needs of those she loves, she can't fathom how John could forget her but still love her. *Her* experience of loving someone is to become absorbed in caring for their needs. When *he* doesn't reciprocate, she mistakenly concludes that he doesn't love her.

When Pam feels unloved, she initially focuses on becoming more worthy of love, rather than on sharing her feelings, wishes, and needs. She tries to become more deserving of love by giving more to her husband and suppressing her negative feelings. There is nothing wrong with giving more to John. Giving always is good. Her problem is that she is not good at receiving. The more she gives without receiving, the more unreceptive she becomes.

Pam thinks she is being strong and self-reliant. But as she becomes less receptive, John experiences less attraction to or interest in her. When Pam gives without also being receptive (feminine) she gradually becomes hard and loses the soft feminine qualities that originally motivated John's interest in her. When she suppresses her emotions, she gradually disconnects from her natural feelings of love, joy, gratitude, and trust. John, being focused on his work, is not even aware of the change.

SYMPTOMS WOMEN CAN LOOK FOR,
ACTIONS THEY CAN TAKE

To help women recognize that a relationship problem is growing, here are a few warning signs:

1. Your partner consistently forgets to do things for you.
2. You don't feel comfortable asking for support.
3. Your partner does something for you, but you feel it is not enough.
4. You don't feel safe to be upset, and find yourself hiding your feelings.
5. You find yourself getting upset over very little things and avoiding the real issues.
6. Your partner doesn't seem to be passionately attracted to you, and you don't care.
7. You feel resentful that you are giving more than he is.
8. You feel that if he would change, you would be happy.
9. You feel guilty or petty being unhappy.

Most women have experienced each of the above symptoms at some time when in a relationship with a man. It is natural to feel these things, especially if you don't understand how men and women are different.

Some suggestions for her to counter these symptoms follow:

1. Accept that he is different from you and practice asking for support.
2. When you are upset, practice sharing your upset, but try sandwiching it with positive feelings of trust, acceptance, and appreciation.
3. As you are sharing, periodically reassure him that he is not being blamed and that his listening is helpful and appreciated.
4. When you feel resentful, talk with lady friends or practice that love letter technique (Chapter 16) to find forgiveness. From a more forgiving attitude, share your feelings.
5. Practice asking for support and making it OK that he doesn't always say yes. Give him the opportunity to support you in his own ways.
6. Acknowledge whatever he does for you. Don't take anything for granted.
7. Take care of yourself before you take care of him. If you are tired or under a lot of stress, don't martyr yourself by giving more. Give less so that he knows you need more support.
8. Whenever he makes suggestions to support the relationship — "Let's go out to dinner" or "Let's go on a vacation together," for example — be especially careful not to correct, criticize, or improve his ideas.
9. Join or start a support group of women. Meeting weekly if possible, read sections of this book together and share your experiences of using this new information.
10. Make friends with someone who has a good relationship, and share with them. If you can't find a friend, then find a mentor or therapist to assist you.

11. Read and discuss sections of this book with your partner. Find out his ideas and reactions and work on accepting him. Share with him your feelings so that he will have a greater understanding of you.

HOW JOHN CAN CHANGE

John can change only by understanding Pam's needs. First, he must realize that she needs his assistance to explore how she feels inside. He has to respect that she has needs but isn't aware of them. His job is to help her discover what she needs. Then he will naturally be motivated to participate more in the relationship.

The problem men have is that they generally are unaware that they are losing interest. They are just aware that they are interested more in their work or play than in their relationship.

To help men recognize that a relationship problem is brewing, listed here are a few warning signs:

1. You have become so focused on your job that you consistently forget to pick up items that you promised your partner you'd bring home from the store.
2. You have promised your partner you'd fix things around the house, and then become distracted with other projects of your own.
3. You don't understand your partner's feelings and find yourself telling her how she should and shouldn't feel.
4. You wonder why your partner gets so upset about little things.
5. You often find yourself half-listening to your partner or children because you are preoccupied with a problem from work or you are distracted by the TV.
6. You start turning off or becoming impatient when your partner begins to talk.
7. You are no longer passionately attracted to your partner when you have sex.

There probably isn't a man on the planet who hasn't experienced each one of these, probably a number of times. Each is an example of focused awareness, which, by the way, isn't bad. Without focus, nothing would get done. But each of the above situations is an example of too much focus — focus that keeps a man from being aware of others' needs. Focus becomes a negative when it is not balanced by openness.

By recognizing these signs of being overly focused, he can begin to open his awareness by listening to his partner. Some men, if they are too focused, find it unbearable to even consider taking time to listen to feelings. This stress of "having to listen" can be avoided if a man encourages his partner to write out her feelings and then schedules time to listen.

PLANNED INTIMACY

This scheduled time is called Planned Intimacy. Its purpose is for a man to listen to his partner's feelings and understand her needs. The best way for John to do this is to read out loud Pam's feelings as written in her letter. This procedure is most effective when she learns to express her negative feelings in a loving and nonresentful way. Not only does Pam write out her feelings, but she also writes a short response letter that she would like to hear in return. This helps Pam to get in touch with her feelings, and insures that John will have the words and awareness of what Pam needs. In this way, John will be able to respond to her feelings in a loving, caring, respectful, attentive, and considerate way.

As John learns to listen and Pam learns to share, both gradually become more balanced. In time, they communicate without having to solely depend on writing letters and scheduling time to read them. John steadily gains the ability to turn off work when he is relaxing and spending time with his wife. Pam learns to freely share her feelings, needs, wishes, and preferences without sounding critical and demanding.

One of the most essential ways a woman reading this book can receive more support is to become conscious of the things that she truly needs. If she is in a relationship, she could underline the points that relate to her, and then ask her partner to read the book and do the same, so that each could better understand the other's needs. Listening to my "Relationship Tape Series" (see Chapter 18) is another way to gradually absorb this material and be inspired with a new understanding of how the sexes differ.

CHAPTER TEN

The Art of Fulfilling Relationships

Men generally assume that once a woman is fulfilled, she should stay that way. Once he has proven his love, she should know it forever, and never need to be reassured or reminded. From the male point of view, this attitude makes perfect sense.

Women find this attitude hard to accept. It is just plain inconsistent with a female's internal reality. She needs to be reassured that she is special, worthy, understandable, and lovable. Men also need to be reassured, but they get that encouragement mainly through their work. Women, however, primarily need reassurance through their relationships.

When a man's work fails, he begins to doubt his worthiness. In a complementary way, when a woman is ignored by her husband, she begins to doubt her worthiness. She needs ongoing signs, symbols, and verbal reassurance that she is loved. Men too have this need for reassurance through relationship. But as long as a man is in a relationship, he will tend to be unconscious of this need. The mere fact that he has a relationship reassures him of his competence. The happiness of his wife will tend to bolster him, while a woman needs direct, caring attention to reassure her.

If a male is in a relationship, he isn't apt to worry about rejection unless it happens. He doesn't consciously feel a need to be reassured, because his successes in the world give him that reassurance. As a result, he doesn't readily respect a woman's ongoing need to be reassured again and again.

His focused reasoning goes something like this: "Even though I am preoccupied with work these days, she should know that I love her today, tomorrow and forever, unless I tell her differently." To a woman this is just as absurd as the following comments would be to a man: "Even though he is broke and out of work, he should know that he will be rich again, because he was rich at one time before the business went bankrupt" or "Although he

167

came in last today, he should know he's a winner because at one time he did win a tennis tournament."

Certainly a man's failures challenge him to realize his worth independent of his successes. But it is equally true that as he follows his failures with increasing success, his sense of self-worth is strengthened. After his business has failed he must regroup himself and try again. As he begins to succeed, his confidence becomes more solid. This can be likened to the process of building muscles: by breaking down one's muscles, they grow back stronger. In a similar way, through a series of setbacks the man who is able to try again strengthens his self-esteem. This is how a man builds self-worth and self-confidence.

A woman's self-worth is challenged when her partner withdraws or temporarily ignores her. This painful experience is a time to center herself and realize her worth independent of his love. However, it is equally important that her feelings of insecurity are followed by reassurance and support from her partner. This reassurance is necessary to strengthen and deepen her self-confidence, trust, and self-esteem.

If she approaches her partner with blame, however, it is predictable that he will resist and she will go uncomforted. In Chapter 16 you will be introduced to the Love Letter technique, a way to reach out and ask for support without offending your partner.

VERBAL REASSURANCE

Every day, a woman needs to receive some form of verbal reassurance that she is loved. This means saying things like "I love you, I love you, I love you, I love you, I love you, I love you, I love you, I love you. . . ." There is basically one way to say it and it needs to be said over and over.

Men sometimes stop saying "I love you" because they want to be new and original. They imagine that a woman would grow tired of it or become bored by it. But saying "I love you" is never redundant. Saying it is actually a process of allowing her to "feel" his love. He may love her, but if he doesn't say it she won't feel it. One way a man can relate to this is by comparing the simple statement "I love you" to a phrase that he never tires of hearing. That phrase is "Thank you." Rarely does a man weary of being told "thank you" after he has done something for someone.

Another phrase that is very validating for a woman is "I understand." If (and only if) a man does understand, then it is very helpful to say this out loud. When a man says "I understand," a woman is assured that she has been heard. A complementary phrase that men appreciate is "That makes sense." When a man hears "That makes sense," he feels equally supported.

SYMBOLS OF LOVE

A woman needs symbols of love. When a man brings a woman flowers, for example, they validate her beauty and femininity as being of great value.

Women need to be given flowers on an ongoing basis. To her, flowers are symbols of a man's love. They make his love concrete. It is unfortunate, then, when a man assumes that she will tire of them and therefore stops giving them to her.

Big presents or very little presents, all serve a very important romantic function. They help her know that she is special. She feels special when he treats her in a special way. Giving presents is a way of honoring this need in women to be reassured.

This is hard for men to understand because their basic nature is different. They focus in on a point, while a woman's nature is to expand outward. As she expands out she easily forgets herself. When she receives gifts or other tokens of love, she is reminded of who she is and is able to feel more trusting, appreciative, and accepting.

Little notes are also effective symbols of love. They are affectionate reminders that simply reassure. It is not necessary to be original or even creative. Just say the basics, over and over again. As long as your notes express what you feel, they will be effective. Some of the basic reminders are: "I love you, I miss you, you are the delight of my life, just a reminder to say I care."

A nice addition is to occasionally purchase a loving, funny, or beautiful card. These little reminders can be written on cards that accompany a small present or a flower, or they may stand alone. When giving a card, try hiding it in a place where the recipient will be surprised. This works wonders. These reminders can also be expressed by surprise phone calls whose simple purpose is to say "I love you."

Many men instinctively know and do this in the beginning of a relationship, but stop after a while because they mistakenly assume that the gesture will get old or is no longer necessary.

WHEN SIGNS OF LOVE DISAPPEAR

Often in relationships, a woman ends up feeling unloved because her man stops giving her the same quality of attention he did in the beginning of the relationship. When the quality of attention changes, she, not understanding men very well, assumes he's unhappy with her and doesn't care for her. *The quality of attention is the most important sign of love.*

Let me give you an example:

When Phil and Ann came for a counseling session, she complained that he didn't love her anymore. Phil couldn't understand what she was talking about. He knew he loved her; it didn't make any sense to him that she didn't know it. He was terribly frustrated.

After some discussion, Phil began to realize that when Ann said "You don't love me," what she really meant was "You don't treat me the same, special way you used to." He wanted to know more, so I asked Ann to close her eyes and remember how Phil's love used to make her feel.

She explored her feelings, then she slowly said, "It made me feel warm, it made me feel loved, it made me feel special, it made me feel happy, it made me feel calm, it made me feel peaceful, it made me feel playful, it made me feel free, it made me feel accepted, it made me feel noticed, it made me feel desired, it made me feel secure, and it made me feel fulfilled."

I asked her to go deeper and she added, "soft, delicate, loving, appreciative, deserving, trusting, and vulnerable."

Next I asked her, "When you feel this way, what are you most grateful for?" Ann listed the following:

"I feel grateful to be loved and cherished. I feel grateful to be a special part of Phil's life. I feel grateful when he treats me with respect. I feel grateful when he goes out of his way to comfort me. I feel grateful when he listens to me and makes me feel heard. I feel grateful when he initiates new activities and adventures for us to share.

"I feel grateful when he notices that I need to talk and asks me how I feel, and takes extra time to listen. I feel grateful when I can share my sadness and he holds me—that makes me feel so comforted. I feel grateful when he notices a new outfit or haircut and appreciates it. I feel grateful when he wants to be with me. I feel grateful when he surprises me with little gifts or notes. I feel grateful when he calls me when he's on a trip, and gives me his number. I feel grateful whenever he anticipates my needs. Then I trust that he really cares and is there for me and not just for himself."

As Phil listened, tears ran down his face. When she finished, he said, "As you spoke, I remembered some of our happiest moments, and I realized how things have changed over the years. Somehow, until now, I just hadn't noticed." Giving his wife a hug, he said, "I've missed you too."

Until then, Phil had been so focused on other things, he'd forgotten how important and wonderful being needed by Ann made him feel. He realized how important her love was to him, and remembered how special and precious his wife really was.

That day he learned that when his wife doesn't feel loved, she isn't being irrational; it's an important signal that she is not getting what she needs. He now knows that when her needs are overlooked, they run the risk of losing track of their special love.

If a man doesn't stay in touch with his partner's feelings, not only does he forget what's important, but she does too. She probably won't know exactly what she needs, but she'll begin to resent him. She may not know what she is missing, but she will know she is missing something.

When a man is willing to hear a woman's needs, they both win. Ann learned the power of letting Phil know how important he was to her. By letting him hear how positive his love made her feel, he became more motivated to support her. Expressing her gratitude helped him feel appreciated, accepted, and empowered.

LITTLE THINGS MEAN A LOT

Before I came to understand how a woman's awareness was different from mine, I couldn't understand why my wife would get upset when I forgot to do what seemed to me like little things — little things like bringing home a newspaper, picking up the dry cleaning, fixing a window, painting kitchen cabinets, or telling her that someone had invited us to a party. In this context, big things would be earning money, telling the truth, being monogamous, "being there" in times of emergency, paying the mortgage, etc.

From time to time, when I'd forget something, she'd come unglued, often telling me she didn't feel that I loved her. How, I wondered, could she interpret my forgetting to pick up a newspaper as a signal that I didn't love her?

Finally I came to realize that from her point of view, remembering the little things was an expression of my love. Those "little things," being her needs, were related directly to her. When I'd forget them, it was hard for her not to interpret my action as a lack of concern and caring for her. When I'd treat them as unimportant, I was actually making her feel as if she were unimportant.

When a man ignores something a woman considers important, she easily feels he's ignoring her. I found that being responsive and responsible about the little things was a significant way I could express my love for her and give her reassurance. Since she really is the most important person in my life, once I understood the importance of "little things," it became more automatic to pay attention to her wishes. In fact, once I understood that this was a legitimate need of hers, I could bring my masculine focus to bear on solving the problem.

Now that I understood how my wife was affected by my absent-minded professor routine, I was able to understand her feelings when I would forget things. I no longer felt compelled to tell her she shouldn't get so upset. She, on the other hand, has grown to understand my masculine tendency to focus, and doesn't take my forgetfulness as personally.

If men only knew how important these "little things" are to women, there would be more happy women. Some women are embarrassed to let a man know how important they are. All it takes, however, is to to remember the "little things" a woman needs, and you will see what a difference it makes.

INCREASING A MAN'S CREATIVITY

Reassuring a woman isn't the only reason to honor little things. As I started following through on more of my wife's wishes and preferences, I also found that doing the little things often helps me gain momentum for doing other things that I might be putting off. Such changes in focus can actually help release me from concentrating too much on tasks that may be wearing me down.

Shifting one's focus of attention is also a very powerful problem-solving technique. After you have focused for a long time on solving a problem, if you can fully let go and then temporarily redirect your focus to something else less demanding — one of the "little things" your female partner needs, for example — this gives the unconscious mind an opportunity to solve your problem. At some point the solution will emerge in your awareness when you are not even thinking about the problem.

This principle dramatically affects productivity. For a man to most effectively solve a work problem, after a full day's work forget the problem and focus on your relationship. At some point when you have completely forgotten the problem, the answer will tend to pop up in your mind. In terms of male and female awareness, you are swinging from being overly focused to being more open. As a result, creativity is enhanced. Paying attention to little things and to a woman's feelings and needs enlivens a man's feminine side. Consequently, he is more balanced and able to express his creative potential. Both partners win.

WOMEN LOVE SPECIAL TREATMENT

Women love to be singled out and treated specially by the men in their lives. I learned this the hard way, when my wife and I had our first big family party. I'd gone to my office while Bonnie had gotten the house ready. When I returned home, I was so proud of myself because I'd actually remembered to bring home the video camera. Although taking videos of a family party was something that I valued, I could have easily become absorbed by work problems and forgotten.

When I got home, everyone had already arrived. I went straight to the living room to set up the recorder, lights, and camera. As I moved equipment around, the kids ran to greet me. Gradually each family member found their way into the living room and we exchanged hugs and small talk as I continued to work on preparing the video equipment exactly right.

When I was finished, I went to the kitchen to say hello to my wife. I, of course, was expecting Bonnie to be delighted that not only had I remembered the camera, but I had gotten it all set up. Instead, she was distant and aloof. It turned out she'd expected me to first greet her, and then go about setting up the camera. Instead, she was the last person I spoke to. I was surprised, because from my male point of view, if she wanted to see me, she could have come into the living room at any time.

When we finally had a chance to talk, she told me she was hurt because it seemed to her that I was ignoring her. She wished I had come home, gone directly to her and given her a big hug, greeted the others, and then set up the camera. By setting up the camera first, I hadn't made her feel special. From her point of view, my focusing on the camera meant the camera was more important than either her or our guests.

ROMANTIC LOGIC

Certainly, if I was defensive I could have judged my wife as being unreasonable and demanding. But from a romantic point of view, what she said made sense. I certainly love it when either Bonnie or the kids get excited to see me. That always makes me feel special and good. Why shouldn't she enjoy that feeling?

I realized how important it is to women that we men single them out. Women actually don't know how special they are to us unless we tell them and demonstrate it. Since a woman can see so many possibilities, she can easily imagine that a camera, or something else, might be more important to a man than her. It never occurs to a man that his wife might feel like that. After all, he knows he loves her, so he assumes she knows it too. But she doesn't, not automatically; she has to be told, over and over again.

As I came to understand this difference, I also realized it would be easy to give my wife the special treatment she needs. To this day, whenever I arrive home, the very first thing I do is find her, give her a kiss and a hug, and ask her about her day.

When she visits my relationship seminars I go to her first and give her a hug, even if there are people waiting to talk with me. I used to give preference to the people waiting to talk — after all, this was their time, and I could talk to my wife any time. This attitude is definitely not romantic, and makes a woman feel unimportant and mundane. The simple formula to make a woman feel special is to treat her differently and first. Don't save the best for last.

This romantic logic explains the importance of doing little things to increase a woman's comfort and convenience. Opening the car door for her is a good example. When a man opens the car door, he demonstrates his willingness and desire to support her. It is not that she can't open or close the door. It is not that he thinks she is weak and he is strong. This simple act is a gesture of his love for her and his willingness to care for her. It is a symbolic expression or reminder to her that she is important to him.

Such special treatment really makes a woman feel loved, which is one of the reasons that relationships go so well in the beginning. Early in a relationship, men are focused on their women and give them special treatment as a matter of course. Once the relationship is established, men tend to think their partners know once and for all that they're special. A man finds it redundant to keep repeating his loving actions unless he realizes how important and needed they are. A woman never tires of hearing and seeing the ways her man loves her.

ONE SECRET TO MAKING A WOMAN FEEL LOVED

Possibly the most important way a man can make a woman feel loved is completely the opposite of what most men think. Most men unconsciously think that if they don't complain about the relationship, their partners will feel loved and valued. After all, if a woman doesn't complain about him, he will feel appreciated. Men don't understand that when a male acts as though everything is fine in the relationship, his partner infers that the relationship is not important to him. That makes her feel as though she is not important to him.

Generally a man tends to get upset and worry most about problems at work. When he comes home, his mind is still on his job. His partner gets the message that work is more important to him than she is. If this man can learn to identify his frustrations, disappointments, and worries in the relationship, he will communicate to the woman that she is important, appreciated, and needed. Herein lies one secret to making a woman feel loved: a woman gains in self-worth when her emotional support is acknowledged, desired, and appreciated.

Jean, 36, constantly complained of not being appreciated by her husband Paul, 43, who is a very successful doctor. Although Paul was the traditional breadwinner, Jean took exception to being the traditional homemaker. Paul resented that he made all the money and his wife wasn't willing to be responsible for the domestic duties.

When asked why, Jean said, "I resent being his maid. All he does when he comes home is complain about what a lousy job I do caring for him and the house. He says he works hard and he wants equal effort from me. I don't mind giving more, but no matter how much I give he doesn't appreciate me. He just criticizes me or points out what I haven't done. It hurts when I feel that he considers me his maid."

Paul went on to explain that he just wanted her to have the house clean and dinner cooking when he came home. In a frustrated tone he said, "It only takes two hours of her day to make me happy. All she has to do is keep the house clean and make a nice dinner. Then she is free to do anything else she wants. All I ask is two hours of housework."

To Paul's remark, Jean responded, "It makes me furious, when I feel as if I am just a maid to him." Paul had no idea that he was sounding so condescending to his wife. Jean was hearing that all he needed from her was housework. On the other hand, he thought he was saying, I value you so much that I only expect you to do a couple of hours of work.

I then asked Paul why it was so important to him that the house be cleaned and that his dinner be prepared. Becoming emotional, he answered, "It means that she really appreciates how hard I work for us. So much of the time she says money is not important to her. That makes it seem as though I am doing all this for nothing. I am trying to secure our future, and she thinks I just care about myself.

"It is painful when I think that she doesn't appreciate me. If I could come home and feel her love for me and her appreciation for what I do for her, it would make my life worth living. Otherwise I become resentful of her. I need her appreciation of all that I do for her. Without that I do become overly critical."

As Jean listened, her face began to glow and tears ran down her cheeks. For the first time, she could feel how important her loving support was to Paul. She saw that in fixing his meals she was not just being his cook. Instead, it was a way she could make him feel appreciated for his efforts to support the family financially. By hearing his frustrated need for her loving appreciation, Jean was able to feel like an important part of his life.

From this heartfelt interaction Jean was able to wholeheartedly release her resentment and enjoy being a homemaker as well as pursue her other interests. Paul realized that by showing her he needed more from her emotionally, rather than just needing more in terms of her labor, he was able to make her feel more valued, loved, and special.

This is difficult for most men, because they are generally unaware of what *they* really need in a relationship. To help a woman feel loved and valued, a man needs to share his frustration and disappointment when he is not getting the appreciation and emotional support that he needs. Not only does this support a woman in feeling her importance, but it also lets her know how to effectively give more support. As a man learns to communicate his emotional needs, this not only increases a woman's self-worth, but also inspires her to give more.

As we have seen, one of the major reasons women don't feel loved is that men have no reference point to instinctively give women what they need, nor are men able to articulate what they themselves need. In the next chapter we will explore in greater depth our primary emotional needs.

CHAPTER ELEVEN

How to Give and Receive Emotional Support

The rules governing successful relationships change as society changes. Political, technological, and scientific advances have shifted most of humanity above the immediate worries of survival and security. No more are men and women primarily in need of each other to ensure their physical survival and security. Today, men and women are drawn together in relationships not only to support each other's physical needs, but also to fulfill their higher psychological or emotional needs.

When the physical needs for survival and security are generally fulfilled, relationships take on a new orientation: the emotional needs take precedence and, consequently, new problems and conflicts emerge. These conflicts arise because a whole new set of needs begins to surface into consciousness. In a sense, it is as though the emotional needs become more demanding. They have been there all along but were in the background. As they rise to the fore, our psychological needs play a key role in the success of our relationships.

One can easily observe this shift in relationships. This explains why during a period of financial hardship, a couple may get along great. It is he and she against the world. Finally they achieve a higher degree of financial security. Rather than enjoying greater peace and fulfillment, they experience increased conflict or dissatisfaction. When the battle is over in the outside world, they find it at home.

Mike was 22 when he married Ellen, who was 26. For eight years Mike and Ellen were quite satisfied in their marriage. When they started out, they were both poor. Ellen worked as an airline flight attendant to finance Mike through law school. They remembered those times as hard but filled with loving, fun, and tender moments together. The couple seemingly had no problems in their relationship. It was as though they were a team fighting the world to ensure survival and security. They could easily ignore their problems because they imagined that one day things would be different.

177

Eight years later, Mike was a highly paid and successful lawyer and Ellen was a mother of two children. Although everything seemed to be working in the relationship, it was not. As soon as their material needs were taken care of on the outside, they began to notice how dissatisfied they were with each other. Mike was no longer interested or excited by his wife. Ellen pretended that everything was fine. Three months after they had moved into their beautiful new four-bedroom house, Mike fell in love with his secretary.

When Ellen found out, they came for counseling. She realized that she had been equally dissatisfied. After some hard work on their relationship, they were able to patch it up. Mike and Ellen were lucky. Many couples don't seek out help, but just get divorced.

When a relationship undergoes this shift from being physically based to being emotionally oriented, a couple needs to know it is inevitable that new problems will come up. The old ways of relating to each other will not be satisfactory or fulfilling.

Because women are generally more conscious of their emotional needs, the woman is first to experience a lack of fulfillment. Her male partner, in turn, begins to feel a lack of fulfillment in response to the woman's dissatisfaction. As they become more successful, he grows more intolerant of her dissatisfaction, because there are fewer physical reasons to account for it. He reasons that because they are more physically abundant, she should be happier.

The reality is that because they are more financially secure, emotional needs emerge that require his continued support and attention. He tends to resist because he thinks that having achieved material prosperity, he has completed his job. Neither is happy and both tend to blame each other. One of the biggest problems is that they both resent having these difficulties in the first place.

These new problems cannot be avoided. If the two *understand* and *accept* that this is inevitable, then they will not be as resentful of each other. *They will not question the relationship; instead they will question their old styles of relating and communicating.* Rather than changing partners, they can focus their energies on improving their abilities to give and receive emotional support.

HIERARCHY OF NEEDS

Abraham Maslow's "hierarchy of needs" demonstrates that as the lower physical needs get fulfilled, quite automatically the higher emotional needs are more deeply felt. From the strong basis of successfully supporting the physical needs for survival and security, one can build a relationship that nurtures the higher emotional needs. From the platform of a solid, loving relationship, a person can then succeed in fulfilling their highest need, which is to express their inner potential in service of others. Maslow described this as the need to self-actualize. To actualize means to realize or make actual. To self-actualize is the "make actual" one's inner potential through making a difference.

This need to self-actualize is fulfilled through expressing our inner potential to be of service to others and make a significant difference in the world. The prerequisite for this is having successful and loving relationships. A heart opens to others frees us to fully express our inner potential without restriction.

Having a successful relationship allows us to stay in touch with and actualize our inner creative potential. A study of 500 of the nation's most successful people revealed that almost all had significant and highly romantic relationships with one person. Before they could truly achieve lasting success in the world, they had apparently needed to build a successful marriage.

To build a relationship requires hard work and persistence, especially at those inevitable times when it seemingly would be much easier to get emotional support elsewhere and leave one's partner — if not physically, then emotionally. When problems arise, if one merely leaves the relationship and starts a new one, after a time the same problems will come back. They will always do so, until new strategies for relating are learned. Not only will this person experience the same problems in every new relationship, but they lose the opportunity to continue building their personal power through facing life's challenges and mastering its many lessons.

The difficulties that come up in relationships test our ability to love and understand others as well as ourselves. These inevitable problems are not to be avoided but solved. They are opportunities to experience increased self-awareness as well as greater joy and fulfillment.

In simple terms this means that as we grow in our ability to master the outer world, our relationships will demand more attention. They will appear to have more problems and we who are in them will be increasingly dissatisfied. To a certain extent, most relationships in the modern world are undergoing this stress. This is one of the major causes of marital dissatisfaction and the reason that divorce rates have increased in every modern country.

This stress will continue to affect everyone until we master the laws of relating in order to fulfill our higher emotional needs. When children can grow up in an environment where their parents exhibit this emotional mastery, then they will not experience this stress. They will naturally learn the strategies for successfully relating through their parents' examples.

CREATING EMOTIONAL SUPPORT

It is significantly easier to offer true emotional support when one has received that support in childhood. It is also easier to correct a situation in which one is not getting their needs fulfilled, if one is already familiar with the kind of support they need. People have chronic difficulties in their relationships because they do not have concrete experiences of what is possible, of how a loving and supportive relationship looks and feels. If their parents were dysfunctional, how can they even conceive of what real emotional support is like?

For example, if one was ignored or disrespected as a child, it is hard for them to gracefully draw in attention and respect. Because they haven't had the experience of drawing in respect by being themselves, they may end up resentfully demanding it — which pushes others away. Or, they may resort to denying their true selves in order to earn it. The problem with being demanding or denying one's self to receive emotional support is that even if one does succeed, the support is hard to let in. It never seems to be enough.

Gail, a travel agent, was 42 when she woke up one morning on a vacation and realized that she was "completely unhappy," dissatisfied with her life and her relationship. She felt empty and alone. She felt that no one had ever "really" loved, respected, or appreciated her.

With the help of some counseling, her husband Glen tried everything to support her and convince her that she was important and loved. In assisting them, I could see that he loved her deeply but she was unable to let it in. I also discovered the ways he unknowingly made heartfelt communication almost impossible.

She said, "I can see he is trying hard to please me. I even feel guilty for not appreciating everything he does do. I don't know why nothing he does is enough. But when I speak he really doesn't hear me. He doesn't see who I am. I don't think he really loves me."

As deep emotion began to well up within her, she took a deep breath and she began to cry, "Nobody loves me. Nobody has ever loved me. The only person who loved me was my father, and he died when I was seven."

For the first time in a long while, Gail began to soften and share her inner pain with Glen. She was amazed that he didn't reject her. As she became able to share and not merely complain, he was able to hear her and respond with profound compassion and understanding. With some assistance, Gail started to open up and reveal her insecure, sad, and even angry feelings. This was completely new to her; she was used to holding everything in and trying to appear loving and nice.

As she exposed this "not so together" side of her, Glen responded with greater love. This confused Gail. She asked, "How can you love this part of me. You've always said how much you loved how strong, good-natured, and independent I was."

"I do love that part of you," Glen said. "But I also love this soft and warm part of you. It makes me feel needed and important to you. I wouldn't want you to be this way all the time, though. I also like the other, strong side of you."

Gail said, "This is confusing . . . how am I supposed to know how much you can take? How am I supposed to know how to be, in order to be lovable?"

Taking her hands gently in his, Glen leaned closer and with tears of love in his eyes said, "I love you just the way you are. I love you when you are happy and I love you when you are sad. I love you most when you are just being you. Whenever you are *trying* to appear happy when you are not feeling it, then it is not you. It is hard for me to deeply feel my love for you when you are not being or sharing the real you. I love this soft, warm, vulnerable part of you."

She smiled and responded by saying, "I love this warm, caring, understanding part of *you.* For the first time I feel I am really being loved. I feel safe. I can say that I like who I am."

Gail was able to let in Glen's love because, for the first time, she had really opened up to him. As long as she had pretended to be what she was not, when Glen would love her, her false persona was getting the love. The more her strong side had been appreciated, the more she had felt her vulnerable and needing side was weak and unacceptable.

As Gail shared the complete truth of who she was, she was able to let in the love she truly deserved. Through taking responsibility to be herself and truthfully share her feelings in a nonresentful way, she was able to draw Glen's emotional support to the deeper and more hidden parts of her that needed his love the most. As she received his support, she began to love both sides of her. Increasingly able to respect herself, she began to appreciate and trust his love.

In the previous example Gail learned to successfully share her emotional needs with her husband and reach out for his assistance. As he learned to give her what she needed, she was able to learn what he needed. This process is greatly facilitated if we have a clear picture of how we need to be supported, as well as how our partner's needs might be different.

THE SEVEN POSITIVE ATTITUDES

There are seven basic emotional needs or attitudes that are essential to creating a truly loving and emotionally supportive relationship. They are the needs for love, caring, understanding, respect, appreciation, acceptance, and trust.

These seven loving attitudes are present to various degrees when a person feels emotionally supported. Positive sentiments like fulfillment, peace, happiness, gratitude, satisfaction, excitement, and confidence are automatically generated when we are able to fulfill our primary emotional needs.

Love. Love is a connecting, uniting, sharing, or joining attitude. Without judgment or evaluation it says, "We may be different but we are also alike. I see myself in you and I see you in myself." On a mental level, love is expressed through understanding. Acknowledging a sense of relatedness, it says, "I relate to you in this similar way." On an emotional level, love is expressed through empathy. It acknowledges a relatedness of feeling. It says, "I relate to your feelings; I have had similar feelings." On a physical level, love is expressed through touch.

Caring. A caring attitude acknowledges one's felt responsibility to respond to the needs of another. To care is to show deep interest or heartfelt concern for another's well-being. When we care about someone, it is a sign that we are affected by their well-being or lack of it. The more one cares, the more he is naturally motivated to fulfill or support others. Caring is also an acknowledgment of what is important to a person. Caring for a person validates that they are special.

Understanding. An understanding attitude validates the meaning of a statement, feeling, or situation. It does not presume to already know all the answers. An understanding attitude starts from not knowing, gathers meaning from what is heard, and moves toward validating what is being communicated. Through understanding we are able to see the world through another person's eyes. An understanding attitude says, "Before I judge you, I will take off my shoes and walk in yours for a while."

Respect. A respectful attitude acknowledges another person's rights, wishes, and needs. It yields to another's wishes and needs not out of fear, but through acknowledging their validity. Respect acknowledges the value and importance of who a person is, as well as their needs. Respect is the attitude that motivates one to truly serve another because they deserve it.

Appreciation. An appreciative attitude acknowledges the value of another's efforts or behavior. It recognizes that the expression of another person's being or behavior has enriched the well-being of the appreciator. Appreciation is the natural reaction to being supported. Appreciation inspires us to give back to others with a feeling of fullness and joy. Appreciation acknowledges that we have benefited from the gift offered to us.

Acceptance. An accepting attitude acknowledges that another's being or behavior is received willingly. It does not reject, but affirms that the other person is being favorably received. Indeed, acceptance is accompanied by a sense of gratitude for what we have received. It is not a passive, overlooking, or slightly disapproving attitude. To accept a person means to validate that they are enough for you. It does not mean that you think they could not improve; it indicates that you are not trying to improve them. Acceptance is the attitude that forgives another's mistakes.

Trust. A trusting attitude acknowledges the positive qualities of another's character, such as honesty, integrity, reliability, justice, and sincerity. When trust is absent, people commonly jump to negative and wrong conclusions regarding a person's intent. Trust gives every offense the benefit of the doubt, positing that there must be some good explanation for why it happened. Trust grows in a relationship when each partner recognizes that the other never intends to hurt. To approach one's partner with trust is to believe that they can and are willing to support.

MALE AND FEMALE NEEDS

What is most interesting and significant regarding these primary emotional needs is that *some are more significant than others according to one's sex.* Love, the first of the seven needs, is equally important to both men and women. The importance of the other six emotional needs varies according to one's sexuality. The male side of a person primarily has the need to be trusted, accepted, and appreciated, while the female side of a person primarily needs to be cared for, understood, and respected.

Because men and women don't understand that their primary needs are different, they make a very common mistake: they give to their partner what they themselves would want, assuming that this is what their partner also wants. Then they are shocked when their partner does not return the favor.

For example, many times a woman will act toward a man with so much caring and understanding that he feels she doesn't trust him. She gives caring and understanding because that is what she primarily needs from a partner. She mistakenly assumes that he will rejoice in her caring attitude as a wonderful gift, and respond to her in the same way. Instead, he may respond by being neutral, or may even interpret her support as smothering and annoying! When he resents her caring behavior, she is perplexed and confused.

On the other hand, a man may be so accepting and trusting that a woman assumes he doesn't care at all about her, and resents him. A man will give his partner trust and acceptance because that is what he needs the most from her. If she gets upset, for example, he may give her some space to work things out and completely ignore her. From his perspective, he is offering acceptance and trust. He is trusting her to handle her problem alone, and accepting her by not trying to change things. She, however, interprets this as abandonment and rejection. She feels greatly uncared for.

In both of these examples, because our couple did not fully understand each other's different needs, they were unsuccessful in supporting each other — when not only were they trying to support, but they thought they were doing a good job of it!

This is exciting information. When it is properly understood, it gives one an awareness of why they may not be receiving the support they deserve in relationships. So many people in intimate relationships report that they give so much and yet their partner does not give back. Yes, they are giving, but not necessarily what their partner really needs. If one truly succeeds in giving, the result is that the receiver rejoices in supporting back. It is very natural; what we give out comes back to us. Give and you will get back is the promise of every relationship.

The main reason this golden rule doesn't always work in our relationships is that what we give is not always what our partner needs. Both sides think they are giving, but no one is getting. This statement and perception only reinforces that they are both victims.

To realize our power to create what we need, we must accept that *when we are not getting, then we are not giving. Or more precisely, we are not giving what our partner needs.* To receive more in our relationships we must learn how to give not what we would need, but what our partner needs. When we succeed in truly fulfilling their needs, they will spontaneously begin to respond to our support by supporting us in return.

The success of our giving, then, is determined by our partner's willingness to support back. If our partner is unaffected by our gifts, rather than blaming them as unappreciative, we must be accountable and explore ways we can more successfully give.

Giving, for most people, is like putting money in a parking meter. They resent the parking meter for not accepting dollar bills when it only accepts coins. If we are to successfully give to our partners, we must be accountable to give in the currency they cherish. When we don't give what our partner can use, we are like the businessman who complains that his customers are not buying his product, rather than finding out what his customers truly need and then supplying that.

To sum all this up, one of the major causes of frustration and resentment in relationships is that men tend to automatically give to women what men need, while women give men what a woman would most appreciate. This exciting information is probably one of the insights that you will remember most from this book. Applying this knowledge has dramatically improved thousands of relationships literally overnight. In the next chapter we will explore more deeply how men and women differ in their primary emotional needs.

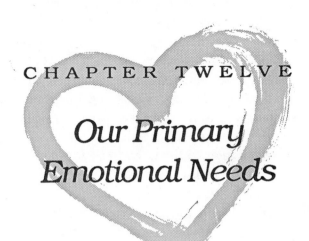

CHAPTER TWELVE

Our Primary Emotional Needs

All men and women have an equal need for love. But regarding the six other basic emotional needs, three are primarily needed by men and the other three are primarily needed by women. Most conflict and dissatisfaction in relationships stems from our inability to fulfill these primary needs. When these needs are not fulfilled it is easy to have our feelings hurt, for which we blame our partner.

A man is most often hurt, offended, or drained when a woman does not *trust, appreciate,* or *accept* his motives, abilities, thinking, decisions, and behavior. Because a man tends to identify with his actions, when he feels his actions are not being trusted, appreciated, or accepted, he will exhibit all the symptoms of being wounded, offended, or resentful. Deep inside he begins to doubt his adequacy and competence.

A woman primarily needs to be cared for, understood, and respected. She is most vulnerable to feeling hurt when her feelings especially are not being *respected, understood,* or *cared for.* When she is not respected by someone she loves, she quite commonly begins to doubt her worthiness and her rights. This is most painful to her.

THE UNIVERSAL NEED TO BE LOVED

The most important of the seven primary emotional needs is the need for love. To love someone is to acknowledge the goodness of who they are. Through loving a person we awaken their awareness of their own innate goodness. It is as though they cannot know how worthy they are until they look into the mirror of our love and see themselves.

We are first able to see ourselves through the mirror of another person seeing our goodness. When we are "seen" with love, we become aware of our goodness. Then we are able to know and love ourselves more.

As we mature in that self-awareness, we become less dependent on others to see ourselves. However, as long as we are growing in self-awareness we will always need to be loved, just as we always have the need for physical survival. Over time this need to be loved is overshadowed by the need to be of service to others, just as in an earlier stage, the need for physical survival and security takes a back seat to the need to be loved.

Love is also a connective feeling. Love relates to another. It says you are like a part of me. When a man loves a woman, he is able to feel and connect with the goodness of his own female side. When he is loved by her in return, he awakens to experiencing the worthiness of his male side. Likewise, when she is loving him, she is recognizing and experiencing the goodness of her masculine side. As he loves her she is able to also experience the merit of her female side.

Through giving and receiving love, men and women can more fully love themselves and experience their inner goodness. In this way they feel more whole and complete.

Love is an attitude that embraces another as one would embrace oneself. It upholds, nurtures, and supports. Whenever we are truly feeling love, there will also emerge a selfless desire to serve the well-being of the loved one.

Through love we feel our connectedness to ourselves and others. When we are loved, we experience the truth of who we are. When we are loved, we feel that we are worthy and "enough." When we are feeling loved, it is easier to be our true selves.

Giving the Gift of Love

As little children we all come into this world giving the gift of love to our parents and all those we meet. We look upon them with wonder, seeing only the beauty and goodness of their souls. We see them as great beings, certainly worthy of all we can give. If that love is returned to us, then we are able to love ourselves. It is as though God gives us the ability to love outwardly, but we need our parents to reflect back that love so that we can love ourselves.

Unfortunately, if that love is not returned to us, we begin to reject or "disown" parts of who we are. Generally we reject, deny, and then change ourselves to win our parents' love and acceptance; we become someone else in order to be loved. To the extent that we disown parts of who we are, it is hard for us to love similar aspects of other people. Once we have disowned parts of ourselves it is also hard to receive love.

To let in the love we deserve, we must risk being ourselves again in the context of a loving relationship. As we grow in our ability to receive love, it becomes easier to truly give of ourselves and realize our deepest potential.

THE FEMALE NEED TO BE CARED FOR

Relationships are an ongoing process of giving, receiving, and sharing. The success of a relationship is based on our ability to give of ourselves. Our ability to give, however, is directly related to our ability to receive. One cannot continue to give unless one is also receiving support. To receive support we must first feel worthy of being supported. To acknowledge and feel worthy of being cared for, we need to have someone care for us.

It is essential that those with whom we are in relationships are responsive to and caring about our needs. The need to be cared for is the need to have someone respond to our needs to the best of their ability. A caring attitude allows us to open up and trust that we are special and entitled to receive support.

Women are especially vulnerable to caring or lack of caring from a male partner. He can make her feel heavenly and then drop her into hell. When a man is caring of a woman, she trusts that her needs are valid and not selfish. But when a woman is in an uncaring relationship or environment, it is very hard for her to assert her needs without feeling guilty for being too needy or selfish. She easily judges herself as weak and unworthy of sharing her feelings and needs.

Men are vulnerable to caring in a different way. When a man is in a relationship with an overly caring woman, he may become weak and dependent. She gradually takes on the role of a mother to him, and he regresses to behaving like a spoiled and demanding child. He may swing back and forth from being dependent to being resentful of her smothering, overly caring love.

Because women are so aware of their need to be nurtured and cared for, it is easier and more automatic for them to nurture and be caretakers. Men must work much harder to develop this attitude. As we explore the seven primary emotional needs, we will see consistently that what women need, they can give easily but men must work to develop, and what men need, men can give more easily but women must work to develop. The better we understand this concept, the more we can be understanding, tolerant, and forgiving of our partners when they don't fulfill our emotional needs. We can begin to appreciate that what is easy for us to give, may not be so easy for them to give.

THE FEMALE NEED TO BE UNDERSTOOD

The need to be understood is crucial if we are to fully understand ourselves. The more we share ourselves the more we are able to know ourselves. In order to know one's own needs, thoughts, and feelings, they must be communicated to and fully understood by another. To understand means to share or take on the thoughts and feelings of another, even if they are very different from your own.

Understanding is sharing and validating their point of view, rather than judging it as invalid. It is being willing to discover the valid reasons why they see and experience the world the way they do, instead of explaining to them why they shouldn't see it that way.

Again, this need to be understood is essential and primary to being female. When a man doesn't devote the time and attention necessary to understand a woman's feelings and needs, she can easily become confused and will have a greater tendency to overreact to situations. While a woman shares herself, if her man only waits passively, hoping that soon she will finish, he affects her in a way that actually adds to her confusion or upset.

When a woman is upset and confused and a man begins to judge her as nuts or crazy, it is very easy for this woman to begin doubting her sanity. It may well be that many women have been committed to mental hospitals simply because men were incapable of understanding and validating their upset feelings.

It is interesting to note that even the dictionary defines insanity as "behavior not based on rational, logical thought." If this were a valid definition, almost every woman would be diagnosed as insane. It is a woman's normal and quite sane nature to act on her instinctive and intuitive feelings, rather than always relying on her logical and rational thought processes.

For example, a woman does not decide to have a child just because she has weighed the pros and cons and concluded that it is a good idea. Even if she does think it is a good idea, her decision is supported by the intuitive *feeling* that it is time to be a mother. Relying on her intuition, she may do things just because she feels like it, and then later one may discover that there was also a good reason for her actions.

Conversely, men tend to make decisions based on logic and reasoning. Later on they may substantiate their decision by making sure it feels good. Just as a man's logic is fallible, so is a woman's intuition. Yet both are valid ways of knowing and deciding.

When women try to think like men and make logic more important than their feelings, they tend to become frustrated and confused, especially when they are upset and under pressure to make decisions. Generally when a woman is confused she is trying to figure something out. She needs instead to relax her mind and explore her feelings. Through going within to her intuition, she can then be decisive.

In a similar but complementary way, a man needs to mull over or think a problem through before he decides. Men who make their feelings more primary than their thoughts become indecisive and procrastinate. These immobilized men need to get out of their feelings and into their minds. One way a man benefits from listening to a woman (once he becomes competent at this art) is that he automatically gets to put his own feelings aside and use his thinking to understand what she is feeling and why she is feeling it.

For a man or a woman, the ideal place to make decisions is balanced in mind and feelings. When a man "listens to understand" he automatically becomes more balanced; a woman likewise becomes more balanced when she shares and is understood. However, this can only come about when he has learned the language women speak and she has learned to speak in a way that he can hear. Practicing the Love Letter technique (see Chapter 16) trains women to share their feelings in ways that men can understand. Writing also helps one to understand what one is feeling without the assistance of a listener.

Ultimately, understanding is essential to our female side. It aids us to discover the truth that lies within us and frees us to release negative feelings and discover our positive feelings. Through learning to communicate with positive, loving attitudes, we can cultivate the understanding that we need to resolve or, better yet, avoid conflict in a relationship.

THE FEMALE NEED TO BE RESPECTED

As one shares in a relationship, it is essential to maintain one's sense of self. Respecting one's partner means not trying to change or manipulate them, but rather, supporting them in being themselves and upholding their rights. Respect honors another's needs, wishes, values, and rights. To respect is to keep one's agreements and commitments. It is to give equal importance and sometimes greater importance to another.

The need to be respected is the need to be oneself in a relationship without giving up who one is. When a person feels respected they don't feel they have to earn their rights; they don't feel unworthy. The need for respect is the need for fairness as well as the acknowledgment that one is entitled. Respect recognizes that a person deserves support without having to earn it.

Because of their expansive nature, women are especially vulnerable to the need for respect. It is difficult for a woman to maintain her sense of self when she is expanding out to love a man. She needs him to constantly remind her of her rights and worthiness. When a man doesn't esteem who she is or respect her rights, very easily she becomes unsure of her rights and self-worth.

This is, of course, proportional to how open she is to this man. The more emotionally attached she is, the more she is susceptible to his level of respect. If a man is not respectful of a woman's needs, feelings, and rights, eventually she will have to close her loving feelings to him so that she can find herself again. Loss of sexual interest is common at this stage. Having sex with a man makes her vulnerable to his level of respect for her.

Men are usually quite unaware of how much women need to be respected, because when men are not respected they react very differently. When women are not respected they tend to give more to prove their worthiness. Men, however, are apt to become self-righteous and indignant about their needs, and to demand more than their share. They may even give less until they get what they deserve.

Unfortunately, as children we were all overly vulnerable to our parents' ability to respect us. If they did not respect our needs, it was hard for us to even know what we deserved. Girls are especially affected by how their father respects their mother and how much their mother respects herself.

As stated before, it is a common reaction for a male to feel even more worthy of respect when others don't respect him. Under certain circumstances he may become aggressive to earn respect. For example, most fights are started when a man is not feeling respected. It is also interesting to compare this concept with military basic training (which, although times are changing, is still designed primarily for the training of male soldiers). In boot camp, a trainee is systematically demeaned as worthless. This stimulates his aggression to prove he is worthy of respect. He sets out to earn his respect through increasing achievement. Gradually he feels that he is truly worthy of respect and appreciation.

While a man's first reaction to being disrespected is commonly aggression and dominance, a woman's is submission. A woman is most vulnerable to this submissive reaction when she is in a relationship with a man whom she loves. When as a result she comes to resent her partner, their roles may begin to switch. To compensate for her submissiveness she may become more dominant and demanding, while he becomes passive and dependent.

THE MALE NEED TO BE APPRECIATED

The primary need for appreciation is generally confused with the need for respect. To appreciate a person is to acknowledge that what they do or how they express themselves is of value to you personally, and that some benefit has accordingly been received. We need respect, on the other hand, to experience the validity of our needs, feelings, values, and rights. Appreciation is an act of evaluating, while respect validates.

Respect acknowledges that we are important, valuable, and useful; it says that who we are serves a valid purpose. A respectful attitude acknowledges our potential to be of service.

Appreciation acknowledges that the value of our actions, intentions, results, and decisions — ultimately, our value, usefulness, and importance — has been received. It is the feedback that tells a man his behavior has served a purpose. If he can feel appreciated, then he is much more willing to explore and understand why his actions have failed.

Without appreciation, a person begins to feel inadequate and incapable of giving support. Without respect, a person may feel unworthy of receiving support.

Appreciation allows us to experience our intentions, decisions, and actions as valuable. It is the necessary support that inspires us to repeat an action that works or motivates us to change what doesn't work. Even when we fail to achieve our desired results, there is always something in what we did that can be appreciated.

Without enough appreciation we lose our will to give. When a man fails to reach his goal, if he is unable to feel there was some value in his actions, he may give up. Or he may have the opposite reaction, and stubbornly repeat the action until he is appreciated.

Men are especially vulnerable to this need to be appreciated. If a man is not appreciated, he loses his motivation and becomes passive, lazy, weak, dependent, insecure and apt to procrastinate.

When a woman doesn't get appreciated her reaction is quite different. She tends to be even *more* motivated to earn appreciation. When her partner ignores her, her first impulse is to try harder to please him. Expecting men to do the same, she is confused when a man doesn't try harder to earn appreciation. She mistakenly assumes that he doesn't love her. When she is not getting enough from a man, she may begin to unconsciously or consciously manipulate him into giving more through withdrawing her appreciation. She is then confused and resentful when he reacts by giving even less.

When women are critical of a man's behavior they have no idea how damaging this is to his personal power. A man's painful response to not being appreciated is equivalent to what a woman experiences when a man judges or invalidates her feelings, needs, wishes, and rights. So when a woman begins to pick his behavior apart — criticizing the way he does things, correcting his thinking, challenging his decisions, and being dissatisfied with what he provides for her — a man loses his power. He retaliates with negative, demeaning judgments and disrespect, and withdraws from her. He is drained of the magical power that her loving appreciation gives him.

Conversely, when a man is being appreciated by a woman, nothing can get him down for long. Being appreciated is a male's primary need. It lets him know he can make a difference; he measures his worth through his ability to make a positive difference in the lives of others. Thus appreciation becomes a fuel that motivates his every action. Even when he is unable to resolve his problems at work, if he can come home to a grateful and happy wife his stress from work can be more easily released.

The strongest drive in a man is the desire to please a woman. This willful desire gives him power. It first manifests as the sex drive. Later, as he is able to blend it with the desire to love, respect, understand, and care for a woman, it becomes even more powerful. When a man can be appreciated physically, mentally, emotionally, and spiritually, then his power is maximum.

When Women Seek Appreciation

A man strives to earn appreciation to feel worthy of the right to make a difference. He seeks an opportunity to serve. However, respect, not appreciation, is a woman's primary need. A woman is misguided if she seeks appreciation to realize her worthiness of receiving support. Regardless of how much she has given, she deserves to be respected and honored for who she is. When a woman finds herself seeking to earn appreciation, many times she is overlooking her own needs.

For example, she makes too many sacrifices for her job, and then says she resents not being appreciated. What she really resents, however, is giving so much and then not being supported or respected. When she is not being respected, even if people do appreciate her it will never be enough. Certainly a woman in the work world needs and deserves appreciation for her hard work in the same way a man does. But to support her feminine side, she has a greater need for respect.

Especially in her personal relationships, a woman needs her values, needs, intuition, feelings, and wishes respected. Many times a woman will be strong at work and feel entitled to respect there, but when she falls in love with a man who ignores her, she begins feeling unworthy of asking for more support. This is a sign that her feminine side is deprived of love. She must fulfill her primary needs for understanding, validation, and respect. By learning to be feminine and get her feminine needs fulfilled, she will find that she can be even more successful at work.

By her nature, a woman is able to discover her true dignity and worthiness by "being" rather than by "doing." Through *being* loving, appreciative, accepting, trusting, respectful, understanding, and caring, she earns respect and becomes more graceful. In cultivating positive attitudes a woman manifests her feminine power, the power to attract the support she desires. This power can make her more successful in the workplace when combined with her masculine power to create results.

When a woman has developed more of her masculine than her feminine side, this evokes in most men a resistance. Men don't readily want to support her. Deep inside a man, his strongest desire is to fulfill a woman. He feels secure when he knows he can make a difference. When she appears too independent, a man feels there is nothing he can do to help her or fulfill her. He may be offended that she mistrusts his willingness to support her, and threatened because he cannot make a difference and be her hero. If she can slay her own dragon, then this knight in shining armor is out of a job.

When a woman is able to balance her feminine with her masculine energy, men are much more willing to support her, assist her, and work with her. Some women have a special grace that allows them a power to enlist others in their service. Men who have a balance of male and female are also able to evoke this kind of support.

The easiest place for a woman to develop for feminine side is in relationships that are personal rather than work oriented. When she then brings her feminine qualities into the work world, where she is competing with men to be appreciated, she is less threatening to men.

Developing her feminine side also enables a female to sustain her self-respect and avoid becoming a martyr. When a woman tries to prove her worthiness through *doing* (in an attempt to be appreciated) she finds herself burning out and never truly feels entitled to respect or support. Even if she does express her entitlement, she tends to do so in a resentful, bitter, and demanding tone. But through the qualities of her *being*, expressed through heartfelt loving attitudes, her presence can draw out from her man warmth, respect, and the desire to serve.

Her wish is truly his command. Yet she does not need to command, because he wants to serve and please her. It is the ungraceful woman who feels the need to command her man and all that results is power struggles and strife. In later chapters, we will explore further how a woman can develop her powers of "being."

When a woman actively seeks appreciation in a relationship, she unknowingly competes with her man for the opportunity to be of service. When he feels her competing he generally pulls out of the race, because he is not getting his fuel, which is her appreciation. He begins to feel drained in the relationship the more she demands his appreciation. In most cases he may be very grateful for her services, but her quest to earn his appreciation has the effect of making him lazy. When she is trying to earn merit badges, he is content to sit back and go into "idle."

This does not mean that a woman should never serve her man through her actions. But when she gives through actions, it must be without the demand for appreciation. *When she serves her partner it should be with the desire to express her appreciation, rather than earn his.*

Women unconsciously give with strings attached when they do not feel cared for, understood, and respected. These women do not understand that a woman's ability to truly appreciate a man's actions earns her the right to have her wishes fulfilled.

THE MALE NEED TO BE ACCEPTED

Acceptance is an attitude in response to being affected by some action or offering. When a person is "accepted," he is received willingly. This attitude cultures a man's belief in his abilities. When one's actions are unconditionally accepted then one feels free to explore how he can improve those actions. For this reason, acceptance is the basis of behavioral changes in a relationship.

Needing another person's acceptance does not mean that you are asking them to hold a passive, overlooking, slightly disapproving attitude toward you. It requires an affirmative belief that you are quite enough as you are, and that you are being favorably received. Gratitude is a symptom of acceptance.

This need to be accepted is especially important for men. Sometimes women appear to accept a man based upon his potential. This is not true acceptance. They are waiting for the day that he changes, and then they will be able to accept him. But men need to be accepted for who they are today, not who they will be tomorrow. A man will tend to become stubborn and resistant to change when he senses that he is not being accepted.

When a woman does not accept a man, she will feel compelled to change him. She will tend to offer suggestions that will assist him in changing, even when he has not asked. Some men are open to suggestions as long as they have requested them. But a man typically feels unaccepted when a woman is preoccupied with changing him or "improving" him. She imagines that she is respecting his needs by wanting to help; he feels disrespected, manipulated, and unaccepted. When a man does not feel accepted, he will unconsciously or consciously resist change.

A man is motivated to change by hearing and understanding a woman's feelings and needs. When he senses that his attempts to support her will be welcomed and appreciated, then he is easily inspired to fulfill her wishes. Her

193

acceptance ensures that if he fails he will not be disapproved of, but will be willingly received with some gratitude for his efforts.

Acceptance allows him to feel that who he is today is enough to please and satisfy his mate. With this kind of confidence he is more willing and able to give his partner the respect and understanding that she deserves. Most women do not know this secret about men. They mistakenly believe that the way to motivate a man to change is to complain, nag, or disapprove.

Whenever a man feels his imperfections are unaccepted, it may take days before he can come back to his true, giving self. One of the ways he unconsciously or consciously gets revenge for his partner's nonacceptance is to repeat the very behavior that she resists.

She does not understand this, because when a man is unaccepting of her behavior, one of her first reactions is to change or improve her behavior — if in doing so she can more successfully support her partner. In this respect women are much more secure than men; they can listen to feedback about ways they can improve their behavior without as much resistance, sensitivity, or defensiveness. Certainly a man can take feedback, but he needs to be feeling good about himself and, especially, to be willing to hear it. Rarely is it effective to give unrequested criticism or advice to a man.

The equivalent vulnerability in a woman is connected to her feelings. To improve or correct a woman's feelings when she has not asked is equally painful for her. A man is sensitive to correction when he is feeling his need to be accepted; if he already feels accepted, he can easily take the feedback. A woman is sensitive to feedback regarding her feelings when she is not feeling understood.

THE MALE NEED TO BE TRUSTED

Trust is a firm belief in the ability, honesty, integrity, reliability, justice, and sincerity of another person. The need to be trusted is the need for an acknowledgment that one's character is believed to be upstanding. When trust is absent that people consistently jump to the wrong, negative conclusion regarding a person's intent, whereas trust gives every offense the benefit of the doubt. Trust says, "There must be some good explanation why this happened." Trust grows in a relationship when each partner recognizes that the other never intends to hurt, but seeks only to support.

Trust is the third primary need for a man. To approach a man for support feeling trusting is to approach him with the feeling that he can and will help. On the other hand, to ask for help without trust is to reject him before he has a chance. When he is not trusted he will automatically begin to withdraw. Not only does lack of trust make it very difficult for him to respond, but it offends and hurts him.

It is a woman's trust in a man that draws him to her. When a woman is trusting of a man, she is able to draw out the best in him. Of course, if she trusts him to be perfect, he will let her down. But if she trusts that he can and will help, then he gets the message that he is of value and that his best is enough for her to accept and appreciate. Her trust will draw out of him increasing greatness. Through a woman's loving trust a man is supported in realizing his powers, abilities, skills, and talents.

When her partner is not supporting her, trust allows her to assume there must be some logical reason, and that when she lets him know her needs, he will respond to the best of his ability.

When a woman trusts a man, she feels safe to share her vulnerable feelings. If this man is indeed worthy of her trust, he will be greatly empowered by her trusting him to support her at such a delicate time. A trusting woman also intuits how much a man can support her, and doesn't demand or expect more. She is able to appreciate and accept what she gets. She does not naively go around sharing her vulnerabilities with just anyone. At the same time she does not withhold her vulnerable feelings from the people who are in truth trustworthy.

This issue of trust makes communication very difficult. Say a woman doesn't trust a man with her delicate feelings. If she decides to test the waters by sharing a more diluted version of her feelings, a man will sense he is not being trusted and begin to withdraw. She then concludes, "Since these diluted feelings turned him off, I'm sure glad I didn't share them all." If she had been more honest, he would have been more receptive.

A man will generally withdraw when a woman takes back a trust that she had previously bestowed. There is a time when a man is not put off by her lack of trust, especially at the beginning of a relationship. When at first a woman doesn't fully trust a man, it serves as a challenge for him to prove himself. If he has never tasted the nectar of her trust, he will patiently seek to prove his worthiness. But once she has opened herself to him and trusted him fully, and then due to some disappointment she begins to mistrust, then he experiences that something has been taken away. In an indirect way he is wounded emotionally.

Many times a woman will withhold her feelings because she is afraid her partner is not really interested. She rationalizes her uncommunicativeness by making some excuse for him, but inside she doubts that he would respond caringly to her feelings. She may end up denying her needs, thinking she has avoided rejection. In reality she has built a wall between him and her.

When a woman doesn't trust a man's loving intent and does not give him a chance to again be her knight in shining armor, she prevents him from being attracted to her. It is the trusting glimmer in a woman's eye that enchants a man to get out of his self-absorption and respond to her needs.

It is of course a woman's responsibility to find, again and again, that trusting part of her. But men have to share this responsibility for earning a woman's trust. If a man hurts a woman without apologizing, he is unknowingly building walls. Most of the time a man doesn't realize the importance of compassion or an apology. It is, however, a woman's responsibility to let a man know what she needs to hear.

Although a man's primary needs are to be loved, appreciated, accepted, and trusted, he also has the other primary needs — but to him they are secondary. In the same way a women primarily needs to be loved, respected, understood, and cared for, but she also has secondary needs to be appreciated, accepted, and trusted.

In review these male and female needs are listed below:

Male Primary Needs	Female Primary Needs
1. To be loved	1. To be loved
2. To be accepted	2. To be cared for
3. To be appreciated	3. To be understood
4. To be trusted	4. To be respected

Not only do we all have primary needs, but we also have primary and secondary natures. A man's primary nature is to complement a woman's primary needs. A woman's primary nature is to complement a man's primary needs.

When a man cultivates his caring, understanding, and respectful attitudes, he is able to be of maximum service to a woman. When a woman cultivates her feminine nature, she is able to be of maximum service to a man. In the next chapter we will explore how our primary natures complement each other.

CHAPTER THIRTEEN

The Secret of Complementary Natures

As men and women mature, they develop and express themselves differently. As a man matures and grows in personal power he primarily develops his caring, understanding, and respectful nature. He moves from being cold, calculating, self-centered, and distant to being fully present, warm, and human. As a woman matures and discovers her personal power she expresses more of her accepting, appreciative and trusting nature. She moves from being manipulative to being empowering, from being chaotic or frantic to being graceful and fluid.

When men and women learn to develop their complementary natures in balance, the potential for peace and love in a relationship as well as for dynamic growth is insured. When a man develops his caring, understanding, and respectful nature he automatically supports a woman's primary needs, that is to be cared for, understood, and respected. When a woman develops her nature to accept, appreciate, and trust she automatically supports a man's primary emotional needs. In learning to most effectively support each other, they are required to nurture those attitudes that increase their own personal power and maturity. Let's look at the three sets of complementary natures.

CARING AND TRUSTING

As a man becomes more caring he supports his partner in becoming more trusting. Vice versa, as a woman becomes more trusting she supports a man in becoming more caring. Many times a man is willing to support a woman much more than she could imagine. But when her reactions imply that he is unworthy of her trust or when she reacts to him as if he were the enemy, quite automatically he stops caring for her welfare. She then imagines him to be untrustworthy because he appears so uncaring.

Sometimes it may seem to a man that he is just too tired to care for or to respond to another's needs. This, however, is a misconception. It is not that he is too tired, but that he is too uncaring to have the energy. Energy, creativity, and power stem from caring. As a man begins to care more, he discovers new resources of energy and vitality within himself. When he is uncaring, he is easily exhausted and unmotivated. For example, if a man is not trusted in his relationship, he is depleted of energy and has little stamina. He may come alive at work, where his talents are trusted and relied upon, but when he returns home he is exhausted.

Look to a man as a "hero," and he is energized; view him with mistrust as "the villain" or "the problem," and he stops caring. When a man is considered to be the problem, then he cannot become the solution nor is he motivated to be supportive. As women learn to trust, giving their men the benefit of the doubt rather than jumping to the wrong or worst conclusions, they will find men becoming more caring and supportive.

One of the reasons a man can be so caring, considerate, and concerned in the beginning of a relationship is that a woman looks to him then with greater trust, adoration, and admiration. In a sense her trust gives him the power to be more caring. She draws it out of him. She can trust in the beginning because she has not yet been disappointed by him. She imagines he is different from the others.

This trust empowers him but cannot make him perfect. Because he is human he will inevitably let her down, and she will begin to doubt and mistrust. As she becomes more mistrustful he becomes more uncaring. An uncaring man has a greatly reduced capacity to give and tends to be self-centered. This person may have great energy reserves to serve himself, but in trying to have a relationship he can be easily drained and exhausted. He must learn to be less self-centered and more caring. A trusting woman who loves him can do wonders for his power.

To become more caring is, for a man, no easy task. It takes time and support. Unfortunately, women are easily impatient and intolerant of a man's tendency to be uncaring, because a female's primary nature is quite different. For her to be caring is very easy; it is not her big lesson to learn as a woman.

A woman's challenge in relationships is being able to trust and then, when she is disappointed, being able to appreciate and accept and trust again. Since childhood little girls have been nurturers and caretakers, while little boys are risk-takers. Just as it is difficult for men to learn to care for others, it is difficult for women to learn how to trust.

When a woman has been let down repeatedly in a relationship, she will tend to deny her trusting nature. Moreover, she soon begins to mistrust a man's love for her when he appears unmoved or detached in response to her upsets. In a similar way, all it takes for a man to stop caring is to be mistrusted or unappreciated for his efforts in a relationship. If he feels his ability to please his partner is doubted, then very quickly he stops caring about her happiness.

These two primary natures, caring and trust, are in themselves complementary. This explains the common scenario of the mother who is always worried about ten things at once and the father who stays glued to the couch, acting as though everything is fine. She is overly caring and thus worried; he is overly trusting and accepting, becoming passive.

Being overly caring, this mother can easily become too cautious or untrusting. In caring for a child she is apt to be overprotective. Just the opposite, in the name of being trusting, a father can easily be uncaring. He may be too trusting and mistakenly assume everything is fine when it is not. In this case he is not caring enough; his daughters especially get the message that Dad doesn't care.

The fact that it is difficult for a man to care and a woman to trust can create many problems unless these natural tendencies are fully accepted and understood. What commonly happens in a relationship is that he acts in an uncaring fashion and she immediately assumes that he is falling out of love with her. As she mistrusts his love he reacts by beginning to care less about giving to her. This in turn causes her to trust less, and he then cares less. In this way their love begins to wilt over time.

With an awareness of these differences, rather than move in a negative spiral, relationships can progress. Rather than restrict us, they can assist us in developing our creative powers. Let's explore how that looks.

Through expressing himself in a responsible and caring way, a man fulfills a woman's need to be responded to in a caring way. Because this is her primary need, she is capable of deeply appreciating him. As she begins to rely on his support, her trust increases. He then gets his needs for appreciation and trust fulfilled, and is inspired to be of even greater service. Her deep trust and need for him increases his capacity to care and give, encouraging him to be even more caring. As she receives more and more support she grows in her ability to relax and trust, which in turn enriches her creative powers.

To create this kind of relationship, a woman must be aware of how difficult it is for a man to respond in a caring way when her reactions say to him that he is not being trusted. Likewise, with knowledge of male and female differences it is easier for her to correctly interpret his detached behavior. She can be more accepting and forgiving of him when he forgets things or doesn't think of things that would come automatically to her.

Men with this understanding are able to more fully accept a woman's ongoing need to be reassured. Rather than make her wrong for it, he can realize that this is a very important way he can support her in her personal development and happiness.

With this knowledge it becomes easier to take responsibility for getting what you need. First of all, if a woman's partner doesn't seem caring, she doesn't have to take it so personally. Likewise, if a woman needs to be reassured, her partner doesn't have to let this frustrate him.

Also one can see clearly how they can receive more in a relationship. Rather than complain about what they are not *getting*, they can begin to focus on what they are not *giving* their partner. For in giving more to the other they are much more likely to receive back.

UNDERSTANDING AND ACCEPTANCE

Through expressing himself in an understanding way a man can consciously give more support to a woman. This support comes directly back to him, because the more understood she feels, the more she is able to accept and feel grateful for him. Through being understanding he helps her to be more centered and capable of accepting him just the way he is.

When she can cultivate a presence of acceptance, quite miraculously he will begin making changes in his behavior based on his increasing understanding of her needs. The secret truth is that men would be highly motivated to change to support their women if they really understood a woman's reality. Over time, as he is able to truly understand her feelings and needs, he can and will make solid changes to build a mutually supportive and empowering relationship.

As a man learns to "communicate to understand" rather than to correct or fix, he gradually masters the art of listening. In the beginning he will have to consciously resist the temptation to find fault with his partner's feelings. To do this he must realize that she is not asking for solutions, nor is she asking him to make her feel better. She is asking for his understanding of what she is going through. She is asking for some validation for being upset.

When a woman knows that her partner has not heard her, she is compelled to try to change or manipulate him. But when a woman feels heard, then she can relax and trust that things are not as bad as they seem. She can also appreciate all that there is to enjoy, rather than worry about what isn't working. When she feels understood she can better accept things as they are, knowing that she is not alone.

Many times men become so focused that they do not see all the day-to-day problems that gradually need to be solved. To the extent a man ignores them, a woman will feel overwhelmed by them. Simply because she sees them, she feels a responsibility to handle them; she will feel the pressure of solving them herself if she sees her partner oblivious of them. She feels alone with all this work and needs to share the burden of this awareness. Sometimes a man will make a woman feel immensely better just by listening and understanding the pressures she is feeling.

When a woman is upset, she does not demand that her partner solve all her problems before she can accept and appreciate him. Seeing her upset, though, he may think she is demanding solutions to her problems before she will feel better. After all, when a man is upset over a problem he generally can't feel better until it is solved or a concrete solution is at least planned. He mistakenly assumes she thinks the same way.

Women don't demand immediate solutions if they can feel heard. The female gender has an incredible capacity to accept imperfection and incompleteness if their feelings can be fully expressed, heard, and validated.

A woman's acceptance of imperfection can be one of man's most refreshing experiences. Most men have no idea that they have the power to draw this kind of support from a woman.

I will always remember the telling experience of driving my mother around Los Angeles. I wasn't familiar with the freeways and at some point I became completely lost. My mother didn't mind being lost and hardly noticed it; she was just enjoying the scenery. In a flash I noticed that something very special had happened. I felt as though I had been liberated from a jail sentence. I experienced the freedom and inner ease of being fully accepted.

In my intimate relationship at that time, I had been used to getting a disapproving look whenever I seemed absent-minded. In contrast, the drive with my mother was such a profound experience of feeling accepted, that in that moment I humorously decided to test any woman I ever considered marrying to see how she would react if I got lost.

Through learning to cultivate her inner acceptance, a woman insures that her man will be more motivated and capable of hearing and understanding her. As women learn to accept their men without trying to change them, slowly but surely men will become more understanding of a woman's unique needs and want to give more. And as men learn to understand women, they will begin to experience the incredible capacity that women have to forgive mistakes and accept a man just as he is.

RESPECT AND APPRECIATION

In a similar fashion, as a man learns to respect a woman's rights by acknowledging her equality in the relationship, he will experience such increased appreciation from her for what he gives to her. To respect a woman's rights, a man needs to honor her differences. She deserves the right to be imperfect and overreact at times without it being a major offense to him. Respecting her means knowing that she will have her times when she is overwhelmed or confused, and that she deserves not rejection, but his support when that happens.

Respecting her rights calls for including her in all decisions that will affect her in some significant way. When he makes a decision, he should then ask for input. His request can be as simple as "Is that OK with you" or "I would like to _____, how do you feel about that?" or "I think we should _____, what would you like?"

Whenever there is a disagreement, he will, out of respect for his partner, acknowledge a need to continue their discussion until a win/win solution can be discovered.

Respecting a woman involves taking the time to learn her special needs and, to the best of his ability, attempting to anticipate them without always depending on her asking.

Respecting a woman also means to support her in fulfilling her dreams and aspirations. Out of respect, a man acknowledges and supports a woman in feeling worthy, special, and entitled to assert herself and her feelings.

Feeling special is one of a woman's most important needs. Making a woman feel special is the essence of romance. For example, by bringing home a surprise flower for his wife, a man is respecting and honoring her femininity.

Commitment and sexual monogamy are probably the most powerful and basic ways a man respects femininity. Commitment demonstrates to a woman that she is most special to him. Sexual monogamy insures that they continue to share something very special and precious to both of them.

In return for this respect a woman will be able to relax. She will not feel a compulsion to prove herself as an equal, but will automatically feel his equal. She will not be preoccupied with receiving appreciation for what she does, but will be able to focus on appreciating and valuing her man and all that he does to make her life easier. As she serves her man, it will not be with strings attached — her every gift to him will be an expression of her appreciation and gratitude.

Appreciating a man means doing all she can to make his life easier in return. She creates a peaceful and beautiful environment in which he can feel important, valued, special, and competent to make her happy.

When a woman appreciates a man, she desires him sexually and takes time to make herself attractive to him. In a sense she treats him like a royal guest in her palace.

Out of her appreciation, a woman processes her feelings so that she can be in a good mood for him whenever possible. She makes an effort to communicate her feelings and needs before resentment can build up. Appreciation prompts her to let him know that when she is upset or overwhelmed, it is not his fault.

Appreciating a man means feeling genuine joy that this man is in her life. An appreciative woman refrains from expressing critical opinions unless her partner asks for this. Appreciating a man calls for actually receiving his support so that she doesn't become overly tired.

THE BENEFITS OF LOVING

Through learning to cultivate our primary natures, we insure that we are able to give and receive more support in our relationships. Although we have been focusing on romantic relationships, these principles apply to all relationships — professional, family, and friends. Understanding the complementary nature of emotional support gives us a new power to create more support in our lives. If we want more trust, then we need to be more caring. If we are needing to be cared for, we must work on trusting enough to reach out and ask for support.

When a man is not getting the support he wants, the first question he must ask is how can he be more caring, empathetic, understanding, validating, respectful, considerate, and compassionate. These seven qualities, the rainbow of his primary nature, spring from the three primary qualities of caring, understanding, and respect.

It is important to recognize that by developing these traits he is not just being supportive of his female partner; he directly benefits as well. Through expressing and developing these loving qualities combined with his basic masculine programming, he will become balanced and powerful. A man's most effective tool to de-stress and find his power is to act, think, or decide with a caring, understanding, and respectful attitude.

Sometimes all a man need do to feel better is to do something that is respectful of the needs of another. When he does something in support of another, he can make a difference. But if he is not respectful, then when he acts he will not make a positive difference. As a result he will feel less inspired to give and only willing to serve himself. In serving himself, he can never be fully satisfied.

A man must have a purpose to serve, a cause or direction. When he stops caring he begins to burn out. Prisoners of war have reported that it was thinking about people they cared about that gave them the strength to survive. When a man does not care he becomes lifeless, empty, and devoid of purpose.

When a man stops caring his life also becomes boring. To temporarily break free from his boredom he may begin taking big risks such as car racing, mountain climbing, breaking societal taboos, breaking laws, gambling, high-risk investing, etc. When a man is about to lose his life climbing a mountain, or about to lose all his money or his freedom, all of a sudden he begins to care about his life, his money, or his freedom. At such times he gets a huge adrenalin rush similar to a drug high. Unfortunately, this feeling of happiness is only a temporary illusion that leaves him even more bored, depressed, and dissatisfied. To create a more lasting happiness, he needs to cultivate relationships and develop his ability to care for other beings.

Through culturing loving relationships, a man doesn't have to take dangerous risks or create emergencies and drama to feel that he cares. As he listens to and understands the feelings of others, he becomes more aware of their differing needs and feels a greater desire to be of service. By respecting their needs, through service, he is able to feel he is enough, without competing to be better than, to have more than, and to do more than others.

When a man is married he has the opportunity to be even more empowered. In a special relationship, he cares more for his mate and family than anyone else. This special caring empowers him to be more giving and motivated in his life. If his marriage is not loving, it may equally disempower him.

In a similar way, when a woman practices loving her man with increasing appreciation, acceptance, and trust, not only does he benefit but she directly benefits. Trusting allows her to contact her inner source of power and self-esteem. Accepting lets her relax and culture her positive attitudes. Through appreciation she is able to open up and receive the abundance she deserves. In trusting, accepting, and appreciating, a woman gains the power to fully enjoy and delight in her life.

As a woman works to release her negative feelings in order to nurture her positive, loving attitudes, she is not only earning and evoking the support of others, but she is also connecting with herself.

As she gives love in this most important and difficult way, she begins to express the full rainbow of positive feelings that most fully support a man. They are trust, approval, acceptance, recognition, appreciation, acknowledgment, and admiration. When a woman can feel these attitudes, a man feels graced by her love. She likewise blossoms and is able to fully actualize who she truly is at the core of her being.

In the next chapter we will explore more fully how men and women can develop their inner power to fulfill their dreams and make a difference in their lives.

CHAPTER FOURTEEN

Male and Female Empowerment

Power means "to be able." When your power is great you *are able* to manifest your desires, wants, wishes, and needs. There are basically two sides of power; they originate respectively from your masculine and feminine sides. When you develop both sides, then your power is the greatest.

Your masculine power is the ability to create results. Your feminine power is the ability to attract opportunities and support. While masculine power is expressed through effort and action, feminine power is manifested through attracting or drawing in support without lifting a finger; it is effortless.

One kind of power without the other is useless. Listed below are some simple examples of *expressed* masculine power combined with *suppressed* feminine power. In each example there is the ability or power to create results, but without the opportunity or the power to attract support.

1. An author may be able to write a great book, but if no one reads it, the book is useless.
2. A teacher may have tremendous wisdom to share, but if he has no students, then his ability to teach is useless.
3. A person may have developed many skills, but if he or she has had no opportunity to use those skills, then he or she is powerless.
4. A person may be willing and capable of having a great relationship, but if they can't find the right person, they are powerless.
5. A person may work really hard, but never get a break. As a result, work feels like a grind.

At the other extreme is the person who has denied their masculine power but has developed their female power to attract opportunity and support. Some examples follow:

1. A person may attract the partner of their dreams, and then go off in search of another partner.

2. A person may have all the connections and support to be successful but they are too afraid to try; they procrastinate or hold themselves back.
3. A person may have the support they need, but be too undisciplined to develop their skills.
4. A person may attract wisdom or access intuition, but not believe it or make use of it.
5. A person may be "lucky," and then waste their good fortune.

The masculine power to create results is associated with many distinct characteristics. Masculine power is aggressive, assertive, autonomous, rational, purposeful, efficient, responsible, confident, decisive, precise, practical, competent, strategic, analytical, logical, focused, bold, disciplined, willful, and empowered by serving. Through these characteristics your masculine power achieves results, mainly via intention, thinking, and doing. You can increase your masculine power to accomplish your goals, especially by developing positive *strategies*.

Female power is vulnerable, centered, receptive, intuitive, fulfilled, nurturing, joyful, enthusiastic, spontaneous, graceful, idealistic, beautiful, positive, feeling, emotional, open, gentle, relaxed, supportive, and empowering to others. Through these positive characteristics of your feminine power you are able to attract support in particular by being true to yourself, loving, and intuitive. Especially through developing a positive *attitude*, you can increase your power to attract support and opportunity.

As displayed in the chart below, each masculine characteristic has a corresponding feminine characteristic. Combining these complementary powers in harmony enables us to develop and express our full and unique human potential.

Masculine Characteristics	Feminine Characteristics
aggressive	vulnerable
assertive	centered
autonomous	receptive
rational	intuitive
purposeful	fulfilled
efficient	nurturing
responsible	joyful
confident	enthusiastic
decisive	spontaneous
precise	graceful
practical	idealistic
competent	beautiful
strategic	positive
analytical	feeling
logical	emotional
focused	open
bold	gentle

disciplined	relaxed
willful	supportive
empowered by serving	empowering to others

Every person is a unique blend of these different complementary powers. Just as a seed has within it the potential to be a unique and special flower, so also each person is special and has a unique potential. This potential is in no way limited by gender.

You are only limited when as a child you did not get support for the full development of your unique masculine and feminine potential. By being loved, a child is able to naturally unfold and develop both its masculine and feminine powers. If you were not supported this way during your early years, as an adult you can still give yourself the support you need to find balance. It is never too late to have the perfect childhood. First let's explore how one's childhood affects their inner balance of powers, and then we will consider how you can make up for your past.

POTENTIAL AND EXPRESSION OF PERSONAL POWER

Lisa was born with the potential to be about 50 degrees assertive (male power) and 50 degrees vulnerable (female power). As a child she felt safe both to assert herself and to be vulnerable. In this loving environment, she matured and grew up in a balanced way. Both her 50 degrees of assertiveness and 50 degrees of vulnerability got the same support to develop.

As a result, Lisa is equally in touch with her male and female sides. For example, she feels comfortable asserting herself and comfortable crying. Men are not threatened when she asserts herself with confidence, because they also detect her sensitivity. When she cries, she is respected and supported by others.

Lisa's ability to freely access her male and female powers is the ideal. It develops when as children we are loved and supported in the ways that we need. When we are not fully loved, things turn out differently.

Let's look at two more examples of potential and expressed power. Debbie's family was not so loving as Lisa's. When Debbie was born she also had the potential to express about 50 degrees of assertiveness and 50 degrees of vulnerability. But each time Debbie would express her assertiveness, she was put down or rejected in some way. She was told to be sweet and nice, and not be so demanding. Because it was not safe for Debbie to express her masculine side, she gradually suppressed her assertiveness by about 30 degrees. In suppressing her assertiveness she decreased her personal power. As a result, Debbie is not in touch with her inner masculine power. She feels insecure and overly dependent on others. It is extremely difficult for her to ask for support.

Amy, unlike Lisa and Debbie, was born with unequal amounts of assertiveness and vulnerability. Amy had only about 20 degrees assertiveness and 80 degrees vulnerability to work with. But similar to Lisa, her childhood was loving and supportive. As she grew up both her masculine and feminine powers developed in harmony. Through the power of her vulnerability Amy was able to empower, motivate, and inspire others to support her and give her the reassurance she needed from time to time.

Although Amy only had 20 degrees of assertiveness, her 80 degrees of vulnerability made up the difference. She was just as powerful in manifesting her wishes as Lisa, who had 50 degrees of assertiveness. The point this example makes is that our greatest power comes from the free expression of our male and female powers, regardless of how much of each we have.

This is borne out by our examples of Debbie and Amy. As adults, both had only 20 degrees of assertiveness. However, Debbie, who had suppressed her 50 degrees of assertiveness to 20 degrees, did not have the 80 degrees of vulnerability that Amy had to support her 20 degrees of assertiveness. Debbie was nearly incapable of asking others for support. When she did ask, she rarely received the kind of support that Amy would. Debbie's 20 degrees of assertiveness was ineffectual because she was suppressing her masculine powers by 30 degrees. Amy's 20 degrees of assertiveness was all she needed to be fully powerful, because she wasn't suppressing herself.

Another important conclusion from these examples is that the amount of assertiveness or masculine power you have does not determine your ability to get what you want. Your ability to fulfill your desires is directly proportional to how much you are expressing who you truly are and not suppressing some part of your inner power.

It is easy to confuse the concept of power with how much of one quality a person has developed. Maximum power comes from the harmonious expression of both sides. A person may be quite centered and balanced, yet have unequal amounts of masculine and feminine energy. From this centered place they can express and develop their full potential.

DEVELOPING THE LUCKY TOUCH

Another way to describe feminine power is to define it as "luck." Some people work hard and develop skills but do not succeed, because they never get a lucky break. These people have not developed their female power. They have not formed the right relationships to support their success. They do not have the right "connections." Knowing the "right people" and "being in the right place at the right time" are attributes of feminine power. In other words, feminine power creates the opportunities to express our skills and abilities, so that we can succeed in producing the results we desire.

In modern society, we generally do not recognize luck as an attribute that we can acquire. It is not widely realized that by culturing a loving, positive, and fulfilled attitude, "luck" or "grace" can be earned and developed.

In our society, male power is recognized and respected much more than female power. While results achieved through hard work are obviously earned, results achieved through luck seem more mysterious and uncharted. Thus for many people, this abstract and intangible feminine power is not respected. If they cannot see it or measure it, then to them it does not exist. Female power goes unrecognized and hence undeveloped.

Unfortunately, this societal blind spot leads those who are more lucky in life to feel their success is unearned. Because they have not had to suffer as much or work as hard as others, they begin to lose confidence and feel less worthy. As they lose their positive attitude, their luck decreases.

Female power needs to be cultivated through healing our hurts and resentments and through positive attitudes and visualization. Luck automatically develops when we create supportive and loving relationships. If, on the other hand, our relationships are filled with sacrifice and secret resentments — no matter how loving they appear on the surface — they do not generate female power. Instead they weaken us and our success.

If female power manifests as luck, then male power may be considered "skill." One may work hard but if he is not skilled, he will not succeed. Even so, if a person develops their skill, their complete success is not assured. For example, a person may create tremendous wealth, but because they have not also developed their female power, they cannot enjoy their wealth or have loving relationships. To avoid the pain of their emptiness, they compulsively seek to achieve more in a desperate attempt to feel fulfilled. Their success is never enough.

On the other hand, another person may have more luck than skill. When they set out to achieve a goal, they start out lucky. But because they have not developed a skill through the hard work of discipline and practice, they do not follow through and fully develop their potential to be successful.

It may also be the case that a person with abundant female power who has denied his or her masculine power will receive opportunities to be successful, but never use them effectively. In addition a person with more female than male power may become too content or fulfilled, and lose their motivation to do what they are here to do. They do not actualize their inner potential.

To be fully effective and creative, both our male and female powers need to be developed and expressed. When they are not, various negative side effects may occur. In a later part of this chapter we will discuss the symptoms of suppression. But first we will explore how to create balance and develop our male and female powers, even if in childhood we didn't get the support we needed.

THE SECRET OF CULTURING OUR INNER POWER

A surprising benefit of having loving and mutually supportive relationships, especially with the opposite sex, is the spontaneous and simultaneous development of both our male and female powers. *By practicing loving attitudes as an adult, the various suppressions and imbalances acquired during childhood can be healed and balanced.*

Generally speaking, to develop a particular inner power we need to focus our awareness on that power and gradually cultivate it through applying it in our life. If a man focuses on expanding his masculine powers, those powers increase. Unfortunately, in the process of developing his masculine power, his complementary feminine power may be suppressed.

It is difficult to develop opposite qualities at the same time. To express "coolness" without suppressing one's "warmth," for example, is no easy task. It is especially difficult if, as children, we were not loved enough to support this simultaneous development. For a man to develop his masculine side, commonly his feminine side will be sacrificed. On the other hand, if a man focuses on developing his feminine side, then that power will increase, but his masculine power may be overshadowed and stifled.

Because male and female powers are complementary opposites, it is difficult for a male to develop both sides of his power simultaneously. If he chooses his male side his female side suffers; if he chooses his female side his male side suffers.

For example, it can be complicated to work on being aggressive (male power) and also work on being yielding (female power); it is hard to focus on being assertive yet, simultaneously, to try to be vulnerable; it is difficult to develop objectivity and learn to be in touch with subjective feelings at the same time; it is a juggling act to be work oriented and cultivate loving relationships at the same time; it can prove challenging to be giving and yet also be receptive; and so on.

In a similar way, when a woman focuses on developing and expressing her masculine qualities, her feminine powers may easily be overshadowed and suppressed. And if she focuses exclusively on developing her female side, her male power may remain undeveloped, leaving her overdependent. It is difficult for her to simultaneously develop the hardness of her male powers and the softness of her female powers.

One way to slowly evolve and balance your masculine and feminine powers is to develop one, then the other. By alternating back and forth, by being hard sometimes and soft at other times, you stand a chance to be fully integrated and whole. A more effective way, however, to nurture and balance your inner powers is *simultaneous* development.

During childhood, simultaneous development occurs naturally and spontaneously when one is fully loved and supported by their parents, family, and friends. Because to some extent we all grow up in an unloving, confusing, and threatening world, most people squelch and distort many of their inner powers during childhood.

To develop both sides simultaneously, a child primarily needs caring, trust, understanding, acceptance, respect, and appreciation. Without this abundant love and support, children will repress their inner powers to various degrees. There are basically three different conditions that lead to suppression.

THREE MAJOR CAUSES OF SUPPRESSION

The first condition is a lack of safety. If a child does not feel safe to be who they truly are, they will suppress themselves. For example, if Billy is different from his father in a certain way, Billy may withhold that certain part of himself to be like Dad. If little Johnny sees Mom rejecting Daddy, Johnny will not feel safe to be like Daddy, so he will automatically put a damper on many of his masculine characteristics. Little Jane, who is more assertive than Mom, may feel that she has to be like Mom to be loved. As a result Jane stifles her natural assertiveness. Even if Jane is completely accepted by Mom, if she is not fully supported by the kids at school, she may restrain her true self and become more unassertive like Mom. There are literally thousands of situations that could make it feel unsafe to develop one's self.

The second condition that leads to suppression is a lack of nurturing support to help one deal with emotional pain. As a child develops, their masculine and feminine characteristics naturally emerge and are expressed. Should this emergence be met with rejection, the child feels pain. If this emotional pain is not safely expressed, heard, and understood, then the characteristic associated with the emotional pain may be suppressed until a later date when that pain is healed. Through healing the pain of our past, a tremendous amount of suppressed power is awakened.

When Timmy asserted himself to make friends and was rejected, his feelings were hurt. He felt scared that he was somehow inadequate and unworthy. He felt like crying. He needed reassurance that he was normal and that he could make new friends. At home, however, Timmy didn't have the kind of nurturing support that would allow him to cry and share his pain. His parents didn't try to understand why he didn't have more friends. Instead of opening up and sharing his hurt, he just pretended that everything was fine. Denying his pain, Timmy told himself that he didn't need friends and that he was better than the other children.

Because Timmy was unable to share the pain he felt when he was rejected, his power to assert himself weakened. Whenever we are hurt, some part of us has failed or been rejected. If that part is not healed, it gets suppressed, and our power weakens.

The third condition that leads to suppression is lack of appropriate role models. For the different male and female characteristics to develop, a child needs to see or experience them being expressed successfully. When a father is aggressive in being supportive of others, then a child is inspired to develop their inner aggression. When a mother is yielding, flexible, graceful, and capable of getting what she wants, her child learns to successfully express their inner yielding characteristics.

But if the father is abusive with his aggression, then the child may suppress their own aggression so as not to abuse others. If the mother is manipulative in her yielding, then the child may suppress their own feminine power to be soft and yielding.

For a youngster to fully develop their inner powers, they need the support to make a lot of mistakes in the process. They need nurturing to heal the pain of their failures, and they need good role models to reveal to them how to be successful.

In addition, ideally the child needs to experience both parents supporting each other, as well as themselves. For example, if Mom is not loving herself, or Dad is not loving Mom, then a little girl's feminine side will not feel *fully* loved even if both Mom and Dad appear to be loving the little girl. In this same situation, a little boy's feminine side will also not feel loved and supported. Neither child would feel fully "safe" to develop their feminine powers.

Likewise, if Dad is not loving himself, or Mom is not loving Dad, their child's masculine side will not feel *fully* loved and supported even if both Mom and Dad appear to love their child. Their little girl or boy may not feel safe to develop their masculine powers. With each of the above examples, "safety," both physical and emotional, is the prerequisite for a child to develop their masculine and feminine sides simultaneously.

In addition to a lack of love and support, there are many other reasons a child might suppress different aspects of their masculine and feminine powers. Some of these reasons are genetic programming, birth order, number of boys and girls in the family, availability of the parents, peer pressure, cultural conditioning and beliefs, financial security, survival conditions, the political environment, previous life experiences, environment and weather conditions, and education. Let's briefly consider each of the above additional factors.

ADDITIONAL CAUSES OF SUPPRESSION

Natural Predisposition or Genetic Programming

Regardless of their sex, children come into this world with special gifts and powers that are either male or female. Due to these natural, inborn tendencies, youngsters will lean in the direction of developing either their masculine or feminine powers. Also, at different times of their lives, predetermined hormonal changes will greatly affect the natural balance of masculine and feminine powers. If a child's inner balance is different from that of their parents, he or she may unconsciously suppress themselves to be like their parents.

If, for example, a girl is born with more assertiveness than her mother, she could easily suppress that power to be like Mom. In doing so, she would disconnect from her inner masculine power.

On the other hand, she may develop that assertiveness, but at the cost of rejecting her Mom or her feminine vulnerability. In this case her life will be filled with struggle. She will become more masculine and reject her feminine characteristics. She will hide her vulnerability from others and reveal only her masculine side. By rejecting her feminine side, she loses the ability to develop both sides. For simultaneous development, her vulnerability or feminine side needs support to develop.

Regardless of her inner balance of male and female, a girl primarily needs caring, understanding, and respect. This is her first requirement. If this is not met, the appreciation, acceptance, and trust that nurtures the development of her male side will never be enough. Her male side will develop while the female one will be suppressed.

When a girl or woman has a lot of innate assertiveness, others may easily assume that she doesn't need caring reassurance; her assertiveness overshadows her vulnerability. While her assertiveness demands acceptance, trust, and appreciation, her feminine vulnerability requires understanding, caring, and respect. Unless she gets these feminine needs fulfilled, all the acceptance, appreciation, and trust that her male side receives will never be enough. In her struggle to be loved, her female side will starve.

It is important to note that even if a girl is born with many inherent male powers, that doesn't mean she is more boy than girl. On the surface she may not appear to have the same primary needs as other girls. But deep inside she is feminine, and if she is to grow in balance and wholeness, those needs must be understood and supported to the same extent as other little girls whose feminine vulnerability is more obvious.

Because some women are born much more assertive, aggressive, autonomous, etc., than their mothers, they relate more to their fathers. In assuming they are like their fathers and thereby seeking support for the development of their male powers, they can easily become unaware of their feminine needs to be who they are.

While their masculine powers develop, their female side suffers. These women may be successful in business but feel an emptiness at home. They do not recognize what they are missing by denying their vulnerability. To heal they must honor their feminine needs.

Just as a girl may be born with more masculine characteristics than her mother, a boy may be born with more female traits than his father. To win his dad's love, he may unconsciously seek to be like his father by rejecting his feminine powers. This boy will never develop his full potential unless he is able to feel safe in also developing his feminine characteristics.

On the other hand, this boy may instead reject his father and bond more closely with his mom. He will experience a greater need for caring, understanding, and respect. Unfortunately, because he has rejected his male side he may not consciously experience his needs for appreciation, acceptance, and trust.

Even though he may have more feminine qualities than his father, brothers, and friends, he still has the same primary needs as other little boys. Primarily he needs trust, acceptance, and appreciation if he is to express and develop both his masculine and feminine powers.

If he feels he is not trusted, accepted, and appreciated, then it will not appear safe to express and develop his masculinity. For example, if his mother is too protective, too corrective, or too giving, he may suppress his masculine powers and become overly dependent. Though he continues to express and develop his feminine side, he will never feel he has received enough support or that he is good enough. Before he can let in the healing powers of understanding, caring, and respect, his masculine characteristics first need to be loved and supportive with trust, acceptance, and appreciation.

Regardless of their individual balance of masculine and feminine powers, a boy primarily needs trust, acceptance, and appreciation, and a girl needs caring, understanding, and respect. Given that this primary condition is satisfied, a boy with more feminine attributes and powers will need more caring, respect, and understanding than another boy with less of a feminine nature. Likewise, a girl with more masculine characteristics will need more appreciation, acceptance, and trust than another girl with fewer masculine qualities, but first her feminine side needs its support.

In conclusion, natural predisposition does determine the amount of masculine and feminine energies within us. The family environment, however, either gives shape to the balanced expression of our potential, or distorts it through the lack of appropriate love and support.

Birth Order

First-born children tend to feel more responsible and grown up. This can cause a child to either suppress their feminine side so as to become more adult and responsible, or the child may rebel and reject the responsible masculine powers in order to stay a child.

The youngest child frequently has the hardest time trying to develop their masculine side, because they seldom have to be responsible at a young age. This position is generally easiest to handle for a girl, while the first-child position is easier for a boy to handle.

The middle child tends to be more balanced. He or she gets to be both responsible for the younger child and dependent on the older.

Number of Boys and Girls in the Family

If two boys are born successively, they tend to polarize. If one is more masculine, the other is apt to express more feminine and suppress the masculine. The younger tends to suppress his masculine side because it is not safe to compete. Each time he does, it is taken as a threat by the older brother, and the younger may lose love or be punished in some way.

If, however, the first child perceives his father being jealous of Mom's time and attention, that child may suppress his masculinity. Then when another child comes along, this next child may polarize to get Mom's love in a different way. By seeking love in different ways, siblings avoid being a threat to one another.

When there is a series of same-sex children, there will be pressure of the next child born to be the sex that is still missing in the family. For example, Martha was the third girl. Her birth so disappointed her father that he became depressed. This deeply affected the little girl. She tried so hard to be like a good little boy for her daddy. Then a fourth child came, and it was the boy he had wanted. In a flash Martha lost her daddy's attention. This was even more devastating because she had suppressed her feminine side to be loved, and then she lost his love to her brother. Martha the adult is now gradually recovering her lost little girl and giving her the love she needs.

Availability of Parents

When parents are both too busy working, a child will tend to justify their parents' lack of availability and put them on a pedestal. Much of the heartache this child feels from being isolated is denied. They lead a rather mediocre life, because suppressed along with their feelings of abandonment are all their masculine and feminine powers. They may even claim to have had a perfect childhood. But at a subconscious level, this person experiences into adulthood the pain of neglect and rejection.

Rich's parents loved him, but they were rarely home. In addition, every year or two his family would move to another town. Rich had given up on making new friends or joining teams because he always knew he would be leaving soon. It was unbearable to form attachments and then have to break them so quickly.

One of the ways Rich handled this pain was to keep reminding himself that his parents loved him. Since his parents were his only source of love, he felt he could not complain or resent their neglect. Being a child, he also felt he didn't have the right to be upset or unhappy about the moves and his isolation. Instead, he justified and rationalized his situation.

Rich appeared bright and cheerful at all times. He was the perpetual good boy. That was the mask he put on to win love. He learned to keep on this mask until he didn't know the real person inside. The price he paid was that he didn't know what he wanted in life, or what he felt. He was numb.

It wasn't until Rich took a number of my weekend seminars that he realized that even though his parents had done their best, he was hurt and he was angry with them. He was sick and tired of being a good little boy. He started to feel rage and resentment. Then he was able to feel and share his hurt. After that, he was able to forgive his parents and heal the little boy inside.

As a result of this healing, Rich was able to give up being a caretaker for everybody else and take care of himself. He started to feel inner peace and calm for the first time in his life. Through recovering his feelings, he was able to feel alive again — sometimes happy and sometimes not, but at least alive.

When parents are not available for a child and there is no one to share his or her feelings with, then their feelings get repressed along with their aliveness and power.

Peer Pressure

During its first seven years, a child is primarily conditioned by its parents or primary caretaker. Then from around seven years old through puberty, he or she starts forming friendships that can add a whole new layer of suppression.

As a little boy, Stevie bonded with his mother and suppressed his masculine side. Later when he spent time with other kids, he felt pressured to be aggressive, daring, and assertive — in other words, to be much more masculine. To win his friends' acceptance he would act like them. But then he felt he had to hide this new "bad" person from his mother. Not only was he pretending with his friends, but hiding from his mother.

Hiding anything produces toxic shame. Lying, secrets, and pretense are the most destructive aspects of growing up. To cope with the shame of hiding the truth, we may even suppress our shame. Held on to in this manner, it eats away at our self-esteem. Until we get help to open up, share all our secrets, and receive the love we did not get in childhood, we will be prisoners of our past.

Sharing secrets and letting go of false images formed by peer pressure or shameful abusive experiences opens a door that allows the suppressed aspects of our masculine and feminine powers to come out. Ultimately we can learn to do this from our parents. If they are truly open with each other, then a child will naturally feel safe to open up rather than suppress.

Cultural Conditioning and Beliefs

Our cultural beliefs are programmed into children before they have the ability to know what is right or wrong. The child has no choice. For example, when thousands and thousands of times a little boy sees cowboys killing without remorse, he learns that real men or "heroes" don't show feelings or even have feelings.

When TV repeatedly portrays women in traditional roles as happy and satisfied, a little girl learns again and again that it is not safe or OK to be unhappy. She cannot ask for more or assert herself. She cannot go after what she wants, but must wait for it. She must be completely dependent on a man. She learns she does not have the right to be upset — and if she does get upset, it must be resolved before the commercial break.

These are only a few examples of the many ways we are misguided as children to limit ourselves according to our sex. Millions of times while growing up a child receives messages defining and restricting society's vision of how men and women should be.

Financial Security

If the parents are poor, or the family is very large, it is quite common for a child to not feel the right to ask for or have more. Accordingly, the child may conclude that he or she is not entitled to feel disappointed, sad, angry, or hurt. If the youngster feels dissatisfied, it is made to feel selfish and bad.

To avoid the punishment of this guilt, the child may cope by suppressing itself to hold back the upset feelings. When a boy smothers his upset feelings he will tend to extinguish his connection with his feminine powers. A little girl in the same situation, equally unable to share upset feelings, will be even more lost to herself. In curbing her feelings she not only suppresses her feminine power, but also her identity.

As a result of losing her identity, she feels unworthy of expressing her feminine needs to be heard, understood, and cared for. As the girl matures, she may move into a caretaker role, giving to others what she feels unworthy of receiving. She learns she can't trust others; she has to go it alone. Feeling unworthy of being loved, yet dependent on others, she will then settle for much less than she deserves.

Poverty is certainly painful for little boys, but much more devastating for little girls. A boy has a better chance to build his self-esteem by working hard and doing it alone. This is why we hear many more stories of the poor boy who becomes rich. This is not to say he is not wounded by this experience, but in a different way.

Part of growing up for a boy is to separate from Mom and go his own way. A girl separates too, but in another way. She sees how she is like her mother, and then how she is different. Because they share certain basic female characteristics, being like her mother helps her to know herself. To a boy, however, the journey of knowing himself requires seeing how his masculinity is different from his mother's femininity. It is a process of separating from her.

In separating from his family, a young man may prove himself by becoming wealthy and developing much of his masculine power, but his feminine side remains weak. To become rich he may be prone to abusing others in the process. He is disrespectful of others or the law. He cares only for himself.

This man tends to feel a void within because he can't surrender and relate in an intimate way. Deep inside he desperately seeks to be loved, to be held, and to belong to someone. He is as much a prisoner as if he were locked in a box and chained up. To connect to his feminine side, he would have to break down and feel all the pain he escaped by working hard and getting rich. He cannot do this alone. This man cannot relax and be intimate unless he gets help to feel his pain, share his feelings, and release his suppressed feminine side. He must humble himself enough to reach out for love and help. Otherwise, he is incapable of giving a woman what she deserves.

A woman must be very careful of a man like this. Either he may isolate her, or when he does open up, he may feel so much leftover anger at his parents that he displaces it onto her. He needs to share his feelings through group work in seminars or through group counseling. By hearing the pain of others he will gradually be able to hear and heal his own pain, and thus to become a whole man.

Survival Conditions

Being raised during a war creates in a child the fear that Daddy and Mommy could die and that the child would be left alone. Our deepest fear, the possibility of abandonment, is at the root of all our anxieties. The real likelihood that Mommy or Daddy might die in the war is too great a pressure for most children. The child will then form this lasting belief: "I am not capable of taking care of myself. I will never get the love I need. I am powerless to get what I need."

Growing up during a war will certainly generate these kinds of anxieties, but any form of danger to a parent can prompt these fears. Also, if one parent is abusive of the other, these deep feelings of abandonment may also emerge.

When a child feels abandoned or sees the possibility of abandonment, the same insecure feelings may arise. Unfortunately, at that time we are very impressionable. Subconscious beliefs may form that will last a lifetime unless they are healed. Even as an adult, when we are no longer dependent on parents to survive, the child inside will continue to feel, "I cannot take care of myself, I cannot get the love I need."

Whenever you are feeling abandonment anxieties, here is a helpful affirmation to write or repeat: "My little boy (or girl) inside is afraid of being left alone. He is scared because he can't take care of himself. Little children are not supposed to take care of themselves. When I was a child I was powerless, but now as an adult I am capable of getting the love I need. I am no longer powerless to take care of myself. I can get the love I need. I can take care of myself."

To help yourself heal anxieties rooted in your childhood, you also may wish to order some of my healing tapes (listed in the back of this book). These will allow you to connect with and heal the inner child that was wounded and suppressed in your youth.

Political Environment

If you were to grow up in a country where free speech is not allowed, you would automatically develop a deep fear of being taken away if you said the truth. This kind of fear blocks us from being real and consequently our inner powers become suppressed. When we cannot freely express ourselves, our ability to develop our full potential is greatly limited.

Previous Life Experiences

Traumatic experiences from our past that have not been dealt with will continually seek an opportunity to be expressed so that we can be heard and healed. When painful feelings are suppressed, it is especially our female side that suffers. Our ability to grow is greatly restricted until our past is healed.

Chapter 16 describes the Love Letter technique. This technique allows you to unfold your full potential by healing the pain that is blocking the spontaneous development of your male and female powers.

Environmental and Weather Conditions

In teaching seminars around the world I have noticed distinct emotional differences associated with colder climates as opposed to warmer climates. People in colder climates tend to have more control over their emotions. This gives greater freedom to their masculine sides. When people in warm climates get emotional, they are likelier to lose control.

As a result family abuse is much more prevalent in warmer regions. A child witnessing a parent lose control not only fails to learn how to maintain self-control, but begins to live in fear. Once the parents' feelings are out, however, they tend to express more love and affection.

In colder climates people are more reserved and guarded. They are not as wounded by others, but their self-made prison creates its own pain: They hold onto their feelings. They may intellectually forgive the transgressions of others, but in their hearts they still carry their pain and resentment. What can open their hearts is the awareness of pain they are feeling and the knowledge that it is self-induced.

Education

Children learn to express themselves by watching their parents. By age seven they have subconsciously learned how to react, how to share, how to pretend, how to manipulate, and how to express or suppress their masculine and feminine powers and characteristics.

When a little boy sees his dad being aggressive and assertive in serving his family, that is how he learns to be masculine. When he sees his father loving his work, that is what he will strive to create in his own life. His masculine side flourishes.

When a daughter sees her mother being vulnerable, responsive, loving, and graceful, she learns how to develop her feminine side. When she witnesses her mother loving herself, being real, and having a positive, trusting attitude, she learns the power of her own femininity.

When he does not know his father or another positive, strong male role model, a boy cannot find his masculinity. If he has not been shown how to be a confident, creative, and loving man, it is difficult for him to attain his masculine powers. This is something a woman cannot teach him. One of the worst things that happened to suppress the natural development of masculine power took place when the Industrial Revolution forced fathers out of their homes to go away to work. Boys lost access to their fathers as role models for the expression of their masculine characteristics.

Not only did boys suffer, but little girls too. With fathers out of the home, girls could not learn how Mommy and Daddy related. They only saw their parents when they were tired and worn out from the day's work. When a young girl cannot see her mother relating to a man and the world in a positive and loving way, then it is much more difficult for her to fully develop.

SIMULTANEOUS DEVELOPMENT

Regardless of how we have suppressed ourselves in the past, we *can* learn to fully express and develop our masculine and feminine powers. Through creating loving adult relationships with the opposite sex, we can accomplish the simultaneous development of our male and female powers.

When a man can favor his male powers, but relate in a caring, understanding, and respectful way with the opposite sex, automatically his female powers will begin to emerge and develop in harmony with his male powers. Similarly, when a woman can favor the development of her female powers, but relate in a trusting, accepting, and appreciative way with men, her masculine powers will emerge spontaneously and develop in harmony with her female power. Through favoring the powers of one's own sex and learning to support the needs of the opposite sex, one can achieve this simultaneous development.

This kind of balanced woman can be strong, assertive, and aggressive (male qualities or powers) without threatening the opposite sex, because her masculine side is naturally balanced by her female powers to be centered, receptive, and vulnerable. A balanced man can be centered, receptive, and vulnerable (female powers) without losing the respect of others, because he is also autonomous, assertive, and aggressive.

This formula, however, does not work the other way around. If a man favors the development of his *female powers* over his male powers and he practices being caring, understanding, and respectful of his partner, he will not achieve simultaneous development and integration. The predominance of his female powers will smother his male powers. He may continue to grow but will become increasingly imbalanced.

Likewise, if a woman does not favor exercising her female qualities, but instead develops and expresses her *male powers,* her female power is restrained. This suppression will continue even if in her relationships with the opposite sex she expresses her male powers in a trusting, accepting, and appreciative way.

Simultaneous development also does not occur if a man favors the development of his male power but rejects the opposite sex by being uncaring, judgmental, and disrespectful. This kind of man can become very developed in his male power, but never gives his female power a chance to blossom.

By the same token, simultaneous development does not take place when a woman favors the unfolding of her female power but rejects the opposite sex by being mistrusting, unaccepting, and unappreciative. This kind of woman may be very powerful in her femininity, but her male power will not have a chance to mature. Her ability to attract support will be through manipulation and control.

Incidentally, it is not absolutely necessary to have an intimate relationship with the opposite sex to initiate this concurrent development of male and female energies. If a man favors his masculine characteristics and relates to others in a caring, understanding, and respectful way, he will experience simultaneous development. Likewise, a woman need not have a man in her life for this simultaneous development to occur. As long as she favors the expression of her female characteristics, and relates to others in a trusting, accepting, and appreciative manner, she will attain simultaneous development.

BALANCING OUR MALE AND FEMALE POWERS

Taking the example of an intimate sexual relationship, let's explore in greater depth how a man and woman can grow together through loving and supporting each other. As we have seen, when a man learns to express his caring, understanding, and respectful nature in the service of a woman, he is able to develop simultaneously both his male and female powers. By favoring the expression of his male powers (aggression, assertiveness, etc.) while respecting his female partner, automatically the complementary female powers (vulnerability, centeredness, and so on) are developed and integrated into his awareness.

Through relating in a caring, understanding, and respectful way with his female partner, his male powers are balanced by his latent female powers. His decisiveness is balanced with intuitiveness, his ability to exert effort is balanced by an ability to relax, his efficiency is balanced by a willingness to nurture and relate lovingly, his responsibility is balanced by an ability to enjoy and be happy. As he directs his male powers toward being more loving, caring, understanding, and respectful, his female power is increased and integrated.

On the other hand, when he is resisting his partner, this resistance is a reflection of his own imbalance. Resistance arises when either his masculine or feminine power is suppressed. This imbalance restricts his ability to spontaneously give his partner the caring, understanding, and respect that she needs. At such times, he can move through his resistance using the following formula: *Through favoring his masculine powers and through directing them in a caring, understanding, and respectful way, his resistance will gradually lessen and peace, love, and balance will prevail.* In his way he will become most effective and creative and capable of expressing his inner potential.

The resulting state of inner balance will boost his creative potential and power to create the desired results to their peak. In addition, his ability to recover quickly from stress will improve dramatically. From this perspective, loving others and resolving conflicts in his relationships becomes a practical means to increase a man's personal effectiveness.

When a man both develops his caring, understanding, and respect and favors the expression of his masculinity, then his awareness is able to integrate the complementary powers: not only is he aggressive but he is also yielding, not only is he assertive but also vulnerable, not only is he efficient but he is also nurturing, not only is he logical and decisive but also feeling and intuitive, not only is he practical but also imaginative and so forth. This secret is one of the extra blessings of creative loving relationships.

If, however, a man does not focus on developing and expressing his masculine powers, his ability to initiate action, be decisive, think clearly, stay committed, work hard, and so on, he will weaken. As his male power decreases his female power may correspondingly increase.

Imagine the masculine to be represented by light and the feminine, by dark. When the light decreases the dark must increase. Similarly, when a man is not developing his masculine power, he swings like a pendulum in the opposite direction and becomes more feminine. In much the same way, if a woman does not develop her feminine side, her masculinity will increase accordingly.

For example, when a man is not motivated to work hard (part of developing his male power), he is inclined to avoid work and to play more. In denying his male power, his female power has a chance to develop more fully. Having a good time, being playful, and pursuing personal fulfillment are all qualities of his feminine power. This man tends to become passive and lazy.

On the other hand, when a woman is not motivated to relax and enjoy her life (an expression of female power), she comes to be obsessively driven to work hard. In denying her female power, her male power is favored. This kind of woman tends to become compulsive and martyrlike.

Let's illustrate this with a male example. Dave's overly protective mother never allowed him to make his own choices while growing up. His ability to make decisions was not nurtured with trust; he did not receive forgiveness for his mistakes and appreciation of his willingness to take risks.

As an adult, Dave has not developed this decisive aspect of his male power. Rather than make choices and plan his day (male power), he tends to be more spontaneous, doing what he feels like doing in the moment. This spontaneity and intuition are aspects of his female power.

There is nothing wrong with developing female power. To work hard and produce results (male power) is no more important than the ability to relax and be happy (female power). But to become whole, Dave needs to consciously practice culturing his masculine powers. When he relies too heavily on his feelings and intuition, he becomes lazy and procrastinates.

Most people favor one side of their power instead of both. Many people can work hard and produce results, but cannot relax and enjoy their success. To them, their success is never enough. Others can be relaxed and happy, but they cannot work hard and achieve goals in their life. They want to make a difference in the world but they don't have that power.

To reach our full potential, both sides of our personal power need to be activated. Without the ability to have successful relationships, and thus to evolve both sides simultaneously, people tend to go out of balance and express their inner powers in four different ways. They are:

The Sensitive Man. This man has favored the development of his female powers. In denying the development of his masculine powers, his feminine side became stronger. Instead of being aggressive and assertive, he is more sensitive and vulnerable. By suppressing his masculinity he has lost much of his personal power, and is thus less effective.

The Macho Man. This man has favored the development of his male powers and rejected the expression of his female powers. Thus imbalanced, he is assertive but insensitive to others, and to various degrees incapable of feeling. In suppressing his feminine powers he has lost his ability to have loving relationships and to enjoy his life.

The Independent Woman. In denying the development of her feminine side, this woman has favored the strengthening of her male powers. Instead of being vulnerable and receptive she is aggressive and assertive. She is unable to use her feminine power to draw in support. In suppressing her femininity she has also lost the ability to have loving relationships and the power to inspire and empower others. She feels she must do it all alone.

The Dependent Woman. This woman has favored her female powers to create what she wants and has rejected her masculine powers. She is warm, receptive, and vulnerable, but also manipulative, demanding, and somewhat irrational. In that she has denied the natural development of her masculine powers, she thus feels powerless, anxious, and overly dependent on others.

In the following sections, we will explore in greater depth the various symptoms of imbalance as indicated by the four groups: Sensitive Man, Macho Man, Independent Woman, and Dependent Woman.

MR. SENSITIVE

This person has suppressed his male powers in favor of developing his female powers. In letting out his female powers he may become more yielding, vulnerable, receptive, playful, soft, imaginative, flexible, feeling, relaxed, or warm. But in the process, by repressing his male powers, he may become passive, lazy, indecisive, dependent, indulgent, irresponsible, less energetic, or weak.

In his relationships, the Sensitive Man may well be caring, understanding, and respectful of his partner. But he weakens himself by not expressing his masculinity. Consequently he doesn't follow through and express his masculine power.

Let's run through some examples of what happens when a man suppresses his male side:

1. His vulnerable female side overshadows his aggressive side; he becomes weak, too dependent, and easily manipulated.
2. His feeling female side overshadows his analytical side; he becomes confused and unclear.
3. His idealistic female side overpowers his practical side; his head is in the clouds and his feet are not on the ground.
4. His nurturing female side overshadows his efficiency; he loses his strength and wastes time and energy; he cannot lead, direct, or make money.

5. His intuitive female side overshadows his male ability to react rationally; he becomes indecisive or "spaced out."
6. His open and expansive female side overshadows his masculine ability to stay focused; he becomes easily distracted and loses his direction and ability to follow through.
7. His emotional female side overshadows his ability to react logically and with love. He becomes moody and petty.
8. His gentle and kind female side overshadows his masculine boldness; he becomes "wimpy" and easily taken advantage of; he will deny his own or his partner's needs in order to be polite or please others.
9. His supportive female side eclipses his masculine willfulness. He loses his personal initiative and leadership qualities; his self-sufficiency is repressed and he begins to feel overly dependent; he becomes motivated through the fear of disapproval.
10. His relaxed female disposition suppresses his hardworking, disciplined masculine power; he becomes too easygoing, passive, laid back, indecisive, and lazy.
11. His fulfilled and happy female side overshadows his sense of purpose; he "goes into idle" and becomes passive, losing his motivation and sense of confidence and power.
12. His joyful and playful female side eclipses his responsible male side; he becomes irresponsible and indulgent.
13. His centered female side outweighs his assertive male side; he becomes withdrawn, uninvolved, passive, or bored.

All of the above examples are symptoms of a man who has developed his feminine side and has suppressed his male power to receive love.

However, when some men begin to feel their female power, they instinctively reject it. To earn love they reject their female attributes and thus limit the integration of their male and female powers. This tendency creates the "Macho" temperament.

MACHO MAN

In the macho state of imbalance, a man develops his masculine power but rejects his feminine side. This kind of man becomes more whole and integrated by developing his ability to be caring, understanding, and respectful, especially to women. Let's look at some of the possible consequences when a man suppresses his female powers:

1. Developing masculine efficiency without also being nurturing (his female side), he becomes overly serious and burns out; he becomes insensitive to the needs of others, appearing cold and callous.
2. Developing his analytical side without also being more feeling (his female side), he becomes unfeeling and inconsiderate.

3. Developing practicality without also being idealistic (his female side), he becomes boring and repetitive.
4. Developing his aggression without also being vulnerable (his female side), he becomes controlling, detached, uncaring, competitive, destructive, and violent.
5. Developing his rational masculine side without also being intuitive (his female side) he becomes skeptical and close-minded.
6. Developing his focus without also being open and flexible (his female side), he becomes inconsiderate, unconscious of others, and incapable of change.
7. Developing his logical side without also being emotional (his female side), he becomes unemotional and shut down; when hurt he becomes moody and sulks.
8. Developing his precision without also being graceful (his female side), he becomes rigid, controlling, and demanding.
9. Developing his autonomy and self-sufficiency without also being receptive (his female side), he becomes defiant, indifferent, and unresponsive.
10. Developing his willfulness without also being relaxed and able to take it easy (his female side), he becomes tense, competitive, and addicted to work.
11. Developing his purposeful side without also being fulfilled (his female side), he becomes bitter, dissatisfied, distressed, and self-righteous; his work is never enough.

Each of the above conditions is a symptom of the macho temperament. It is doubtful that someone would have all of these qualities, yet it is certainly possible. In any case, this analysis helps us to understand the delicate balance of our male and female sides.

When a man works to express his male powers with the loving attitudes of caring, understanding, and respect, his awareness is capable of integrating the complementary powers of his male and female sides. Without this higher, more loving consciousness he cannot develop the opposing characteristics.

THE INDEPENDENT WOMAN

When a woman does not develop her female nature to appreciate, accept, and trust men, she will tend to become overly defensive, move in the direction of her male powers, and suppress her female power to draw in support. She may become more efficient and effective in her actions, but she will come to be less feeling, intuitive, relaxed, receptive, and supportable. Her female powers will gradually lessen.

In some cases she may appear trusting, accepting and appreciative of others, but she is not really open to receive. Although she can express these positive attitudes, in reality she is not open to letting others support her and fulfill her needs. She denies her female qualities and swings to her male side in order to feel more secure.

This imbalance of male over female powers in a woman helps us to understand the independent or overly responsible female personality. The Independent Woman tries to be everything for herself or everyone. She is compulsively motivated to be efficient, reasonable, practical, constructive, decisive, task oriented, logical, bold, self-sufficient, willful, and purposeful.

She may be self-sufficient, but at the expense of becoming cold, resentful, overworked, exhausted, hard, and closed. A woman who has denied her female powers in favor of her male powers will have little joy and fulfillment in life. She will be unable to relax because there will always be something worrying her.

When a woman does not get the love she needs, she starts to go out of balance. She becomes more masculine to the degree that she is unable to fulfill her feminine needs. Let's look more closely at how this change may affect her:

1. Her male efficiency overshadows her female nurturing; she becomes compulsively organized and overly responsible.
2. Her male analytical side outweighs her female feelings; she becomes cold, critical, and suspicious.
3. Her male practical side overshadows her female idealism; she becomes narrow, uncreative, and unromantic.
4. Her male aggressive nature eclipses her female vulnerability; she becomes pushy, defensive, manipulative, and demanding.
5. Her male rational side predominates over her female intuition; she becomes excessively analytical, frustrated, and confused.
6. Her disciplined male side outweighs her relaxed female side; she becomes compulsive and worries about everything.
7. Her male logic eclipses her female emotions; she becomes sharp, opinionated, and detached.
8. Her male precision overshadows her feminine grace; she becomes a perfectionist; demanding more without tact or consideration for the feeling of others.
9. Her male autonomy and self-sufficiency outweigh her female receptiveness; she becomes overly self-reliant, unsupportable, and unwilling to ask for assistance or support.
10. Her male willfulness overshadows her female supportive side; she becomes tense, intolerant, judgmental, and impatient.
11. Her male assertiveness eclipses her feminine centeredness; she becomes overly independent and forgets her needs for intimacy.

In the above ways a woman who doesn't feel loved and supported will begin to repress her natural female qualities and develop more fully her male traits. However, some women, when they move in the direction of their male power, instinctively reject it. This then creates the "Overly Dependent" or "Little Girl" or "Martyr" personality.

THE DEPENDENT WOMAN

The dependent temperament occurs when a woman rejects her male powers, thus becoming overly dependent on others to get what she needs. Let's look at some of the possible ways a woman might reject her masculine power:

1. Being playful and joyful without also developing her responsible male side, she becomes wasteful, indulgent, and inefficient.
2. Being in touch with her feelings without also developing her analytical male side, she becomes unreasonable, confused, and irrational.
3. Being idealistic without also developing her practical male side, she becomes ungrounded, "off the wall," and too romantic to ever be satisfied.
4. Being nurturing without also developing her efficient male side, she becomes helpless, hopeless, and overwhelmed.
5. Being intuitive without also developing her rational male side, she becomes superstitious and naive.
6. Being open and expansive without also developing her focused male side, she becomes scattered, indecisive, and undirected.
7. Being emotional without also developing her logical male side, she becomes overreactive, illogical, and random in her thinking.
8. Being graceful and nice without also developing her precise male side, she becomes covert, indirect, vague, and manipulative.
9. Being receptive without also developing her autonomous male side, she becomes needy and desperate.
10. Being vulnerable without also developing her aggressive male side, she submissive and weak.
11. Being positive and good without also developing her strategic male side, she becomes a martyr and makes unnecessary sacrifices.

These examples describe some of the possible transformations a woman may go through when she rejects her male side. Some women will from time to time swing from being the "Independent Woman" to the "Dependent Woman." Other women remain fixed in one temperament. In a similar way, some men move from being "Mr. Macho" to being the "Sensitive Guy" while others remain stuck in one disposition.

It is very common for a woman to be overdependent in a relationship, get hurt, and swing in the other direction for a while, becoming overly independent. Then at some point she will begin to feel her suppressed feminine needs and seek to fulfill them. At such times she swings back toward being overdependent. This cycle continues until she learns how to be feminine without suppressing her masculinity.

Unbalanced men, too, commonly swing from being cold and macho to being nice, tolerant, and sensitive. A man may try to fulfill a woman and then, when he feels he has failed, he will swing back to being uncaring and macho. In general a man needs to learn how to be masculine without suppressing his feminine side.

ROLE REVERSAL

Just as a man can alternate between being Macho Man and being Sensitive Man, he may also take on the roles of Independent and Dependent. This is role reversal. If he does not get the love he needs through being macho or sensitive, he may begin to identify more with his feminine side. Instead of swinging between macho and sensitive, he will seesaw from being Independent to being Dependent.

When during childhood a boy feels helpless or powerless to get the love he needs, he may go into role reversal. More commonly though, men go into role reversal when they get married and do not get the love they need.

In much the same way, some women who marry but fail to get the love their feminine side needs begin to identify with and seek to fulfill their male side. In doing so they swing between being Macho and Sensitive. This is how a woman may experience role reversal. It may also begin in childhood if she felt powerless to get her feminine needs fulfilled.

A person in role reversal especially needs to practice loving themselves. When a man in role reversal succeeds in loving himself, then he will come back to being both macho and sensitive. From this position he is capable of favoring his masculine side and giving caring, understanding, and respect.

Instead of looking for love outside himself, he needs to love himself. In loving himself he must practice trusting, accepting, and appreciating himself. He needs to take an inventory of his resentments and forgive the people who have hurt him. In forgiving his father he can begin to trust, accept, and appreciate masculinity. This strengthens his ability to love himself.

Likewise a woman in role reversal, oscillating between being Macho and Sensitive, needs to practice loving herself. It is difficult for her relationships to work in this state of imbalance because she cannot receive love. By forgiving her mother she can begin to feel the feminine is worthy of caring, understanding, and respect. Through caring for, understanding, and respecting herself she can get back in touch with her feminine needs. This increases her ability to love herself. As she identifies more with her feminine side, she will come out of role reversal and begin to swing from being Dependent to Independent. Then she can practice developing her feminine characteristics and supporting others with trust, acceptance, and appreciation.

Just because men or women in role reversal primarily need to love themselves does not mean they should avoid intimate relationships. That is always a personal choice. It means however that they should not look to their partners to find balance. They must work instead on releasing resentments from the past, giving up blame, and finding forgiveness within themselves. Until this forgiveness is achieved, it is hard to be successful in receiving and giving love.

HOW A WOMAN FINDS HER POWER

As a woman learns to successfully support a man through fulfilling his primary needs to be appreciated, accepted, and trusted, then quite automatically she becomes more balanced and capable of expressing her male powers without overshadowing her female powers. Not only does he benefit, but she gains the ability to express both her female and male sides in harmony.

To support her effort to be more trusting, accepting, and appreciative, she should also practice nurturing her female side and developing her feminine characteristics. They include being vulnerable, centered, receptive, intuitive, fulfilled, nurturing, joyful, enthusiastic, spontaneous, graceful, idealistic, beautiful, positive, feeling, emotional, open, gentle, relaxed, supportive, and empowering to others.

Reviewing the following list from time to time can remind her of the direction that will give her real power. She can affirm:

"I am a strong, loving, and vulnerable woman, and each day I am learning to trust, accept, and appreciate more."

"I am a strong, loving, and centered woman, and each day I am learning to trust, accept, and appreciate more."

"I am a strong, loving, and receptive woman, and each day I am learning to trust, accept, and appreciate more."

"I am a strong, loving, and intuitive woman, and each day I am learning to trust, accept, and appreciate more."

"I am a strong, loving, and fulfilled woman, and each day I am learning to trust, accept, and appreciate more."

"I am a strong, loving, and nurturing woman, and each day I am learning to trust, accept, and appreciate more."

"I am a strong, loving, and joyful woman, and each day I am learning to trust, accept, and appreciate more."

"I am a strong, loving, and enthusiastic woman, and each day I am learning to trust, accept, and appreciate more."

"I am a strong, loving, and spontaneous woman, and each day I am learning to trust, accept, and appreciate more."

"I am a strong, loving, and graceful woman, and each day I am learning to trust, accept, and appreciate more."

"I am a strong, loving, and idealistic woman, and each day I am learning to trust, accept, and appreciate more."

"I am a strong, loving, and beautiful woman, and each day I am learning to trust, accept, and appreciate more."

"I am a strong, loving, and positive woman, and each day I am learning to trust, accept, and appreciate more."

"I am a strong, loving, and feeling woman, and each day I am learning to trust, accept, and appreciate more."

"I am a strong, loving, and emotional woman, and each day I am learning to trust, accept, and appreciate more."

"I am a strong, loving, and open woman, and each day I am learning to trust, accept, and appreciate more."

"I am a strong, loving, and gentle woman, and each day I am learning to trust, accept, and appreciate more."

"I am a strong, loving, and relaxed woman, and each day I am learning to trust, accept, and appreciate more."

"I am a strong, loving, and supportive woman, and each day I am learning to trust, accept, and appreciate more."

"I am strong, loving, and empowering to others, and each day I am learning to trust, accept, and appreciate more."

Another affirmation is: "I am a strong and loving woman, and I deserve to be loved just the way I am. Each day I am becoming stronger. It is safe for me to trust. I accept others the way they are; I do not need to change them. I appreciate the increasing support I have in my life."

HOW A MAN FINDS HIS POWER

Whether he is aware of this or not, when a man is able to support his female mate he is indirectly nurturing his own female side. By giving to her, his own female side is validated and feels cared for. By understanding her, his female nature becomes more understandable to himself. By respecting her needs, he begins to respect his own complementary female needs. One of the greatest things about being in a loving relationship is this: by focusing on giving to your partner in the ways that he or she needs most, you directly benefit as well.

Through expressing his masculine traits in a caring, understanding, and respectful way, a man can become fully integrated and balanced within himself. These masculine characteristics include being aggressive, assertive, autonomous, rational, purposeful, efficient, responsible, confident, decisive, precise, practical, competent, strategic, analytical, logical, focused, dignified, disciplined, willful, and empowered by serving others. It is helpful for him to review this list of the masculine qualities of power. He may affirm the following:

"I am a strong, loving, and aggressive man, and each day I am learning to be more caring, understanding, and respectful."

"I am a strong, loving, and assertive man, and each day I am learning to be more caring, understanding, and respectful."

"I am a strong, loving, and autonomous man, and each day I am learning to be more caring, understanding, and respectful."

"I am a strong, loving, and rational man, and each day I am learning to be more caring, understanding, and respectful."

"I am a strong, loving, and purposeful man, and each day I am learning to be more caring, understanding, and respectful."

"I am a strong, loving, and efficient man, and each day I am learning to be more caring, understanding, and respectful."

"I am a strong, loving, and responsible man, and each day I am learning to be more caring, understanding, and respectful."

"I am a strong, loving, and confident man, and each day I am learning to be more caring, understanding, and respectful."

"I am a strong, loving, and decisive man, and each day I am learning to be more caring, understanding, and respectful."

"I am a strong, loving, and precise man, and each day I am learning to be more caring, understanding, and respectful."

"I am a strong, loving, and practical man, and each day I am learning to be more caring, understanding, and respectful."

"I am a strong, loving, and competent man, and each day I am learning to be more caring, understanding, and respectful."

"I am a strong, loving, and strategic man, and each day I am learning to be more caring, understanding, and respectful."

"I am a strong, loving, and analytical man, and each day I am learning to be more caring, understanding, and respectful."

"I am a strong, loving, and logical man, and each day I am learning to be more caring, understanding, and respectful."

"I am a strong, loving, and focused man, and each day I am learning to be more caring, understanding, and respectful."

"I am a strong, loving, and bold man, and each day I am learning to be more caring, understanding, and respectful."

"I am a strong, loving, and disciplined man, and each day I am learning to be more caring, understanding, and respectful."

"I am a strong, loving, and willful man, and each day I am learning to be more caring, understanding, and respectful."

"I am strong, loving and empowered by serving others, and each day I am learning to be more caring, understanding, and respectful."

Another affirmation is: "I am a strong and loving man and I deserve to be loved just the way I am. Each day I am becoming stronger. I do care for others. I can understand others without judging them. I am willing to respect others the way I respect myself."

LOVE IS THE REAL SOURCE OF POWER

Sometimes women fear that they will become weak if they really open up and trust and rely on a man. A woman many anticipate that her female side will develop but her male power will weaken. This concern is unfounded. When a woman is able to successfully support her man, she indirectly cultivates her male side.

When a woman can accept her man, she is then able to accept her own masculine side. By trusting him she learns to trust her own masculinity. Through appreciating him she also appreciates her own masculine nature. This increased self-acceptance, self-appreciation, and self-trust increases her masculine power but at the same time develops her female powers.

Without loving or serving others, if a woman wants to develop her male side she is apt to do this through denying her female side. Relationships afford a woman the opportunity to cultivate her female side while automatically developing her male side.

Likewise, a man naturally develops his female side by cultivating the male attitudes in service to a woman (and/or the world). He both uses his male power to create through action and expresses his power in a caring, understanding, respectful way. Automatically his feminine qualities become integrated into his awareness.

A NEW POSSIBILITY

This concept of emphasizing that men should focus on developing their male characteristics and women should focus on their feminine side does not represent a backslide to our past with its defined roles for men and women. Rather than defining roles, we are defining ideal attitudes to be striven toward and perfected. Nowhere in history do we see a man being abusive to his wife or his environment if he was practicing the virtues of caring, understanding, and respect. These three primary attitudes can be observed, however, in the lives of the eminent men who have molded our history by assisting mankind to make great leaps of progress.

Nowhere, too, do we see in history a woman capable of truly trusting, accepting, and appreciating who was also easily taken advantage of, passive, or weak. These three loving attitudes of trust, acceptance, and appreciation are embodied by the great women who have made their mark on our history. They are also exemplified by the thousands of women who didn't stand out, but quietly and dynamically supported a man who did.

The latter did not feel demeaned or abused; rather, these women shared in their partners' successes. For them, it was not necessary to receive the recognition, glorification, and appreciation that their masculine counterparts sought out. They intuitively understood their male partners' need for appreciation and wisely did not seek to compete in any way.

Although many women may choose to continue in a supportive role to a man, it is not necessary. This more traditional version of a woman's role is changing as we more fully develop our inner abilities. Cultivating our primary sex characteristics along with loving attitudes is not in any way a step backward, but presents a new vision of what is possible for men and women in relationships.

HARMONY IN THE WORKPLACE

Through developing these primary attitudes, a man and woman can work side by side as equals without creating the tremendous resistance that men and women now experience in the work world. Men and women who understand their differences can share the same responsibilities but still enjoy the creative energy that their polarity engenders.

Many women have denied their feminine powers and needs to avoid resistance and to succeed in the workplace. They have molded themselves to become what men expect from men, rather than being true to their female nature. It is my hope that with this information the work world, a male dominated area of life, will begin to recognize the practical effectiveness of caring for, understanding, and respecting feminine needs and powers. Not only will this give more support to women, but it can also save men from burning out.

Women in the workplace who are committed to developing their female nature — to appreciate, accept, and trust — will also greatly assist men by giving them the support they deserve. By culturing these attitudes women will learn how to express their masculine powers without rejecting their feminine powers.

When women learn to employ their power without competing with the masculine power, they will also ensure increasing support from men. As women come to express their feminine powers, men will be less offended or threatened and will gradually gain greater respect for their female coworkers. A woman's expression of masculine power tends to threaten a man to the degree that she is denying her female power. When a woman can maintain her female qualities while also expressing her male power in balance, she more effectively wins the respect and support of men.

Some women have already experienced the power of this approach in the workplace. As women learn to express their female nature in this arena, they are finding that they can earn respect and achieve success in a different way, a feminine way.

For this process of finding balance in the workplace and in our relationships to be most effective, we must be aware of the symptoms of going out of balance. One of our biggest problems is that when we are out of balance we usually do not know it. When we go out of balance we begin to use love as a way of manipulating and controlling. We may think we are being loving and supportive, but in truth we are not. Sometimes we may ask for a form of love that is not what we need or really want. In the next chapter we will explore some of the hidden sources of discontent that emerge in relationships.

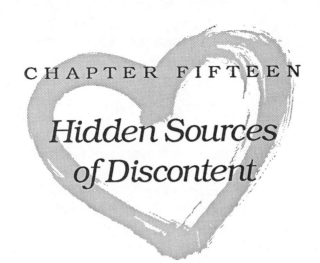

CHAPTER FIFTEEN

Hidden Sources of Discontent

An important reason we may fail to achieve fulfillment in our relationships is that we give out the wrong messages. For example, a man may put out the message that he wants a mothering mate, then reject her when she is overly caring. A woman may give out the message that she wants her man to need her more, and then reject his neediness. The problem with mixed messages is that when we get what we think we want, we are not satisfied.

The solution to this problem lies not in trying to be satisfied with what we get. The only way to *get* what we truly need is to *realize* what we truly need, and ask for that. In the above example the man is asking for the caring love of a mother when what he primarily needs is the trust that he can take care of himself unless he asks for support. True, sometimes he may need his partner's motherly caring. But his primary need as a male is her trust that he can support himself and her. This trust is expressed each and every time she gives him an opportunity to "be there for her."

In the second example the woman is asking her partner to need and trust her to let her in, to let her be more helpful to him. Hers is, however, a mixed message: her real desire is for him to be more caring and considerate of her needs.

Another common double message confuses respect and appreciation. A woman may busy herself in giving to a man, thinking that she desires to earn his appreciation. The message she puts out is that she wants to be appreciated, when what she really needs is to be respected more and for him to do more for her. Conversely, men put out the message that they want respect, when in truth what they are subconsciously seeking is appreciation.

In the above examples women were putting out the message that they wanted their mates to be more trusting and appreciative, while the men were signaling that they wanted more caring and respect. As we have seen in previous chapters, men primarily need the reverse — trust and appreciation — while women fundamentally need caring and respect. In this chapter we will explore how and why men and women give out mixed messages.

REPLACEMENT NEEDS

Men possess the feminine needs to be cared for, respected, and understood, but these are subordinate or secondary to their emotional well-being. A man's primary needs are to be loved, accepted, appreciated, and trusted, while his secondary needs are to be understood, respected, and cared for. The priority of these needs, however, can get confused in his awareness.

When a man's primary needs go unfulfilled, they may be automatically repressed and "replaced" by the secondary needs. This can make relationships very confusing: what you earnestly feel you need may not be what you really need. In our lack of awareness we may be akin to the alcoholic who genuinely feels that he needs a drink. What he truly needs is love. But because that need is unfulfilled, he finds a replacement need and seeks to fulfill that.

Listening as a Replacement Need

Very commonly, women feel a need to be heard. This is a normal primary need for a woman. After this need goes unfulfilled for some time, however, it will be replaced by its complement — the need to listen. Women frequently exhibit this pattern. The more a woman needs to share and to be heard, the more she is compelled to hear another's feelings. She is not aware of her primary need, but feels a secondary need.

Many times when a woman's true primary need is to share what she is feeling, instead she will think, "I have to know what my partner is feeling." Her primary need to be heard is replaced by a secondary need to listen. One problem with this is that she will be giving out the wrong messages. The other major dilemma is that no matter how much her partner shares, she will feel it is not enough. A secondary need can never be truly satisfying unless the primary need is recognized and fulfilled.

Overeating as a Replacement Need

This relationship of primary needs to secondary needs is somewhat comparable to an overeater's compulsive need to eat. The overeater may genuinely feel the need to eat. But because this is not their primary need, eating leaves them wanting more rather than leaving them satisfied and fulfilled.

The compulsion to overeat is a signal that some more primary need (generally the need for emotional support) is being replaced by the need to eat. Although eating is a primary need when one's body is truly hungry, it can also be adopted as a "replacement need": to repress the emotional pain of not feeling loved, a person feels the urge to eat.

A replacement need is generally one that a person feels more competent in fulfilling. If a person feels powerless to fulfill their primary need, they may become obsessed with fulfilling another need over which they have more control. It is much easier to pig out in the kitchen than to reach out for emotional support.

Because the need to eat, at that moment, is just repressing and replacing their unfulfilled primary need for love, eating food cannot fulfill their craving. So they keep eating, imagining that after one more bite they will feel satisfied. They stuff themselves with food to stuff (repress) their painful feelings. A similar phenomenon occurs in relationships. When a person's primary emotional needs go unfulfilled, they automatically get replaced by secondary emotional needs.

PRIMARY AND SECONDARY NEEDS

For example, when a man does not feel *trusted* by a woman, to avoid feeling the resulting pain he may develop a compulsive need for her to care for him. He may become as demanding as a little boy. The problem arises, however, that no matter how *caring* she may be, he will feel it is not enough, just as the overeater never satisfies their hunger. In most cases he does not even know that what he is missing and needing from her is her trust. He mistakenly demands more caring and consideration, then rejects her for smothering him.

In a complementary way, when a woman does not trust a man she will tend to mother him or become overly caring and responsible for him. Because she is responding to and fulfilling his secondary need to be cared for (and not his primary need to be trusted), it will never be enough, no matter how much she cares.

At some point he will begin to reject her caring and deny his secondary need to be cared for. Like a pendulum that swings back and forth, he will send her double messages: "I need you to care for me" and then "your caring is suffocating me." In a similar way the overeater swings from feeling the need to eat and then denying the need to eat by adopting strenuous diet plans. The way out of this unstable oscillation of the replacement need is to fulfill the primary need.

Although the situation is not always this clear-cut, if we can identify our primary needs and focus on fulfilling them, we can gradually minimize the urgency and demanding quality of our secondary emotional needs. If we are not fulfilling what we primarily need, no matter how much we meet our secondary needs we will be unfulfilled and dissatisfied. Let's explore our primary and secondary needs and see how they can easily get confused and reversed.

CARING AND TRUST

Caring is a feminine need while trusting is the complementary masculine need. When a man is caring toward a woman he is able to instill trust in her. Likewise, when a woman trusts a man he will spontaneously be more caring toward her. Masculinity flourishes when it is trusted. Femininity flourishes when it is cared for.

For example, an overprotected boy commonly becomes overly soft and dependent. An overprotected girl, by comparison, would flourish in the safety of a caring environment. She would grow up with a stronger sense of herself. This is not to say that a boy doesn't need a caring environment. But if he is not trusted enough, he will not develop his masculine powers. He may become overly dependent on those who care for him, and not trust himself.

Trusting him might mean trusting that he can do things and not always trying to help or improve him; trusting that if he makes a mistake he will learn from it; trusting that he is doing his best, and that he has good intentions.

If a woman cares for a man but does not trust him, he will unconsciously resent and reject her "caring." Most likely he will not even know why. Although he cannot articulate his reaction, he will be offended and pull away. All he knows is that her caring is annoying and makes him feel weak. Actually, it is not the caring that weakens him, but her secret lack of trust.

Many times it is when a woman feels she can't trust her partner that she goes out of balance and becomes "overly caring." She denies her need for his support because she doesn't trust that she can rely on him. She reacts to her own mistrust by becoming overly caring of others or by not caring at all. She swings from being overly caring to being unduly self-reliant and independent. What she doesn't realize is that she is putting out the message that she is strong and doesn't need help.

People who go into professions such as nursing commonly have a problem trusting others to be there for them. Consequently they become overly caring and trustworthy people. Because they can't trust others to fulfill their needs, they follow an unconscious compulsion to fulfill the needs of others in the ways that they secretly wish someone would fulfill theirs. To put it more simply, the need to be cared for gets replaced by the need to care for others. Instead of feeling "I need you to care for me," the message is "I need you to trust me as I care for you."

When a little girl is ignored you can watch her compensate by becoming overly caring toward her dolls. This does not mean it is wrong for a girl to care. It means that excessive caring is a symptom of her fear and inability to receive the caring she needs.

Why Wounded Men Leave

"Wounded" men will at first be drawn to these caring women. If a man is not sure of himself, for example, he may be attracted to the independent or mothering woman. But as he heals he will begin to feel trustworthy and to resent her lack of trust. When he feels more secure he will reject her, or she will reject him when he stops needing her as much. In this case, he gives out a double message. He acts as if he wants her to be strong and independent, but then leaves her for a more vulnerable woman.

It is a common female complaint that women care for a man while he is down, but when he is back on his feet and has no need for them, he rejects them. He is automatically drawn to a more trusting woman who feels secure enough to need him. Although a man needs to take responsibility for this injustice, his overly caring partner also needs to recognize that she was denying her primary need to be cared for. They were both sending out mixed messages.

Men Need to Be Needed

Men love to feel needed. A woman's ability to "trust" allows her to need a man. The woman who needs her man empowers him. This "needing" communicates the message, "I have these needs and I trust that you can and will support me." "Needing," however, is not the same as "neediness." A "needy" woman is not saying "I need you. " Instead she is saying, "I have these needs and I don't trust that you can or will fulfill them. I am helpless."

This same mistrust is also communicated to a man when a woman behaves in an uncaring way. She reacts in an aloof manner as if to say, "You cannot hurt me. I won't give you a chance to let me down. I don't need you or anybody. I don't trust you to give me what I need. I can do it alone. I have trusted before and have been burned. It is too painful." Although she appears strong and self-reliant, the opposite of needy, the basis of her attitude is still mistrust. A man gets this message and is unconsciously emotionally wounded. He will begin to withdraw or become irritable or feel drained.

The complement to this is when a woman feels hurt because the man she loves doesn't care for her. If she is open to him and loves him and he remains uncaring and cold, she is hurt in much the same way that a man is hurt when he loves her and she is mistrusting.

One of the reasons men are so gallant and empowered in the beginning of relationships is that he feels she is trusting him. Her trust enlivens his whole being. He becomes a much more caring person. This trust is the most valuable gift a woman can give a man, just as his caring is the most important gift he can give her.

In a new relationship, she feels that she has finally found a man she can trust. But when he disappoints her a few times, her underlying mistrust returns. As a result, he is no longer as motivated and caring. He loses his momentum.

Some women feel that they are trusting, when in truth they are walking around with a suitcase of repressed mistrust. A sign of her underlying mistrust is this familiar situation: She feels in the beginning of the relationship that "he is different from other men, I can trust him." Then when her romantic vision of him shifts, she reacts by feeling, "I knew it, he was no different, he was just like the rest of them — untrustworthy!"

Trusting a man is the opposite of hoping one day he will change. Trusting is a woman's feeling that this man really does care about her. It is knowing that he does care even when he is preoccupied. It is being open and willing to share her hidden feelings and wishes. This building of trust is the foundation of a successful relationship.

UNDERSTANDING AND ACCEPTANCE

When a man is overly accepting but not understanding, a woman feels he is too passive and condescending. What a woman really needs from a man is true understanding and then consideration based on that understanding — not "lip service."

In a complementary way men primarily need a woman's acceptance. Certainly men like to be understood, and at times feel greatly misunderstood. But what generally precedes a man's feeling misunderstood is a woman's lack of acceptance.

This need for acceptance is primary to a man, and most painful when he doesn't receive it. A man wants to be received and accepted by a woman. When a man doesn't feel accepted, his needs may become confused. Thus he puts out the double message that he wants to be understood. He demands to be heard and he demands to be right, all because deep inside he feels he is being rejected. He feels that he is inadequate.

A man needs to remember that when he is demanding to be right, he really needs to understand the other person. He needs to listen more. That will greatly assist his ability to figure things out and feel accepted. When he is frustrated because he doesn't feel heard, he usually needs to stop and ask, "Before we go on, I'd like to know what you have heard me say." This will give him a chance to feel accepted, and then he will be less rigid. When dealing with a man who has to be right, to assist him in being more flexible you can use the statement, "I think I understand what you are saying; you are saying _____. Is that correct?"

Why Women Make Great Listeners

A woman needs most to be *understood*. She wants a man to share her innermost feelings and thoughts. This sharing is her primary need. Sometimes a woman's primary need to be understood is suppressed and replaced by her secondary need to be accepted. In her compulsion to be accepted, she will try to earn a man's love and acceptance by being a great listener. She instinctively believes that if she can hear his feelings, then he will be more accepting. After all, if *she* can be heard and understood, she becomes accepting.

For this reason, when a woman needs to be heard and understood, she will often feel that she needs her man to open up and share his feelings. She wants *him* to open up and share, because *she* secretly needs to share and be heard. She primarily needs to be understood, but feels the secondary need to be accepted. This woman will make a great listener.

As she listens attentively, what she doesn't give her partner is real acceptance. Inside she is secretly wishing he would change. She hopes that if she listens to him he will change. Indeed, she expects him to change, because she knows how easily she can change when she is heard or understood.

Why Listening Doesn't Work

When he doesn't change, although she is quick to make excuses for his shortcomings, she is increasingly frustrated with him. She constantly expects him to be more than he is. As a result she readily misinterprets his behavior. Overly hurt by his actions and comments, she believes that "if he loved me he would not do these things."

Frustration with his inadequacies is the theme of how she hurts him. But she doesn't see how she abuses him, because she is so absorbed in feeling her own hurt. To release her pain she tries to be more understanding of his behavior and to make excuses for him. On the surface she may feel sorry for him, but she really feels sorry for herself. What she needs to do is to explore and share her hurt. By fulfilling her primary need (to be understood), she will be able to fulfill his primary need, which is to discover again her true acceptance of him.

How a Woman Can Find Her Acceptance

Women appear adept in the art of understanding, but in an indirect way a man consistently gets the message that he is unacceptable and inadequate. He gets this double message: although she is dissatisfied, she also understands the problem. She feels noble because she is excusing his imperfections but in truth never really accepts them. Her "understanding" is just another way of trying to change him.

So many times I have counseled men who hate listening to their wives ask them questions about their feelings. They don't want to be understood. They don't want to share. And most of all, they don't want to be asked a lot of personal questions. There are many reasons for this reaction, but it boils down to him being hurt by her unacceptance of who he is. He really doesn't want someone trying to improve him. Her nonacceptance causes her to question his behavior, as if to understand it better. But on an emotional level she asks him to open up, because she does not really accept his imperfections. She demands more of him before she can feel satisfied. What a man needs is acceptance for who he is today, real acceptance that is not conditional on who he can be tomorrow.

The woman who doesn't accept a man feels responsible to improve her man. She feels that she knows the way, and tries to teach and guide him.

This overly understanding woman is consistently frustrated. Her frustration is painful to him. She thinks she alone is being abused and rejected, and is not aware of how she is rejecting him and causing him to shut down.

A woman who has successful loving relationships with men tends to accept a man's limits in being able to give to her. Knowing what to expect, she is not waiting for the day he changes. She feels gratitude for the gifts he is able to give her. She does not feel a compulsion to correct, direct, or change him. She continues to share her needs and wishes, but from a realistic and accepting perspective. To be this accepting she needs to be understood.

RESPECT AND APPRECIATION

A woman may think she respects a man, but if she does not also appreciate what he does for her, then he will not value or feel her respect. He may even be offended that she doesn't respect him. When a man's need to be appreciated is not fulfilled, he may confuse the issue by feeling his secondary need to be respected. In demanding respect he is never satisfied. This is confusing to her because she thinks she does respect him.

Many times, to the degree that a woman does not appreciate the way a man treats her, she will overly respect him. This means that she will respect or honor his *will* by being obedient, or she will respect or esteem his *potential*, but as far as how he is treating her today, she will be dissatisfied. If her respect is not balanced by genuine appreciation, he may easily abuse her submissiveness by being overly dominant.

How Her Unhappiness Poisons Him

When a woman doesn't appreciate the way a man does things, she may automatically begin to "respectfully" (and sometimes very disrespectfully) attempt to improve him. She will try to change and manipulate him. In this state of imbalance she is constantly concerned with trying to get him to change.

This compulsive intention is what hurts him. Like a poison that affects him in an unseen way, it arises from her basic unhappiness. The more unhappy she is, the more she tries to change him. This need to change him is also a "replacement" need. It is a compulsion that overshadows her need for his respect, which would assist her in feeling better.

Respect is her primary need. She must have his respect if she is to appreciate and enjoy him. When his actions and words do not convey a respect for her rights and needs, it is hard for her to appreciate what he does for her. It is harder for her to access her inner happiness. Whenever a woman feels the compulsion to change her man, she should look further inside and there she will find her primary need to be respected. She can ask herself, "How do I need to be supported?" and then, "How can I let my partner know my needs without being demanding?"

When her primary need for respect is not fulfilled, a woman may confuse the issue by feeling more intensely (or compulsively) her secondary need to be appreciated. She complains that she is not being appreciated, when what she really needs is to be respected. This sends a double message to a man. To appreciate her more, he has to become more passive. He doesn't recognize that she needs more active support.

Men and Control

When a woman's rights are not respected, she becomes compulsive about telling a man how he should do things differently. Over and over he gets the message that his way is not good enough. Most men immediately resent this as control. Some men, at first, welcome a woman's attempts to improve them and even become dependent on it. But eventually or periodically, they will rebel and resent it. They get back at women like this by becoming overly controlling.

Certainly any man can stand some improvement. But when a woman feels a compulsive need to improve him, he will end up being wounded and disempowered.

Sometimes a woman may over-appreciate a man. Just as hurtful, this over-appreciation is again an unconscious attempt to change him in some way. To over-appreciate is an indirect way of saying "What you really give me is not enough. Therefore I will exaggerate my appreciation in hopes that you will become a person who deserves this much appreciation." Although this woman appears to appreciate her man, he gets the message that he is not enough.

The female compulsion to improve, which arises from a core of dissatisfaction and unhappiness, is very painful to men. This is one of the reasons that men are so threatened by women with power. Men are unconsciously afraid of being improved, corrected, and controlled. A man senses his partner's hopes to change and improve him, and to protect himself he attempts to suppress her power.

The more a woman learns to appreciate a man, the more he will respect her. In a similar way, the more a man respects a woman, the more she will appreciate him.

Respecting Without True Appreciation

What a man needs most from a woman is her genuine appreciation for what he *is* doing for her — not her respect for what he *could* do for her. Women imagine they are appreciating a man by believing or hoping that one day he will change and be trustworthy. This is not true appreciation.

One type of woman respects a man's potential but is constantly looking at what he is not giving her. According to her, all the problems in the relationship have to do with what he is not doing for her. She feels compelled to change him or teach him or heal him, so that she can receive the treatment she would prefer. She chooses to be with him yet continues to be dissatisfied with what she gets. This woman does not recognize that her negative attitudes poison and weaken him over time, just as his disrespectful behavior hurts her. To a great extent, even she is fooled by her respect for his potential: she gives out the message that he is enough, but she is continuously dissatisfied.

Another common symptom of not appreciating a man is the combination of respecting his wishes and will but secretly resenting his lack of support. This woman easily compromises, sending the apparent message that she is generally satisfied. This woman will do as her husband directs, and then secretly be dissatisfied that she never gets her needs fulfilled. She does not enjoy giving of herself, but continues to make sacrifices for him. She then expects him to sacrifice in return. She gives out the message that she is strong and doesn't need help, then complains that no one helps her.

She gives through her behavior, but does not bestow sincere appreciation, which is what he primarily needs. At the end of such a relationship she will often say, "I gave so much and I got nothing in return." In giving "so much" she was respectful of her partner's apparent needs and requests. But if she feels that she got nothing back, then throughout the relationship she failed to give him what he most needed — her gratefulness. She might have loved him and respected him, but she was lacking in true appreciation.

Sometimes women who feel burned in this way by a man don't understand what is meant by appreciation. Appreciation, in this example, would be a feeling that says, "He really made me happy. I gave to him and he gave so much to me. I will always remember the wonderful times we spent together."

Appreciating Without Respect

Typically, a man will give a woman a lot of appreciation, but when she has needs he will resist. He truly appreciates her, but doesn't respect her needs, wishes, and desires. He appreciates her devotion to his need but is not devoted to her. A symptom of his disrespect is that he judges her feelings as weak and her desires as selfish. He is a good receiver but not good at giving.

She, on the other hand, is great at giving respect by compromising and fulfilling his apparent desires, but not good at appreciating his support. She tends to resent his self-centeredness but feels too proud to share her wishes. If she is to receive and appreciate his support, she must be able to share her wishes without demanding. A "wish" is free of demand. Asking for support works better when she is able to remember and feel what she appreciates, even while she is wishing for more.

A woman becomes hard when she forgets what she appreciates about a man. When a woman is unable to be soft and receptive, she hurts a man in the same way that a man hurts a woman by being selfish and self-centered. A selfish man can be great at giving appreciation, but he is truly unable to give of himself in a caring, respectful way. A self-less woman is great at respecting another's wishes. But because she is inept at sharing her own wishes, she is unable to be appreciative in her attitude.

Learning to Appreciate

Say a woman respects her partner's wishes and desires but doesn't appreciate being treated the way he treats her. True appreciation is the acknowledgment that one has received what he or she needed or wished. The feeling that she has received nothing from a man reveals that she also was unable to give him the appreciation and trust that he primarily needed. She may feel as though she has given more, but in truth, what she gave was not what he primarily needed.

One might ask how can she "appreciate" when he is ignoring her, for example. At such times she needs to explore her negative emotions and come back to appreciating what he does do. This appreciation will motivate him to respect her needs. When women do not know how to sort out their feelings and release the negative emotions, then their innate and natural feelings of appreciation get repressed.

The question is not "How can I change him so that I have something to appreciate?" Rather, it is "How can I appreciate more fully what he does and who he is, so that I can support him better, be happier, and inevitably get more back?"

WHEN LOVE IS CONFUSING

Relationships become confusing when we are unable to clearly distinguish between what we really need and what is just a replacement need. We give out double messages, which, needless to say, make our relationships very confusing.

To be clear about our needs and to fully understand our partner's needs, good communication is essential. What generally blocks good communication is the inability to fully experience and communicate our inner feelings, desires, and needs. In the next chapter we will explore practical techniques for improving communication of our inner feelings. We will also learn how to ask for the support we need and to give the support others deserve.

CHAPTER SIXTEEN

The Love Letter Technique

The love letter technique is probably the most important skill a person could learn to have a successful and lasting loving relationship. Thousands of people practice this technique to release resentment and other negative feelings in order to become centered again in the positive attitudes of love, understanding and forgiveness. It has saved thousands of marriages and has helped others experience divorce in a more loving and peaceful way.

Since it was first published in 1984 in my book, *What You Feel You Can Heal*, it has been rewritten in three other best-selling books by other authors, and is used by numerous therapists, self-help groups, twelve-step programs, church groups, college counseling courses, and hundreds of other support groups. The love letter technique is the ultimate method for processing and transforming negative feelings into positive feelings.

In brief, the love letter has two parts. The first part consists of writing out the complete truth about how you feel, while imagining that you are being heard and understood. The second part is then to write a loving response to your letter. In this response letter, imagine the person you have written the letter to responding with an open heart. Write a response to you expressing the feelings and acknowledgments that you need to hear.

THE PURPOSE OF A LOVE LETTER

The purpose of writing a love letter when you are upset is to expand your awareness, to incorporate positive, loving feelings without having to repress your negative emotions. Writing a love letter assists you in transforming any negative attitude into a positive one. It allows you to open your heart.

Writing love letters helps you to incorporate all of the new and loving strategies in this book. No matter how much you know about having a good relationship, if your feelings are hurt it is difficult to be loving and supportive.

The love letter helps you give yourself the support you need when your partner can't. When you are writing a love letter, you are taking the time to listen to yourself with love, caring and understanding. If you are not willing to take the time to love yourself by listening to your feelings, you cannot realistically expect others to do this for you. When you feel the need for emotional support but you are not getting it, this is a sign that you need to give to yourself by writing a love letter.

The purpose of a love letter is not to dump negative resentments, judgments, and criticisms on your partner. It is not written to try to change them or correct them, nor to point out their inadequacies. If used in this way it will not work. It will become just another weapon to get even with your partner, or a means to manipulate them by making them feel guilty. The love letter works when it is written *for you to feel more loving.*

WHAT A LOVE LETTER ACCOMPLISHES

When your feelings are not being heard by another, it is essential that at least you hear them. Then once they have been expressed, it is essential that you imagine the response you need to feel supported and heard. Writing a love letter assists you in removing the blocks to giving and receiving love. Through experiencing and exploring the full range of your feelings, negativity gets released quite automatically.

In writing out the response letter, your subconscious mind gets to feel and hear the support it deserves. Through being responsible to express what we need to hear, we open our hearts to feel and accept the support that does exist. The response letter also helps the reader of your love letter know what you need from them in response to your letter.

The precise structure of the love letter format assists you in experiencing and feeling deep levels of emotion. As you continue to write, your awareness spontaneously expands until you discover the positive feelings that are always already there but generally hidden.

Whenever you are upset or disturbed, the reason is that your awareness is contracting onto the negative side of things. But through exploring the negative feelings inside, your awareness begins to expand and see the good side of things. Instantly, you are free from the gripping influence of negative emotions. You are suddenly aware of a wealth of positive feeling and emotion.

To bring about this catharsis and transformation, there are four levels of negative emotions you need to consciously experience or feel. Then, as a result, you can experience the positive feelings of love that were blocked by the negativity. Thus after writing out the four levels, you always finish the letter by writing out the fifth level, the level of love. By writing out these emotions they are more consciously experienced and thus more fully released. These different levels are:

Level 1: Anger
Level 2: Sadness
Level 3: Fear
Level 4: Remorse
Level 5: Love and other positive attitudes

Through following this emotional map one can most effectively explore the depths of negative emotions, and discover again and again the loving feelings that are so quickly forgotten at times of stress. After writing the love letter, write a letter in response. Write out expressions of apology, understanding, agreement, acknowledgment, love, and gratitude. In the response letter to your love letter, write out what you need to hear, what would make you feel good, and what you feel the other person's response would be if they were able to hear you and respond with an open heart.

HOW TO WRITE A LOVE LETTER

In writing a love letter, you write out the feelings of one level and quite naturally your awareness moves to the deeper feelings of the next level. Begin by writing out any feelings of anger. As long as you are feeling anger, continue writing at level one. At some point you will notice a softening of your awareness. Then choose to explore the feelings of level two.

Put in writing the feelings of sadness. As you fully explore level two your awareness will shift automatically to experience the deepest and most vulnerable feelings of level three. Write out your feelings of fear. As you write out the feelings of the first three levels, you may notice the emotions becoming more intense. This is a sign they are being released and a catharsis is taking place.

Spontaneously you will begin to feel a sense of responsibility. Then move to level four. Write out your feelings of remorse and apology. This shift will most effectively release you from holding on to any negative feelings. Automatically a surge of positive and loving feelings will emerge into your conscious awareness.

At this point you will probably feel much better. It is still vitally important to write out your positive feelings. Express love, appreciation, respect, understanding, acceptance, caring and trust. Setting down your positive feelings will make them last longer. Each time you write a love letter you will be strengthening your ability to sustain a positive and loving attitude, especially during stressful, upsetting times.

When writing a love letter, imagine that you are sharing your feelings with someone who is really listening to you and willing to support you. If you are upset with someone, you may address the love letter to that person. But keep in mind that you are just sharing your feelings with them; you are not trying to tell that person about himself or herself. You are not giving a critique of them. Rather, you are sharing feelings with them so that they will better understand how to support you.

You can benefit from writing a love letter to someone even if you don't give it to them. If someone can't support your feelings, by all means write the letter to them, but do not give it to them. By writing the letter you will feel better. It is much more powerful to be able to share your feelings with the person you are writing to, but if they cannot support your feelings with love and understanding, sharing them will only upset both of you.

To help you discover the full range of your feelings, the love letter format includes lead-in phrases for each level. Write out the lead-in phrase and then complete the sentence. This sentence completion technique helps to draw out your feelings. Lead-in phrases are especially helpful when you are not sure how to express what you are feeling.

These precise lead-in phrases not only help you bring up feelings, but they also lead you to deeper and deeper levels of emotion. You may choose to use just one, over and over at each level, or to use them all. It is up to you to use the phrases that best assist you to express your feelings. Most of the lead-in phrases are "I sentences," which can help you stay in your feelings.

Whenever you feel upset, find a pen and a couple of pieces of paper and just start writing. Writing out what you are feeling will always help you to become more centered. Following the love letter format ensures that you will quickly find your loving center again.

THE LOVE LETTER FORMAT

Dear _____,

I am writing you this letter to release my resentment and negative emotions, and to discover and express the positive feelings that you deserve. I am also writing this letter to ask for your support without demanding it.

Level 1: Anger
I don't like . . .
I resent . . .
I feel frustrated . . .
I feel angry . . .
I feel furious . . .
I want . . .

Level 2: Sadness
It hurts . . .
I feel disappointed . . .
I feel sad . . .
I feel unhappy . . .
I wish . . .

Level 3: Fear
It is painful . . .
I feel worried . . .
I feel afraid . . .
I feel scared . . .
I need . . .

Level 4: Remorse and Apologies

I apologize . . .
I feel embarrassed . . .
I am sorry . . .
I feel ashamed . . .
I am willing . . .

Level 5: Love, Understanding, Gratitude, and Forgiveness

I love . . .
I appreciate . . .
I realize . . .
I forgive . . .
Thank you . . .
I would like . . .
I trust . . .

Love, _____

Remember, whenever it is hard to be loving, that is the time to write a love letter. Following the love letter format will help you fully process your negative feelings and bring out the true and loving feelings within you.

Give yourself the time to explore each level. Even if the feelings don't seem to be there, take a deep breath, relax, and search for them. Take whatever comes up and write that out. Try to spend equal time at each level. When one level is missing, sometimes that level needs most to be explored.

Love letters generally take about twenty minutes to write. Take about four minutes to explore each of the five levels. Don't worry about spelling or punctuation. Just continue to feel the emotion as you write it out. Whenever you get stuck, just start writing the lead-in phrase. Then write out whatever feeling or thought comes up, even if that feeling is unrelated to the lead-in phrase or even unrelated to the person to whom you are writing this letter. Writing a love letter is a tool to assist you in opening your heart. By repeatedly using this tool you will gradually develop the skill of keeping your heart open at all times.

THE RESPONSE LETTER

After writing a love letter, take a few extra minutes to write a response. For many people this is what allows the love letter to be most healing. In formulating a response you are indirectly giving yourself the love you deserve. We generally get upset because we are telling our feeling self that we are being abused in some way. To write a response letter is to tell our subconscious mind or feeling self what we deserve to hear in response.

After writing a love letter, your feeling self is wide open to receive positive input. A response letter allows you to take responsibility to affirm the love and support that you deserve. The response letter does not need to be long, but it can be if you choose. It should include

1. apologies expressed in a way that makes you feel heard and supported;
2. understanding and validating statements that express a warmth and compassion for your feelings;
3. loving statements that praise, agree, appreciate, and acknowledge what you deserve; and
4. whatever else you need to hear to feel good.

Response letters also gradually train the people in your life to know how you need to be supported. Throughout this book we have explored how different we all are. It is unrealistic to expect our loved ones to know the right words. By writing a response letter and sharing it with your partner, you give them a chance to express their love and support through a channel that will be most effective for you

WHY THE LOVE LETTER WORKS

The love letter works because it assists us to become aware of how we are truly feeling. When we are upset or bothered, by becoming fully aware of what is bothering us, automatic "self-correction" takes place and we begin to feel loving again. Increasing our awareness of how we are feeling facilitates self-awareness and thus connects us to our inner resources, including love, wisdom, and forgiveness. The effectiveness of the love letter technique is based on four principles.

1. Feeling and expressing emotions increases self-awareness and thus connects us to our true selves.
2. Feelings unfold in layers. Through fully experiencing one layer, another, deeper layer unfolds to consciousness. Each new level brings increasing awareness.
3. The action of *writing out* feelings dramatically increases awareness and, especially, releases us from the grip of unresolved past feelings.
4. The action of writing a response letter increases the awareness of what we need as well as our entitlement to receive that support. By expressing that desired support, we indirectly give that support to ourselves and become more capable of loving ourselves.

PRINCIPLE 1
EXPRESSING EMOTIONS INCREASES SELF-AWARENESS AND CONNECTS US TO OUR TRUE SELVES

Negative emotions are the symptoms of imbalance. They are signs that we have lost an awareness of our true self. By feeling, experiencing, and learning from our negative emotions, we automatically come back to balance and experience the positive and loving feelings of our true self.

Our negative emotions are like clouds that block the radiance of the sun. When the clouds blow away, the sun can be seen again. When our negative emotions are released, our already-present loving attitudes can be felt again. Ironically, the recognition of negative emotions leads the awareness back to positive center.

Every negative emotion has the potential to bring us increasing awareness so that we may effectively cope with the stress of change. Negative emotions help us to realize what has happened to push us out of balance. With this understanding we automatically come back into balance.

These primary negative emotions are really healing emotions. They are a divine gift to aid us in increasing our awareness and coming back into balance. Just as physical pain is nature's way of telling us that some correction needs to be made, negative emotions are the expressions of emotional pain. The increased insight achieved through feeling our negative emotions assists us in discovering, forming, sustaining, changing, or correcting our beliefs, expectations, and desires. In this sense emotions motivate and guide us in relating to external reality.

By resisting our negative emotions we lose touch with the positive feelings that always lie dormant within us; we disconnect from our potential to adapt harmoniously to external changes and stress. People resist negative emotions only because they do not have the skill to release them. Writing love letters gradually frees you from the need to resist and repress negative emotions. You are then able to experience the profound depths of who you are and what you have to offer this world, as well as what you need in order to heal.

To be superficially aware of our negative emotions is not enough. To come back to center we need to explore the full range of our negative emotions. By becoming aware of our deeper negative emotions, we are able to release them and come back to our true self, which is always positive.

PRINCIPLE 2
EMOTIONS UNFOLD IN LAYERS

The second principle is that emotions unfold in layers. When one experiences a negative emotion, there is generally some deeper feeling underlying it. Through experiencing one level of emotion, another level spontaneously emerges into conscious awareness. When the full range of negative feeling is experienced, one is able to feel more loving and positive.

For example, Bill was reading the paper one evening and Mary felt ignored. Mary was angry that Bill was ignoring her. However, at a deeper, more vulnerable level, she was sad that Bill was not as affectionate as he used to be. She missed his attentiveness and affection.

When she expressed her anger, Bill reacted by explaining that he was not ignoring her, but was just focused on something really important. Then she felt even more hurt and angry. From there they continued to argue about whether or not he was ignoring her.

In this example, Mary never got a chance to discover her more vulnerable feelings of missing Bill's affection. If she were to write a love letter, she would have discovered the sad feelings that were underlying the anger. If she continued to explore her sadness, her most vulnerable feelings would begin to surface. She would begin to experience her fears.

Let's imagine now that Mary did write a love letter. In the process, she experienced being afraid that Bill was going to continue ignoring her. She was afraid that Bill would never have romantic feelings for her again. As she wrote out her negative emotions, she began to soften and remember all the wonderful things about him. Her resentment dissolved and she realized that he wasn't purposefully ignoring her.

When Bill read her letter, he was able to hear the complete truth and thus react appropriately. Now he could understand why she was so upset, and he also had time to realize that he had not given her the understanding and respect she needed and deserved. In reading Mary's letter you can see how her feelings softened and became more vulnerable. It is as follows:

MARY'S LOVE LETTER

Dear Bill,

I am writing you this letter to release my resentment and negative emotions to find my positive loving feelings, which you deserve. I am also writing this letter to ask for your support without demanding it.

(1. Anger) I resent it when you ignore me. I resent it when you walk right past me as if I do not exist. I feel frustrated because I am feeling left out and ignored. I feel frustrated because you think everything is fine in our relationship. I feel frustrated when you sit there reading the newspaper. I want to be more important than the newspaper. I want you to notice me. I feel angry that you didn't even bother to give me a hug or ask me about my day. I am angry that you went right to the newspaper. I deserve to be noticed when you get home. I want you to be happy to see me. I want to feel special.

(2. Sadness) It hurts when I think about you all day and look forward to seeing you and then you don't even notice me. It hurts to feel as though I am all alone. I feel disappointed that we are not more intimate. I feel disappointed that you are not as affectionate as you used to be. I wish we were more intimate. I feel sad that when you came home you were not excited to see me. I wish you would ask me how my day went. I feel sad that you didn't seem happy to see me. I miss your affection. I would like you to be interested in my day.

(3. Fear) It is painful to feel you don't love me anymore. I feel worried when you don't even think to give me a hug and a kiss. I feel worried that you take me for granted. I hope that you really do still love me. I feel afraid that you will continue to ignore me. I'm afraid that you will think this is really no big deal. I am afraid you will always forget me. I need your loving reassurance. I need your hugs and kisses.

(4. Remorse) I feel embarrassed for resenting you so much. I feel bad for offending you. I am sorry for not trusting that you love me. I am sorry for not appreciating how much you do try to make my life easier. I am sorry that I was not more flexible. I apologize for being so demanding. I am willing to be more flexible and more accepting.

(5. Love and asking for support) I love being with you. I love when you are interested in me. I love feeling that I am a special part of your life. I love when you make my life easier and support me. I love that you want to please me and try to do the things that are important to me.

I would like to have a hug and a kiss when you come home. Would you be willing to share a few minutes of special time when you come home? I love being close to you and trusting you more and more. I love learning to give you the support that you need. I trust that you do love me and that we can both get what we need.

Love, Mary

MARY'S RESPONSE LETTER:

Dear Mary,

I am sorry that I have been ignoring you when I get home. I am sorry that I have hurt you. You deserve to feel special because you are special. I love coming home knowing that you will be there. I generally don't realize how important a hug and a kiss can be. I also miss the early days of our relationship when hugs and kisses were so spontaneous.

I have been so busy at work that I have made our relationship less important. I did forget. I am sorry that I have been ignoring you. I understand how angry it makes you and how much it hurts. Please forgive me.

Love, Bill

Because Mary was able to explore the complete truth about her feelings, she was able to experience her loving emotions again. From this more loving place, she could ask for support and communicate the response she needed to hear without demanding it or making Bill wrong. By fully expressing each level she easily and effortlessly moved to deeper levels of her feelings, until she was able to transcend her resentment and negativity and to experience the love that Bill deserved. From this loving place she then could imagine his support as she wrote the response letter.

One of the reasons arguments generally don't work is that neither person ever feels enough support to vertically move through their deeper feelings and find love. When most people share feelings, they either stay on the surface or they argue. Arguing prevents probing into deeper levels.

When one is unable to move to the deeper levels of feeling, then in order to feel better they become dependent on repressing negative feelings. By exploring these deeper levels one is able to regain contact with the true self, regardless of how repressed it has become. Through repeatedly writing love letters, awareness of one's true, loving self becomes greater and more stable.

PRINCIPLE 3
WRITING OUT FEELINGS RELEASES US FROM THE GRIP OF UNRESOLVED PAST FEELINGS

Writing out your feelings heightens your awareness of your emotions. This greater awareness allows you to go deeper and to more effectively release the negativity. Sharing your feelings out loud also increases awareness and allows you to go deeper, but only if you feel completely safe and heard.

When we share upset feelings out loud, we may feel a need to protect, defend, justify, or explain our feelings. This just holds us up and may actually prevent us from going deep enough to release our resentments and negative emotions.

Overreactions may result from a "displacement" of upset feelings. When Mary is upset with Bill, ninety percent of her upset may be from something else that happened to her that day. Or her upset may be the result of resenting him for other reasons. Either way, it all comes out in response to his reading the paper.

When we are stuck feeling upset, most of the time, we are overreacting because of past unresolved feelings. Mary may be upset with Bill not only for ignoring her, but also because her father used to ignore her when she was growing up. Ten percent of her upset has to do with Bill and ninety percent has to do with her unresolved feelings toward her father.

Thus we may overreact because we transfer the unresolved feelings of the past onto present situations. This transference happens automatically and unconsciously. All we consciously know at these times is that we are very upset. But when we look back at the situation, we can easily see that our reactions were unwarranted in relationship to what happened.

When past feelings come back to haunt us, it is then difficult to break free and react appropriately to the situation. At such times, when we feel gripped by the unconscious, we can regain control by consciously writing out the feelings that are coming up.

It is generally very difficult not to succumb to the influence of the past when it comes up, because this flood of intense feeling "feels" as though it is being caused by what is happening right now. When Mary is upset with Bill, it feels as though Bill's present actions are all that is upsetting her.

Through the action of writing we are able to center ourselves again in present time, rather than be overwhelmed by a flood of past feelings. When the past feelings inevitably come up, we can more easily release them because they are obvious overreactions and appear irrational.

When past feelings come up and they are confronted, it has the effect of making them more real. If Bill responds as though Mary's reaction is unfair, which is almost inevitable, Mary will feel even more intensely that Bill is the source of her negative feelings. If he tells her that she is overreacting — when she is indeed overreacting — he only adds fuel to the fire. What she really needs is Bill's support in writing a love letter, so that she can become more centered. To avoid intensifying the past feelings, Mary can choose to write out her emotions. By the end of the letter, she will probably realize on her own that she was overreacting.

PRINCIPLE 4
WRITING A RESPONSE LETTER
INCREASES OUR WORTHINESS

People are generally much better at being upset than being able to identify exactly what they need to feel better. Through writing a response letter, one can become more aware of what they need to feel supported. As this awareness increases, the need to be upset decreases, even if that need is not immediately fulfilled. By taking responsibility to identify his or her needs the writer is also released from feeling so dependent on others to feel OK, worthy, or lovable.

Many times, the instinctive drive to express negative emotions is resolved merely by identifying the unfulfilled need. It is as though negative emotions arise to reveal the pain of unfulfilled needs. Take, for example, a frustrated little girl. She gets louder and louder until her needs are identified. The identification and acknowledgment of her needs helps her to relax. When her needs are validated, then she can relax even more. She becomes capable of waiting her turn.

When a person's needs are not identified and validated, they may develop an unconscious pattern of intensifying their hurt to receive validation. If they feel they have to prove their worthiness to be upset, then the tendency to stay upset increases. To bear out the validity of their unfulfilled needs, the emotions cry out louder.

For many, the intensity of emotion signals greater hurt; greater hurt then implies that the unfulfilled need is more valid, which in turn signals greater worthiness of compassion and support. This logic, of course, is self-defeating. When a person is in need of support, but unconsciously feels unworthy of support, they will tend to overdramatize their emotions by rejecting or overlooking whatever support is available. Rather than experience both the negative emotions and their positive feelings, they fixate on negativity. The mind remains fixated on feeling negativity to validate its pain, and thus resists acknowledging the positive. This occurs when we don't want to feel better, or when we are stuck in any undesirable emotional state.

There are always valid reasons for a person to be upset, but there are also valid reasons to feel really good. When the conscious mind is able to hold together both the good and the bad, resolution automatically takes place and one feels better.

Writing a response letter naturally brings forth a greater awareness of the validity of one's needs. With this greater awareness, the inclination to overdramatize our emotional pain (or fixate on negativity) subsides, and our ability to receive love and support increases. We can more fully envision receiving the support we need.

Writing a response letter also helps our partners learn how to support us when we are upset. Opening a door that was previously closed, it shows the way for our partners to love us more. A response letter does not criticize them or demand anything from them. More importantly, it becomes a powerful means for us to support and love ourselves.

To write a loving letter to ourselves affirms that we deserve that love. Rather than remaining victim to the moods of others, we become more self-reliant and less dependent on others to make us feel good. Ultimately, the inner child is hurting when our emotional needs are not being fulfilled. At such times we must learn to love ourselves, forgive ourselves, and believe in ourselves. Through writing a loving response letter, our inner child or emotional self will receive the love it deserves. As the inner child is healed, the adult aspect of us becomes much more capable of communicating our needs and attracting the support we deserve.

WHEN TO WRITE A LOVE LETTER

One of the biggest problems with writing love letters is that when some people really need to write a love letter, that is the last thing they want to do. They would rather be resentful and stuck. This is because they are being gripped by the unconscious mind. To overcome this tendency, get in the habit of writing short love letters. Then whether you want to or not, you can willfully pull out a sheet of paper and start writing. Writing love letters is a discipline that becomes easier to do the more you practice it.

There are many situations that call for writing a love letter. The following should give you some ideas.

When there is an upset between partners, both agree to go into separate rooms and write a love letter to the other as well as a response letter.

When partner A is upset and partner B cannot listen without getting defensive or upset in return, then to avoid an argument, partner A writes a love letter (including a response letter) and then reads the love letter. Partner B then reads the response letter back to partner A.

When you are feeling resentful, writing a love letter assists you in releasing your resentment and finding forgiveness.

When you are upset, writing a love letter helps you feel better through exploring your feelings and releasing the negative emotions.

When you are confused, overwhelmed, or exhausted, writing love letters helps you become centered again.

When you are resisting through withdrawing, grumbling, or shutting down, writing a love letter assists you to open up.

Writing a love letter is the most powerful tool two people can use for making up after fighting or arguing.

When you are upset with yourself, writing a love letter to yourself helps you forgive and love yourself more.

When you are generally feeling depressed, anxious, irritated, or apathetic, writing a love letter enables you to once again feel inspired, confident, tolerant, motivated, enthusiastic, and even excited.

When you are giving up an addiction, writing love letters is the ultimate tool to assist you in processing, releasing and healing the painful feelings that the addiction was holding down.

When you are trying to heal the wounds of a painful childhood, writing love letters allows you to bring up and heal those feelings.

Whenever you experience a traumatic change in your life, such as a divorce, the death of a loved one, a financial loss, a failure, a rejection, a change of job or location, writing love letters helps you cope with the stress of such a change.

When you need to receive spiritual support, writing a love letter to God assists you in fully opening your heart in prayer.

In each of these cases writing out your feelings is the best technique. Whenever you want to feel better, that is the time to write a love letter.

SHARING AND READING LOVE LETTERS

To fully heal emotional hurt it is important to share your feelings. When you share your feelings in a context of love and support, negative feelings and emotional wounds are most effectively healed. You are also increasing your self-awareness when you write the love letter. This expanded self-awareness generates the self-love necessary to release negativity.

Probably you have noticed that when you are feeling good about yourself, it is difficult to stay upset. Ultimately every upset is just a symptom of not loving ourselves. Writing out feelings allows us to give ourselves the caring, understanding, respect, appreciation, acceptance, and trust that we deserve. Through sharing our feelings with another in a context of love, that loving self-awareness is magnified.

If you have ever stood up in a group of people to share about yourself, you probably noticed a tremendous rush of energy. This energy boost comes from an increase in self-awareness, and that comes from the anticipation of a whole group of people being aware of you. The more you share yourself, the more self-aware you will become.

Sharing yourself with those who love you increases loving self-awareness. Sharing yourself with those who do *not* love you can easily hurt you unless you are firmly rooted in your self-love.

If you cannot share your feelings with your partner, then it is important to share them with your friends. If it is not comfortable to share with your friends, it is essential that you get a therapist with whom to share your feelings. Find someone who will be able to hear your feelings and support you.

One time a lady told me that love letters did not work for her. I asked her how many times she had written them, thinking that I would suggest that she write several to help develop the skill. She told me she had written over a hundred. I was amazed by her commitment. I then asked her why she had written so many if they didn't work. She said they had worked for the first six months, but for the last few months they hadn't worked. When I asked her with whom she had shared her letters, she said no one! By not sharing her feelings, love letters stopped working.

Love letters work because the subconscious mind believes that these feelings are being shared. If you are writing love letters but none of them are shared, then by choosing not to share them, you begin giving yourself the message that your feelings are unworthy of being understood and are not acceptable to others. This negative judgment prevents the feelings from being fully released. *An essential part of the healing process is to share your love letters.*

When you are sharing a love letter with someone, it can also be a very supportive experience to listen to this person read out loud the letter you have written. This process gives you an even greater loving awareness of what you have felt. Sometimes, however, you may feel a need to get the emotions out by reading it yourself. If the letter is not too long or if you have the time, it is ideal to do both.

HOW TO READ A LOVE LETTER

There are four main rules for reading another person's love letters. They are:
1. *As a general rule, when you receive a love letter, read the end of the letter first to connect with the love.* This will then give you the strength and awareness to hear the other negative feelings.
2. *Never stop reading a letter until you have gotten to the end.* If you are going to read a person's love letter, promise to read the whole letter. It is unfair to hear their negative feelings without also hearing their loving feelings and apologies.
3. *Do not make any comments while reading the letter.* This allows the writer to feel fully heard. If the reader doesn't like what is being said, that is understandable. Most people would prefer that their partner never have any negative feelings, but that is not reality. Rather than disagree, question, correct, or invalidate what the letter is expressing, just take a deep breath and keep reading or listening.
4. *Do not criticize the letter or what was said in the letter.* Regard love letters as a sacred opportunity for a partner to share their feelings without having them used against them. If you feel like criticizing a person's love letter, don't. Just write your own love letter. By all means avoid arguing after the sharing of love letters. If you are feeling like arguing after you both have written love letters, that is a definite sign that the two of you need some space from each other for a while.

It is very typical, however, that once you have read a love letter you will feel more loving and understanding. If that is the case, thank your partner for writing the letter and give them a big hug. Review the letter using the phrase "I understand" in relationship to some of the main points that you strongly relate to. You may say things like, "I understand it is difficult when . . ." or "I understand it hurts when . . ." or "I understand that it makes you angry when . . ." or "You deserve . . ." "I understand you feel disappointed that . . ." "I also wish . . ." and so on.

If you do not feel more loving and understanding or you do not feel like giving them a big hug, put on the brakes and do not criticize the letter. Let your partner know that this was a hard letter to hear and that you need some time to think about what was said, and that you need to write a love letter.

It is natural to feel positive until someone starts complaining about you. At that moment you begin to remember all the complaints and resentments that you have been storing up. If one has been storing up bad feelings, reading another's love letter will increase their awareness of their own bitterness. They will need to take some time before they can fully process those resentments that come up.

If reading your partner's letter has upset you, letting them read the letter to you may sometimes help you to receive the love. You may need to hear the letter several times before you are willing to receive the love at the end of the letter. Reading a love letter may be the necessary catalyst to help you feel and release your own accumulating resentment.

Again, when you feel like criticizing a person's love letter, resist the urge and go write out your own love letter. A man especially may need to mull his partner's letter over for a while. After some time he will begin to see the writer's point of view. At such a time it is then very helpful for him to thank her for writing the love letter.

Women should realize that reading love letters is generally harder for men. Even though a man may not say much in response, he has heard as much as he can. One should feel grateful that their partner has read the letter, and not expect them to respond. If they can respond, that is an extra bonus.

LOVE LETTERS AND PROBLEM SOLVING

I remember that for the first three years my wife and I used the love letter technique, we wrote the love letters and just felt good that we were back to feeling loving again. Then at a later time, when we were not feeling so sensitive, we would discuss our problems and look for win/win solutions.

As your understanding of each other increases and trust builds over time, it becomes easier to discuss the actual problems that are mentioned in your love letters. I do not recommend that you discuss solving the problems to a great extent when you have just made up. Enjoy being loving awhile, and then tackle the problems.

Love letters do not solve problems: they just assist you in getting back to the love. They inform others of how you could be supported, but do not demand. From a loving frame of mind you are then capable of approaching problem-solving from a place of wanting both sides to win.

Love letters expand your ability to care, understand, respect, love, appreciate, accept, and trust. With these positive attitudes it is much easier to solve the inevitable problems and conflicts that arise in a relationship.

WHEN YOUR PARTNER WON'T READ YOUR LETTERS

If your partner doesn't want to hear your love letters, don't use that as an excuse for not writing them. Remember, the purpose of writing love letters is to help yourself feel more loving so that you can be more supportive. It is not to receive more support from your partner. However, love letters do give them the opportunity to understand you better.

If a partner doesn't want to hear your love letters, it is probably too hard for them to hear negative feelings. As they see that writing love letters makes you more loving, they will gradually appreciate that you write them. Eventually, when they feel securely loved, trusted, accepted, and appreciated, they will become curious and want to read your letters.

You may want to give them this book or my book, *What You Feel, You Can Heal,* to help them understand the importance of all feelings and the need to share them. After some time, if you continue sharing your apologies and love, they may begin to trust the full range of your feelings. It is such a relief to feel that all your emotions are acceptable and understandable to your partner.

Sometimes it may be necessary to leave out the resentment, anger, and frustration section. Write it out on a separate page but don't share it with your partner. Some people have been so hurt by childhood abuse, anger, and frustration that they cannot listen to negative feelings. Others have been trained that having such feelings is bad. In these cases, you may choose to share only the apology and love sections of your letters.

WHAT TO DO IN AN EMOTIONAL EMERGENCY

Have you ever felt like fighting with your partner right before going on a trip or right before guests are due to arrive? These are examples of emotional emergencies. There is no time to talk things through, and there is insufficient time to write a love letter. There is nothing to do but repress your feelings and pretend to be nice and loving. As a result you do not enjoy the trip or party together.

There is, however, something that you can do:

You can take two minutes and write a mini love letter.

Take out a piece of paper — a napkin, an envelope, anything will do — and write just one sentence for each of the five levels of feeling. It is amazing how quickly you can release the negative feelings, rather than stuff them and hold on to them.

For example, while getting ready to leave on a vacation, Bill feels resentful that Mary gave him a disapproving look when he expressed that they were late for the airport and needed to rush. Instead of being upset with her, Bill took two minutes to write a mini love letter and a response.

(Love Letter)
Dear Mary,

    1. I resent it when you disapprove of me. I want you to appreciate me.

2. I feel disappointed that now we are fighting instead of being happy.
3. I feel afraid that we are going to fight in the car.
4. I am sorry for overreacting and being so unforgiving.
5. I love you so much and I want to enjoy this trip. Let's have a great time.
   Love, Bill

(Bill's Response Letter)
Dear Bill,

I am sorry for disapproving of you. You are wonderful. Thanks for understanding my imperfections. I love you. You are so important to me.
   Love, Mary

Bill did not even need to share this letter. In two minutes of writing he was released from the gripping influence of negative feelings and resentment. Whenever you think you don't have time to write a love letter, you can always write a mini love letter.

CREATING TIME TO WRITE LOVE LETTERS

Sometimes busy people think they can never create the time to write a love letter. They should consider how much time and energy they waste by worrying too much and being frustrated or unhappy. They should consider the mistakes they make simply because they were not more creative and centered. Writing love letters keeps you connected to your intuition, which ensures that you make fewer mistakes and use your time, energy and resources more efficiently. Taking the time to write love letters actually gives you more time.

Most often, couples who argue for hours and days will say they are too busy to write love letters. Imagine how much more time you would have to enjoy each other if you did not argue or fight. Creating the time to write love letters is essential if you want to be an emotionally fit person and sustain loving relationships. Writing love letters is akin to brushing your teeth. If you don't brush your teeth, then plaque builds up and you get gum disease. If you don't regularly process your feelings, then resentment builds up and cripples your ability to fully love.

POINTS TO REMEMBER
WHILE WRITING A LOVE LETTER

1. *Just begin!* Sometimes the hardest part of writing a love letter is starting. Try to keep a pen and paper handy. When your partner needs to write a love letter, support them by getting them a pen and paper.
2. *Don't edit your feelings.* Let them all come out. Even if only a part of you has the feeling, let it be expressed. Allow the hurt and wounded child within to come forth. Don't try to be reasonable or rational. Stick

to "I" sentences and short comments. When sentences are longer than two lines, you are getting too intellectual. Don't analyze what happened. Rather, share how you feel in reaction to what happened.

3. *Don't expect yourself to be aware of love when you start the letter.* When you begin a love letter, you may feel resentful and not much else. Just start writing out the resentment, and you will see how naturally your awareness will progress to the deeper levels of feeling. Don't wait till you are feeling love to write the letter. The purpose of writing the letter is to help you feel more loving.

4. *Repeating levels.* You may find, after you have written out the first three levels, that when you start writing out the apologies of the fourth level, you get angry again. That's fine. Just go with the flow. Begin expressing the anger and then work your way down to the fourth level again.

5. *Don't finish until you reach the love.* If you stop writing before you get to the love, it is not a love letter. Come back to the letter in a while if you don't have time to finish it. It is never healthy to share your letter if you have not gotten back to the love. If you just can't find the love, try the role reversal technique. Write a love letter to yourself from the person you can't forgive. By standing in their shoes awhile, it is easier to forgive them.

6. *Balance the sections of your letter.* Try to give equal attention to each level of a letter. Don't write three pages of resentment and one page of hurt, two paragraphs of fear and guilt, and one line of love. That is not a love letter. There should especially be a lot of love at the end of a love letter. If you leave out a particular level, that may block you from fully releasing the negativity and fully feeling good and loving.

7. *Write the love letter for yourself.* Don't write the love letter for the purpose of changing your partner, mother, or anyone else. Write the love letter so that you will feel better and so that you can give them more support. Even if a person refuses to write you a love letter or refuses to read yours, it doesn't mean that you can't benefit from writing the love letter.

8. *When discussions turn into arguments, stop talking and go into separate rooms, and both of you write out your feelings.* Come back and share the letters with each other. Bill reads Mary's letter and then Mary reads Bill's letter. In most cases they will feel better and more loving. The argument is over and they make up with a hug. The original problem they were fighting over may not be solved, but now at least they feel they are on the same team.

9. *When reading love letters doesn't seem to help, you can do the following:*
   a. Write another letter: You may need more time to feel the deeper levels of your painful emotions, or you may need time to process what was said in the letter to you.
   b. Read your letter out loud to your partner; this may help release the emotions.

c. Reread your partner's letter and have them reread yours.

d. Put the love letters aside for an hour, and take some time apart from each other. Try to discuss your feelings with someone else who can give you the support you need. Or simply go out and do something that makes you feel good. When you feel better about yourself, it is easier to love your partner.

10. *Go with your feelings.* When writing love letters, express whatever feelings come up. It may be that you start out talking to your husband, but then, you begin feeling emotions from childhood or other things that are bothering you. Just continue to let these feelings come up and be expressed. As you practice the love letter technique you will find that whatever you think you are upset about is rarely the real source of your upset. Writing love letters is a journey into the depths of your inner feelings as well as a process of healing the past.

EIGHT COMMON KINDS OF LOVE LETTERS

Although love letters are written primarily for yourself, they are generally addressed to others. When you write a love letter you imagine that the person is going to read it with understanding. There are eight common kinds of love letters:

1. A love letter to an intimate partner
2. A love letter to a friend, child, or family member
3. A love letter to a business associate or client
4. A love letter to yourself
5. A love letter to God
6. A role reversal love letter
7. A "monster" love letter
8. A displacement love letter.

1. A Love Letter to an Intimate Partner

To avoid the buildup of resentment, it is recommended that couples write and share love letters on a regular basis. Whenever you find making up awkward or difficult, writing a love letter makes it very simple.

Intimate relationships are an excellent context in which to share our feelings, because our intimate partners have the potential to give us the most love and support. If, however, your intimate partner is not capable of giving that support, you can write a love letter without sharing the negative feelings. It is helpful in that case to have a therapist or a friend who can read your letter and support you.

2. A Love Letter to a Friend, Child, or Family Member

Love letters are excellent for resolving tension between family members, between parent and child, and between friends. To heal the past, many people have successfully written love letters to their parents. One recovering alcoholic framed the love letter he received from his daughter.

As soon as children can write, they can pen love letters to their siblings as well as to their parents. Parents can sit down and assist the child in writing a love letter.

When parents are upset with their children they can write a love letter to become centered again, but they must not share it with the children. When writing to children it is important that there are no overreactions, which can be very confusing to them. You may just write a letter to feel centered, and then talk to your child. Sometimes parents simplify and rewrite their letters, then give them to their children.

One mother who was always telling her teenage son what to do decided instead to start writing love letters just sharing how she felt. Immediately he started being more supportive.

Love letters work to dissolve tension in friendships. If you feel your friend cannot support the expression of anger and frustration, then don't share that part of your letter with them.

3. A Love Letter to a Business Associate or Client

Love letters can reduce tension in the workplace and make you more successful. When you are resenting the people you work with, you will be less effective. By releasing your resentment you can avoid work burnout and draw in more support.

If someone is bothering you at work, write them a love letter to release your resentment. As a result, you will be able to cope and communicate more effectively with them. Remember, though, it is not safe to share a love letter with anybody who might reject your feelings or not want to hear them. *It is generally not safe to share love letters in the workplace.* You can still write the letter to feel better yourself.

If you are resenting your clients, inevitably business gets worse for a while. To improve things, remember to write a love letter. Writing love letters can help bring you out of a slump, and then your productivity will tend to pick up.

4. A Love Letter to Yourself

If ever you are upset with yourself, it is very helpful to write yourself a love letter. Sometimes we are our worst enemies. At such times, write a love letter to yourself, expressing your anger, fear, etc., and then the loving feelings.

Remember, it is unrealistic to expect others to love you when you are not loving yourself. Writing a love letter to yourself allows you to fully release your negative emotions and strengthen your ability to love yourself.

5. A Love Letter to God

If you have a relationship with God, then write love letters several times a week sharing your feelings with God. When you have finished the letter you can feel God's love for you. Then write a short letter from God to you expressing that love and support. Give expression to God's love for you.

Some people do not have a conscious relationship with God but do recognize a relationship with the universe. These people can enrich this relationship by writing their letter to the universe, the life force, or whatever label works for them.

Writing a love letter to God is the ideal form of prayer when you are upset. At the end of the letter you can add the lead-in phrase, "I pray . . ." The definition of prayer in this context is to humbly ask for support.

Love letters are miraculous because truth works. In every spiritual tradition, truth has been hailed a master healer. Christ said, "The truth will set you free." The rishis of ancient India said, "Truth alone is victorious." Every seeker of God or goodness has been committed to the truth. The love letter format is a systematic way to explore the truth about ourselves that is most illusive and threatening. It gives us an emotional map to guide us through the darkness of negative emotions and bring us into the light of love, responsibility, and compassion.

6. The Role Reversal Love Letter

When it is hard to find the forgiveness and love at the end of the love letter, that is a sign that you need to increase your ability to understand the other person. By standing in their shoes for a while, it is easier to forgive them. The ultimate technique for finding forgiveness is to imagine that you are that person and write a love letter from that person to yourself.

This is hard to do, because when we are not forgiving, it is because we don't want to understand the other person's feelings. If you are skilled in writing your own feelings, writing a role reversal love letter will be much easier. You will find quite miraculously that years of resentments can melt away in a matter of minutes.

7. The "Monster" Love Letter

When you are very upset, it can help to write out your feelings without editing them in any way. Just let your feelings come out, no matter how destructive or victim-like or blaming they may sound. Follow the standard format but don't share the letter with the person you are writing to. Don't try to be rational or fair. Go ahead and use generalizations and "you" sentences.

After finishing this letter, put it away. Reread it a week or a month later when you are feeling more positive. It is very freeing to review your monster feelings when you are not feeling negative.

8. The Displacement Love Letter

When you are upset, you may feel as though you are upset about one thing, but deep inside you are often upset about something else. This is called

267

displacing feelings. For example, you may be angry with the boss, but you come home and take it out on your partner or children.

In a displacement love letter you begin writing to one person, but as you continue writing, you discover that you are really upset about something else or with someone else. At this point in the letter, you would then begin writing to this different person. In this case the love letter helps you find out and then heal what is really bothering you.

It is also quite common that when we are upset in our relationships, our upset is greatly intensified because it reminds us of a painful experience in the past. Our upsets in present time tend to be clouded or intensified by the unhealed memories of past traumatic experiences.

A woman may be upset with her partner for ignoring her. While writing a love letter she discovers that she is actually still upset that her father ignored her; her husband's treatment is reminding her of unhealed wounds. She then starts over and writes the letter to her father. In sharing the letter with her partner, a friend or a therapist, she has a chance to heal this old hurt and be free to respond in a more accepting way to her husband. Approaching him with the attitude of acceptance, she can more effectively ask for his support.

SAMPLE LOVE LETTERS

1. Two Love Letters Written by a Couple After an Argument

Mary was upset with her husband Bill. She was looking forward to sharing his day off with him, but he ended up sleeping late. She felt so much resentment that when he did get up, she couldn't enjoy the time they did have. After some discussion they got in an argument. To avoid wasting the rest of the day in resentment, they stopped talking and she wrote the following letter. Writing it allowed her to forgive and accept Bill's need for sleep, and to enjoy the rest of the day with him. Reading it gave Bill a greater understanding of what was upsetting her.

(Note: These two love letters are included because they demonstrate the different ways feelings can be expressed. Not everyone writes letters this long; some people are just more expressive. In many cases a shorter letter will suffice.)

Dear Bill,

I resent that you slept late today. I resent it when you only think about yourself. I resent that we made plans together for the day, and now I find out that you have taken the day into your own hands. I resent feeling left out. I feel frustrated waiting around until you wake up after we made other plans for the day. I want you to let me know what you are planning. I want you to talk to me if you want to change plans. I want to know what you are thinking.

I feel frustrated that you ask me what I would like, and then you do what you want to do anyway. I feel frustrated when you mislead me into thinking that you are thinking about me. I want to share in our relationship. I feel used for sex, going to movies, and food. Where am I supposed to go when you don't need me. Am I supposed to disappear? I feel angry because I think you don't think I deserve to be consulted on a day like today.

I feel angry that you didn't tell me that you had decided to sleep late. I feel angry that you didn't give me the courtesy of having an opportunity to adjust my day. I deserve to be informed when you change our plans. I feel angry that you were so selfish. I am so angry that I don't get any consideration in this. I expect you to include me. Whatever happened to asking me what I would like to do? Are you just humoring me or what?

I feel angry because I think you feel that I am there just for you to play with according to your desires. I feel angry that you didn't let me know what you were planning. I feel angry that you probably didn't even have a plan. I expect you to tell me if you want to change the plans. I expect to know what is happening.

It hurts when you don't hold our time together on the weekend as special as I do. I feel disappointed that we are not enjoying this day together. I feel disappointed that you don't consider my time as important. I wish you had told me what you were going to do. I wish we could have gotten an early start. I feel sad that I waited around while you were sleeping late. I feel sad that I didn't know how late you were going to sleep so that I could figure out what I wanted to do with that time. I feel sad because I got up extra early to make a nice picnic and then sat around waiting for you.

I feel sad that I am unimportant and not special to you because we spent more time together this week. I feel sad that you were not excited to spend time with me without the children around. I feel sad that we fought. I feel sad because I feel so disrespected. I feel sad because I was really looking forward to this. I feel sad because I have rejected you when I could have enjoyed your company and had a good time. I would like that. I would like to still have a special day together. I would like to have a picnic. I would like you to let me know what to expect when we have a special day together.

I feel worried that you don't want to be with me today. I feel worried that you don't like family life. I feel afraid that you will give yourself to your work and I will get the leftovers. I feel worried that you like your work more than me. I feel worried that I have hurt you and that you are making me wrong. I hope that you will forgive me. I hope that we can have a good day. I hope that this gets resolved.

I feel afraid that you are going to withhold your love. I am afraid that you will not forgive me for being so disapproving. I am afraid that you will stay shut down to me. I need to feel safe. I need you to open up to me. I need you to forgive me. I need you to make me feel special. I need to feel your loving attention. I need to know that you do care.

I feel embarrassed that I was so resentful and intolerant of you. I feel bad that we didn't get things straight. I feel bad that I have probably shut you down. I feel bad that when I get upset I am not considerate of your feelings;

I see how that hurts and pushes you away. I am sorry that I have overreacted and judged you. I know that you try so hard to give me what I need, and mostly you succeed.

I am sorry that I assume that you did this to me. You probably had really good reasons for doing what you did and had no intention of hurting me or pushing me to the side. I am sorry that you felt so attacked when you did get up. I am sorry that this was not a perfect day for us to simply be together in the sunshine of our love. I apologize for being critical of you. I am willing to start over and create a very special day. I want to have another chance at today. What happened was an opportunity for me to love, respect, and accept you, rather than make you wrong.

I love being your wife. I love it when we take walks. I love when we spend time together. I love feeling your loving attention on me. Thank you for taking my car to be washed. Thanks for driving the kids to the movies the other day. Thanks for taking me out last night. I had a good time. I appreciate that you work so hard to support us. I respect that sometimes you need time for yourself to rest and relax. I forgive you for keeping me waiting this morning. I understand that you didn't realize that I had put everything on hold. I am concerned that you may still be resenting me. I trust that you will forgive me. I trust that you do love me. I trust that we can have a wonderful time together.

I love you, Mary.

After the argument Bill also was feeling upset, so he wrote the following love letter.

Dear Mary,

I resent it when you look at me like I am a bad child. I resent being talked down to. I resent being corrected. I resent being made wrong for sleeping late on my day off. I feel angry that you resent me so much. I feel angry that you made such a big deal of this. I feel angry that you expected me to get up early in the morning on my day off. I expect you to be more flexible. I expect you to be happy that I am having a nice morning in bed. I expect you to realize that I need my sleep.

I feel frustrated when it seems I am the bad guy who ruins your day. I feel frustrated that we are wasting this day not loving each other. I feel frustrated when you think I am lazy, selfish, and inconsiderate. I want you to be happy with me. I want you to be more flexible. I want to feel free to sleep late on my weekends off. I also want you to feel free to do as you please.

It hurts when I think you don't appreciate me. It hurts when you look for things to justify feeling unhappy and unsupported. I feel sad that you felt so unsupported by me. I feel disappointed because I don't even want to talk to you. I feel sad that you didn't do something that you wanted to do this morning. I feel sad that my taking care of myself has to be a source of pain for you. I feel sad that you think I don't care about you. I want you to know how much I really do care. I want you to feel loved and supported by me. I want to sleep late when I am tired. I want to have better communication between us.

I feel disappointed because we wasted so much time arguing. I feel disappointed because I don't feel appreciated by you. I feel disappointed because I think you always want more from me. I feel disappointed because I was hoping this would be a beautiful day for both of us. I wish that we could change everything and forget our resentment and be nice to each other. I wish that I had told you last night that I might sleep late. I wish it didn't have to hurt you so much.

It is painful to feel your disapproval. It is painful to feel like I failed you. It is painful to feel responsible for your unhappiness. I feel afraid that you will hold onto this and feel like a victim. I feel afraid that you will bring this up again and again. I feel afraid that you will continue to disapprove of me when I take care of myself. I think that you are jealous that I do take time for me when I need it. I need you to release your disapproval. I need you to accept and love me the way I am.

I feel worried that you really do believe I didn't care whether or not you waited around. I feel worried when I think that you feel so hurt by me. I feel worried because I really didn't mean to hurt you. I feel worried that you really don't accept or trust me. I deserve to be trusted. I am a very loving man. I hope that you find your love for me. I hope that you will be more accepting and forgiving. I hope that we will make up and have a beautiful day together.

I feel sorry that you waited two hours for me. I feel sorry that you expected to enjoy the whole day and I slept part of it away. I feel embarrassed that we didn't communicate better the night before. I feel embarrassed that we argued. I feel embarrassed that we were both so unforgiving. I am sorry that you were hurt. I am sorry that I didn't warn you. I am sorry that I was so defensive in the argument. I apologize for being insensitive and inconsiderate of you. I am willing to be more understanding and considerate.

I love you. I love when you make picnics. I love how caring you are. I love spending time with you. I look forward to spending time alone with you. You are my special sweetheart and I love being with you. I appreciate that you got up early to make the picnic. I appreciate that you wanted it to be a special day for us. I respect that you need to know what my plans are. I respect that we need to align our expectations better. I forgive you for being so upset with me. I understand that it took the whole romance out of our special day. I am concerned that you really don't feel how important you are to me. I trust that we will have a wonderful day together. I trust that you will release your resentment. I trust that you love me very much.

I love you, Bill

After writing their letters Bill and Mary felt more loving and centered. Then they shared their letters. Bill read Mary's letter out loud and then without much comment, Mary read Bill's letter. Having read the letters they felt much closer and gave each other a big and loving hug. They then went off and had a wonderful day together. It is important to note that, after reading the letters, Bill and Mary avoided trying to teach each other about how they could improve or change. It is enough to share how your partner affects you; it becomes unwanted criticism when you impose your opinions on how they should change or improve.

Bill and Mary assured me that without writing these letters they would not have enjoyed the day together and would have collected more reasons to be upset with each other. I suggest that whenever tension builds up, write love letters as soon as possible. Otherwise, resentment builds at an accelerated rate.

2. A Sample Love Letter to God

Jane is 48 and was feeling upset that her boyfriend Jim didn't want to get married. She wrote the following love letter to God.

Dear God,

I am writing this letter to release my resentments and negative feelings in order to feel loving again. I am also writing this letter to ask for your support.

I resent that I do not have any children. I resent that I have this time clock. I resent that my dreams have not come true. I feel like crying. I feel frustrated that I am not married. I feel frustrated that I feel so alone. I want to be married. I want to have a child. I feel angry that Jim doesn't want to get married. I feel angry that my life has passed me by. I feel angry that other people have relationships and children and I don't. I was expecting to get married and be happy. I was expecting to have children.

It hurts when I feel that I will never have a child. I feel disappointed that things are not working out the way I had dreamed. I feel disappointed when I think I will never touch my own baby's soft skin and hold him/her close. I wish that I were married. I wish that I had at least one child and a warm family life. It makes me sad when I feel my time has passed. I feel sad that my time has been taken away. I would like to be married to Jim and pregnant with his child. I would like him to want the same. I feel sad because I can almost see how beautiful our child would be. It hurts to feel so alone in my dreams.

It is painful to feel that I am living someone else's life. It is painful to feel somehow that you have failed me. I've always prayed and been good. I feel worried that I am being punished. I feel worried that I am doing something wrong. I feel worried that I am missing something very important. I hope that I can release this pain. I hope that I can learn this lesson. Maybe I need to release this dream and create new dreams of importance. I feel afraid I will never experience a real loving relationship. I feel afraid that Jim does not really love me. I feel afraid that he will leave me and I will have to start over. I feel afraid that I will keep making the same mistake.

I feel embarrassed that I have turned my back on you. I feel embarrassed that I have resented my life. I feel embarrassed that I focus on what I don't

272

have and don't appreciate what I do have. I feel embarrassed that I am always struggling to change things rather than relaxing and feeling grateful. I am sorry that I demand so much. I am sorry that I do not see the good of things. I am sorry that I don't pray more often. I am sorry that I doubt and worry so much that I cannot enjoy the gifts of today. I apologize for feeling abandoned by you. I apologize for not trusting in your love and grace. I am willing to fight less and surrender more.

I love you God. I love being alive. I love Jim. I love all the babies of the world . . . perhaps this is the unconditional love I so much want in my life.

I appreciate that Jim does love me and we have so many good times together. I appreciate that I have a good job and good health. I respect that there are many different ways that we are supposed to live our lives. I understand that I am put on this earth for a different purpose. Thank you for the good life I have lived. I am grateful. I am concerned that I fight and struggle too much. I trust that you will open my hand with love when my fists get tight. I trust you will lead me in the right path. I trust you. I love you.

    Love, Jane

As a result of writing this letter, Jane felt more loving and accepting of her life. She was able to be less demanding of Jim and to enjoy him more. Most important, she was able to remember her connection with God and feel God's love for her.

Ultimately, there is always an abundance of love and support available to us in our lives. It is our lesson to learn how to access that support. Through writing love letters we are able to release the negativity that collects in our hearts. In this way, we open ourselves to receiving the love and support we need so that we may fully give of ourselves in our relationships.

Writing love letters is so very powerful because it frees us to explore and heal our inner feelings regarding all our different types of relationships, without depending on the cooperation of the people in our lives. In the next chapter we will explore how being overly dependent on others for love and support can be our biggest mistake in trying to have loving relatinships.

CHAPTER SEVENTEEN

Making Peace with the Opposite Sex

To make peace with the opposite sex, the attitude of support is essential. But as we have already explored, the meaning of support is very illusive. We may think we are supporting when in truth we may be making things worse. It is ironic that conflict most often arises in our relationships when we are trying to be supportive.

When we feel dependent on someone, "supporting" them quite unconsciously turns into trying to change them. This compulsion to change our partners is at the root of all conflict in relationships. This is why it is crucial that we understand and accept that men and women are supposed to be different. Real support means appreciating and respecting these differences. Frustration is minimized when we work with the differences rather than impose our way of being.

With this basis it is truly possible to have enriching relationships with the opposite sex. But there is yet another requirement to end the conflict between the sexes. It is the underlying reason we try to change our partners. It is the real basis of our compulsion to improve and fix others. Without fulfilling this requirement — even with our new knowledge of how to support the opposite sex — conflict is inevitable; peace, love, and cooperation are obstructed.

THE IMPORTANCE OF SELF-LOVE

This single most critical requirement for building loving relationships is self-love. Without self-love our relationships with the opposite sex, and especially our intimate relationships, are filled with conflict and pain. When self-love is low, all our knowledge of how to have good relationships goes out the window.

When we are not loving ourselves, our actions and reactions are tainted by our need to be filled up with love. Out of our emptiness, we consciously or unconsciously seek to be filled. This need creates the compulsion to change our partners. We want to change them so we can get what we need. Even when we feel we are truly loving, our "love" may be compromised by the need to receive in return. When we are empty, we have little choice but to give conditionally with the expectation of return.

Essentially for a man to fully give to a woman, he first needs to appreciate, accept, and trust himself. These are the primary ways he needs to love himself in order to give unconditionally. When he is not loving himself in these ways and his partner is unhappy or gets upset, he becomes defensive and takes it personally; instead of listening and giving her the support she needs, he pouts. He feels a need to defend himself and ultimately feels a compulsion to change her feelings so he can feel good again.

He becomes controlling and demands particular responses from her. He demands that she feel positive; otherwise, he takes it personally. His defensiveness prevents him from supporting her. At those times when she is overwhelmed, overreacting, and exhausted by the stress of life, he tends to withdraw, grumble, and shut down to a greater extent.

For a woman to give unconditionally, she first needs to care for, understand, and respect herself. These are the primary ways she needs to love herself. When she is not loving herself in these ways, then she tends to overextend herself. She gives more than she has to give. She cares more about others than herself. She tries to be good and denies her own needs and feelings. She sacrifices herself for love and mistakenly expects that others should sacrifice too. She expects to receive what she puts out.

Her giving is sincere, but this underlying demand is not supportive. The more empty she grows, the more overwhelmed, overreactive, and exhausted she becomes. In these states, it is next to impossible for her to support her partner. When he feels her giving with strings, he does not feel supported; he tends to withdraw, grumble, and shut down to her.

These self-defeating tendencies can be overcome with unconditional love. But to give unconditionally we need first to be loving ourselves. Unconditional love is the expression of inner fulfillment. We cannot love unconditionally when we are needing love from ourselves.

When two adults approach each other to be filled up, neither is truly giving and both end up feeling used and empty. Mature relationships with the opposite sex are fulfilling when both members are giving. Mature relationships require mutual support. Relationships are mutually supportive when one approaches the other with the need to share and support, rather than the need to receive or to be filled up.

Imagine that every person has a "love tank." When that tank is filled with love, then they are capable of overflowing with love. They are capable of giving without demanding something in return. This person can be likened to a multi-millionaire philanthropist. He effortlessly shares his wealth because all his needs are satisfied. He is able to give to others without needing something in return. He rejoices in having opportunities to use his wealth constructively.

In a similar way, when we love ourselves and feel our worth, then we feel a compelling need to share and support others. From the feeling of self-love, we are capable of loving others without requiring something in return to make us feel good about ourselves. This unconditional love is the basis for successfully relating with the opposite sex. It is the fuel of commitment and marriage.

Peace is reflected in our relationships when our love tanks are full. Love is abundant when we are loving ourselves. From this higher perspective, we realize outward conflict to be the expression of our own inner turmoil and emptiness. Rejection is only painful when we also reject ourselves. To make peace and to experience increasing love and cooperation in our relationships, we must resolve our inner conflicts and negative emotions, rather than blame our partners in relationship. It is essential that we do not accuse our partners of not loving us when we are not loving ourselves.

PRACTICING UNCONDITIONAL LOVE

To practice unconditional love, we must take responsibility for loving ourselves at those times when our partner is not loving us. When we want to change our partner or we demand more, we must realize that we first need to fill our own love tanks, and then we can best support our partner. Instead of seeking to receive more from our partner, we need to give more to ourselves, so we may overflow in supporting our partner.

Let's explore a common example of the role a lack of self-love plays in a relationship conflict.

Bill and Mary went to an art fair with their three-year-old, Laurie. Bill had been away for a while on a business trip and was looking forward to spending this time together. Likewise, Mary and Laurie had been missing Bill and were looking forward to having a fun day together as a family.

Within a short period of time, however, they parted paths. Bill decided to sit with Laurie for a while at a magic show, while Mary perused the art. Bill was trying to make Laurie happy and Mary was trying to accommodate Bill's desire, even though she wanted to share the experience of the art fair with Bill.

While Bill sat with Laurie at the magic show, Mary enjoyed the art. Three times, Mary came back to the magic show and invited Bill to join her. Each time Laurie cried and wanted her dad to stay longer.

At Mary's third request, Bill said, "Just fifteen more minutes."

Mary responded with anger.

Bill become cold and judgmental of her.

Mary became more angry and critical. They had a brief argument and then decided to go home. Their potentially beautiful day at the art fair had been interrupted by hurt feelings. Mary ended up feeling mistrustful and unloved, while Bill felt moody and grumbly for days.

Let's examine this situation and understand what really happened. When Mary was loving and appreciative of Bill, it was easy for him to support her and care about her needs and feelings. But when Mary got angry and resented

Bill, it became very difficult for him to support her. He experienced Mary as the cause of his upset. Mary was opposing him; Mary was preventing him from being kind and nurturing; Mary was the problem.

Bill's experience often tells him that Mary "makes" him angry. In our illustration his experience told him that he was willing to be supportive until she changed everything. Unfortunately, he was only experiencing part of what was really happening. To him it appeared that the problem was outside himself. It appeared that Mary's anger and rejection was the problem. This appearance was an illusion. In reality, he was responsible for his resistance to loving her.

Instead of hearing her, he blamed her. Granted, his experience told him that she was responsible, but from a higher perspective he was responsible; the problem only appeared to come from outside. It is because Bill was not loving himself that he reacted so defensively. He could not feel Mary's love because he did not love himself.

Because Bill was not loving himself, his awareness fixated on the negativity in Mary's response. He did not recognize the reason for her being upset, that he is important to her. He did not take into consideration all the other times she had appreciated him. Bill was unable to feel her love because he was not loving himself in the moment.

When he is not loving himself, he becomes dependent on Mary to feel good about himself. If Mary is not capable of supporting him at that moment, he makes her responsible for his pain, instead of being responsible for his own sensitivity and insecurity.

If Bill feels unappreciated by Mary, it hurts because he is not appreciating himself. When Mary feels rejected by Bill, it hurts because she is also rejecting herself. Before the art fair she was already doubting her worthiness to be loved, so when he ignored her it hurt a lot. Ultimately, whenever we feel we are not being loved enough, it hurts because we are not loving ourselves enough.

Bill's inconsiderate behavior triggered Mary's own feelings of low self-esteem. Instead of asking Bill for the support she would like and working with him to get it, her reflex reaction was to become angry and blame Bill.

On the other hand, Mary's momentary lack of appreciation for Bill triggered his own feelings of low self-esteem. Rather than listening to her hurt with understanding and compassion, Bill's reflex reaction was to become cold and detached. He felt hurt by her momentary lack of appreciation for him. The true source of his hurt, however, was his own lack of appreciation for himself.

If Bill had been truly appreciative of himself, then in that moment when Mary got angry with him, he would not have reacted defensively, but would have responded with compassionate understanding and listened to her feelings. If Mary was truly loving herself and taking care of herself, then when Bill was inconsiderate, she would have been more accepting of his unconscious behavior, working with him to get what she needed.

MATURE RELATIONSHIPS

Mature relationships with the opposite sex work best when both partners are giving. If two people are blaming each other, depending on each other to feel OK, conflict is inevitable. When both parties take responsibility for their hurt and negative emotions and behavior, then they can begin having a mature relationship.

It is not necessary to be perfect to have a mature relationship. A mature relationship can work even when one of the partners is temporarily incapable of giving. It can even work when *both* partners are temporarily unable to support each other. Let's look at a few examples:

When Mary is out of balance, under stress, or just not loving herself, she is incapable of giving. If Bill happens to be full within himself that day, he can be fulfilled by supporting Mary. He can give her the time, attention, and understanding she needs. He can give without demanding that she appreciate his support. He feels good in supporting her even if she doesn't feel better right away. However, Mary can only receive this support to the degree that she doesn't make Bill responsible for her hurt.

Let's take another example. If Bill is empty for a period of time and Mary is full, then again the relationship can work. Mary gives from fullness, and Bill receives her support by not making her responsible for his hurt. If he blames and thus makes her responsible, then he stays empty longer. As long as he makes her responsible to fill his love tank, he cannot fill his own tank.

It is essential that they both take responsibility for their hurt feelings. Whenever it seems as though they are not getting the love they need, they are looking in the wrong direction. When Bill is looking to Mary for love but not getting it, he needs to first take responsibility for loving himself.

As long as Bill makes Mary responsible for his upsets, then he doesn't have the power to feel better without changing Mary. As long as Mary blames Bill for her hurt, then she cannot feel better unless he changes. This attitude — that our partner is responsible for us — makes us dependent on changing our partner to get what we need. It causes within us a powerful compulsion to change our partner so we can feel better. As a result we weaken in our ability to feel better out of love for ourselves. We become too dependent on another.

The biggest test of a mature relationship occurs when both Bill and Mary are feeling empty at the same time. At such times they are both incapable of giving. To avoid conflict and resentment they must look to themselves or elsewhere for the love they need. Their relationship can work as long as they fulfill the two requirements of a mature relationship. The first is that they are not actively blaming the other for their own emptiness and hurt. The second is that they are both taking responsibility to get the love and support they need from an appropriate source. Through fulfilling these two requirements, we can most effectively dispel the illusions that create unnecessary conflict.

THE GRAND ILLUSION

The belief that another person causes our unhappiness is the grand illusion. It permeates every conflict that arises in relationships. Whenever we feel hurt or offended that our partner is not loving us enough, in truth it is we who are not loving ourselves. When it appears that we are being rejected, the pain of that rejection is felt only because we are already subconsciously rejecting ourselves.

This recognition that we are responsible applies to our adult self. It does not apply to children. When we were children we were subject to being wounded by the abuse of our family and circumstances. When a child is rejected, that child is hurt. When a youngster is unfairly criticized or punished, that child is abused. When a child is blamed, that child is wounded. When a child doesn't receive love, acceptance, appreciation, trust, kindness, compassion, validation, encouragement, admiration, understanding, forgiveness, and respect, it is hurt. This psychological hurt is as real as the wound of a cut or a broken arm. Psychological injuries leave scars that obstruct our full development.

A child is a victim of his or her environment. The adult self is not. A child has not yet developed a sense of self. Without a developed sense of self, trauma and abuse distorts the child's view of itself.

In childhood we are completely dependent on our parents, family, and friends to form our sense of self. We are highly impressionable. As adults we are capable of defining ourselves regardless of how others view us. This ability to define ourselves without depending on others is maturity. Through developing this ability we become capable of loving ourselves when it appears others are not loving us. This ability frees us from being victims of our past.

It is never too late to have the ideal childhood. If we take responsibility to parent ourselves, we can heal the wounds of the past and develop the positive qualities of our true selves. As adults we can learn to love ourselves, even if our parents were not capable of loving us. We can give ourselves the love we need.

We enter into this world with an incredible capacity to love, yet we have little ability to love ourselves. We have not yet formed a sense of self. We gradually build a sense of self according to how our love is returned. Based upon loving feedback and support, we can gradually learn who we are and what we deserve. Without loving feedback and support, we fail to learn who we are, and form a negative and untrue self-image.

Billy (at three years old) sees his parents as great, glorious, grand, OK, important, special, beautiful, strong, etc. If these great beings ignore, blame, judge, and reject him, then he feels he is not enough; he is inadequate, unworthy, bad, stupid, unimportant, invisible, and so on. If his parents are able to return his love, then he gradually learns to feel worthy of such love. He can feel accepted, special, wanted, important, lovable, strong, confident, self-assured, smart, intelligent, handsome, bright, and so forth.

When a child's love is not returned or reflected back, the child's development suffers. Rather than naturally exploring and developing different aspects of self, the child develops coping mechanisms. Billy learns to get love by repressing and denying certain aspects of self. In this process of desperately seeking love, attention, acceptance, respect, etc., instead of finding himself, Billy loses parts of who he truly is.

For example, when Bill's father ignored him, it hurt to feel unimportant. It hurt to go unnoticed. Acknowledgment is an essential psychological nutrient. Without it, Bill did not learn to fully appreciate and accept himself. He was somewhat unsure of himself and insecure. He repressed his more assertive side. As a consequence he did not learn to set limits.

In Mary's case, when her father ignored her it hurt to feel she was not special. It hurt to feel invisible. Attention is another psychological nutrient. Without it, Mary did not learn to fully respect, understand, or care for herself. She became good at caring for others but would ignore herself. As a result of suppressing her own needs, she had a difficult time asking for support.

Twenty-five years later, Mary feels angry and ignored by Bill. She is overly sensitive to his giving more attention to Laurie. Bill gets upset with Mary because she gets angry with him. Bill overreacts to her anger. Instead of understanding her hurt, he feels offended and defends himself with coldness and detachment.

Let's probe more deeply into what happened that day at the art fair. When Bill didn't say "no" to his daughter, he began to subconsciously doubt his worthiness of acceptance and appreciation. When Mary got angry with him, he was already unconsciously blaming himself for not setting limits, so the impact of her blame was greatly reinforced. Bill overreacted because he was being influenced by the unresolved pain of his childhood.

Imagine a friend patting you on the shoulder. Under normal circumstances that would feel fine. But now imagine that you have a large bruise on your shoulder. If a friend pats you there this time, it hurts a lot. Now imagine that you have an open wound. A friend comes up and again pats you on the shoulder. It hurts even more. In a similar way, when interactions in our relationships activate the sensitivities of our past, we become overly sensitive to our partners.

As a child it was appropriate that Billy experienced hurt when he felt rejected. As an adult, however, he is now responsible for his feelings. It is unfair and unproductive of him to blame Mary for them. If he holds her responsible for his feelings, he has become as a child again. It is, however, appropriate for Bill to feel and acknowledge that his inner child is hurt. As a result he doesn't blame Mary as much, and can more effectively move in the direction of releasing blame and forgiving. He can give himself the support he needs to fill up his love tanks. In this way he dispels the illusion that Mary is hurting him.

This grand illusion is analogous to the illusion of the sun moving across the sky. Even though we understand with our minds that the sun is stationary and the earth is moving around the sun, our senses still experience the sun's motion. The sun's movement is an illusion.

The grand illusion in relationships is that Bill experiences Mary as the source of his upset. He fails to realize that he is just overly sensitive because his love tank is empty. He is looking to Mary to fill it up when only he can do that. Ultimately he cannot receive her love if he does not love himself. The same, of course, is true for Mary. She cannot expect Bill to fill her love tank; that is her own responsibility.

WHO IS TO BLAME?

Who is responsible for this couple's hurt?

From one perspective Bill has hurt Mary and Mary has hurt Bill.

From a second perspective, Bill's father's neglect has made Bill sensitive to Mary's anger. Mary's father has made her sensitive to Bill's lack of consideration for her.

From a third perspective, Bill is responsible for his hurt, because he is not fully loving himself. He is looking to Mary for the love his father failed to give him. He looks to her for the love that he is not giving to himself. It is inappropriate to look to his mate for this love. From this same perspective, Mary is responsible for her hurt, because she is not loving herself; instead she is expecting Bill to fill the void left by her father.

From a fourth and more spiritual perspective, the whole conflict is a test. It is an opportunity for Bill to discover and heal his inner hurt from his past, develop greater confidence in and consideration for his wife, and learn how to be more supportive of her. For Mary it is an opportunity to discover and heal her hurt from the past, develop a greater sense of worthiness and trust, and learn the importance of letting Bill know her preferences.

All four perspectives are essential to having a successful, mature relationship. Whenever there is conflict and tension in a relationship, there is generally more of the first perspective and less of the other three; that is, blame predominates. Bill blames Mary, Mary blames Bill, and neither takes responsibility for their hurt. By taking responsibility for healing our own hurt, we are freed from needing to change our partner to feel better.

Bill is expecting Mary to make up for his deficiency in self-esteem. Mary is looking to Bill to make up for her lack of self-worth. At times like this, instead of looking to each other for love, they need to look to themselves for love or look elsewhere. It is impractical to think one person can always be there to support us.

LOOKING FOR LOVE IN THE WRONG PLACES

Generally when you are not getting enough love and support, you are looking in the wrong direction. Part of the grand illusion is that there is a scarcity of love. In truth there is an abundance of love. There only appears to be a scarcity of love when we are looking for it in the wrong places. So many times people have love in their lives but negate it, because it is not coming from the person they want it from.

Gwen, 38, a mother of three, was married to Hal, 39, an executive in an advertising agency. She had lots of girlfriends who supported her, she had a great therapist, she was involved in a support group at her church, she liked her work, she felt her children loved her, and recently even her relationship with her mother had greatly improved.

But after ten years of marriage Gwen was very unhappy. Her major complaint was that everybody loved her except her husband. He didn't even laugh at her jokes. She felt so deprived. She felt that without his love it was all meaningless.

In attending one of my Relationship Seminars, Gwen realized something very startling about herself: the more others supported her, the more deprived she felt of Hal's love. Her resentment would then push away whatever love he could express.

Instead of being grateful that she was receiving so much support, she was making Hal wrong for not being the one to support her. She realized that she was expecting him to completely fulfill her. She had mistakenly believed that if she wasn't getting everything she needed from Hal, then something was wrong with their relationship and with her.

With this awakening she could relax. She didn't have to work so hard to make Hal love her more. She realized that God was giving her the support she needed but in different ways than she thought. In accepting Hal and releasing her resentment, she was surprised to see Hal's behavior change remarkably. He spontaneously became more supportive and even began laughing at her jokes.

One of the biggest problems in relationships with the opposite sex and especially marriage is that we set our partner up as the sole source of love. We forget that *all our relationships are valid sources of love.* We negate the value of love from its many sources when it is not coming from our primary relationship.

If you are single and are telling yourself that you can't be happy until you have a partner, then you are rejecting the importance of being single, loving yourself, and receiving love from other sources. In every case, the formula for filling your love tank is to diversify. Don't put all your eggs in one basket.

Rachell is a talented interior decorator. When she started therapy she was 42, single, and had no children. She was feeling very alone and unsupported in her life. Her parents and her brother had stopped talking to her. She was very hurt. She felt depressed and hopeless because she wasn't married, didn't have children, and didn't have a positive relationship with her family.

After about a year of regular therapy Rachell was on talking terms with her brother, but still her parents rejected her. Her dad, however, had, responded with a card to one of her letters. She had worked on exploring and releasing her negative feelings, replacing them with forgiveness, understanding, and love. At times she had felt much better, and full within herself, even though she didn't have the loving relationships she wanted.

In therapy, Rachell practiced writing love letters to her family members and then wrote the responses she needed to hear. Through releasing her negative feelings she was learning to accept that she might never change them and that they might never be viable sources to fill up her love tanks. She was learning to give herself the love she missed from them. In learning to let go of trying to change them, she was able to open up new channels for love to enter.

She took a short leave from therapy during the Christmas holidays. After the holidays she came back to therapy very depressed. She complained that her parents didn't invite her to celebrate Christmas. She was particularly hurt because on this particular Christmas, her mother's sister, Aunt Thelma, called and invited her to join her cousins for Christmas.

Rachell complained, "Even my aunt invited me but my own mother wouldn't. And my brother, who generally lets me stop by to see my niece on Christmas morning, told me I couldn't stop by. I love my little niece. I couldn't believe he would deprive me. Then I received a call from the mother of my godchild Danna. I love her like my own child. Her mother invited me to come by and visit them Christmas morning. Can you imagine that, I was invited to see my godchild, but I couldn't even see my own niece."

After a long pause, I asked, "Did you go to your aunt's and goddaughter's house?" Looking very hurt, Rachell said, "No, I spent Christmas Eve alone and the next morning I just stayed in bed and cried."

She then asked me why I looked happy. I told her, "I am happy that you have progressed so far. Even though you spent Christmas alone, God is rewarding you for all your work on healing your heart by at least showing you that the love you need is available. Even though your mother is not capable of loving you, God has supplied you with a replacement mother and family. Even though you couldn't visit your niece, God provided you with an invitation to see your goddaughter."

Rachell burst into tears, realizing that she had grown and she wasn't as alone as she had thought. She had just been so fixated on needing love from her mother that she couldn't appreciate that it was available to her from different sources.

By forgiving her mother, Rachell stopped making her mother responsible for her happiness. This then opened a door through which she could draw in the love she needed. Rachell began to trust that she wasn't alone and that she could get her love tanks filled even if she never talked again with her parents.

THE NINE SOURCES OF LOVE

For relationships to work, our love tanks need to be full. It is not possible to feel full when we are looking for love from one major source. That is like trying to be healthy by taking only vitamin C. Just as our body needs a variety of vitamins and nutrients, so also our psyche needs various kinds of love. There are many sources of love and all are important.

As a rule of thumb, whenever your intimate relationship is not fulfilling you, it is time to be responsible to fill up your love tank from another source. Generally when you are needy for a particular person's love and you are not getting it, then you are looking in the wrong place. By choosing to look elsewhere to fill up your tank, you can then come back to that relationship and give and receive love unconditionally.

There are nine major kinds of love and support. This support comes from different kinds of relationships. Each relationship is like a different vitamin or nutrient. The nine major kinds of relationships are:

1. Vitamin G — A relationship with God or a Higher Power
2. Vitamin P — Relationships with one's parents
3. Vitamin F — Relationships with family and friends
4. Vitamin SS — Relationships with members of the same sex
5. Vitamin S — A relationship with self, work, and pleasure
6. Vitamin O — Relationships with the opposite sex
7. Vitamin PC — Relationships with our children and/or with a dependent, pet, other animals, or ecology
8. Vitamin CS — Relationships with the community and society
9. Vitamin W — A relationship with the world

Each of these relationships provides a particular kind of love. Just as different foods provide different vitamins and minerals, so all of these relationships provide the essential support to make us emotionally and spiritually healthy.

Just as every person has unique deficiencies and needs for different vitamins, different people have different relationship needs. Each person has his or her own unique requirements for the various kinds of love and support. But even though we may need different degrees of each kind of love, every person has a basic requirement for each one. We all have a need for love from all of these different relationships.

To various extents unique to every individual, each of these vitamins plays a significant role in our development at different times in our lives. There is a natural sequence of unfoldment of our needs for these different kinds of relationships. In a very general sense, each of the nine different kinds of relationships sequentially emerges in importance for our development and maturity about every seven years.

Our first relationship is with a Higher Power. This spiritual presence sustains us in the womb and throughout our life. The second essential relationship, which emerges in our first seven years, is our relationship with our parents. Then in our next seven years, our relationship with family and friends becomes essential for our development and maturity, and so on.

This unfoldment does not discount the importance of our relationship with God and parents but reveals that as the child develops, its needs become more complex, and the love of God and parents can only fill part of the child's love tanks. In a sense, a new compartment of the love tank has opened, and only the love of family and friends can supply the support needed. The child's ability to receive the support of vitamin F (family and friends) is hinged to a great degree on the continuing foundation of the other two kinds of support, i.e., God and parents. In the following sections we will explore this unfoldment more deeply.

1. VITAMIN G
(A RELATIONSHIP WITH GOD)

A relationship with God or a higher power is the essential basis for all other relationships. Some people laugh at the need for spirituality while others just underestimate its value. But to fully love ourselves and others, we need to feel that we are here in this world for a reason. Spirituality gives us a sense that we are all connected and that we are supported by a higher power in fulfilling our life's purpose.

When our relationship with God is strong we are never alone. Even when we are betrayed we can turn to prayer and our relationship with God. If we deny our relationship with God, we may continually feel abandoned and rejected, and fail in our other relationships.

The more we reject God, the more we seek to have this need for God fulfilled through our other relationships. No partner can successfully be God to us; no human being can be perfect. If we expect our partner to be perfect, we are sure to be disappointed again and again. Another way of saying this is: if we are vitamin G deficient, then no matter how much we get of the other vitamins, we may stay sick.

When we feel that God doesn't exist or if our relationship with God needs attention, then we will begin to make others our God. We will look to others to find strength and fulfillment. We become overly dependent on false sources of support. A frustrated or denied relationship with God leads some to substance abuse. To the drunk, his bottle is his God. To the drug addict, cocaine is his God. It promises him salvation. To the workaholic, money is his God.

To the co-dependent, her mate promises her salvation. To put one's partner on a pedestal is to set them up to fail us again and again. A human partnership will always disappoint us when our need for God or a higher power is not being fulfilled. It may start out seeming perfect but later on it will disappoint us.

This transference happens because the need for vitamin G gets replaced by some other need. A person may feel they need a mate of the opposite sex when really they are needing to feel God's love. Thus vitamin G gets replaced by vitamin O (relationships with the opposite sex).

Replacement needs are always deceptive. Our true need gets replaced by another need that does not have the capacity to fulfill us. For example a person may feel compelled to overeat in order to feel fulfilled, when they need instead to be filled with love. A person may need to share and heal their feelings, but instead they consciously feel a strong urge to suppress their pain through drinking or some other addiction. In every case addictions are false needs that have replaced our real needs. The addiction not only fails to fulfill us, but it actually prevents us from feeling our true needs.

Some people feel they have outgrown the need for spirituality. This could not be further from the truth. Certainly as we mature our understanding of God and spirituality changes, but it is not outgrown. Many people have appropriately rejected their simplistic childhood beliefs about God, but have not taken the necessary time and attention to form an adult perspective of spirituality and God. Such a relationship is vital to all other relationships. It requires work, attention, and caring, as does any other relationship.

The most common symptoms of a lack of spirituality are addiction and co-dependency. Addiction is any compulsion that does not promote personal well-being. When our relationship with God is weak, we are not connected to the source of life within us. In feeling disconnected we experience an emptiness and craving that can be temporarily satisfied through excessive sensory stimulation. This stimulation temporarily releases us from feeling our inner suffering.

Every form of stimulation can be used as an addiction. Eating, drinking, working, sleeping, meditating, sex, talking, etc., are all quite innocent. But when overdone, they can become destructive to our well-being. Anything we do repetitively that is destructive to ourselves or others is an addiction.

Not all replacement needs are destructive. We can replace our need for vitamin G with any of the other nine forms of relationships. In this case the other relationship may not be harmful as an addiction, but it will not be ful-filling. At best it can provide temporary relief, but then leaves us feeling empty.

Co-dependency involves a compulsion to serve, please, and support others in ways that do not support our own well-being. Preoccupied with other people's wants and needs, the co-dependent neglects their own. Indeed, the co-dependent seeks a kind of redemption through assuming responsibility for the feelings and behavior of others. Because they do not feel God's support, they feel a compulsion to be godlike to others.

When they fall back again and again to being human with human needs, wants, feelings, and reactions, they are severely judgmental of themselves. This creates a painful sense of worthlessness, inadequacy, and helplessness. They are then temporarily released from their pain by once again sacrificing themselves for others. To the co-dependent, taking care of others becomes another form of addiction to relieve their emotional pain and get "high" on feeling virtuous and godlike.

Another symptom of a weak spiritual life is looking to others to define ourselves as worthy, special, and important. When we do not feel the support of a higher power, we begin to feel that we are separate and all alone — which in truth we are not. This mistaken belief conflicts with our inner experience of feeling the need for support. On one hand we have needs we simply can't fulfill on our own, and on the other hand, we believe that we are all alone. To feel the need for support and at the same time to feel we are all alone is a very powerful internal conflict. It creates fear, guilt, and rage, and manifests as an excessive need to control others and our external environment.

The need for a relationship with God is our first need for love and support. When we are in the womb of our mother, we are connected to our God source. In this state everything is done for us; we are not responsible for anyone or anything. We are supplied everything we need by our higher power.

This awareness that we are supported by a higher power is our first and most powerful relationship.

One of the reasons little children are so beautiful and radiant is that they are fully connected to God. Although they have not yet developed an intellectual belief about God to define their experience, they are intimately connected to this source. We feel so good and happy around children because they reconnect us to our own innocent experience of God. A spiritual relationship supports us in feeling innocent, good, and worthy of unconditional love.

Vitamin G is our most important relationship in the womb, and it remains important throughout our life. Its importance, however, is diminished in the sense that, as we grow older, other relationships are also necessary to fill our love tanks. From the foundation of our relationship with God, we then begin to form our next significant relationship: a relationship with our parents. As we emerge into this world at birth, we not only need to be receptive to God's love and support, but also to the love and support of our parents.

2. VITAMIN P
(A RELATIONSHIP WITH OUR PARENTS)

As children we are completely dependent on our parents to fill our love tanks. Many psychologists believe that our basic sense of self is determined in our first seven years. It is during this time that our relationship with our parents is so important.

Certainly we outgrow being dependent on our parents, but this vital relationship remains important throughout our lives. It is a source of continued support. To ceaselessly work on having a loving relationship with our parents creates an inner emotional security. This sense of safety frees us to continually grow and develop. It helps us to love ourselves even when we make mistakes or need help. This form of support gives us more self-assurance at times of stress and pressure. To feel our parents' love and support is a tremendous asset in confronting life's challenges.

Most of our emotional problems stem from a deficiency of vitamin P. When we have a shortage of vitamin P in our lives, quite automatically we begin to look to our intimate relationships to fulfill the deficiency. We look to our partners to give us the support we needed from our parents but did not get. We expect our mates to be responsible for us and treat us like powerless, delicate and needy children when in truth we are adults attempting to have a mature and equal relationship. This can be a very subtle destructive pattern.

In an adult relationship we should not expect our partners to feel responsible for us. However, his expectation will continue to emerge if we have a deficiency of vitamin P. If we were neglected as children, then when we become adults this need for vitamin P will persist. If we cannot fulfill this need through loving interactions with our parents, another means of getting vitamin P is through therapy.

Therapists in this case are really parental surrogates. They are paid by your adult self to be a parent to your inner child. For an hour a week they are nurturing and attentive to the needs of your inner child. They listen with the understanding compassion of a loving parent. They are always on your side. This kind of personal support is essential to heal the wounds of our inner child, especially in the case of those who were abandoned, neglected, or abused in some way by their parents.

It is very common for people who have unhealed hurt in their relationship with their parents to project this need for parental love onto their mates. In such cases their partners are doomed to fail. Even a good therapist cannot re-parent his or her own mate. The roles must be kept clear. If a therapist's mate is working through childhood issues, the therapist will support his or her mate by responsibly hiring another therapist to support their partner.

When a husband tries to be a father to his wife, or when his wife expects him to be like a father to her, it is inevitable that her unresolved negative feelings of childhood will be transferred onto him. Just as she felt mistrustful of her parents, she will mistrust her husband.

By entering therapy to explore her hurt feelings, she can discover that her feelings of hurt have more to do with her childhood than with her mate. Her therapist, being uninvolved in her day-to-day life and thus more immune from receiving her transference, can help her to explore her feelings without her feeling the need to protect herself.

This kind of safety is essential for her to process and release her negative feelings. Once she projects her childhood feelings on her mate, no matter how caring and supportive he can be, she will not feel safe to share and explore her feelings. At such times the help of a counselor or someone else she respects is essential. Even if her mate is worthy of such trust, it is impossible for the hurt little girl inside to feel that trust until more healing has occurred.

After they grow up, many people misguidedly wish to have nothing to do with their parents. They leave home and try to forget the negativity of their past. But eventually they enter into a relationship and begin to feel the same way they felt growing up. They feel rejected, unimportant, unappreciated, unwanted, ignored, unfairly judged, misunderstood, criticized, blamed, controlled, and unsupported in a variety of other ways. They blame their partners instead of recognizing that they are replaying the pain of their past.

Instead of reacting appropriately to their partners, their hurt child reacts in a childish way. They may become selfish, demanding, needy, or insecure. They may irresponsibly whine and complain, avoid and procrastinate. They may throw tantrums, accuse, blame and yell. Or they may submit, placate, and sacrifice their own needs. These people may reject, withdraw, withhold, or even punish. Or they may react in a mistrustful, defensive way. Once their inner child's hurt is stimulated, all their adult skills for relating and negotiating are forgotten. The inner wounded child takes control and reacts, while the adult becomes powerless to respond appropriately.

To whatever extent vitamin P (relationship with parents) is deficient, a person will project their unresolved feelings from childhood onto their adult relationships. When a couple enters the sexual stage of a relationship, their bonding can be so intense that the repressed and unresolved feelings of early childhood begin to surface and emerge into the conscious awareness.

It is important to realize that when these feelings come up, they are immediately projected on people and circumstances in present time. It takes time, practice, and a lot of healing to develop an awareness that doesn't project these feelings. When a person is not being affected by his past, it is easier for him to recognize and take back a projection. But people who have had traumatic childhoods especially need the support of a therapist to help heal the past by fulfilling the deficient vitamin P.

Some people may need therapy their whole lives — not because they are dysfunctional, but because they are deficient in vitamin P and their parents are incapable of supporting them. To have supportive parents or surrogate parents is a great blessing. But if they are not available, one can enlist a therapist to give them the support they need.

People who were abused in childhood tend to experience abusive relationships in their adult lives until they learn to reach out and get the support of others who can fulfill their need for vitamin P. Sometimes a friend can fulfill this need, or a lawyer or priest. Anyone you greatly respect and who loves you can fulfill your need for vitamin P. Ideally a person goes to therapy to heal their childhood enough so that they can create vitamin P in their lives without having to continue in therapy.

Major steps in healing the past are exploring old hurts and forgiving our parents. Gradually we are able to recognize and feel that they did the best they could. Then as our forgiveness grows and the hurt is healed, we are able to remember the times they were supportive and feel that love supporting us in our present-day lives.

This can happen even if our parents won't talk to us. In our hearts we realize and feel their love, which was frustrated by their own pain and self-hatred. We begin to acknowledge that the abuse we received was not deserved, but happened because they were dysfunctional. Then we are able to heal the child that took the abuse personally.

Some people delude themselves into thinking they have healed their past. They intellectually forgive their parents, but in their guts they are still bitter. They do not feel genuine compassion and love for their parents. At some level they are still hurting and angry. As long as they don't think about or deal with their parents, they assume their past is handled. In their adult relationships, however, they continue to take things personally and react from their hurt child to people and situations. They unconsciously repeat the same kinds of relationships they had with their parents.

When a child feels loved and supported by its parents, it is free to grow and develop naturally. When a child feels unloved or unsupported, it develops coping mechanisms that result in suppression, repression, and denial of true feelings, real needs, and wants.

To win Mommy's and Daddy's love, the child suppresses its true self to conform to their designs and wishes. In abusive situations the child learns protective mechanisms such as lying, placating, denying, and pretending. The authentic self is lost.

When parents are dysfunctional, many children react by feeling responsible for the parent. If the parent is unable to be responsible or take responsibility for their own feelings and behavior, then the child takes on this responsibility. Not only does the child try to make things better, which no youngster could ever do, but it holds itself guilty for the parents' dysfunctional behavior.

If the mother is unhappy or depressed, the child feels somehow responsible.

The child feels inadequate and powerless to help her, although in reality it is not responsible for her happiness. If the father is physically abusive, the child takes responsibility for provoking his violence. To take on this guilt is too great a strain for the child. Consequently, this person may be insecure throughout their adulthood no matter how competent they become. They will continue to experience anxiety for no apparent reason.

Exploring these anxious feelings and linking them to the experiences of childhood uncovers the hurt child. From there, with the loving direction and compassionate kindness of a therapist or surrogate parent, this inner child can eventually emerge as a mature adult, free of insecurities, self-doubt, and anxiety.

It is important to note that we do reach maturity to various degrees, no matter how much abuse we received. In a sense, parts of us have developed while other parts remain childish. For example, a person can react from his hurt child in his relationship at home, while at work he acts and responds quite appropriately as a mature adult. A part of him has matured while another part is still a child.

Maturity is that stage in our development when we have developed a sense of self and are not largely dependent on others. At this stage we are capable of unconditional love. It is only when we know who we are that we have something to share in a relationship. Only when we are capable of loving ourselves, accepting our limitations and imperfection, can we truly love someone else and accept their limitations.

It is appropriate for a little child to be needy. Needing to be filled up is a fitting relationship between a child and parent. Neediness and self-absorption, however, ruins adult relationships. Ideally, childhood would have been a time when our love tanks were filled up. Ideally, we were not required to do anything but be ourselves to receive love. Under these conditions we would slowly but surely learn to love ourselves. Then as we become adolescents and young adults, we would be capable of successfully loving ourselves and others.

Maturity begins when we are no longer narcissistic and dependent on others, but can actually give without needing to be filled up in return. From the fullness of maturity, we are capable of truly filling up through giving to others. Maturity takes time to develop. To take on a mature relationship, it is essential that we counteract the unresolved feelings of childhood by getting regular doses of vitamin P.

3. VITAMIN F
(RELATIONSHIPS WITH FAMILY AND FRIENDS)

After a child is about seven years old, another relationship need arises: the need for family and friends, or "vitamin F." Our relationship with God and parents continues to be important, but now the need for support from family and friends becomes a major factor in our development. Feeling the love of God and the love of our parents is not enough anymore to fill our love tanks. Vitamin F has become a requirement for our growth.

From age seven to fourteen supportive relationships with our family and friends are essential for our development. In these relationships we learn to experience ourselves as separate from our parents. This is not to imply that family and friends are not important before age seven. It means that at this stage, vitamin F is most important and impactful. Traumas that occur during this time are healed through fulfilling our need for family and friends.

Based on the support of family, friends, and schoolmates we learn to freely express ourselves. We begin to develop subjective awareness. Seeing ourselves through the eyes of others, we form an image of ourselves. This is our first glimpse of who we are. If we are loved and supported, we come to see who we truly are. But if we are not supported, we form a false sense of self. We may see ourselves as clumsy and awkward, and continue feeling that way long after we have become adults. We may see ourselves as too small or too big. We may see ourselves as not good enough or not smart enough. These impressions stick with us if we do not receive enough love and support from our family and friends. Even loving parents cannot counteract this kind of deficiency.

Without the support of family members and friends we may become inhibited. Or we may rebel and be overly uninhibited, as if to prove that we don't care what anyone thinks of us. Certainly as adults, what others think of us should not define who we are. But when we have been wounded through a lack of vitamin F, it is very automatic to continue being affected and limited by the perceptions and opinions of others.

Adults deficient in vitamin F tend to fixate on negative feedback and ignore positive feedback. If someone appreciates and loves them but then becomes critical about one aspect of them, they may feel completely criticized. They may be overly shy or unable to ask for what they want. Some women, for instance, can ask for what they want, but as soon as they have fallen in love, they fold. They regress and become incapable of assertion in their relationship.

A slightly different example of this principle is the woman who feels her thighs are "too" fat. As a result, she feels as though all of her is too fat. This kind of generalization as it relates to self-image is common in those who were in some way deprived of vitamin F.

Another consequence of vitamin F deficiency shows itself after you make a sales presentation or meet someone new. After the meeting you critique yourself, focusing on what you didn't say right and not recognizing and appreciating all the good things you said.

Vitamin F deficiency is most adequately fulfilled though group therapy or group seminars. Actually any kind of group activity in which you feel supported can meet your ongoing need for vitamin F. Especially through sharing in a group do we heal the wounds of childhood and learn to let in vitamin F. Thorough vitamin F we are then able to build a positive and realistic self-image.

In the beginning sharing in a group requires a lot of willpower. Generally, sharing in a group is difficult when you are deficient in vitamin F. Most people who lack vitamin F shy away from groups. They may be good at sharing one on one, but in a group they feel uncomfortable. They reject the very thing they need the most.

However, the more difficult it is to share, the greater the gain. Just by being part of a supportive group seminar, listening to and supporting others, you, can experience tremendous healing. Eventually as you feel better and better about yourself, you will dare to stand up and share. Vitamin F supports assertiveness.

Sharing in a group can be highly transformational to the degree that one is truly supported by the group. To heal a vitamin F deficiency, it is important to share yourself in a group that is capable of supporting you. As the self-image improves and the wounds are healed, you may continue to participate in group therapy and seminars to fulfill your needs for family and friends, especially if you live away from family or they are not available to support you.

As a result of meeting your need for group support, you can see yourself more clearly. A positive self-image develops that can support you wherever you go. Even when others are not supportive, you can sustain this positive image of yourself.

The ability to laugh and have fun also comes from vitamin F. One becomes more spontaneous and uninhibited. People who are too serious need to heal their vitamin F deficiency and get the support they need to lighten up. When we feel we are all alone without family or friends, life becomes exceedingly heavy.

Some people deficient in vitamin F give up their friends as soon as they get into an intimate relationship. This sets the stage for problems. An intimate partner is not the same as a friend. Both partners are interdependent; their lives are much more entwined than in a friendship. Certainly they can be friendly to each other, but an intimate partner cannot supply the kind of support a friend can. One cannot expect to receive vitamin F from a person when you are having a sexual relationship with them.

Some men require a woman to give up her friends and devote all her time and attention to him. This generally happens when he makes her his mommy and looks to her to get vitamin P. She complies by giving up her friends and losing that support. Gradually her love tank will get emptier and so will his. Inevitably they both develop negative patterns.

Holidays with the family, family and school reunions, and parties are great for filling up with vitamin F. If one doesn't have a good relationship with their family, it is important to work on healing that while simultaneously getting support through regular group therapy or group seminars.

4. VITAMIN SS
(RELATIONSHIPS WITH THE SAME SEX)

From about age fourteen to twenty-one, relationships with the same sex are essential for our development. This is a time to explore who we are as sexual beings, as our sexual differences come more into the foreground. It is at this time that we are seeking to understand who we are without being dependent on our parents or family. We now need to bond with members of our own sex.

During this period our self-esteem is greatly affected by how we are accepted by the members of our same sex. For example, boys at this age get in fights and become friends. They go on adventures together and bond closely. They play together on teams, join clubs, or form gangs. Having a best friend during this time is also conducive to feeling good about oneself. Just by interacting with a member of the same sex, sharing similar experiences, desires, and feelings, one feels automatically validated and accepted. This acceptance is essential for the development of male self-esteem.

Girls bonding with girls is essential during these years. Having a girlfriend or several girlfriends to share with automatically validates the female psyche. It is important that a girl learn to define herself without depending on her parents and family. She looks to her girlfriends for this support. Through sharing common feelings, desires, and experiences, her femininity is validated and she is able to fully develop her emerging feminine awareness.

Ideals and values begin to develop during these years. It is important that they originate from within and not from external parental sources. This is why young people commonly rebel against their parents. To develop self-esteem they must find their own values within themselves.

Through interactions with members of the same sex, a teenager experiences common values as if they are emerging from within. In a sense, up to this point one's knowledge of self came through others and was dependent on others. The teenager now learns about self, developing values and self-respect by relating with those who are most similar to his emerging sexuality, members of the same sex.

With the support of members of the same sex, teens are able to explore and develop the self in a more autonomous manner with the safety of acceptance at every step. Validation of their emerging sexuality is essential. Through acceptance by members of the same sex, the teenager gets the necessary doses of vitamin SS.

A deficiency of support from members of the same sex obstructs self-respect and lowers self-esteem. It can inhibit the full development of one's sexuality. Boys can suppress or restrict the development of their emerging masculine qualities: being willing to work hard, compete, strive, earn respect, and apply discipline, commitment, and cooperation, thus becoming action-oriented and decisive. Girls who don't receive the support they need can restrict the development of the emerging feminine qualities: of being loving, adaptable, nurturing, intuitive, graceful, supportive, and expressive. Without peer support, boys can become weak and girls can become hard.

When a mature woman wants to connect with the qualities of her feminine side, working on and enjoying relationships with the same sex is a must. Likewise, when a man wants to work on discovering and developing his masculine qualities, he needs to spend time with the same sex.

Ideally, each week women should share time and feelings with other women. Simply sharing with other women who support her validates a woman's femininity in a deep way. The love that a man can give a woman can never replace her need for love and support from other women.

Men are much more capable of giving in a relationship when they sustain close relationships with other men. Many men give up this need and expect to get this kind of support from their partners. But without the support of other males, a man is apt to behave in ways that will shock or threaten his female partner and thus provoke subtle disapproval. Men need an outlet to express their adolescent selves without eliciting the disapproval of their female mates.

Women often disapprove of the emerging male adolescent energy as crude, callous, or insensitive. Certainly it can be that way when it is not in balance with the whole person. But this male energy needs support to come out before it can be integrated into the whole person.

Men, on the other hand, tend to judge the emerging female energy as irrational, illogical, or petty. Similarly, it can manifest that way when it is not integrated with the whole person. Women need support to explore and integrate this feminine energy, and when it is first surfacing it is hard for men to validate it. Just being with members of the same sex automatically validates our sexuality.

Men generally need to *do things* together to get their dose of vitamin SS. They need to compete together, take risks together, watch sports together or go to *Rambo*-type movies.

Violence should not be ignored as an ingredient in the male need for vitamin SS. It is something that every man needs to accept and transform within himself. This is a part of adolescence. To a certain extent mankind is still very adolescent in its need for violence. Gradually this is being healed as we mature. Going to some of the violent movies may help a man accept his inner violence and see that it stems from a desire to serve justice and protect the innocent. From this perspective he can transform the violent tendency of his masculine power into the service of the highest good.

Women need to share together, go for walks together, enjoy beautiful surroundings, and go shopping together. Attending cultural events, relaxing, and having lunch together are other ways for women to connect, share, and bond.

Most important, of course, is communicating in person or on the telephone. It is essential that women support each other in order to develop self-respect.

5. VITAMIN S
(THE RELATIONSHIP WITH ONE'S SELF)

From ages twenty-one to twenty-eight a positive relationship with one's self is essential. This is the onset of maturity. Up to this point we were dependent on others. Henceforth we can be responsible for loving and healing ourselves. Now we need to be completely autonomous and find out who we are, what we are here for, what we want, what we need, and especially, what we can be and what we can do.

Through the support we gain by loving ourselves, we can begin the process of healing our past and discovering our inner potential. In this stage we are responsible for getting the love and support we need. We are responsible for how we feel. We can no longer blame others for our unhappiness. We are just as free to get the support we need and free to reject it and suffer.

By the time we are twenty-eight there is generally a major change in how we relate with others, usually triggered by some kind of crisis in which we decide to stop letting others determine who we are. We determine to give up living for others or seeing ourselves through the eyes of others.

Supporting ourselves means taking risks and forgiving ourselves for the mistakes we make, while also appreciating ourselves for our successes and achievements. In this stage it is we who abuse ourselves or support ourselves.

If we have not had a lot of support in our past, it is much harder to support ourselves at this time. But by being responsible for ourselves and striving to be all that we can be, while getting the support we need, we can overcome the deficiencies of the past.

Laziness and not taking risks are two major symptoms of a deficiency of vitamin S. To discover who we are, it is essential that we apply ourselves and diligently seek out the secrets of the universe. In reaching to the heights of success, we are able to test our potential and discover our inner gifts, talents, and strengths.

Being kind and nice to self are ways to love one's self. When we give ourselves permission to discover what we enjoy and then do that, we are loving ourselves. This is also a time when we begin to take care of ourselves. Exploring various self-improvement and health strategies and philosophies is another symptom of supporting one's self. We support ourselves through discipline and service, testing our abilities and skills. Through this gradual process of trial and error we discover who we are and discover our inner potential.

One of the most powerful ways we can love ourselves is to seek out the support we need. To be disciplined in approach and committed to self-healing is self-love. If there is no one to listen to our hurt child, then we need at least to listen to our own feelings. How can we expect others to listen to our hurt feelings when we are not willing to sit down and explore them ourselves? Writing love letters is a very powerful tool for loving ourselves, especially if we were deficient in vitamins P (relationship with parents) and F (relationship with family and friends) while growing up.

In this stage our ego develops to the extent that we are really capable of loving ourselves without depending on others. From this basis of loving ourselves we are then able to forge successful, mature relationships.

Only when we are loving and supporting ourselves can we truly love another. If we have not learned to love ourselves in spite of our own limitations and imperfections, how can we love another human being who is also imperfect and limited?

6. VITAMIN O
(RELATIONSHIPS WITH THE OPPOSITE SEX)

From age twenty-eight to thirty-five, relationships with the opposite sex are indispensable for the next stage of development. We should note that generally from the time of puberty on, one may feel the need to have relationships with the opposite sex. Nevertheless, vitamin O is not essential for development until this stage. Prior to the accomplishment of loving one's self, one is not capable of fully loving a member of the opposite sex without losing one's self.

In this stage, one is at least biologically mature. Only the deficiencies from his or her past prevent the blossoming of maturity. This level of maturity signifies a time when we are not so dependent on the love of others or from self to fill up, but we are dependent on the actualization of our loving potential to experience fulfillment. In other words, through giving of ourselves to others we are enriched.

Now we are capable of giving unconditionally. To whatever degree we are already full within ourselves, we can only experience our fullness through sharing it. In this stage if we are not sharing, supporting, and serving, then we are not fulfilled.

It is from this basis of knowing and loving one's self that a man finds completeness through loving a woman. Through loving her, his own female begins to emerge and complement his masculinity. Likewise, a woman who has learned to love herself can learn to fully love a man without losing herself. Through loving his masculinity, her own masculinity begins to emerge and balance her femininity. In this stage, each person's development requires the opportunity to serve the opposite sex.

When a man and woman come together from a place of mutual fullness, they can create a greater fullness. A man's fullness automatically complements a woman's fullness and vice versa. Through fulfilling each other they begin to actualize their human potential to be loving, accepting, understanding, caring, trusting, appreciative, and respectful.

Certainly men and women can have successful relationships before this stage of maturity, but these relationships will not have the same quality or serve the same purpose. Before maturity we are self-absorbed. We give to get back. This is natural; there is no judgment on this.

In our adolescence (Stage 4, when we need vitamin SS or same-sex relationships for our growth), relationships with the opposite sex assist us in learning more about ourselves through recognizing our differences. In Stage 5, our major lesson is to support ourselves (vitamin S, a relationship with self), and one of the ways to get support is to give support. Relationships with the opposite sex in Stage 5 are a means to discover who we are, and to learn how to get what we need.

When we reach maturity in Stage 6 (vitamin O), the orientation shifts. Now the most important way we can support ourselves is to successfully support someone of the opposite sex. Through supporting a woman on the basis of loving and accepting his masculine self, a man is now more capable of integrating his masculine self with his feminine self. His female self gets permission to emerge, but his established masculine self is not overshadowed. In loving a woman he is able to serve another, and yet he too benefits from the gradual emergence and integration of his own female qualities.

On the other hand, when a man loves a woman before he fully accepts himself, he inevitably loses himself again and again. And when a woman loves a man before she fully understands herself, she will to some degree lose herself in a relationship.

True surrender and unconditional giving cannot be sustained until maturity — until one experiences self-love. Of course, to whatever degree a person loves themselves, they can love the opposite sex without losing themselves. The actual process of losing one's self in love, then falling out of love and coming back to loving one's self, is a valid process of learning to support one's self. For some this process begins at puberty.

With this expanded vision of our differing and ever-changing emotional needs, we can reevaluate and improve our strategies for having a relationship with the opposite sex. From this perspective, it is easy to see how we lean too much on our partners and then blame them for our emotional hurt or discomfort. Now we can more responsibly conclude that whenever a relationship with the opposite sex is not working, the cause is either a lack of knowledge of how to support the opposite sex, or a deficiency of the five previous kinds of love. Thus the five common deficiencies most responsible for relationship problems are as follows:

1. Conflict and tension result when at least one partner expects the other to love them when they are not even loving themselves (a deficiency of vitamin S).

2. Disapproval and judgment are the outcomes when at least one partner is not getting enough support from the same sex (a deficiency of vitamin SS).

3. Unhappiness and heaviness arise when at least one partner is not getting enough support from family and friends (a deficiency of vitamin F).

4. Hurt and emotional insecurity result when at least one partner is not feeling the support of their parents or surrogate parents (a deficiency of vitamin P).

5. Abuse, addiction, and co-dependency ensue when at least one partner is not feeling the support of God or a higher power (a deficiency of vitamin G).

Certainly when a relationship is not working, the cause might be a combination of any of the above conditions and deficiencies. But from this analysis, we can conclude in general that when a relationship with the opposite sex is not working, the first step toward improving things is to stop blaming one's partner or one's self. Then, take responsibility to heal your hurt, realizing that your inner deficiencies, not your partner, are creating the problem.

Being responsible does not mean feeling guilty. It does mean getting the support required without demanding it from one's intimate partner. Fill up your own love tank, and then return to the relationship ready to give rather than seeking to receive.

7. VITAMIN C
(A RELATIONSHIP WITH CHILDREN, PETS, OR THE EARTH'S ECOLOGY)

The natural outcome of a mature relationship with the opposite sex is, of course, having children. One can certainly be a responsible parent before this stage. But at this level of maturity, having and serving children is an essential part of our development. For those who do not choose to bear or adopt children, a pet often serves as a surrogate child.

This seventh stage occurs between ages thirty-five and forty-two. During this period we are capable of serving and giving of ourselves without receiving back. In the previous stage we needed a partner to complement our selves. In this phase we require someone who needs what we have to offer. We need to be responsible for another. We need to be a parent. Without this opportunity to be responsible for the well-being of another who is dependent on us, we may suffer a depression.

By this time we may have a tremendous amount of support, but without being responsible for others we will now experience an emptiness. Some couples who can actually be supportive of each other lose interest in the relationship because they don't have this opportunity to share in being responsible for the well-being of another.

At this stage of life, a relationship must have a purpose other than one's own personal fulfillment. The fuel of a relationship at this stage is sharing a partnership to serve the fulfillment of a child or surrogate child. Without this purpose outside the self, the relationship may suffer.

Sometimes a woman will want to have a child to insure a relationship with a man. This certainly is a mistake. But if two people who love each other keep drifting apart and they are in their mid-thirties, this principle may be contributing to their problems. For a mature person, a relationship is too confining and narcissistic if it does not serve a purpose. Having children may be the necessary challenge and commitment to solidify the relationship.

Just as mature relationships are based on the previous stage of loving oneself, a successful relationship with one's children is also based on a mature relationship with a mate. Ideally, a woman needs the support of a man to raise a child most effectively. She also needs to have a positive relationship with her masculine side as evidenced by a good relationship with the father of her child. This is equally true of men. A father cannot supply appropriate love for a child if he is rejecting his own femininity, as evidenced by his rejection of the child's mother.

Many times when children are having problems, this is an expression of the parents' problems with each other. Responsible parents know that to work on their own adult relationships is the most successful way to deal with their children's problems.

Divorced parents are sometimes too hurt to care about the other enough to work on having a loving but divorced relationship. Their expressed or unexpressed resentment and tension will create problems in the child. Ideally, divorced parents receive ongoing counseling to continue resolving their conflicts, so that the children don't have to work them out. If this is not possible, the next best approach is to work individually on finding forgiveness and understanding through personal therapy and/or writing love letters.

It is important for single parents to realize that it is not selfish to take care of their own needs for a romantic relationship. Many single parents feel guilty if they spend time developing a new relationship with the opposite sex. On the contrary, having relationships is essential if they are to be successful parents. Otherwise, a parent who is not full within themselves, with all the necessary emotional vitamins, looks unconsciously to the child to fill them up. This is very inappropriate and harmful.

Looking to a child to fulfill your deficiencies puts the child in the position of companion, which is too big a strain. The child will feel overly responsible; at the same time he or she will feel powerless and inadequate. In certain ways they will grow up faster, but a part of them does not grow up. The child never gets a chance to be a child and progress through the necessary stages to develop an autonomous identity. Single parents need to devote time and attention to getting their emotional needs satisfied elsewhere, rather than looking to their children.

This situation of adults looking to children to fill them up manifests even more strongly in marriages that don't end in divorce. When couples continue to be married but deny the problems that exist, their children will again take on these problems, just as in the case of single parents. In the case of both single-parent families and dysfunctional marriages, the solution lies in being responsible to get support and in not looking to the children for love. Ignoring the problem does not make it go away.

Couples in this stage who are childless need to have some form of parental relationship with a dependent. Otherwise, they may begin to parent each other. This is a sure way to create increasing conflict and resentment.

If couples or singles at this age have no children or dependents, it may be very helpful for their own inner fulfillment to have a pet. This need can also be satisfied by serving the poor or working for some other humanitarian cause. Yet another way of fulfilling this need of maturity is through serving

Mother Earth by preserving and protecting the earth and the animal kingdom. This kind of compassionate concern strengthens the heart.

A lot can be said about how we are destroying our world. It is vital that at every stage of maturity, we contribute to a safe and healthy world. But at the seventh stage, it is also a part of our own development. To become aware and involved in preserving our world, the "Greenpeace" organization is an excellent resource. While a discussion on the various ways we contribute to pollution and animal abuse and what we can do about it is beyond the scope of this book, everyone's involvement in service to the earth is highly recommended.

8. VITAMIN CS
(RELATIONSHIPS WITH THE COMMUNITY AND SOCIETY)

During Stage 8, the mature person needs the opportunity to serve his community and society in order to continue developing. This stage generally occurs between ages forty-two and forty-nine. All the other stages support him or her in being able to give selflessly, free from the temptations of power and corruption.

To continue developing at this stage of life, a person needs to include some form of social service and practice social responsibility. Certainly one can be socially responsible before this time, but at this stage of life one can be most fulfilled through this kind of relationship. Missing this kind of participation can put a great strain on one's intimate relationships.

This stage of development is partly responsible for what's known as the mid-life crisis. At this time in a person's life he or she markedly begins to feel the deficiencies of their past. It is quite common for people to emotionally regress at this time because they are not capable to giving to others, which is a requirement of this stage.

Many people in this age group who have not received the support they need to develop this far rebel against their responsibilities and regress to being the self-absorbed and narcissistic person of the first five stages. They decide to live for themselves and not for others. To whatever extent they haven't learned to love themselves, they will have accumulated a lot of resentment for all the sacrifices they have made up to this point. That resentment comes up and is projected into their present life and relationships.

It is important for people in this stage to carefully consider life changes such as divorce, having affairs, moving, or changing jobs. Some people in this stage who were previously living for image and money tend to shift and care more about society's needs. Others who have sacrificed themselves to this point may overindulge in fulfilling their childhood and adolescent desires. Many people unnecessarily "blow up" their lives, hurting others and making it even more difficult to get the support they need.

For example, a married man of forty-two may begin to feel his adolescent desires to have sex with younger women. He may feel that he cannot be happy unless he works this out. From one point of view he is right. He needs to work it out. But he doesn't have to betray his wife and family to do it. He may be able to explore these feelings and process them in therapy without having to act them out.

For others, turning their lives upside down is the only thing that forces them to seek out professional help. But it is a sign of wisdom to seek out help without having to blow everything apart.

As our values change in this stage, certainly we will make life changes. I caution against making sudden changes without getting lots of support. Almost everyone at this level is still greatly restricted by unhealed wounds of the past stemming from deficiencies of the other emotional vitamins. In this stage, serving society is essential to their development. But because of past deficiencies, it is equally important to continue working on all the other relationships.

If we don't deal with our emotional pain due to these deficiencies, the emotional pain may take the form of physical pain. Because we are denying that we are dying emotionally, we begin to develop annoying ailments or even to prematurely die physically from disease. Sickness is generally the result of not healing our past emotional wounds.

Corruption and abuse of power in society are other ways some people avoid feeling their emotional pain. Some people develop illness as they mature, while others abuse their fellow human beings and society in general. As explored in a previous chapter, it is the male side of us that avoids feeling our hurt by hurting others, while our female side avoids feeling our emotional pain and emptiness through self-abuse or sickness.

People at this age and beyond who seem to be full of life are generally very involved in life and in their communities. They have a twinkle in their eye that says they love themselves and they love serving others.

9. VITAMIN W
(A RELATIONSHIP WITH THE WORLD)

This ninth stage is essential for our development from the age of forty-nine and fifty-six. This is a ripe period for global leadership and transformation. Beyond this stage, one has developed, at least biologically, one's full potential and has achieved full maturity. At this point their lives are committed to service to the world, and healing of their past to remove any blocks to expressing their full potential.

During this ninth stage, global consciousness is the primary nutrient. Certainly at every stage of maturity, world peace becomes a growing concern. But during this time period we especially need to be active in global consciousness to complete our development of maturity. Traveling the world is another way in which we get a good dose of vitamin W. Seeing and feeling ourselves a part of the world is a major source of support.

Those who have not received the support and healing to mature to this level may rebel against this emerging global consciousness and become cynical, abusive or narcissistic with their power. Others begin to retrogress to a childish state to unconsciously process their unresolved feelings through various diseases. It is amazing to see how many people in their mature years regress to being like, and feeling powerless like, children. If they will not consciously process their childhood they may finally die from it. To avoid the pitfalls of old age, we must be diligent to heal as we grow older, continuing to mature through our relationships and deriving support from the age-appropriate sources.

This framework of nine sources of love supports us in realizing again and again that when we are not getting the love we need in our relationships, it is generally not our partner's fault. It gives us a new direction to look for the love we need, instead of following the compulsive demands of our reactive self, which looks for love in the wrong places. Using this model helps us to experience an abundance of love and support in our lives. Through dispelling the illusion that there is a scarcity of love and support, it becomes practical, indeed realistic, to visualize a world of peace, love, and abundance.

WORLD PEACE

World peace is a dream that we all share. Achieving it demands a maturity of the soul. Fortunately, it is not necessary that all reach this point of maturity to manifest this dream. Only a small percent may be necessary.

Various emerging theories, taking examples from modern physics and anthropology, lead us to believe that it will only take a small percent of people to reach a new threshold of maturity for the whole global consciousness to shift.

Just as water heating up starts with a few little bubbles before it bursts into a full boil, so now a small portion of mankind's population is achieving and living higher values of integrity and love. When enough people change, it is possible that everyone will automatically change.

In a study by anthropologists, it was observed that a small group of monkeys on an island started washing their food. Gradually more and more monkeys on that island began to do the same. At a certain point, all the monkeys started washing their food. A critical mass was apparently reached, and then all the monkeys changed.

What is most surprising is that on all the surrounding islands — separated by miles of ocean — where monkeys were not previously washing food, there was an immediate shift and all the monkeys started washing their food. This has been called the hundredth monkey effect. When the so-called hundredth monkey started washing food, a critical mass was achieved and then thousands of monkeys automatically started washing their food.

A similar occurrence can be viewed in dysfunctional families. If the children are disruptive because the parents are fighting, then when the parents are able to make peace, the children become more cooperative.

Mankind is also on the verge of such a shift. It is possible for massive changes to take place if a small percent can rise to a higher level of maturity.

As a whole, mankind is still plagued by war, violence, disease, and corruption. In a sense the human race continues to be held back by the issues of childhood and adolescence. It is the responsibility of those whose souls have matured to look honestly at their lives and strive to be examples of love.

Through learning to love ourselves and having loving relationships we not only free ourselves from violence and sickness but we affect the rest of mankind. In simple terms, this means that when you make the effort to grow in love, you make it easier for others to love.

THE CHALLENGE OF RELATIONSHIPS

As we learn to overcome our differences in our relationships with the opposite sex, we are challenged to love ourselves and to give of ourselves unconditionally. Through studying and diligently applying the principles of this book, not only are you ensuring your own increasing happiness and fulfillment, but you are creating a better world for your children to grow up in. You are making it impossible for corruption, disease, and abuse to continue in our society and world.

I believe there is hope for the world because there is hope for our relationships. Each day I witness the information in this book transforming the relationships of good people who could not otherwise sustain truly loving relationships. I watch people letting go of their protections and defenses and learning to share and communicate to solve their problems. More importantly, I have witnessed the wisdom contained in this book transform the quality of my own life, helping me to be more loving to my wife and family and making me more socially conscious. This gives me hope.

We cannot expect countries to remove their defenses when we maintain psychological defenses in our relationships. We cannot expect our leaders to end war when we cannot resolve conflict in our own families. We cannot expect countries to trust each other when we cannot even trust our family members. We cannot expect peace between countries until we learn to have peace at home.

There is hope for our world, however, because people *are* making peace in their relationships and homes.

There is hope for the world because world peace begins at home.

World peace begins with you.

CHAPTER EIGHTEEN

Daily Exercise and Follow-Up

A DAILY EXERCISE

Each day ask yourself this simple question:

Who are the people that need your love?

Feel in your heart a willingness to be of service to them. Imagine them reaching out to you for love, support, validation, forgiveness, reassurance, and encouragement. Feel the walls of fear and resentment surrounding your heart melting away as you slowly raise your palms up and outward. Send out your love. . . .

Renew your commitment to be all that you can be.

Reflect on what is really important to you.

Feel the promise you are here to keep. Feel your purpose.

Remember that you are special and that your love is needed.

Feel peace.

THE FOLLOW-UP

As I mentioned in the Introduction, the powerful influence of reading this book can fade away as you forget the information. I caution you because as you forget many of the insights in this book, you will not realize that you have forgotten them. It is not that you stop knowing this information, but rather, you may consciously forget what you already know. Thus you will not be automatically applying it in your relationships.

Ultimately, reading this book has only reminded you of or given expression to what you already knew at some level of your being. Rereading this book will remind you of what you already know but have forgotten. Reviewing and working with this book will keep its insights fresh in mind as you gradually develop new habits for relating.

Listed below are some of the ways you can fully remember and integrate the insights of this book:

1. Make a list of the special people in your life. Feel in your heart a willingness to share with them the precious gifts you have received through reading this book. Give or lend them a copy of this book as an expression of your love and support. The most important step in receiving wisdom is to share it. Share it and it becomes yours.

2. Set up support groups with your friends to give and receive support. Set aside time for writing and sharing love letters and for reading aloud and discussing sections of this book. If you would like more specific guidelines for support groups, I invite you to write my office.

3. Listen to *The Relationship Tape Series*. Practice the healing exercises contained in the *Healing the Heart Tape Series*. All tapes are available through my office. Listen to this new information as you drive your car or before going to bed. Use the healing exercises again and again. To learn more about healing the hurt from your past, ask your local bookstore for a copy of my first book, *What You Feel You Can Heal*, or write to my office.

4. Write me a letter sharing the impact of this book in your life. I intend to use your questions and feedback in creating my next book. Share examples of how the information relates to your life or how it has helped you. Your stories and examples will inspire others.

5. Attend the weekend seminar, *Men, Women and Relationships*. The seminar is not just for couples, but is equally attended by single people. If you are single, don't wait until you have a relationship to take the seminar.

If your relationship is working, don't wait to have problems before you attend the workshop. Your relationship is worth "an ounce of prevention." Many couples come to heal their relationship, while others take the seminar to assist them in ending a relationship in the most loving way possible. If you have just ended a relationship, the seminar will assist you in the healing process so that you can start again without making the same mistakes.

If you, your support group, company, or church would like information about the weekend seminar, *Men, Women and Relationships*, which is taught throughout America, Europe, and the Far East, write to:

Dr. John Gray
20 Sunnyside Ave., Suite A-130
Mill Valley, CA 94941

DR. JOHN GRAY

Cordially Invites You . . . to enrich your relationships
through listening to audio cassette recordings of his seminars
and reading his classic book, *What You Feel You Can Heal.*

WHAT YOU FEEL YOU CAN HEAL

Dr. John Gray brings 18 years of experience as a therapist, seminar leader
and author to this comprehensive handbook for healing the heart. This 214-
page book is the ultimate guide for enriching relationships and increasing
one's self-esteem. Through practicing the simple but profound techniques
contained within this book, thousands of couples have renewed their relationships while individuals have increased their self-esteem. Warmly written
and whimsically illustrated, this easy-to-read and entertaining book will take
you through the steps required to break through love's barriers.

1 book, 214 pages, $12.95

INNER HEALING

Learn two powerful exercises for feeling better when you are upset. The
first cassette contains a gentle guided process to increase self-love and heal
your inner child. In the second cassette, Dr. Gray reveals how, in 20 minutes,
you can free yourself from the gripping influence of negative moods. By
practicing this revolutionary new technique you can heal the hurt and pain
which gives rise to unwanted anger, anxiety and resentment. Experience the
healing power of love and forgiveness. 2 cassettes $19.95

SECRETS OF PASSIONATE RELATIONSHIPS

Learn the seven secrets for creating and sustaining loving and passionate relationships. Understand and appreciate how men and women are different. Discover how you unknowingly sabotage your relationships. Realize
the eight ways to get the love you need now! 6 cassettes, $59.95

SECRETS ABOUT MEN AND WOMEN
(AND THE SECRETS OF GREAT SEX)

Learn the hidden reasons why men pull away and why women get upset. Find out how your past relationships keep you from enjoying your present
relationships. Discover how men and women react differently to stress. Avoid
the six major mistakes. And most of all learn new and practical techniques
for giving and receiving love and support. Then relax and be entertained by
the secrets of great sex. 6 cassettes, $59.95

You may order the book, *What You Feel You Can Heal,* or any of the tape
albums by sending a check or money order to: John Gray Seminars, 20
Sunnyside Ave., Suite A-130, Mill Valley, CA 94941. Make checks payable
to Heart Publishing. To expedite delivery, use your Mastercard or Visa and
call (415) 381-5735. Add 10% for shipping (plus 6.25% for California orders).

Other Books of Interest Available From
Beyond Words Publishing, Inc.

WHAT YOU FEEL YOU CAN HEAL
by Dr. John Gray

Dr. John Gray brings 18 years of experience as a therapist, seminar leader and author to this comprehensive handbook for healing the heart. This 214-page book is the ultimate guide for enriching relationships and increasing one's self-esteem. Through practicing the simple but profound techniques contained within this book, thousands of couples have renewed their relationships while individuals have increased their self-esteem. Warmly written and whimsically illustrated, this easy-to-read and entertaining book will take you through the steps required to break through love's barriers.

$12.95, softcover

SEEING BEYOND 20/20
by Dr. Robert Kaplan

An internationally noted authority in vision training gives readers a practical, solidly researched 21-day program for self-help in working toward clearer vision. Dr. Kaplan, who himself was plagued with double vision, combines clinical evidence with case examples, the theory of whole-brain perception and the wisdom of alternative therapies from around the world. Topics include nutrition, aerobics for the eyes, the eyes as a biofeedback device and the relationship of inner vision to outer sight.

$12.95, softcover

WORKING WITH MEN
Professional Women Talk about Power, Sexuality, and Ethics
by Beth Milwid, Ph.D.

In the spirit of Studs Terkel's *WORKING*, psychologist Beth Milwid interviewed women across the country in a variety of industries and professions with the purpose of uncovering the truth about today's working women. These accounts provide insight and advice "from the trenches" and give an insider's look at the pressures that female colleagues, spouses and friends face very day. She discovered a new coalition developing inside corporate America . . . based not on gender, race, or age, but rather on talent, mutual respect, and values.

$12.95, softcover